## Praise for *A History (*

"No one has attempted to write the history of autism so comprehensively before. Adam Feinstein's highly readable but remarkably thorough book contains a treasure-trove of conversations with the scientists, clinicians, lobbyists, and parents who have shaped the development of autism in both research and policy. The timing of this book is opportune, as the pioneer generation becomes 'emeritus.' History-telling is never wholly objective, but Feinstein (the science-writer, parent, and international conference organizer) is better placed than almost anyone to document the extraordinary changes that have happened to the autism community worldwide since the 1940s onwards. This book is an important contribution to the history of medicine and a unique resource for future generations who will build on their predecessors."

*Simon Baron-Cohen, Director, Autism Research Centre,*
*Cambridge University*

"The material in *A History of Autism* is selected and worded with such enthusiasm, such personal engagement, that it is contagious. I couldn't stop reading. This book is a monument; a milestone that we all owe to autism's history."

*Theo Peeters, Centre for Training in Autism, Belgium*

"From the many years before Kanner's 1943 description when the condition was known by other names, through all that has happened to the present time, along with a glimpse of the future, Feinstein explores the evolutionary journey of autism in an enlightened, educational, and entertaining fashion. Nowhere will you find a more comprehensive, carefully documented and eminently readable account of the history of autism than this book."

*Darold A. Treffert, University of Wisconsin Medical School*

"Adam Feinstein provides an essential historical context for autism; one of the most contentious childhood diagnoses today. This is a grounding book for those ready to look beyond pet theories, 'magic bullets' and 'treatment of the day.' This book will navigate you beyond the idea of any 'one autism' and leave you with the clarity, hope and opportunity for new directions inherent in that realization."

*Donna Williams, author and autism consultant*

"Of interest to researchers, clinicians and parents, this volume provides a detailed perspective on the history of autism and related disorders. Writing from the perspective of a parent, Adam Feinstein brings the people and concepts vividly to life in this insightful and comprehensive book."

*Fred R. Volkmar, Child Study Center Yale University*

"The field of autism has been in need of a solid historical account of the many changes since Kanner first coined the term autism in 1943, and Feinstein's book finally fills that gap. His novel approach of telling the story of autism through interviews with the pioneers, their associates, and their family members is creative and fascinating. What wonderful stories these people tell, how well the author passes the stories on, and what a terrific way to relate the history of the field.

"Feinstein's deep understanding of the field leads to excellent questions and penetrating discussions. This wonderful combination will be irresistible to anyone interested in how the field got to where it is now and where it might be going."

*Gary B. Mesibov, University of North Carolina School of Medicine*

"This book outlines, from an unusual point of view, the history of the development of the concept of the spectrum of autistic conditions. The author's account is brought to life in fascinating detail by his interviews with leading professionals (or their children who survive them), parents, and adults with autistic conditions. He reveals the controversies between professionals and the problems that still exist for families in different countries, as well as the progress that has been made. A book to be highly recommended to anyone with an interest in autism."

*Lorna Wing, Honorary Consultant to the National Autistic Society, UK*

"Adam Feinstein's book is a valuable contribution to the autism literature. No other author has sought out the important scientific contributors to autism research; it is fascinating to read their current views, as well as a summary of their original contributions."

*Susan E. Folstein, John P. Hussman Institute of Human Genomics*

"The story of autism only began remarkably recently. In this unique book you can listen to the voices of the opinion makers and learn what they thought about autism in times past and present. Pioneers who pushed the boundaries of knowledge since autism was first identified talk freely about their ideas and experiences."

*Uta Frith, University College London*

# A History of Autism

*Conversations with the Pioneers*

Adam Feinstein

**WILEY-BLACKWELL**

A John Wiley & Sons, Ltd., Publication

This edition first published 2010
© 2010 Adam Feinstein

Blackwell Publishing was acquired by John Wiley & Sons in February 2007.
Blackwell's publishing program has been merged with Wiley's global Scientific,
Technical, and Medical business to form Wiley-Blackwell.

*Registered Office*
John Wiley & Sons Ltd, The Atrium, Southern Gate, Chichester, West Sussex,
PO19 8SQ, United Kingdom

*Editorial Offices*
350 Main Street, Malden, MA 02148–5020, USA
9600 Garsington Road, Oxford, OX4 2DQ, UK
The Atrium, Southern Gate, Chichester, West Sussex, PO19 8SQ, UK

For details of our global editorial offices, for customer services, and for
information about how to apply for permission to reuse the copyright material
in this book please see our website at www.wiley.com/wiley-blackwell.

The right of Adam Feinstein to be identified as the author of this work has been
asserted in accordance with the UK Copyright, Designs and Patents Act 1988.

Wiley also publishes its books in a variety of electronic formats. Some content that
appears in print may not be available in electronic books.

Designations used by companies to distinguish their products are often claimed as
trademarks. All brand names and product names used in this book are trade names,
service marks, trademarks or registered trademarks of their respective owners. The
publisher is not associated with any product or vendor mentioned in this book. This
publication is designed to provide accurate and authoritative information in regard to
the subject matter covered. It is sold on the understanding that the publisher is not
engaged in rendering professional services. If professional advice or other expert
assistance is required, the services of a competent professional should be sought.

*Library of Congress Cataloging-in-Publication Data*
Feinstein, Adam, 1957–
A history of autism : conversations with the pioneers/Adam Feinstein.
   p.; cm.
   Includes bibliographical references and index.
   ISBN 978-1-4051-8654-4 (hb : alk. paper) – ISBN 978-1-4051-8653-7
(pb : alk. paper)  1. Autism–History.  I. Title.
   [DNLM:  1. Autistic Disorder–history–Interview.  2. History, 20th
Century–Interview. WM 11.1 F299h 2010]
   RC553.A88F45 2010
   362.196′85882–dc22

                                                        2010006818

A catalogue record for this book is available from the British Library.

Set in 10/12.5pt Plantin by Graphicraft Limited, Hong Kong
Printed and bound in Malaysia by Vivar Printing Sdn Bhd

2   2011

Unless otherwise indicated, all photographs are the author's.

For Johnny

# Contents

# Acknowledgments

First and foremost, I owe an immense debt of gratitude to Dame Stephanie Shirley. This book would not have been possible without her enormous generosity and support in financing my travels around the world to speak to the pioneers in the field of autism.

I must express my huge appreciation to Professor Uta Frith, who was also on the steering committee which saw this book through to its completion and, as one of the world's foremost authorities on autism, gave me friendly advice combined with constructive criticism.

The other member of the steering committee, alongside Dame Stephanie and Uta, was the project manager, John Carrington, whose calm and smooth running of the financial elements of the whole operation was enormously helpful.

Through my travels, I have spoken to hundreds of people who provided many hours of insights. I could not possibly thank them all and I apologize for any that I have inadvertently omitted.

In London, I have to express my profound gratitude to Dr. Lorna Wing and her colleague, Dr. Judith Gould, for our many conversations which have clarified a vast number of issues. I am doubly indebted to Dr. Wing because she also kindly agreed to act as external reviewer of the manuscript. I am also extremely grateful to Professor Sir Michael Rutter for his invaluable insights, both in person and by telephone and e-mail, and to his colleagues at London's Institute of Psychiatry, Dr. Patricia Howlin and Dr. Francesca Happé. I would also like to thank Marc Bush for his insights into Hans Asperger's pre-Kanner writings.

My profound gratitude goes to all those parents who, together with Lorna Wing, were involved in setting up the National Autistic Society

(NAS) and the Sybil Elgar School in London and who shared their reminiscences with me. They include Michael Baron, Gerald de Groot, Peggie Everard, and Wendy Brown. I must thank the current NAS archivist, Norman Green, for kindly allowing me access to important past interviews, and Richard Mills, the NAS's director of services and director of Research Autism, for many fascinating ahd helpful discussions while I was working on the book.

Elsewhere in the UK, my deep gratitude goes to Professor Simon Baron-Cohen in Cambridge for many enlightening conversations and also Dr. Phil Christie in Nottingham for his accounts of his own work and that of his colleague, Professor Elizabeth Newson. I am indebted to Professor Rita Jordan in Birmingham for her enlightening views on educating children with autism and to Ros Blackburn for her articulate expression of life with autism from the inside. In Wales, my sincere thanks go to my Autism Cymru colleague, Hugh Morgan, and in Northern Ireland, to Arlene Cassidy, for their early memories and their continuing tremendous efforts on behalf of individuals with autism. I am very grateful to Ruth Hampton, the current chairman of the Scottish Society for Autism, for her hospitality and for helping to organize interviews with two leading Scottish psychiatrists, Dr. Sula Wolff and Dr. Fred Stone, as well as with some of the parents involved in establishing the Scottish Society for Autism, including Marian Critchley, Robert and Yvonne Philips, Chris and June Butler-Cole and Andrew Lester. Fred Stone, who provided me with some fascinating memories of his work on the historic Creak Committee, sadly died in June 2009, while Sula Wolff—considered one of the founders of child psychiatry in Britain and a woman whose joyful enthusiasm and compassion for children with autism was enormously contagious—passed away in September 2009. I must also thank Jim Taylor, head of education at New Struan School in Alloa, for his friendly support and insights.

In Scandinavia, I would particularly like to thank Professor Christopher Gillberg in Gothenburg, Sweden, for his immense generosity with his time, and Bent Vandborg Sørensen in Aarhus, Denmark, for his great kindness and friendship in offering memories of the beginning of the autism movement in that country, and in opening up contacts elsewhere in the region.

In continental Europe, I was very fortunate to enjoy the help in Vienna of Dr. Kathrin Hippler in arranging meetings with Hans Asperger's colleagues, Dr. Elizabeth Wurst and Dr. Maria Theresia Schubert. Kathrin also provided me with valuable documentation in Vienna, and a PhD student there, Roxane Sousek, clarified an important point. I am enormously grateful to Hans Asperger's daughter, Dr. Maria Asperger Felder, for sharing so many personal recollections in Zurich and for giving me access to valuable documentation. I must also express my deep gratitude to Dr. Gerhard Bosch in Frankfurt. At over 90, he is probably the world's oldest living autism pioneer but he kindly spared the time to talk to me about his work from the 1950s onwards.

I greatly appreciate the kindness of Isabel Bayonas, the founder of Spain's National Association for Parents of Autistic Children (APNA), for arranging interviews in Madrid with Dr. Angel Díez-Cuervo, Dr. Mercedes Belinchón and Dr. Carmen Nieto. Carmen kindly supplied me with a number of useful documents and other material. I am also grateful to Isabel for her hospitality and for sharing her own memories of those crucial early days in Spain of the 1970s.

The magnificent French team of researchers in Tours was a source of friendship and valuable reminiscences. A special debt of gratitude here goes to the pioneer in studying the biological causes of autism, Professor Gilbert Lelord, for his charming hospitality, and to his colleagues, Dr. Catherine Barthélemy and Dr. Monica Zilbovicius. I appreciated the observations of Dr. Denys Ribas and Dr. Roger Misès in Paris and Dr. Jean-Claude Maleval in Rennes, who provided alternative perspectives. In Belgium, Theo Peeters shared his friendship and compassionate understanding of autism with me, as did his Antwerp colleague, Hilde De Clerq. I thank them, as well as Irène Knodt-Lenfant in Brussels for her insights into life as the mother of an autistic boy adopted in Haiti and as the founder of a center for adults with autism.

The leading Italian autism activist, Donata Vivanti, and one of the country's most prominent autism researchers and clinicians, Professor Michele Zappella, also provided me with extremely useful information, for which I am grateful.

In the United States, Leo Kanner's close colleague, Professor Leon Eisenberg, was immensely helpful—both in person at Harvard Medical School and in subsequent e-mail exchanges. His illuminating recollections of his work with Kanner were invaluable. It was with great sadness that I learnt of Professor Eisenberg's death in September 2009. I am also grateful to three other key interviewees in Boston: Dr. Margaret Bauman, Dr. Thomas Kemper, and Professor Helen Tager-Flusberg for their friendly support and insights.

In Huntington, West Virginia, Ruth Sullivan, first elected president of the Autism Society of America, was delightful and very informative company, as was Dr. Darold Treffert, the leading world expert on autistic savants, in Fond du Lac, Wisconsin; I also greatly appreciated the opportunity to speak to Leo Kanner's son, Albert, in Madison.

Dr. Gary Mesibov was enormously supportive at the TEACCH headquarters in Chapel Hill, North Carolina, as he has been in many subsequent exchanges, and I must also thank Gary's colleague, Dr. Brenda Denzler, for organizing my interview with Eric Schopler's three children—Bobby, Tommy and Susie—and his first wife, Betsy, as well as with two of the first TEACCH parents, Mary Lou (Bobo) Warren and Betty Camp. I am very grateful to all of these Chapel Hill interviewees for sharing their memories, as I am to Dr. Lee Marcus, a clinical psychologist, who was also involved in the early days of the TEACCH program.

In New York, my sincere thanks go to Professor Isabelle Rapin, Dr. Mary Coleman, Dr. Theodore Schapiro, Dr. Richard Perry; at Yale, in New Haven, to Dr. Fred Volkmar and Dr. Ami Klin; and in Baltimore, to Dr. Susan Folstein, Dr. Rebecca Landa and Dr. Andrew Zimmerman, as well as to Andrew Harrison, who allowed me access to valuable Leo Kanner documents at the Johns Hopkins University archives.

I also appreciated the chance to speak in Chicago to Bruno Bettelheim's colleague and successor as director of the Orthogenic School, Jacquelyn Seevak Sanders. Dr. Peter Tanguay and Dr. Manuel Casanova gave me valuable time and information in Louisville, Kentucky, while Dr. Cathy Lord at the University of Michigan at Ann Arbor also shared her experiences with me. My thanks go to all three.

Lee Grossman, president of the Autism Society of America (ASA), and Jeff Sell, the vice-president of advocacy and public policy, were very helpful in allowing me access to ASA documents at the organization's headquarters in Bethesda, Maryland.

On the West Coast, I must thank Dr. Robert Reichler in Seattle, for his memories of working with Eric Schopler; and, at UCLA, Dr. Laura Schreibman for her reminiscences of Ivar Lovaas, and Dr. Ed Ornitz, Dr. Ed Ritvo and Dr. Marian Sigman for their equally valuable observations on their pioneering early studies.

I also greatly appreciate the clarification of a number of important issues—especially on Asperger's syndrome—provided by Dr. Tony Attwood in Australia.

In Asia, my immense gratitude goes to Merry Barua at Action for Autism in New Delhi for providing me with contacts in India (and for the tremendous work she is doing there) and to Qazi Fazli Azeem in Pakistan. In China, my sincere thanks go to Professor Sun Dunke,

## Acknowledgments

Professor Jia Meixiang, Professor Liu Jing, Dr. Guo Yanqing, and Sun Menglin for their hospitality and insights during my stay in Beijing. I would also like to thank my Chinese guide, Sun Wei, for helping to make that visit so pleasurable and Tian (Hope) Huiping for sharing her experiences of setting up the first private school for autistic children on mainland China—and for her honest account of being the mother of a child with autism.

The Japanese child psychiatrist, Dr. Tokio Uchiyama, gave me many useful details of early developments in the field of autism in that country, for which I am grateful.

In the Middle East, I greatly appreciate the recollections which Edna Mishori—a true pioneer in improving facilities for, and understanding of, autism in Israel—shared with me. I must also thank Dr. Talat al-Wazna, the secretary-general of the Saudi Autistic Society, for offering me valuable information about the understanding of autism in that country and neighboring Arab nations.

Two of the world's best-known women with autism—Temple Grandin and Donna Williams—provided me with illuminating insights into their condition and I am very grateful to both of them. I must also thank Philip Hadley for kindly facilitating my meeting with Temple.

In Latin America, Judith de Vaillard in Mexico City provided useful observations on the peculiar problems facing the autism pioneers in that country, while Edna García de Martínez was refreshingly honest about the difficulties that still exist. I thank them both. I would also like to thank Dr. Lilia Negrón in Caracas for keeping me abreast of the situation in Venezuela.

During the writing of this book, I have been working with an excellent team at Wiley-Blackwell. I am grateful to them all: Andrew McAleer, Annie Rose, Karen Shield, and my very thorough copy-editor, Annie Jackson.

I must thank my beautiful wife, Kate, and my equally beautiful daughters, Lara and Katriona, for allowing me the time and space to write this book. And of course, my final words of gratitude have to go to my son, Johnny who, at 17, has grown into a good-looking, mischievous young man. The teachers and carers who have looked after him so affectionately and knowledgeably at his wonderful school deserve a special mention but it was Johnny himself who patiently—and sometimes not quite so patiently—permitted me to complete this project.

Adam Feinstein

# Foreword

The Shirley Foundation has a focus on pioneering strategic projects in the field of autism spectrum disorders. In 2007, its trustees initiated this study of the development of the autism sector. The aim was a work of scholarship to capture the essence of the past 60 years while the facts were still in living memory. The project was driven by a volunteer steering group of Professor Uta Frith FRS (herself a pioneer in the field) and me, with businessman John Carrington chairing us.

I knew and admired the author, Adam Feinstein, from the portal site, AutismConnect, and via Autism Cymru, two previous Shirley Foundation projects. He traveled worldwide to meet the sector's pioneers and their families and colleagues. In separating trends from bad science, his conversations are both intimate and insightful. His family and professional experiences give him the depth of understanding which pervades this book.

Ground-breaking men and women, pragmatists and dreamers alike, have been the agents of progress in fathoming the different autisms that impact the lives of over a million families worldwide. Individually and severally, I thank them and those who follow them in unraveling this perplexing disorder.

Dame Stephanie Shirley
In memory of her late son, Giles

# Introduction

The first time I remember the word "autism" spoken was on a flight out of Heathrow. I was talking to a distinguished-looking Frenchman sitting next to me about what was worrying me most: our three-year-old son, Johnny, had inexplicably stopped speaking and now always kept to himself in his playgroup. My neighbor turned to me and said: "I am quite sure that your son has autism." I listened politely and took the man's business card without looking at it. About six months later, a team at St. George's Hospital in London diagnosed Johnny using the same word. I quickly began to read everything I could find about autism and, a few months later, I glanced at that business card still lying in my jacket pocket: the name on it was Dr. Eric Fombonne, which I now recognized as belonging to one of the world's leading autism experts.

Johnny is now 17 and, in the intervening years, I have put much of my energy into trying to understand the disorder. I launched a monthly international autism newsletter, *Looking Up*, and now edit two autism-related websites, AutismConnect and Awares, run by Autism Cymru.

This present book has come about as the result of the generosity of Dame Stephanie Shirley, a successful British businesswoman whose own autistic son, Giles, died at the age of 35. She wanted this book written and made it possible for me to travel round the world and talk to leading experts on the disorder, not only in Europe and the United States, but also in China, India, Russia, Latin America, and Australia.

My journey has been exhilarating and stimulating. I have spoken to hundreds of professionals and parents and all the pioneers in the field. I made many good friends. It was extraordinary to be able to talk to

1

**Figure 1** The author, Adam Feinstein, and his son, Johnny (photo by Lara Feinstein)

Leo Kanner's closest colleague, Professor Leon Eisenberg, and Kanner's son, Albert, as well as to Hans Asperger's daughter, Dr. Maria Asperger Felder, in Zurich, and to his colleagues in Vienna. There were moments of sudden enlightenment and others of hilarity. I will never forget meeting the world's two pioneers in the neurology of autism, Dr. Margaret Bauman and Dr. Thomas Kemper, for breakfast at my Boston hotel and finding that the place which we had been assured was the quietest in the building turned out to be the noisiest spot in Massachusetts, with a hotel page announcing the shuttle bus to the airport every five minutes. Happily, I was able to conduct this interview again later.

Speaking to high-functioning, articulate and self-aware individuals with autism—like Temple Grandin and Donna Williams—has offered many clues to the nature of the disorder. One of the most extreme examples of the preference for objects over human beings—which Kanner noted in his first 1943 paper—came from Ros Blackburn, a British woman with autism, whom I interviewed in Paddington, West London, not long after the train crash there. I asked Ros whether she felt sympathy for the victims of the accident and she told me she felt as concerned for the paper from briefcases strewn across the upturned train carriages.[1]

Autism is one of the most complex of all psychological disorders. Indeed, many academics would argue that we are not talking about a single disease. One of the world's leading living autism authorities,

Dr. Lorna Wing, invented the concept of the autistic spectrum and coined the term "Asperger's syndrome." Some—including Wing herself—insist that all these variants of the condition share a core deficit, the social one. Others, like Dr. Mary Coleman in New York, go so far as to say that there may be dozens of different diseases, each related to a specific medical condition.

Autism has probably always existed. That, at least, is the logical assumption if we accept that it is a neurological disorder, rather than one induced by bad parenting or some modern environmental factor. A complete history of such a complex disorder would require several volumes. This book is not an attempt to give an account of the first cases through to the present day. What I have tried to do is to record and analyze my conversations with the leading pioneers in the field—and so shed new light on the evolution of our understanding of the concept.

It is, nevertheless, worth giving a brief account of the way the first descriptions of behavior which we would today recognize as autistic began to emerge.[2] In a 1974 paper, Natalia Challis and Horace W. Dewey claimed that many of the holy (or "blessed") fools of ancient Russia exhibited elements of autistic-like behavior: many were non-verbal, apparently insensitive to pain, and indifferent to social conventions; some had epilepsy (it is believed that around 30% of people with autism suffer from epilepsy).[3] Intriguing claims have been made that the changelings which appear in fairytales could have been autistic children.

In the eighteenth century, a number of cases began to be reported of what we would now recognize as autistic behavior. In 1724, a boy, who would later come to be known as Wild Peter, was seen running up and down naked in the fields near the German town of Hamelin. He never learned to talk and, although his sense of smell was acute, he was insensitive to noxious odors such as his own excrement—a characteristic often seen in autism.

Professor Uta Frith has made a detailed study of Hugh Blair, an eighteenth-century Scottish landowner whose marriage was annulled on the grounds that he was an "idiot"—although Frith and Professor Rab Houston contend that Blair was actually autistic. His behavior was certainly bizarre: he would eat with a cat on his shoulder sharing his food and was always watching drops of water falling (like Raymond Babbitt, the autistic character played by Dustin Hoffman in the 1988 film, *Rain man*).[4] The behavior of the eighteenth-century monarch, King Christian VII of Denmark, would probably have met the criteria for Asperger's syndrome today.[5]

One of the best documented early cases of what we now recognize as autistic behavior emerged at the end of the eighteenth century. Aged around 11 or 12, Victor, the Wild Boy of Aveyron, was discovered naked in southern France while looking for acorns to eat. In 1801, he was taken into the care of a French doctor, Jean-Marc Gaspard Itard. A fellow doctor, the celebrated Philippe Pinel—considered by many as the father of modern psychiatry—believed that Victor belonged in the same category as the incurable idiots he had worked with at Bicêtre Hospital. Itard did not believe Victor was congenitally retarded, but rather that he had lost his human faculties in his struggle to survive. Some thought Victor had been reared by wolves. When found, he had a thick scar across his neck, as if his throat had been cut, suggesting that someone had tried to kill him, perhaps because he was autistic and strange in behavior and whoever he had lived with was unable to cope.

In 1809, a British hospital doctor, Dr. John Haslam, wrote an account of a boy who had contracted a severe case of measles at the age of 12 months and whose subsequent behavior, it now appears, resembled that of a child with autism. Another British doctor, Dr. William Howship Dickinson, who was a physician at London's Great Ormond Street and St George's Hospitals in the mid- to late nineteenth century, wrote three volumes of case notes, dictated to nurses or assistants, which include 24 cases in which children presented symptoms characteristic of autistic spectrum disorders.[6]

In 1887, Dr. John Langdon Down differentiated between early-onset and late-onset disorders. Dr. Darold Treffert, who is also the leading world expert on the savant syndrome, believes that Down was referring to "regressive autism."[7] Down also wrote about individuals he called "idiot savants" who had great musical, artistic, or mathematical skills. Such people today frequently have a diagnosis of autism.

In 1898, a psychologist, Dr. M. W. Barr, described an encounter with a 22-year-old retarded man who had a phenomenal memory and echolalic speech, not unlike some individuals recognized as autistic savants today (for example, the pianist Derek Paravicini). Anyone who has met Derek will be struck by the similarity between his personality and performances and the descriptions provided by Mark Twain of one of the most celebrated nineteenth-century savant pianists, Thomas Wiggins Bethune—known as Blind Tom Wiggins—who was born to slave parents in Georgia, in the United States, and who knew more than 7,000 pieces of music from memory but had a vocabulary of just 100 words. Twain reported:

4

He lorded it over the emotions of his audience like an autocrat. He swept them like a storm, with his battle-pieces; he lulled them to rest again with melodies as tender as those we hear in dreams; he gladdened them with others that rippled through the charmed air as happily and cheerily as the riot the linnets make in California woods. . . . And every time the audience applauded when a piece was finished, this happy innocent joined in and clapped his hands, too, and with vigorous emphasis. It was not from egotism, but because it is his natural instinct to imitate pretty much every sound he hears.[8]

In fiction, claims have been made that three nineteenth-century creations—Dickens's Barnaby Rudge, Herman Melville's Bartleby and Arthur Conan Doyle's Sherlock Holmes—were based on observations of autistic behavior.

One American academic, Dr Majia Holmer Nadesan, believes that the conditions permitting the diagnosis of a child with autism are less rooted in the biology of their condition than in the cultural practices and economy of their times. In the 1800s, she maintains, the standards for classifying individuals as disordered were far less nuanced and the standards of normality much broader. Prior to the late 1800s, she claims, children would not have been subjected to any form of "developmental" or psychological examination unless their condition was particularly severe and their parents economically privileged.[9]

In the first half of the twentieth century, workers in the field of abnormal child development began to attempt to define subgroups within so-called childhood psychoses. In 1906, Sancte de Sanctis in Italy described children with what we would now recognize as autistic behaviors. Two years later, Theodor Heller in Austria reported six cases of the onset of a disorder in the third or fourth year of life after normal development, resulting in a rapid loss of speech and other regression. Both men used the term *dementia infantilis*, in accordance with the German psychiatrist Dr. Emil Kraepelin's term *dementia praecox* for the disorder now known as schizophrenia.

The term "autism"—from the Greek *autos*, meaning self—was first employed in 1911 by Dr. Eugen Bleuler, who was director at the time of the Burghölzli Hospital in Zurich (among his most celebrated patients was the Russian ballet dancer, Vaslav Nijinsky, and his most celebrated interns included Carl Jung). The term appeared in his paper, "Dementia praecox oder Gruppe der Schizophrenien," and then emerged in English for the first time in a review of his paper in the *New York State Hospitals Bulletin* in August 1912.

In 1911, Bleuler distinguished two modes of thinking: logical or realistic thinking and autistic thinking. For Bleuler, autistic thinking was not a pathology confined to a group of children who exhibited a withdrawal from other people and the external world (as it would be for Leo Kanner in 1943). Bleuler considered autistic thinking a normal mode of thinking in both children and adults. It was evident, he said, in dreams, pretend play and reveries, and in the fantasies and delusions of the schizophrenic. Bleuler, unlike Freud, believed that the ability to conceive of alternatives to reality was not a primitive process but one which was relatively sophisticated. For Bleuler, reality-directed thinking came first and autistic thinking later. Nevertheless, many French professionals remain convinced to this day that Bleuler's use of the word derived from a contraction of Sigmund Freud's "auto-eroticism."

Bleuler also coined the term "schizophrenia"—because he did not agree with Emil Kraepelin that premature dementia was the ultimate outcome of dementia praecox—and he originally included autism as one of what he called "the four schizophrenias." This group was united by the "four As"—associated disturbance, affective disturbance, ambivalence and autism. As Professor Uta Frith has noted, it is clear that "autistic thinking in Bleuler's sense has nothing to do with autism as we know it."[10]

Writing in the 1920s, and reflecting the potently psychoanalytical trend which persists in France to this day, Eugène Minkowski—who introduced Bleuler's work to a French audience in his 1927 book, *La schizophrénie*—considered autism to be not a withdrawal to solitude or a morbid inclination to daydreaming, but a deficit in the basic, non-reflective attunement between the person and his world, that is, a lack of "vital contact with reality."

For Minkowski, autism was the disorder which generated schizophrenia, rather than being a mere symptom of schizophrenia. Minkowski considered that Bleuler's profile of autism led to an interpretation of the disorder as a voluntary withdrawal from the world, and if not voluntary, then certainly a defense mechanism. Minkowski coined his own terms: *autisme riche* (rich autism) and *autisme pauvre* (poor autism). By the former, he meant individuals whose fantasies were intense and by the latter, those who were capable of high achievement in a restricted field, but with an absence of fantasy. Lorna Wing told me she thought this distinction was altogether spurious.[11]

In 1920, Dr. Lightner Witmer—widely considered to be the founder of clinical psychology—published the first detailed case report of a psychotic child. The boy, exhibiting many features of what today would be called an autistic child, had "no desires except to be left alone."[12]

In 1926, a Russian psychiatrist, Dr. Grunya Efimovna Sukhareva,[13] published an account in a German journal of six boys displaying what she termed "schizoid personality disorder of childhood."[14] Reading the translation of that paper by the German-born child psychiatrist, Dr. Sula Wolff, it becomes clear that Sukhareva was depicting the core deficits and major hallmarks of Asperger's syndrome more than a decade before this condition was described by Hans Asperger in Vienna.[15]

In the late 1920s, Sterba diagnosed a boy with developmental infantile psychosis. He had gaze avoidance, "striking poverty of creative imagination," a "special predilection for systematization" (a remarkable, and very early, use of the term which Professor Simon Baron-Cohen now employs to support his "extreme male brain" theory of autism), rituals, pronoun reversal—but also an excellent memory.[16]

In 1933, Dr. Howard Potter wrote about children who, he said, had a childhood form of schizophrenia. In this important paper, Potter noted that, in every institution for "mental defectives," children—who would now be called autistic—could be found who were classified as "idiots."[17] The following year, Earl described a group of adolescents who were mentally retarded and who developed behavior he called catatonic, but which had major similarities to severe autistic behavior.[18] (Lorna Wing has long believed that many individuals diagnosed with catatonic schizophrenia actually have autism with catatonic features.[19])

Just before the outbreak of the Second World War, researchers at the University of Nijmegen, in the Netherlands, described a group of children with autism-like behavior and actually used the term "autistic" in the way we would understand it today.[20]

Who came first, Leo Kanner or Hans Asperger? Until recently it was thought that Kanner's landmark paper appeared in 1943 and Asperger's article on a similar condition was published independently, the following year. In fact, as his daughter confirmed to me in Zurich (see chapter 1), it was Asperger who first used the term "autistic" as early as 1934, so in chronological terms, at least, he appears to have been the pioneer.[21]

Clearly, both men played an enormously significant part in introducing this mysterious disorder to the world—although, for various reasons analyzed in the next chapter, Asperger's writings took far longer to emerge in the English-speaking world. Professor Sir Michael Rutter, one of the world's leading authorities in the field, feels that Kanner was the first to organize clinical descriptions efficiently and effectively.[22] This is similar to the recent discovery that the first person to study the moon through a telescope was not Galileo but a virtually unknown British astronomer, Thomas Harriot. It would be difficult to argue that Harriot made the greater contribution to our understanding of the night sky. As Lorna Wing put it to me: "Nothing is totally original. Everyone is influenced by what's gone before."[23]

Some startling associations did, indeed, emerge during the writing of this book. Professor Simon Baron-Cohen, another of the world's leading autism authorities, told me that, while he certainly did not share Bruno Bettelheim's belief that parents were to blame for their child's autism, Bettelheim's controversial 1967 book, *The empty fortress*, was the book which had "fired him up to work" in the field. "Bettelheim was obviously thinking deeply about concepts like the self. That idea is still around. After all, theory of mind is all about imagining other people's thoughts and what is going on in other people's minds. This is linked to the concept of self-consciousness."[24]

Autism is troubling for parents and bewildering for even the most knowledgeable of professionals. But it is also intriguing. It has become a favorite theme for movie-makers, ever since *Rain man*. Novels such as Mark Haddon's hugely enjoyable and successful novel, *The curious incident of the dog in the night-time*, featuring a narrator with Asperger's syndrome, have kept the condition in the public eye.

It is my hope that this book—as it follows the route from Leo Kanner and Hans Asperger, through the broadening of the spectrum and key research findings along the way through to the present day—will tackle many of the myths and misconceptions and provide new insights into a condition which continues to exert such an enduring and enigmatic fascination.[25]

# 1

# The Two Great Pioneers

*"Nothing is totally original. Everyone is influenced by what's gone before."*
*(Dr. Lorna Wing in conversation with Adam Feinstein)*

*"Whatever will they think of next?" (Reported comment by the*
*Hollywood producer, Sam Goldwyn, on being shown an ancient sundial)*

The two great pioneers in the field of autism, Dr. Hans Asperger and
Dr. Leo Kanner, started work in this area at roughly the same time—
the 1930s. But they were very different human beings and, while their
notions of the condition they first described overlapped to some extent,
there are significant differences that still need exploring—and allegations
of plagiarism and Nazi allegiances which also require examination.

The Scottish child psychiatrist, Dr. Fred Stone, was one of the few
people who met both Asperger and Kanner. Stone told me: "There
couldn't be a bigger contrast between the two men. I met Kanner in
Edinburgh in the mid-1950s. He was very spruce, carefully dressed,
cautious but pleasant. I liked him."[1]

Stone met Hans Asperger at a conference in Vienna in the 1960s.
"He was on duty 'welcoming' people—actually, he didn't welcome
anybody, he just sat there at the door of the lecture theater. I had just
heard about his syndrome from the German-speaking members of my
planning committee. I could not engage him. I think that those who
claim that he may have been suffering from the syndrome that would
later bear his name could be right."[2]

Most people who met Kanner reported on his warmth and charm.
Physically, with his large ears and mischievous grin, he bore a

9

resemblance to the pianist, Vladimir Horowitz. His son, Albert, a retired ophthalmologist at the University of Wisconsin School of Medicine, recalled him as a very cheerful man, enjoying puns and doing the *New York Times* crossword remarkably quickly. "My father was very proud of me. He always used to introduce me as 'my son, Al, the eye doctor, while I am the 'I doctor'!" Albert told me—an impish reference to Al's chosen profession and Kanner's own psychiatric research.[3]

He had a hugely infectious sense of humor. One Baltimore journalist who interviewed Kanner in 1969 recalled that their two-hour conversation was "dotted with Latin phrases, nursery rhymes, travelogues and punstering." His humane spirit emerged during that same interview when he said: "Every child, every adult, everybody wants what I call the three As: affection, acceptance and approval. If the child has that, regardless of his IQ or anything else, he will be all right."[4]

Asperger, for his part, was a courteous, old-fashioned gentleman. Lorna Wing met and talked to him (in English) in London in the late 1970s, not long before his death in 1980. She told me: "We sat in the Maudsley [Psychiatric Hospital] canteen over cups of tea and argued about whether his syndrome was a type of autism and what the relationship was between his and Kanner's ideas. Asperger firmly believed his was a separate syndrome, unrelated to Kanner's, although it had a lot of features in common. I argued for an autistic spectrum. We argued very happily and politely."[5]

For decades, it has been wrongly assumed that Kanner's landmark 1943 paper—"Autistic disturbances of affective contact," published in the now-defunct American journal, *The Nervous Child*[6]—predated Asperger's 1944 paper, "Die 'autistischen Psychopathen' in Kindesalter," which appeared in the journal, *Archiv für Psychiatrie und Nervenkrankheiten*.[7] However, in a lecture given five years before Kanner's paper—at the Vienna University Hospital on October 3, 1938—Asperger was already talking about children with "autistic psychopathy" (in the technical sense of an abnormality of personality). The speech was subsequently published under the title "Das psychisch abnorme Kind" in the Vienna weekly, *Wiener Klinischen Wochenzeitschrift*, also in 1938.[8]

In fact, I have discovered that Asperger was using the term "autistic" even earlier. His psychiatrist daughter, Dr. Maria Asperger Felder, told me that he had employed the word "autistic" as early as 1934 in letters to colleagues during visits to Leipzig and Potsdam in Germany.[9] In a newly published chapter about her father, she cites a letter dated April 14, 1934, in which he discusses the difficulties of diagnostic concepts and suggests the possibility that "autistic" might be a useful term.[10] She also refers to a diary entry from that same year in which he appears to be attacking the "fanaticism" of the German people in following a certain path, and to an unpublished article of her father's, also from 1934, in her possession in which he makes an oblique criticism of the Nazi regime in Germany.[11]

While Kanner described the children he had seen in consultation from 1938 onwards, Asperger had actually been treating his children from as early as 1930 in a therapeutic institution.

Professor Michael Fitzgerald, of Trinity College, Dublin, has gone so far as to suggest to me that Kanner "plagiarized" Asperger's work. Fitzgerald is convinced that Kanner, although by then based in America, must have heard about Asperger's writings and lectures from the many Germans and Austrians immigrating into the US in flight from Nazi persecution.[12] He is not alone. The Swedish autism authority, Christopher Gillberg, told me: "I am pretty certain that Kanner must have been aware of Asperger's work, because he was writing about the work of all other writers who had had anything to say about conditions with symptoms similar to his. Kanner never mentioned Asperger, but it does not make sense that he was completely unaware of someone writing in his own language, given that he was so very well aware of people writing in other languages at the same time that Asperger was working."[13]

It does seem very odd, especially as Van Krevelen, whom Kanner often quoted in his papers, was mentioning Asperger's work as early as the 1950s and Bernard Rimland, in his seminal 1964 book, *Infantile autism*, includes a reference to "Asperger's syndrome," a full 17 years before Lorna Wing officially coined the term. Gillberg noted that he and his Swedish colleagues were aware of autistic pyschopathy as a concept as early as 1973.[14]

Kanner's supposedly pioneering 1943 paper begins: "Since 1938, there have come to our attention a number of children whose condition differs so markedly and uniquely from anything reported so far, that each case merits—and, I hope, will eventually receive—a detailed consideration of its fascinating peculiarities." Could that 1938 reference be an allusion to Asperger's 1938 paper, as Michael Fitzgerald believes?

Kanner's closest colleague. Leon Eisenberg—now in his eighties but still a sharp-minded professor at Harvard Medical School—thinks not. Eisenberg told me: "That 'we' must refer to 'him' [Kanner]. That was the royal 'our.' He would not have deliberately withheld Asperger's name

11

if he had known about Asperger's work at the time." Eisenberg believes the reference to 1938 was an allusion to the date Kanner saw the first of the 11 children in his original study, Donald T.[15]

Kanner never referred to Asperger in any of his papers, whereas Asperger makes a number of allusions to Kanner's work—sometimes in glowing terms. (In his 1968 paper, Asperger refers to Kanner's excellent descriptions of his children.) Nor did the two men meet when Asperger visited the United States in the 1970s. Michael Fitzgerald in Dublin believes that this might have been a sign of Kanner's "embarrassment" at having "plagiarized" his work. Lorna Wing also said she found Kanner's silence on Asperger "suspicious" but was careful to add: "No one is totally original. . . . Asperger may have read Eva Sushareva's 1926 paper."[16]

If Kanner had known of Asperger's work, could his silence on the subject be attributed to professional jealousy? One of the leading world authorities on the neurological and linguistic impairments in autism, Professor Isabelle Rapin, believes this is possible. She told me: "The field of autism is incredibly politicized here in the United States. There are the 'in' people and the 'out' people."[17]

Germany's Dr. Gerhard Bosch—who, at over 90, is probably the oldest living autism pioneer on the planet (as we shall see in chapter 2, he not only began work on autism in the early 1950s but also diagnosed

**Figure 2** Hans Asperger (photo courtesy of Maria Asperger Felder)

individuals with Asperger's syndrome in that decade, using Hans Asperger's term, "autistic psychopathy")—told me that he thought Kanner had never mentioned Asperger's cases because "he was dealing with severe cases. He had another picture and for Kanner, Asperger was describing a very different condition."[18] Bosch met both men but wrote a chapter on autism for a volume on twentieth-century psychology edited by Asperger.

So who were these two remarkable men, both of whom came to play such a seminal role in the understanding of the autistic condition?

Hans Asperger was born on a farm outside Vienna on February 18, 1906. A talented linguist, he had difficulty making

12

friends and was considered "remote." His daughter, Maria Asperger Felder, described him in similar terms in an interview with Professor Uta Frith and Professor Christopher Gillberg, prompting Gillberg to suggest that Asperger himself could have been affected by his own syndrome. When I raised this issue with Maria Asperger Felder myself, she conceded that her father "didn't need much social contact. He was content with his own company. He loved nature. He even climbed the Matterhorn."[19]

In 1932, Asperger was appointed director of the play-pedagogic station at Vienna University children's clinic. He married in 1935 and had five children, including two daughters who themselves became doctors. In the later part of the Second World War, Asperger served as a doctor in Croatia. As his daughter told me: "He saw many wounded and dead and told us about his experiences years later. He was against war. He was a nature- and people-loving person, not a soldier."[20]

In 1944, he became a lecturer at the University of Vienna and was appointed director of the children's clinic in 1946. It was here that his remarkable nursing colleague, Viktorine Zak, developed the first programs for children with what we now call Asperger's syndrome. She used pioneering music, drama, play, and speech therapy to teach the children social skills. She was killed during an allied bombing raid on Vienna and buried with the child she was clutching at the time. In 1957, Asperger became professor at the University of Innsbruck children's clinic and from 1962 held the same position in Vienna.

Asperger's mentor was Irwin Lazar, who had initially shown an interest in the writings of Sigmund Freud and had invited psychoanalysts to join his clinic, but later decided that psychoanalysis was not appropriate for treating children. Lazar treated the child and adolescent victims of the First World War. This interest in traumatized youth demonstrated a humanity which he may well have transmitted directly to his pupil, Asperger. Asperger adapted a method known in German as *Heilpädagogik* (roughly translated as curative or remedial pedagogy or the educational treatment of neuropsychopathological disorders of children). It was a term introduced in Vienna by Clemens von Pirquet. (The German school restricted the approach to individuals with mental retardation, whereas the Austrian concept was broader.) When Lazar died suddenly in 1932, he was replaced by Franz Hamburger, whose interest in a possible affective disturbance in children at a biological level of drives and instincts strongly influenced Asperger's concept of autism. Professor Uta Frith has noted that the staff met at each other's homes

**Figure 3**  Elizabeth Wurst

**Figure 4**  Maria Theresia
Schubert

for dinner once a week and during their informal chats, she speculates, they probably discussed the characteristic features of autistic children.

Dr. Elizabeth Wurst worked closely with Hans Asperger in Vienna in the 1960s and 1970s. They first met in 1969. Sitting in the very same building in the University Clinic where they worked together, Wurst told me: "He was tall and enjoyed telling stories. He was like a grandfather, with white hair and very patient and respectful. He made you feel welcome and he was interested in what you had to say. My first impression was that I would enjoy working here with him."[21]

According to Wurst, one of the first questions Asperger asked the child was: "Do you know what your name means?" It was important for him to see if the child knew anything about his or her own forename. "That was the way he started every interview."[22]

Another of Asperger's colleagues in the 1970s, Dr. Maria Theresia Schubert, recalled that, with the children, Asperger "appreciated the children enormously. He would give them little tasks: mathematical sums, general knowledge questions. The children respected him—but he maintained a certain distance from them."[23] Schubert said that Asperger liked to joke that it helped to be a little autistic if you wanted to do things well—meaning, specifically, that it helped to be focused. She told me: "My first impression was that he was very tolerant. He didn't push people in any particular direction, giving his employees great freedom."[24]

Wurst told me: "Asperger had a very good memory and he had read very widely in literature—Goethe, Lessing, also Sartre and classical literature. He also loved art." Nevertheless, he could be exceedingly harsh at times. Once, Wurst handed Asperger a manuscript she had written and he said to her: "Why have you got so much paper dirty? Why are you quoting these other people writing abut autism? My ideas are good enough."[25] Schubert recalled another instance of his severity. She had dressed up as Eliza Doolittle from *My Fair Lady* at a fancy dress event and Asperger expressed admiration for the costume: "But you have to *be* Eliza Doolittle."[26]

In a radio interview in 1974, Asperger claimed he had begun work as a clinician in 1932 under Franz Hamburger.[27] Hamburger appears to have had strong sympathies with the Nazi Party—certainly this is suggested by a speech he gave as president of the University of Vienna in 1939, published in the *Journal of the American Medical Association*, in which he declared: "National Socialism means a revolution in every sphere of our civilization and culture. No phase of Western culture is unaffected by it. . . . Medicine has now progressed beyond its old frontiers and has broken out of its shell, thanks to the philosophy and deeds of the Führer."[28]

Hamburger's clear allegiance, coupled with Asperger's professed enthusiasm for the Jugendbewegung—a youth movement similar to the Boy Scouts—have led some critics to claim that Asperger himself had affinities with the Nazis. There seems to be no evidence of this whatsoever—indeed, the very opposite is more likely to be the case, as we shall see shortly. Nevertheless, one of the most prominent proponents of this view was Eric Schopler, the great US autism pioneer who founded the TEACCH educational program in North Carolina in the 1970s, and was himself a refugee from Nazi persecution. Dr. Lorna Wing, who first introduced Asperger's work to the English-speaking world in 1981, told me that Schopler fervently believed that Asperger had either been a member of Hitler Youth or at least had close ties to the Nazis.[29] I have made an extensive study of all Asperger's lectures and I have found absolutely no sign whatsoever of praise for the Hitler Youth Movement, only of his enjoyment of the Jugendbewegung, which dated from much earlier and had nothing to do with the Nazis.

It is important to emphasize the social and political conditions under which Asperger gave his 1938 talk. The year before, the Vienna Psychiatric and Neurological Association appointed a committee to study the problem of revised insanity laws for Austria. Prominent in the legislative program sponsored by this group was the establishment of state detention institutions for psychopaths who, although not insane within the legal definition, were nevertheless a public burden. A Professor Berze pointed out in a lecture to the association that, among the psychopaths of the "borderline" type who, in the absence of any definitive mental disease, could not be declared insane were those mentally subnormal criminals who constituted a permanent social menace. The Vienna psychiatrists recommended not only the detention of dangerous psychopaths but a continuous systematic supervision of all psychopathic individuals.

Hans Asperger worked as the Director of the Department of Orthopaedagogy at the Children's Clinic of the University of Vienna, under Franz Hamburger. Some critics have claimed that his thesis was consistent with the eugenic approach, as set out by Hamburger.

This appears to be a serious misconception. The Nazis annexed Austria in March 1938 and it seems clear that Hans Asperger feared they would shortly introduce the eugenics law, already in place in Germany, ordering the extermination of, among others, the mentally handicapped and "subnormal." Indeed, his daughter claims that he personally witnessed some unpleasant incidents during his visits to Germany in the early 1930s.

A PhD student, Marc Bush, has carried out a very detailed stylistic analysis of Asperger's papers of 1938 and 1944 and believes that Asperger deliberately couched them in "Nazi-style" vocabulary to deceive the Nazis, while protecting the children in his charge in Vienna. "That explains why the 1938 paper, or Asperger's follow-up paper in 1944, did not become known in the United States, where you might have expected German-speaking, scientific-minded immigrants to mention them: they saw them virtually as Nazi propaganda and not worth citing. Whereas nothing could be further from the truth."[30]

Asperger's colleague, Elizabeth Wurst, told me: "Asperger had a very clear standpoint against the Nazis. He tried to develop this position. Two of his colleagues . . . emigrated to the United States and when he himself visited the US, he met them and discussed the old times. If there had been any problems with Jewish people in his team, he would not have sought them out in America."[31]

A close reading of Asperger's 1938 paper throws up some fascinating clues to why he wrote this article in the way he did, as well as to how his vocabulary was misinterpreted. The paper begins by appearing to praise the Third Reich and he then refers to the need to avoid "the transmission of sick genetic material"—apparently falling firmly into line with Nazi thinking on eugenics. However, as Marc Bush has so rightly pointed out, in virtually the same breath, Asperger goes on to defend and praise the children (with autistic psychopathy) in his charge. He speaks about "how much we can do to help" abnormal children:

> And if we help them with all our devotion, we also supremely serve our people; not only by preventing them from putting a strain on the community of our nation through their anti-social and criminal deeds, but also by trying to ensure that they may find their place in the living organism of the nation as working individuals.[32]

Asperger continues to stress the value of the children with autistic psychopathy to society:

> We claim—not on theoretical grounds but from the experience of dealing with many children—that this boy's positive and negative features are two naturally necessary, connected aspects of what is really a homogenously laid-out personality. We can also express this as follows: the difficulties which this boy experiences with himself, as well as with his relationship to the world, are the price he has to pay for his special gifts.[33]

Asperger concluded his 1938 lecture thus:

> We must never give up on the education of abnormal individuals, based on the knowledge that, in these people, all of a sudden—at puberty, for example—there may appear strengths and capacities which we would not have suspected existed in these children or we could not have foreseen would have been of any importance.[34]

The Gestapo came twice to Asperger's clinic to arrest him and he was protected on both occasions by Hamburger. Why would the Gestapo have come for Asperger if he was not Jewish? Wurst speculated: "He ran a hospital with so-called 'abnormal' children. Some had Down's syndrome. The question is whether he refused to hand them over to officials. That may be what happened."[35] Could Nazi members also have been in the audience during his 1938 talk? His daughter told me that she thought this was likely.[36]

Asperger himself gave a major clue as to the reasons for the Gestapo's visit in his 1974 radio interview:

> In *Heilpädagogik*, we had a great deal of contact with disturbed, mentally deficient children. We had no choice but to recognize their value and

love them. What is their value? They belong to the population, they are indispensable for some jobs but also for the ethos which teaches us how we humans are committed to one another. It is totally inhuman—as we saw with dreadful consequences—when people accept the concept of a worthless life. . . . As I was never willing to accept this concept—in other words, to notify the [Nazi] Health Office of the mentally deficient [children in my charge]—this was a truly dangerous situation for me. I must give great credit to my mentor Hamburger, because although he was a convinced National Socialist, he saved me twice from the Gestapo with strong, personal commitment. He knew my attitude but he protected me with his whole being, and for that I have the greatest appreciation.[37]

Maria Asperger Felder told me that her father had never joined the Nazi Party. She did not know, she said, how he had managed to continue in his post without becoming a party member.[38]

After the war, Asperger traveled around the world, not just in Europe (he spoke about his new syndrome in the Netherlands as early as 1949) but further afield. He spent six weeks in the United States in 1950 and gave a talk to the newly formed Japanese Society for Child and Adolescent Psychiatry in Tokyo in 1965.[39] His daughter told me he had been entranced by the Japanese gardens—"especially the old men combing the leaves of the flowers to make wonderful patterns."[40] He also traveled to Latin America with his wife and, as a great admirer of Inca culture, visited Machu Picchu in Peru.[41]

Nevertheless, Asperger's writings were not mentioned at a major psychiatry conference in Zurich in April 1957. The veteran French autism authority, Professor Gilbert Lelord, who attended this congress, told me that this might have been a consequence of the Second World War. "Even though Asperger was undoubtedly a victim of the war, German-language papers were not popular at the time," said Lelord.[42]

After he retired, Asperger continued to come into his clinic once a week, on Wednesdays, to give a lecture on *Heilpädagogik*, which was founded in Austria. "He was not interested in psychotherapy—he was convinced that teaching could help the children," Schubert told me. "The most interesting word in *Heilpädagogik* was 'integration'. He wanted to integrate five disciplines: teaching, pediatrics, psychiatry, psychology, and sociology. That was what *Heilpädagogik* meant."[43]

★ ★ ★

**Figure 5**   Leo Kanner
(photo courtesy of Johns
Hopkins University)

Leo Kanner—who pronounced his name "Konner" (indeed, his son, Al, told me his father was always amused when post came to him in the US addressed to Lee O'Connor[44])—was born Chatskel Leib Kanner to orthodox Jewish parents in a small Austrian village called Klekotow on June 13, 1894. Klekotow (called Klelotiw today) was a village near the Ukrainian town of Brody. From 1872 until the end of the First World War, Brody marked the border between Austrian Galicia and the Russian Empire. Jews made up about 70% of the total population and Yiddish was the predominant language. Kanner spent the first years of his life in Klekotow and Brody. He described his own father as socially awkward, obsessively dedicated to Talmudic studies, and eager to acquire large amounts of other, often useless information. His mother enjoyed having her husband perform amazing feats of memory in public. In fact, Kanner's father might well have been diagnosed with Asperger's syndrome today. Kanner himself could also recite long poems from memory—but unlike his father, he did have social skills.

Kanner's close Baltimore colleague, Professor Leon Eisenberg, supported this account of his prodigious memory, telling me: "He was remarkable man. He gave courses in the evening for school teachers. He would ask them to take the same seats each week, to connect their names and faces. But I saw Kanner on the street eight years after a course, and he recalled a student he had met perfectly and the people she sat next to. And this memory may have played a big part in his ability to recognize the first eleven children with early infantile autism which he wrote up, because he had seen them over a period of several years and it took a remarkable mind to sort out the commonalities, given the disparities in these kids who went from—the one I remember in particular who had learnt the 25 or so questions and answers of the Presbyterian Catechism by the time he was eight or nine and another who was non-verbal but had remarkable gifts in performance intelligence that made it clear that there was a child behind that mute appearance."[45]

Leo Kanner could quite easily have become a writer, rather than a child psychiatrist. As a young boy, Kanner moved to Berlin in 1906 to live with his uncle. He wrote his first poem when he was 10 years old, inspired by Hector Malot's touching account of the loneliness of childhood, *Sans famille*, a book young Leo had bought for half a kroner. His parents and friends—who heard him recite verse—encouraged him to continue writing poetry. Indeed, his high-school teachers in Berlin advised him to consider a literary career and for a time he attempted to follow their advice. Berlin, in the years prior to the First World War, was a crucible for aspiring young writers and artists, and representatives of many of the major movements—impressionism, expressionism and surrealism— were living and working there at the time. Impressed by the report of a lecture which Kanner had submitted for publication, the *Berliner Morgenpost* newspaper supplied him with passes for lectures and readings by prominent literary figures and critics so that he could review them for the paper. He received a modest fee of 5 marks for these reviews, but his true reward was the opportunity to hear writers of the stature of Gerhardt Hauptmann read from their works.[46]

In 1917, while already a medical student, Kanner wrote a poem, called "The madman and his mirror image," in which the madman, fearing that his own image in the mirror may come to destroy him, attacks the mirror with a shattering blow. The poem had been inspired by the description his professor of psychiatry had given him of one of his patients.[47]

His reviews won Kanner a reputation as a literary critic but his hopes of a creative literary career were dashed, since no one wanted to publish his poems. Kanner looked back fondly on these years in Germany, but he told a *Baltimore Sun* reporter in 1978 that the decision saved his life: "If I had made it in literature, I'd have stayed in Germany and been killed in the Holocaust."[48] Indeed, some sources claim that Kanner's mother and three sisters were murdered by the Nazis, although his own unpublished autobiography, *Freedom from Within*, does not mention his mother's fate and states that, while his father died just before the outbreak of the Second World War, one of his sisters moved to Belgium, a brother, Max, emigrated to the United States, and another, Josef, left Europe for Palestine.[49]

Kanner studied at the school of medicine at the Friedrich-Wilhelms-University in Berlin. At the outbreak of the First World War in 1914, Kanner, because of his Austrian origin, was recruited into the Imperial and Royal Army of Austria and Hungary and was in the medical service of the 10th Infantry Regiment. After his military service, he continued medical school before another period of military service in the army of the Habsburg monarchy. He became naturalized as a Prussian in 1919. At the beginning of the following year, he started as an assistant physician at the Charité Hospital in Berlin, under Friedrich Kraus. Kraus commissioned him to carry out work on normal heart sounds and their relationship to the electrocardiogram—and indeed, cardiology was Kanner's chief research interest at this time.[50] After earning his doctorate in 1920, he not only worked as a physician but also continued to write poetry and participate in the art and culture of Berlin at the time.

Although he began to teach electrocardiography at the University of Berlin, Kanner already had a great interest in psychiatry. As he recalled in an interview in Louisville, Kentucky, in 1972: "I was fortunate in having an excellent teacher, Karl Bonhoeffer, who is well-known in the history of psychiatry. He was a very noble person. . . . He was not in accord with the Hitler regime and his son and son-in-law were sent to concentration camps."[51]

By now, however, Kanner had a wife and young daughter to support and, with inflation raging in Berlin, he decided to leave Germany for the United States in January 1924. In the same 1972 interview, he recalled: "I was in practice for three years during the time of the horrible German inflation, when I was a multibillionaire!" One of his students on his electrocardiography course in Berlin happened to be based in Aberdeen, South Dakota. "He was very lonely," Kanner recalled in 1972, "and we invited him to our place a number of times for dinner. One day, before going over to our house, he said he had some dealing at the American Consulate and asked whether I would go along with him. So I did. He had me wait, and then he came down with an affidavit all signed out for me and my wife, and he said: 'I think you should get away from all this terrible inflation. Why don't you go to America?' "[52]

Kanner began work as an assistant physician at the State Hospital in Yankton, South Dakota, publishing a paper on general paralysis among the Native Americans he treated there, and another on syphilis the following year. He even had an opportunity to meet the great German psychiatrist, Emil Kraepelin, who was visiting the United States. At the same time, his interest in the arts remained a potent one. Sometimes, Kanner's passions for science and literature coincided: in 1925, the *Journal of Abnormal and Social Psychology* published his article, "A psychiatric study of Ibsen's *Peer Gynt*."

Kanner wrote his first book, *Folklore of the teeth*, in 1924, based on notes he had made while teaching dental students in Germany. He later claimed that writing this book had helped him to master the English language. He was also fluent in Polish, French, Lithuanian, Yiddish, Hebrew, and Ukrainian, apart from his native German. He retained a strong German accent while speaking English until the end of his life.

He joined the Henry Phipps Psychiatric Clinic at Johns Hopkins University in Baltimore in October 1928, working under the leading Swiss psychiatrist, Adolf Meyer. Two years later, Kanner founded the first child psychiatric clinic in any teaching hospital anywhere in the world.

Kanner's early months at Johns Hopkins had an inauspicious beginning. After Paul Schilder had given a lecture on research into the hypothalamus—with particular emphasis on glucose metabolism and sexual behavior—Adolf Meyer asked the audience: "Is there any discussion?" The young Kanner stood up, congratulated Schilder on his talk and then remarked humorously that he now understood why people called their love objects "honey" or "sugar": because of the proximity of the sex center to the sugar center in the hypothalamus. While the audience laughed loudly, Professor Meyer was not amused by what he considered Kanner's inexcusably crass intervention and repeated the question: "Is there any discussion?"[53]

Although Kanner and Meyer came to admire one another, my examination of the Kanner archives at Johns Hopkins has revealed that letters from Kanner asking his boss for an increase in salary fell on deaf ears, even after Kanner won international renown for the publication of his book, *Child psychiatry*, in 1935, and for diagnosing and treating childhood mental disorders.[54]

What influence did Adolf Meyer have on his young protégé? Meyer was founder of the psychobiological school of psychiatry and because he believed each individual's psychiatric disorder was unique, he was unable to accept the classificatory schemas of either Kraepelin or Bleuler. Meyer also rejected Freudian assertions of the presence of hidden psychodynamic factors causing mental disorders. In the first edition of his book, *Child psychiatry*, in 1935, Kanner does make a brief reference to "autism"—in the sense Bleuler used it—as a disorder of the mother–child relationship.[55]

In his 1941 book, *In defense of mothers*, Kanner wrote:

> If you want to go on worshipping the Great God Unconscious and his cocksure interpreters, there is nothing to keep you from it. But do not let your children pay the penalty for your own excursions into the realm of fancy. For there is nothing more fanciful than an unproven, arbitrarily

decreed "psychology," sublimely removed from life as it is lived, scornful of facts and real occurrences, and depending instead on a dreambook type of "interpretation of a mythological unconscious."[56]

On the other hand, Kanner said, rather startlingly, in his 1972 interview in Louisville: "There are wonderful analysts. I can't think of a grander person who has done more for children than Anna Freud. On the other hand, you have that horrible example of Melanie Klein, who saw everything in only one way and that was *her* way."[57]

In many ways, Kanner had an old-fashioned attitude to his consultation work. He was once asked, during a visit to Omaha, Nebraska, how old he was. He replied: "I'm a left-over from the nineteenth century!" He said in a 1976 interview: "People talk about the organicist approach, the analytical approach, the sociological approach. But you don't approach patients; they approach you, because of their need."[58]

Long before his work in autism, he demonstrated profound concern for mentally retarded children at a time when most psychiatrists excluded them from their clinics. Significantly, in the 1930s, he undertook a follow-up study of 166 patients who had been released from Maryland state training schools for the retarded via habeas corpus writs secured by lawyers over the previous two decades. Kanner managed to locate 102 of them, of whom only 34 were doing even moderately well. The vast majority, he discovered, had worked as domestic servants before being dismissed as inadequate to the task and ending up in city slums. When Kanner revealed the truth of what was happening in 1938, his paper received massive media coverage leading to action to end the practice of lawyers being able to obtain the release of the mentally retarded into the community.[59]

Kanner also had great sympathy for the politically oppressed. Leon Eisenberg told me about Kanner's work on behalf of victims of Nazi persecution: "During the 1930s, when it was still possible to help Jews to leave Hitler's Germany, Kanner was quite active on their behalf. To obtain a visa, the potential immigrant needed a certificate from an American citizen in good standing stating that he or she would not only help the migrant to obtain work, but would stand guarantor that the migrant would not become a burden on the public purse. That is, Kanner had to take financial responsibility for the people he was willing to endorse."[60]

Eisenberg pointed out that this was a time of considerable turmoil in the Jewish community in the United States. "The United States had its own anti-Semites. Some well-to-do and conservative Jews were afraid that bringing more Jews to American shores would increase anti-Semitism, Kanner's attempt to get additional financial support from wealthy Jews in Baltimore met with little success."[61]

Eisenberg also pointed out that Kanner had brought distinguished German and Austrian physicians over to the US and got them jobs as attendants in the state hospital. "However far this was beneath their deserts, they were grateful to him for saving their lives. . . . I don't know how many refugees Kanner brought over. I once heard him say '200,' which is a really incredible number for one man."[62] Eisenberg also told me of Kanner's efforts on behalf of victims of Franco's repression after the Spanish Civil War.

★ ★ ★

It may well be that Asperger preceded Kanner in his description of autistic features. Nevertheless, Kanner's 1943 paper, "Autistic disturbances of affective contact," published in the now-defunct American journal, *The Nervous Child*, certainly marked a watershed. Indeed, Michael Rutter believes Kanner's paper is the important one: "I don't actually have a very high opinion of Asperger's writings. They were so rambling and disorganized. Which came first? Well, it depends what you mean. Was Darwin the first person to deal with evolution? Of course not. But what Darwin did was provide an organized approach to it. I think the same thing about Kanner."[63]

In his key 1943 paper, Kanner considered five features to be diagnostic: a profound lack of affective contact with other people; an anxiously obsessive desire for the preservation of sameness in the child's routines and environment; a fascination with objects, which are handled with skill in fine motor movements; mutism or a kind of language that does not seem intended for interpersonal communication; good cognitive potential shown in feats of memory or skills on performance tests, especially the Séguin form board (a widely used instrument to assess children's abilities through non-verbal means such as the puzzle-like placement of common geometric shapes into openings of the same shape).

Kanner also emphasized onset of the condition from birth or before 30 months. For this reason, he refused to see the children as "withdrawing." For him, the children had never been engaged with the social world. All 11 children he examined in the original 1943 paper had difficulty relating to other people, a condition Kanner called "extreme autistic aloneness." This was, for Kanner, the determining feature of autism.

In addition, most of the children had speech delays or unusual language—they echoed what they heard or they reversed pronouns. They also hated changes in routine: in the arrangement of furniture or even the route taken from one place to another. There were also sensory problems. Most were highly skilled at one or two tasks, such as classifying animals or memorizing addresses or train timetables.

Oddly, however, Kanner did not believe that the unique syndrome he was describing was mental retardation; most of the 11 children were, he believed, of normal or above-normal intelligence. This is bewildering, partly because of his own expertise in mental retardation and because his own descriptions of the first 11 children include features of cognitive impairment.

"It is an interesting point," Lorna Wing told me. "I'm only guessing, but maybe Kanner thought the cognitive difficulties followed on from the emotional ones, that their social impairment explained everything else, and that really, if you could get over that, you would find they were brilliant underneath. He firmly believed they had this potential for normal or high intelligence. And I suppose that fitted in with his fervent belief at the time that there was no organic problem and that the only difficulty they had was the lack of social instinct."[64]

Kanner's colleague, Leon Eisenberg, told me: "That is where he went beyond the evidence. He talked about intelligent physiognomy—the appearance of an intelligent look—rather than the dull look which one associates with mental retardation. And the children could do puzzles and remember places and go to the same place in the house, even though they were non-verbal. But I think he was extrapolating beyond the data, and some of these children are not only verbally delayed but cognitively impaired."[65]

Michael Rutter believes that Kanner was focusing on the children's unusual talents in his study. "With the benefit of hindsight, he clearly read more into it than was justified. Since then, there is a lot of evidence for the reality of the savant skills he identified. So that stood the test of time."[66]

Dr. Ami Klin, at the Yale Child Study Center in New Haven, agrees: "Kanner was impressed that some of the children had special skills. But two years after him, a wonderful neurologist, Kurt Goldstein, picked up on one of the children Kanner had seen and wrote an entire monograph showing that there were special things the child could do but also that he was surrounded by a sea of disability."[67] Klin told me he felt Lorna Wing and Judith Gould's landmark 1979 study could be traced back to Goldstein's 1945 paper.

**Figure 6**   Albert Kanner

Kanner's son, Albert, told me that his father brought some of his first 11 children back to the family home and he (Albert) would play with them on the living-room floor—although he never noticed anything strange about them.[68]

Kanner's original sample was also biased, and it may have been this which led to his surprising conclusion about the children being of normal or above-normal intelligence. As the Swedish autism authority, Christopher Gillberg, noted to me: "Kanner's original cases were over-selected, with the children coming from the higher classes, because those were the parents who were aware of his writings. That's why Kanner got the impression that autism all came from the upper classes."[69]

Lauretta Bender, a psychiatrist working at Bellevue Hospital in New York, made much the same point in 1959. She wrote: "It is not clear what he [Kanner] means by saying that there is evidence that autistic children have greater intellectual potentialities, unless he is referring to the family background of his colleagues, professors and intellectual sophis-ticates who have selected his services."[70]

Apparently, Kanner denied this assertion, telling Bernard Rimland that his clientele had come both "from the slums" and the "penthouses."[71] However, Gillberg noted: "There is something very astute about Kanner's observation that the children seem to be very intelligent, because they often are, in very narrow areas."[72]

It may seem odd that both Asperger and Kanner chose to use Bleuler's term "autism," especially given that Kanner was convinced that what he described was a unique syndrome. But Marc Bush has pointed out to me that both men were likely to have studied the same textbook, namely the fifth edition of Bleuler's 1930 *Lehrbuch der Psychiatrie*.

Christopher Gillberg told me he believed they chose the term "autism" because the psychiatrists of the 1930s and 1940s were influenced by the terminology of both Bleuer and Kraepelin. "They always tried to use terms which were already in place to describe various conditions. After all, it took time for people generally to accept that Bleuler's term, autism, could be used to describe a symptom of schizophrenia. So when

Kanner was thinking of children who were aloof and detached, even though he thought it was a separate syndrome, he did see links with Bleuler's definition of autism. And of course, Bleuler's definition *was* all about egocentric thinking—and many of us today consider this to be a core feature of autism. The links between autism and schizophrenia are probably not as far-fetched as they seemed to be in the 1970s. Kanner's journal was called the *Journal of Autism and Childhood Schizophrenia.*"[73]

Indeed, the American psychologist, Louise Despert, whose ideas, as Lorna Wing reminded me, held quite a potent influence over Kanner for a while, described her first cases of childhood schizophrenia in 1938. Could Kanner, perhaps, have been referring to Despert's initial studies, rather than Asperger's, at the start of his own 1943 paper? Six years later, Kanner could be found writing: "The extreme emotional isolation from other people, which is the foremost characteristic of early infantile autism, bears so close a resemblance to schizophrenic withdrawal that the relationship between the two conditions deserves serious consideration." And yet he continued to insist that his syndrome was unique.[74]

As we shall see, this confusion in Kanner's mind between autism and childhood schizophrenia was one shared by professionals around the world for many years to come. And even Hans Asperger, in his little-known 1938 paper, can be found writing: "From such states of severely disturbed personalities there is a continuum to—and no clear dividing-line from—schizophrenia, the main symptom of which is autism, too, in the sense of loss of any contact with the environment."[75]

Six years later, in his 1944 paper, Asperger wrote: "The name 'autism,' coined by Bleuler, is undoubtedly one of the great linguistic and conceptual creations in medical nomenclature." But, just like Kanner, Asperger distinguished between Bleuler's schizophrenia and autism, because

> schizophrenic patients often live in an imaginary world of wish fulfilment and ideas of persecution. . . . However, this type of thinking does not play a role in the children we are concerned with here. While the schizophrenic patient seems to show progressive loss of contact, the children we are discussing lack contact from the start. Autism is the paramount feature in both cases. It totally colors affect, intellect, will, and action. . . . However, unlike schizophrenic patients, our children do not show a disintegration of personality. They are therefore not psychotic, instead they show a greater or lesser degree of psychopathy.[76]

Kanner was aware of the potential danger of introducing the term "autism" to describe the unique behavior he had observed in the late

1930s and early 1940s. In an important—and neglected—lecture he gave in New York in 1965, Kanner declared that he had decided, "after much groping," to introduce the term early infantile autism, "thus accentuating the time of the first manifestations and the children's limited accessibility."[77] In that lecture, Kanner went on to quote Bleuler, who had written:

> Naturally, some withdrawal from reality is implicit in the wishful thinking of normal people who "build castles in Spain." Here, however, it is mainly an act of will by which they surrender themselves to a fantasy. They know it is just fantasy and they banish it as soon as reality so demands. I would not call the effects of these mechanisms "autism" unless they are coupled with a definite withdrawal from the external world.

Commenting on these words from Bleuler, Kanner told his New York audience: "This definition does not quite account for the status of our patients. For one thing, withdrawal implies a removal of oneself from previous participation. These children have never participated."[78]

Interestingly—in view of recent studies indicating that it might be possible to diagnose autism earlier than previously believed—Kanner explained back in 1965:

> [These children] have begun their existence without the universal signs of infantile response. This is evidenced in the first months of life by the absence of the usual anticipatory reaction when approached to be picked up and by the lack of postural adaptation to the person who picks them up. Nor are they shutting themselves off from the external world, as such. While they are remote from affective and communicative contact with people, they develop a remarkable and not unskilful relationship to the inanimate environment. They can cling to things tenaciously, manipulate them adroitly, go into ecstasies when toys are moved or spun around them, and become angry when objects do not yield readily to expected performance. Indeed, they are so concerned with the external world that they watch with tense alertness to make sure that their surroundings remain static, that the totality of an experience is reiterated with its constituent details, often in full photographic and phonic identity.
>
> All this does not seem to fit in with Bleuler's criteria for autism. There is no withdrawal in the accepted sense of this word, and a specific kind of contact with the external world is a cardinal feature of the illness [*sic*]. . . . Nevertheless, in full recognition of all this, I was unable to find a concise expression that would be equally or suitably applicable to the condition, After all, these children do start out in a state which, in a way,

resembled the end results of later-life withdrawal, and there is a remoteness—at least from the human portion of the external world. An identifying designation appeared to me to be definitely desirable because, as later events proved, there was a danger of having this distinct syndrome lumped together with a variety of generalized categories.[79]

★ ★ ★

As Arn van Krevelen, of the University of Leiden's School of Medicine in the Netherlands—the first European child psychiatrist to publish a case of early infantile autism (in 1960)—pointed out in the *Journal of Autism and Childhood Schizophrenia* in 1971, the clinical pictures of Kanner's and Asperger's cases "differ considerably." He said that "Kanner described psychotic *processes*, characterized by a *course*. Asperger's autistic psychopathy represented *traits*, which were *static*."[80] Nowadays, it is the similarities, more than the differences, between the two cases which tend to be emphasized. The term "Kanner's autism" is often used today to indicate the child with a constellation of classic, "nuclear" features, resembling in astonishing detail the features that Kanner identified in his first description. In his 1944 paper, Asperger asserted that the children suffered from a fundamental disturbance that gave rise to highly characteristic problems.

Asperger noted that the syndrome was very much more common in boys than in girls. In fact, he went as far as to say, in his 1944 paper, that "autistic psychopathy is an extreme male variant of masculine intelligence, of masculine character." This concept has been taken up recently by Professor Simon Baron-Cohen in Cambridge, with his "extreme male brain" theory of autism, but Jacques Constant has pointed out that Asperger's notion chimed with the sexist ideology of the times in which Asperger was writing and working, especially *Küche, Kirche, Kinder*. Women, Constant noted, were relegated to the kitchen, church and child-rearing, and this spirit, he insists, infused Asperger's texts.[81]

**Figure 7**  Kathrin Hippler

Dr. Kathrin Hippler, who works with Elizabeth Wurst and has done a great

29

deal of valuable research in this area, agreed that Asperger's papers were written in an old-fashioned style which reflected the time in which he was writing: "He specifically said that girls did not create many original ideas."[82] In contrast, Wurst pointed out that Asperger had two women doctors working in the clinic, including herself. "He was a pioneer in this aspect for the time. We had freedom here."[83]

Jacques Constant also claimed that one of the catalysts for Asperger's interest in autism was his observation that the children he took to summer camps in the mountains reacted with terror, rather than sharing his love of nature.[84] When I raised this suggestion with Asperger's daughter in Zurich, she expressed skepticism, saying she was not even aware that her father had taken the children to the countryside.[85]

Asperger's 1944 paper deals with just four boys between the ages of 6 and 11, although a colleague of his, Swiss-born Dr. Günter Krämer, declared that Asperger's work was based on investigations of more than 400 children. Asperger called children with his condition "little professors" because of their ability to talk about their favorite subject in great detail. He followed one child, Fritz V., into adulthood. The boy became a professor of astronomy and solved an error in Sir Isaac Newton's work which he had previously noticed as a child.

The children were initially referred to Asperger from kindergartens and schools. Wurst and her Vienna colleague, Kathrin Hippler, both agreed that it was surprising that Asperger was not interested in following up the children in later years, as Kanner did. Was this, perhaps, because he felt that his condition was a constant personality disorder? Wurst conceded this possibility, adding: "Asperger was more interested in the child at that moment, to understand what was going on. At that time, not 15 years later."[86] However, Maria Asperger Felder told me that her father was planning more follow-up studies at the time he died.[87]

One of the young Austrian girls taken to see Asperger at his Vienna clinic in 1952 was 6-year-old Elfriede Jelinek, who would go on to win the Nobel Prize for Literature in 2004. In a book-length interview in 1995, the reclusive Jelinek said: "Yes, I was an Asperger patient. Not an Asperger autistic, though indeed not far off." Looking back, she qualified this decision to take her to Asperger as "a crime": "Instead of sending me out to play in the company of kids my age, my mother sent me into the company of severe neurotics and psychopaths."[88] Asperger ultimately diagnosed young Elfriede as prey to an excitement which had yet to find a suitable outlet. She suffered a complete nervous breakdown at 18 before finding a successful outlet in writing.

Asperger believed that his syndrome was never recognized in infancy and usually not before the third year of life or later. A full command of grammar was sooner or later acquired, he said, but there might be difficulty in using pronouns correctly, with the substitution of the second- or third- for the first-person forms. The content of speech was abnormal, tending to be pedantic and often consisting of lengthy disquisitions on favorite subjects. Gestures were limited, or else large and clumsy and inappropriate for the accompanying speech. Perhaps the most obvious characteristic was impairment of two-way social interaction, due primarily to an inability to understand and use the unwritten, unstated rules governing social behavior. Asperger also reported certain skills, as well as impairments: the children had excellent rote memories and became intensely interested in one or two subjects, such as astronomy, geology, the history of the steam train, the genealogy of royalty, bus time-tables or prehistoric monsters, to the exclusion of all else.

**Figure 8**   Sula Wolff

Unlike Kanner, Asperger thought of his condition as a personality disorder with organic causes. In fact, Dr. Sula Wolff, who translated Sukhareva's 1926 paper which described six boys now recognized as having Asperger's syndrome (see introduction), often referred to "schizoid personality disorder" in virtually the same breath as Asperger's syndrome. She was not using it in the sense that Melanie Klein employed the term "paranoid-schizoid." Indeed, Dr. Wolff told me: "No, it's got nothing to do with Melanie Klein, whom I have never respected. My use of these terms is in line with the DSM [American Psychiatric Association] and ICD [World Health Organization] classifications. . . . My children could be either abnormally sensitive or callous."[89]

That last adjective is a significant one. One of the aspects of Hans Asperger's writings which Dr. Wolff laid great emphasis on was the capacity of individuals with the syndrome to show malice. Both Elizabeth Wurst and Maria Theresia Schubert recalled instances when the children at Asperger's clinic did indeed show such delight in another's misfortune.

However, Professor Simon Baron-Cohen, who sees adults with Asperger's syndrome regularly at his Cambridge clinic, strongly disagrees:

"I have to say I have seen the opposite. some of them like to speak bluntly—which can be hurtful—but I don't think this is motivated by malice. It's just that they value the truth and a sense of justice. They value loyalty and they certainly have a strong moral code by which they may have worked out how they would like to be treated and how they would like the planet to be treated."[90]

Baron-Cohen cited the case of the computer hacker with Asperger's syndrome, Gary McKinnon, who won an appeal in January 2009 against his extradition to the United States from Britain after Baron-Cohen declared that he would suffer if he were to be jailed. "He is a man who is focused on the truth. This is because you can *rely* on facts. Social relationships can be very slippery, whereas facts are predictable. He was interested in whether the American government was concealing information. He was motivated by a desire to help."[91]

Here again, Sula Wolff sees things very differently: "Asperger considered the condition he described as a personality disorder and my position has always been that that is so. At the same time, one can also consider Asperger's syndrome to be among the 'developmental disorders'. There need be no contradiction. My guess is that people with Asperger's syndrome, unless also psychotic, can understand what they are doing but are totally preoccupied with their own abnormal reasoning (often paranoid) as a basis for their actions and do not have the capacity to empathize with, or understand, the position of their victims and society at large."[92]

Wolff added: "By substituting the much more palatable concept of a 'developmental disorder' for Asperger's 'personality disorder,' Lorna Wing has certainly done a service to affected people and their families. But I don't think either Asperger's or Sukhareva's work made affected people in any way 'morally suspect.' In current classification systems, the schizophrenia spectrum has nothing to do with the sociopathic group of personality disorders."[93]

Lorna Wing has written: "There is no question that Asperger's syndrome can be regarded as a form of schizoid personality. The question is whether this grouping is of any value."[94] Wing pointed out that, as early as 1925, the German psychiatrist Ernst Kretschmer outlined some case histories of so-called schizoid adults, one or two of which were "strongly reminiscent" of Asperger's syndome, "although he did not provide sufficient detail to ensure the diagnosis."[95]

In his 1944 paper, perhaps surprisingly, Asperger refers to the severe learning problems of his children: "They had their very own way of learning," Elizabeth Wurst recalled. "They didn't like learning by heart,

32

for example."[96] He also refers to the *Humorlosigkeit* (humorlessness) of the children. Maria Theresia Schubert felt he was alluding to lack of understanding of humor—they took words literally at their meaning.[97]

Strikingly, by 1969, Asperger appeared to be no longer using the term "autistic psychopathy." His 1968 paper refers to "Aspergersche Kinder" and "Kannersche Kinder." Kathrin Hippler told me that, by the late 1960s, Asperger realized that people were talking more about "anti-social behavior and personality disorder, and he did not want these to be mixed up with his own syndrome, which might have happened if he had continued to use the term 'psychopathy.' Maybe it was also because he realized there were the two types of autism."[98]

Hippler added that a reason Asperger dropped the term "psychopathy" may have been that he considered it very important that his syndrome "had nothing to do with psychosis. He always differentiated his syndrome from schizophrenia. He took Bleuler's term, but only because of the children's 'withdrawal.' "[99]

Wurst agrees. She told me: "Asperger knew there were children with low intelligence and similar behaviors, but he focused on the children with good levels of intelligence. He knew a lot about Kanner, but he was fascinated in the children with restricted interests. He loved to talk to them and hear about their thoughts."[100]

The main difference between his children and Kanner's, Wurst said, was that his children had creative intelligence. "They also had good speech, even if it was peculiar. And sometimes they had clumsy movements, whereas Kanner's children often had good movements. Both groups had social problems."[101]

Christopher Gillberg is one of those who believes that Kanner's celebrated 1943 paper, unlike Asperger's work, set the cause of autism back, in some ways, rather than represented its first and most valuable introduction to the world. Gillberg is alluding to the emphasis Kanner placed on the coldness and detached nature of the parents of the autistic children he saw in his original study. It was, indeed, Kanner who coined the term "refrigerator mother" long before Bruno Bettelheim used the concept so harmfully to instil a sense of blame in so many parents around the world. In fact, as late as 1960, Kanner told *Time* magazine that children with autism were the offspring of "parents cold and rational who just happened to defrost long enough to produce a child."[102]

Michael Rutter disagrees that Kanner's allusion to cold parenting represented a serious danger. "What we have to differentiate is evidence of a broader phenotype. Kanner switched back and forward, which is a mark of his integrity."[103] By "broader phenotype," Professor Rutter is referring to the finding, notably in his 1977 twin study with Susan Folstein, that family relatives of individuals with autism could themselves show autistic traits.[104]

To understand why Kanner wrote about parents in the way he did in 1943, it is essential to recall the climate in the United States at the time. There was powerful opposition in some circles to any suggestion that genes could affect behavior, as this was thought to be redolent of the Nazis' hideous racial laws. (This also explains why the psychoanalytical approach has clung on so long in France: it was the Vichy collaborationist psychiatrists who took the organicist, genetic line, while the Resistance professionals adopted the psychoanalytical approach.)

And yet the debate raged heatedly on both sides. Indeed in July 1942, when Germany's eugenics program was known to leaders in American psychiatry, the official journal of the American Psychiatric Association published two articles debating a "final solution" for America's retarded. In the journal's lead article, originally a paper delivered at the annual meeting of the association, Foster Kennedy, professor of neurology at Cornell University, argued that all children with proven mental retardation ("feeble-mindedness") over the age of 5 should be put to death to relieve them of "the agony of living" and to save their parents from expense and mental anguish. "So the place for euthanasia, I believe, is for the completely hopeless defective: nature's mistake, something we hustle out of sight, which should never be seen at all."[105]

In rebuttal, Leo Kanner came out against euthanasia but was nevertheless in favor of sterilization. He argued that such individuals might still serve a purpose to society—garbage collection, postmen, for example—as well as give meaning to their parents by virtue of having to care for them. Shockingly, however, no one emphasized the unethical nature of putting individuals with disability to death.

Although Kanner's 1943 paper does apparently make the claim that the parents of autistic children are cold and detached, he always claimed that he had never actually *blamed* the parents. It seems peculiar, then, that he felt the need to announce to the 1969 meeting of the National Society for Autistic Parents (later the Autism Society of America): "Herewith I especially acquit you people as parents." In that famous address, he declared:

I have been misquoted many times. From the very first publication until the last, I spoke of this condition in no uncertain terms as "innate." But

34

because I described some of the characteristics of the parents as persons, I was misquoted often as having said that "it is all the parents' fault." Those of you parents who have come to see me with your children know that this isn't what I said. As a matter of fact, I have tried to relieve parental anxiety when they had been made anxious because of such speculation.[106]

Leon Eisenberg insists that Kanner, in his 1943 paper, "made the rather bold suggestion, for the time, that this was an inborn error of affective contact. Kanner thought—and told me he thought—that the notion that it was inborn, that is congenital, perhaps genetic (but not specified), delayed the acceptance of autism, because those were the days when psychiatry was entirely psychogenic in its orientation, and people were talking about Margaret Mahler's psychosis well before Kanner's autism because her condition was psychodynamic"—and that matched the spirit of the times.[107]

How to explain, then, that Mahler states in her memoirs that Kanner gave her fulsome praise and support?[108] Indeed, in his 1972 edition of *Child psychiatry*, Leo Kanner approvingly cites Mahler's division of child psychosis—"one representing cases of early infantile autism and the other comprising the cases of symbiotic infantile psychosis."[109] And in the 1973 edition of his book, *Childhood psychosis: Initial studies and new insights*, Kanner writes:

> The emotional frigidity in the typical autistic family suggests a dynamic experiential factor in the genesis of the disorder of the child. The mechanization of care and the almost total absence of warmth in child-rearing may be exemplified by the case of Brian. . . . The mother, a psychology graduate student, decided that the children were to be raised "scientifically"—that is, not to be picked up if crying, except on schedule. Furthermore, an effort was made to "keep them from infections" by avoiding human contact.[110]

Kanner goes on to note that psychiatrists generally agree that "emotional deprivation has profound consequences for psychobiological development."[111] He cites Bowlby and Gesell, among others. It may well be that this chapter is a reworking of a much earlier paper (as suggested by the people he quotes from the 1940s and 1950s). Nevertheless, it is surprising that Kanner allowed these lines to appear in a book under his name as late as 1973.

On the other hand, the picture is considerably more complex than this would suggest. I have found several pieces of evidence in the Johns

Hopkins archives of Kanner's willingness to condemn very early on (from 1937 onwards) the "abuse" committed by fellow psychiatrists and pediatricians in blaming the parents for the "defects" of their offspring. And he wrote a book in 1941 called *In defense of mothers*, tellingly subtitled: "How to bring up children in spite of the more zealous psychologists." Later, as we shall see in a subsequent chapter, Kanner condemned Bruno Bettelheim's 1967 parent-blaming book, *The empty fortress*, dubbing it "the empty book."

In a 1972 lecture, Kanner declared:

> I couldn't quite see all this very fascinating and pathological behavior as emanating from the difficulty of the mother's ability towards relating to the child. . . . The parents finally rebelled against this assumption of guilt, of being made to feel the culprits, and have encouraged further research and got together to help themselves, as well as those who were interested in the topic.[112]

In his interview in Louisville that same year, Kanner could still be heard to say:

> [Early infantile autism] is a unique syndrome. You will find a variety of backgrounds, but it is unique and—almost photographically—not identical, but very, very, very similar. . . . I saw 11 children [in the original 1943 study] and I reported it, and that was that. For the first 10 years afterwards, there wasn't too much of a repercussion, and this gave me a chance to study more of these children as they came along. But in the 1950s, there came a time when people overreacted as they react now to the concept of "minimal brain damage syndrome."[113]

In that same 1972 interview, Kanner recalled his paper he wrote for the International Congress of Psychiatry in Zurich in 1957, entitled "Specificity of early infants." By 1972, he said, "the diagnosis is made much more correctly than in the 1950s, when any child who showed any peculiarity was dubbed 'infantile autism' and they created that terrible noun—oh my gosh, I hate it!—the *autist*."[114]

Kanner always claimed that he was most interested in human beings as individuals. He liked to cite a quotation from a treatise on mineralogy and geology by the German poet, Goethe, whose portrait hung over his desk next to that of Adolf Meyer: "The history of science is science itself, the history of the individual *is* the individual."

# 2

# The 1950s

## *The Seeds of Understanding*

After Leo Kanner wrote his original paper in 1943 defining the syndrome he called early infantile autism, people became fascinated with the condition. This led to some illuminating research—and to some extended confusions.

Distinguished professionals around the world began citing case after case of the condition, even while maintaining that it was rare. In 1952, the Dutch psychiatrist, Arn van Krevelen, referred to the instance of a 4-year-old girl whom he described as being as much like Kanner's cases as "one raindrop resembles another."[1]

The German pioneer, Dr. Gerhard Bosch, while working as a junior, then senior, psychiatrist at Frankfurt University's department of child and adolescent psychiatry between 1951 and 1962, presented his first case of what he called "primary autism" in Frankfurt in 1953. "I was dealing mainly with Kanner cases," the 90-year-old Bosch told me. "But shortly afterwards, I began seeing individuals who were more like Asperger's cases. Asperger's writings had appeared in Germany at around that time. I presented my first case of 'autistic psychopathy' in Maarburg in 1958."[2]

Peter Tanguay, the veteran Canadian autism researcher, told me that the curiosity aroused by Kanner's first article may have been partly because "people thought this was a way of testing parent–child relationships."[3] If so, then there was a problem: Kanner's initial paper had heightened suspicions—already quite potent in the headily psychoanalytical spirit of the times—that the parents' coldness could somehow be to blame for the child's disorder. Although Kanner explicitly stated in the 1943 paper that he considered autism to be a "biologically innate"[4] condition, that emphasis appeared to become lost in the psychodynamic passion of the period.

It was a passion Kanner did little to dampen. In his 1949 paper, he refers to "the astounding fact" that his "search for autistic children of unsophisticated parents" had remained unsuccessful. He also alludes to the "remarkable" absence of mental disorders in the children's parents and relatives.[5] This statement contrasts markedly with a 2008 study from the University of North Carolina showing that the parents of autistic children are 50% more likely to suffer from psychiatric disorders.[6]

The idea of a parental contribution to autism continued to appear in Kanner's writings and those of his close colleague, Leon Eisenberg, though with nuances. In their 1956 follow-up paper, "Early infantile autism, 1943–1955," they wrote:

> The emotional frigidity in the typical autistic family suggests a dynamic experiential factor in the genesis of the disorder in the child . . . It is difficult to escape the conclusion that this emotional configuration in the home plays a dynamic role in the genesis of autism. But it seems to us equally clear that this factor, while important in the development of the syndrome, is not sufficient in itself to result in its appearance. There appears to be some way in which the children are different from the beginning of their extra-uterine existence.[7]

They also observed that the parents' personalities might be aggravated by the non-responsiveness of the autistic child, rather than the other way around.[8]

**Figure 9**   Leon Eisenberg

Eisenberg told me that he had followed up Kanner's original sample for his own 1956 paper and reported on their clinical status in adolescence.[9] "I did not treat them, nor did Kanner. He had seen these patients in consultation. Regardless of the 'treatment' they received, my point was that the presence or absence of speech for communication by the age of 5 predicted whether they would do well or poorly."[10]

Nevertheless, Eisenberg published a separate paper in the following year, 1957, in which he spoke of the coldness of fathers of autistic children. One example he singled out was that of a man involved in a train crash. When the rescuers arrived at his carriage to pull him out, they found him sitting happily in the wreckage typing away at his typewriter.[11]

Eisenberg emphasized to me that what he was referring to in this paper was not a causal relationship between father and child, but merely a possible contributory factor. However, as Bernard Rimland would write in his ground-breaking 1964 book, *Infantile autism: The syndrome and its implications for a neural theory of behavior* (about which much more in subsequent chapters):

> There appears to be an implicit assumption that the uniqueness of the parental personalities constitutes evidence only for the "environmental" side of the controversy. It is apparently assumed that the parental personalities are too specific to be biologically determined and not capable of being transmitted genetically.[12]

Rimland also pointed out that the works of W. Goldfarb, René Spitz, Margaret Ribble and John Bowlby on the syndrome of "hospitalism" or "maternal deprivation" were frequently cited as analogous evidence that early infantile autism was psychogenic. But that analogy was poor, since the symptoms characterizing those children did not resemble autism.[13]

Another controversial issue was the continuing confusion between autism and schizophrenia. As Michael Rutter put it: "Everything was schizophrenia at that time. There was a complete neglect of diagnostic distinctions. But Kanner was a very astute clinician. He had a mischievous disrespect for the trends of the time."[14]

Nevertheless, in 1949, Kanner wrote of autistic children: "Possibly some of them are brain-damaged. Possibly all of them are schizophrenic. But in whatever category one wishes to place them, they do present a phenomenological constellation *sui generis*."[15]

Lorna Wing believes that this confusion in Kanner's mind was largely due to the influence of the psychologist, Louise Despert, whom Kanner admired. Even before Kanner's 1943 paper, Despert had presented several case histories in 1938, some of whom may have been schizophrenic but at least one of whom (HL) had behavioral symptoms very reminiscent of autism. In 1947, Despert described another group of "schizophrenic children," whom she classified by "acute" and "insidious" onset. All four in the insidious group had autistic traits.[16]

The American Psychiatric Association's publication of DSM-I—its first *Diagnostic and Statistical Manual of Mental Disorders*—in 1952 did not help clarify this point, since it specifically claimed that the primary manifestation of childhood schizophrenia was autism. Autism was not classified as a separate condition in DSM-I; autism-related behaviors were classified under the diagnosis of childhood schizophrenic reaction (see chapter 7).

"Schizophrenia was not very well understood in adults, let alone children," Peter Tanguay pointed out to me in Louisville. "It wasn't until Issy Kolvin's 1971 paper that we really had the evidence that they were different conditions."[17] In fact, it would be only in 1980, with the publication of the third edition of the American Psychiatric Association's *Diagnostic and Statistical Manual of Mental Disorders* (DSM-III), that autism was formally dissociated from schizophrenia with the introduction of the general category of "pervasive developmental disorders."

The pioneering autism researcher, Dr. Ed Ornitz, who worked at University of California, Los Angeles, from the 1960s, told me that he had conducted a study in 1984 showing that three children with a diagnosis of autism went on to receive a diagnosis of schizophrenia in adulthood. "You will find some schizophrenics with autistic characteristics—they don't relate fully, don't have good eye contact—although the vast majority do not, so there may be a phenomenological relationship between the two conditions. The important question is: could there be a causal relationship? Could there be some shared genetic etiology? I think this is worth researching."[18]

Actually, there was far less confusion in Europe than there was across the Atlantic in the US. Researchers such as Van Krevelen, Grewel, Poppella, and Schachter all published studies in the 1950s suggesting that autism was a separate syndrome. Rimland quotes an interesting 1961 study from Nesnidalova and Fiala in Czechoslovakia[19] stating categorically: "We validated, through the study of our cases and the literature, the authenticity of the differential diagnosis of Kanner's early infantile autism from childhood schizophrenia."[20]

In his important 1965 lecture in New York, Kanner told his audience:

> While the majority of the Europeans were satisfied with a sharp delineation of infantile autism as an illness *sui generis*, there was a tendency in this country [the USA] to view it as a developmental anomaly ascribed exclusively to maternal emotional determinants. Moreover, it became a habit to dilute the original concept of infantile autism by diagnosing it in many disparate conditions which show one or another isolated symptom found as a part feature of the overall syndrome.

Almost overnight [he added] the country seemed to be populated by a multitude of autistic children, and somehow this trend became noticeable overseas, as well. Mentally defective children who displayed bizarre behavior were promptly labeled autistic and, in accordance with preconceived notions, both parents were urged to undergo protracted psychotherapy, in addition to treatment directed toward the defective child's own supposedly underlying emotional problem.[21]

Kanner denounced a number of other abuses of the term "autism" in the 1950s. He said Grewel's suggestion of the term *pseudo-autism* to mean conditions with autistic-like features, rather than *true autism*, had led to haphazard use of the term. "Conditions variously described as hospitalism, anaclitic depression and separation anxiety were put under the heading of pseudo-autism."[22]

He said a tendency had arisen

to set up a pseudo-diagnostic wastebasket into which an assortment of heterogeneous conditions were thrown indiscriminately. Infantile autism was stuffed into the basket along with everything else. . . . Such looseness threw all curiosity about diagnostic criteria to the winds as irrelevant impediments on the road to therapy, which was applied to all-comers as if their problems were identical. The therapeutic cart was put before the diagnostic horse and, more often than not, the horse was left out altogether.[23]

Kanner added (and this was as late as 1965): "We can state unreservedly that, whether or not autism is viewed as a member of the species schizophrenia, it does represent a definitely distinguishable disease."[24]

He drew attention to a number of attempts to describe specific conditions lifted out of the "schizophrenic package," including Margaret Mahler's 1949 coining of the term *symbiotic infantile psychosis* and Bergman and Escalona's discussion, in the same year, of "children with unusual sensitivity to sensory stimulation." He also noted Robin and Vitale's 1954 introduction of a number of "children with circumscribed interest patterns."[25]

Rimland himself was adamant that autism "can and should be distinguished" from schizophrenia. He was mystified at how the conditions could be so closely entangled, saying that this reminded him of the story of two men indistinguishable in appearance—apart from the fact that the tall thin one had a red beard and only one leg. He pointed out that it was not just an academic distinction: the treatment should be vastly different.[26] This is an aspect which has resurfaced over the past few years with the locking up of Asperger's syndrome sufferers in mental hospitals in the United Kingdom after being misdiagnosed as schizophrenics. A dramatic example is that of Piers Bolduc, a British man who was held at Broadmoor high-security psychiatric hospital for 14 years, after being misdiagnosed with schizophrenia as a teenager, and given mind-altering neuroleptic and SSRI drugs. He is now in a unit at a private psychiatric hospital. His mother, Cris, says that he is "totally withdrawn from the outside world, having been locked up for half his life. We last saw him in 1998."[27]

For Kanner, when he was seeing clearly on the issue, schizophrenia was different from autism in that its severe symptoms followed a period of normality; it was marked, in other words, by a withdrawal from the world after a period of normality whereas the children Kanner saw with autism had never participated in the world. The peculiar pronoun reversal seen in autism is also absent in schizophrenia, as are savant skills, and Eisenberg also pointed out the lack of hallucinations in autism.

The Swedish child psychiatrist, Christopher Gillberg, told me: "Autism is not knowing how to form social relationships when you are very young. That is very different from schizophrenia. But there are some similarities between the two conditions in terms of neuropsychological profiles: for instance, the theory of mind deficit. They are not as separate as we used to think, but they are different in terms of onset and some of the symptomatology."[28]

In contrast, Dr. Sula Wolff, the psychiatrist who translated Eva Sukhareva's 1926 paper and continued to associate Asperger's syndrome with schizoid personality disorder, told me that people actually started to disentangle autism from childhood schizophrenia after she and Jonathan Chick published papers in the late 1960s. "But today, people are starting to recognize that there are some common genetic factors out there. There may well be some overlap."[29] Wolff was born in Germany but fled to Britain to escape the Nazis. She often used to recall that she grew up in Berlin as a "pavement child," playing on the streets with the city's urchins, and, as an only child herself, she observed their behavior with a fascination that never left her. A charming woman who always retained a vivacious sense of humor, mischief, and curiosity, she is considered one of the founders of child psychiatry, along with Michael Rutter.

The diagnostic label, "childhood schizophrenia," was actually coined after the publication of a 1947 paper by one of the most interesting personalities working in the field in the 1950s, Lauretta Bender, expressing her view that autism represented the earliest form of adult schizophrenia.

**Figure 10** Lauretta Bender

Bender was based at Bellevue mental hospital in New York. Leon Eisenberg told me that she was "a remarkable woman but she was more or less out on her own. She treated childhood schizophrenia with electric shock. That seemed scandalous to most of us. She claimed that some of these children recovered. I once wrote a paper in which I referred to several studies by Clardy. He was at the Rockwin state hospital—the back-up for Bellevue—and he described the arrival of these children. He considered them psychotic and perhaps worse off than before the treatment. Well, I wasn't there. I didn't see the children either before or afterwards. But it certainly casts doubts on Bender's claims of recovery."[30]

Eisenberg pointed out that Bender also used LSD on children. "She did all sorts of things. Lauretta Bender reached success in her career long before randomized controlled trials had ever been heard of. She didn't see the need for trials of drugs because she was convinced she knew what worked. Lauretta was an old-fashioned psychiatrist. So was Kanner—he never did controlled trials. But he never got much involved in treatment, anyway, because Kanner saw most of his cases as a consultant."[31]

The Scottish child psychiatrist, Fred Stone, got to know Bender. "I had formed an opinion of her as someone I detested, from reading her papers," Stone told me. "I went to an international conference in Spain or Portugal—a five-day event which was the worst-organized conference I had ever been to. After two days of suffering, I decided I'd had enough and as I sat alone in the amphitheater, I was gradually joined by three other people. We all decided to head off to the coast for a swim. They were Lauretta Bender, Mildred Creak [of the celebrated Nine Points Committee], and Kenneth Cameron, the Scotsman who was in charge of the Maudsley

**Figure 11** Fred Stone

Hospital—Jim Anthony's predecessor. All three of us simply played truant for the rest of the conference! And in the course of swimming, relaxing, eating and drinking, my heart softened to Lauretta Bender when she told me about her life and career and that her husband [Paul Schilder] had been killed when he was run over by a car."[32] (In fact, Schilder had been visiting her in hospital in 1940 after the birth of their third child. Bender would not marry again until she was 70 years old and was widowed again just five years later.)

Stone added: "There was a level of frankness—once she got over the fact that I was one of her enemies! She wanted me to understand how she had got where she was. She told me: 'If you were confronted by the cross-section of the patients at Bellevue, where I was the consultant-in charge, you would do everything to try and make life easier for their families. They were undiagnosed psychotic-like children. We had somehow to create an environment which wasn't punitive, which might be helpful, and sometimes we had successes without knowing why.' "[33]

Stone said it was a time of almost complete clinical ignorance. Although he did not remember Bender talking much about autism at that point, he claimed that it was she who was responsible for Mildred Creak setting up the Nine Points group of which he was a member. "I think I remember Lauretta saying: 'Someone has got to get down to basics and nobody's doing that,' and Mildred said she'd do it."[34]

In 1959, Bender wrote an article entitled "Autism in children with mental deficiency." In it, she wrote that there was considerable evidence that various known biological disorders could lead to autistic patterns of behavior hardly distinguishable from these autistic states. She quotes Kanner as saying "Possibly some of them are brain damaged. Possibly all of them are schizophrenic."[35]

Bender noted that her near-namesake, Clemens Benda, had shown that children suffering from anoxia or infection with encephalitis could also be autistic. Benda argued that it was often impossible to differentiate between the "idiotic" and "autistic" child, even in their ultimate course.

Then, in a turn of phrase highly reminiscent of the psychoanalysts of then and now, Bender added: "I have long argued that autism is a *defense mechanism* [my italics] frequently occurring in young schizophrenic, or brain-damaged, or severely traumatized, or emotionally deprived children, who thereby withdraw or protect themselves from the disorganization and anxiety arising from the basic pathology." She said that, because she considered the autistic behavior and thinking to be a secondary or defense symptom, she chose to use the terms *pseudo-defective* and *pseudo-neurotic*.[36]

44

Nevertheless, Bender said, in the majority of the children she had followed from early childhood into adolescence and adulthood, it had not been possible to "get them out of their autistic behavior and many had had to be cared for in protective institutions.[37]

She called attention to two reports by W. R. Keeler on the subject of autistic behavior in blind children with retrolental fibroplasia resulting from their being cared for as premature infants in incubators with high oxygen tension. In her own experience, Bender said, she had witnessed autistic behavior in every type of disturbed young children. In those that she had diagnosed as schizophrenic, she wrote, "it occurred in families of considerable intellectual potentialities, but also in families where both mental deficiency and schizophrenia showed strong familial trends."[38]

Prefiguring Stella Chess's pioneering study 12 years later, Bender added that she had seen two cases of children whose mothers had rubella in the first trimester of pregnancy, "with the associated microcephaly, mental deficiency, cataracts and partial blindness."[39]

Describing Kanner's syndrome of early infantile autism as a valuable concept, Bender claimed that it described only a limited group of children from the particular sophisticated, intellectual strata who had consulted Kanner, but was not a clinical or etiological entity. She insisted that it would be unwise to restrict the concept and knowledge of autism to this group alone, since that would limit the scope of scientific studies and the assessment of the emotionally and mentally ill and retarded children who came to her and others for help.[40]

Autism was not synonymous with psychosis, she said, nor did it indicate a specific type of mental illness. Autistic thinking and actions were a primitive form of behavior, a part of the normal developmental process which might persist and become exaggerated or represent, by withdrawal, a defense against disorganization and anxiety in children with many different types of pathology in their genes, brains, perceptual organs or social relationships. It could provide some indication of the way of life the child adopted at the time the term had been applied, Bender added, but little about the cause or ultimate outcome.[41]

One of the best-known mothers to seek Lauretta Bender's services in the 1950s was Jacqueline Susann, author of the novel, *Valley of the dolls*. She and her press agent husband, Irving Mansfield, had a son, Guy, born in 1946. He was diagnosed as autistic at the age of 3. Her biographer, Barbara Seaman, claims that Susann took Guy to see Lauretta Bender at Bellevue Hospital in New York and quotes Bender as saying:

"I have never seen one single instance in which I thought the mother's behavior produced autism in the child."[42] Bender recommended electric shock treatment for Guy, even though he was only 3. The boy was left in Bender's hands, a decision Mansfield profoundly regretted. He said the shock treatment "destroyed him. He came home with no expression, almost lifeless." The following year, Guy was committed to an institution where he remains to this day. In a graphic illustration of the stigma attached to autism at the time, Susann and Mansfield told no one of their son's true condition. Friends were informed that Guy was asthmatic and had been put in a school in Arizona for the healthy climate. Susann was said to have been tormented with guilt for the rest of her life over institutionalizing her son.[43]

The world's most famous living woman with autism, Dr. Temple Grandin, associate professor of animal science at Colorado State University, was originally diagnosed with brain damage by the Boston-based child neurologist, Bronwyn Cruthers, in 1949. Over dinner in a Chinese restaurant in London, Grandin told me that, in those early years in the 1950s, it was her mother, the actress Eustacia Cutler, who ensured that she was forced to interact with her sister and nanny: "I was allowed to revert to autism for only an hour after dinner. It was all good training. I see a lot of kids today who are not expected to do anything. I was classic Kanner autistic. I had no speech until 3$^{1}/_{2}$, I screamed, I would twiddle with things. But I was taught about time. I was given an alarm clock at 5 years old and I was expected to use it—which I did."[44]

Grandin recalled that her mother was told she should be put in an institution. "But my mother went to a hospital with lots of retarded children and she realized she could work with me because I would hum to Bach."[45]

Fellow pupils called her "retard" at school. Today, Grandin is an extremely successful woman who designs many of the cattle ranches in the United States—she even designed that of the actor, John Wayne—and has written three best-selling books. Yet for many years, she was unwilling to talk about her autism for fear that she would be thought to be crazy. "I still meet people today who don't know anything about autism," she told me, as she showed enviable fine motor skills in manipulating her chopsticks.[46]

The consensus still held in the 1950s that autism was an extremely rare condition. In 1958, Kanner himself wrote that he had seen fewer than 150 cases of autism in 19 years—fewer than eight patients per year—despite the fact that his Baltimore clinic served as what he called "a sort of diagnostic clearing-house" and that the patients came from all over the United States and even from as far afield as South Africa. Bernard Rimland said that Kanner had informed him personally that only 1 child in 10 brought to him after being diagnosed as "autistic" by others was actually a true case of autism.[47]

Kanner did quickly become irritated at the way his term was, in his eyes, being abused. Indeed, in 1956, he even decided to narrow the criteria for early infantile autism to two main ones: aloneness and obsessive desire for sameness, removing the language abnormalities. When I asked Eisenberg what had prompted this move, he replied, rather vaguely: "I was following Kanner's lead. It wasn't that we had extensive discussions."[48]

The world's leading living authority on language impairments in autism, Dr. Helen Tager-Flusberg, was more forthright. She told me that Kanner clearly felt language was not a cardinal factor in autism deficits.[49]

Michael Rutter is also a little bemused by Kanner and Eisenberg's decision to drop the language abnormalities criterion. "I've no idea why they did it," Rutter told me. "Kanner, in his earlier papers, had described such abnormalities. All the evidence was that whatever the mechanisms involved—and we still do not understand these—language impairment was an important feature of autism."[50] Rutter himself, as we shall see, was to conduct a number of studies in the 1960s indicating that this was the case.

The question of etiology began to be seriously addressed for the first time in the 1950s. Although two of Kanner's original 11 cases had epilepsy, he himself did not, surprisingly, attempt to seek an organic cause for his syndrome. Eisenberg told me that Kanner was not moved to ponder a specific etiology until Stella Chess's 1971 study showing that children with congenital rubella could often be autistic. "For the first time, Kanner accepted that there were children with autism who suffered from a brain lesion. Here was a case of a clear cause," said Eisenberg.[51]

Gerhard Bosch told me, in contrast, that he himself had assumed, from as early as the 1950s, that autism—and Asperger's syndrome—were organic. "The fact that epileptic seizures often occurred in these individuals suggested to me that it was a neurological problem."[52]

Genetics appeared likely to play a major role in autism, given the findings of a number of important twin studies. Interest in the field was heightened by Francis Crick and James Watson's 1953 discovery of the double-helix structure of DNA. (Watson told an American audience more than half a century later, in 2007, that scientists were studying the genome and the genetics of autism because it had only recently became possible. As for the autistic phenotype, that had to wait until we understood its structure and definition, Watson added.[53])

The first study on autism in identical twins was conducted by W. R. Keeler in 1957. This was followed by A. H. Chapman's 1956 study of identical, autistic twin girls. The French psychiatrist, Jacques May, described his own identical non-verbal autistic twin sons in his book, *A physician looks at psychiatry* (1958). Kanner made only one mention of twins, in his 1956 paper with Leon Eisenberg. But Rimland points out that "the finding of at least eleven sets of monozygotic twins, all concordant, seems highly significant in terms of the biological etiology of the disease."[54]

Nevertheless, at the time, the prevailing mood of the time was anti-genetic. This is understandable, in a sense, since the Second World War was still raw in the memory and there was a very strong desire to forge a distance from the Nazi policies of eugenics and the creation of a "master race." The concept that genes could influence behavior was thus widely rejected in most quarters in favor of psychoanalytical notions. There was another reason for the weakness of the genetic arguments and the strength of the psychodynamic approach in the United States and elsewhere in the world. As Nolan Lewis pointed out in 1954: "It would seem that most of the prejudice against genetic inheritance stems from a feeling in the realm of wish fulfilment, based on the idea that acceptance of genetic factors would create an attitude of therapeutic hopelessness."[55]

There were other theories. Several studies in the 1950s suggested that a child's autistic symptoms could be traced to a postencephalitic condition or a central nervous system injury. Researchers began to show an interest in the neurology of autism. Without any form of scanning equipment, of course, the major obstacle was a lack of brains for postmortem examinations. One of the only papers in the decade to report such an examination was that of R. J. Schain and H. Yannet in 1960.[56] It involved the single case of a child who showed a reduction of cells in the hippocampus—a finding also reported in epilepsy and other brain disorders. The problem—as it is still today—was to determine whether the finding was specific to autism (especially as about a third of individuals with autism are known to suffer seizures). An intriguing aspect of Schain and Yannet's report is their speculation that the limbic system (of which the hippocampus is a region) could be impaired in autism. This is a much-pursued area of research today, especially as regards another limbic region, the amygdala.

Another area of research in the 1950s was perinatal causes. A number of studies suggested that autism could be due to both overoxygenation and oxygen deprivation during birth.

Observations of unusual behavior continued to accumulate. It is interesting that, as early as 1949, Bergman and Escalona were noting unusual responses to the sensory environment in children very similar to the ones Kanner described.[57] More than 60 years later, the committee drawing up DSM-V—the latest classification of the American Psychiatric Association—is finally planning to include sensory abnormalities in the new definition of autism.

Insensitivity to pain or to heat and cold were reported and, in one intriguing case described by Eveloff in 1960, an autistic girl could not understand why she was unable to grasp the cane painted on a life-like dummy—even after repeatedly running her hands over the surface of the object. In 1956, Goldfarb pointed out autistic children's preference for using the proximal senses—touching, tasting and smelling objects— a feature which Eric Schopler would analyze in greater depth at the University of Chicago a few years later.[58]

The psychoanalyst, Margaret Mahler, many of whose ideas seem decidedly quaint or downright misguided today, reported a phenomenon which is common to very many children with autism: "a peculiar inability to discriminate between living and inanimate objects."[59]

Ed Ornitz saw his first autistic child at the Yale Child Study Center in the 1950s. He told me: "One of my professors—who was a very experienced psychiatrist—started talking with me about the unconscious life. Yale at that time, in 1958, was completely dominated by psychoanalysis. Most of the professors were psychoanalysts. One of the children I was dealing with was flapping his hands and staring off into space, suddenly grimacing when there was an unusual sound in the room, like the air-conditioning. When my supervisor mentioned the unconscious, I replied: 'Can we really relate this child's behaviors to the unconscious?' I clearly remember him turning to me and saying: 'Ed, don't you believe in the unconscious?' To which I could not suppress the response: 'Sure, I believe in it—but I don't worship it!' "[60]

## Treatment

The question of treatment for children with autism began to be discussed in the 1950s. In 1954, Kanner wrote that, out of the first 42 of his cases

49

with infantile autism, "29 did not go anywhere" after psychotherapy. And the 213 children who had improved sufficiently to go to school "are children who have not had anything that is regarded as good psychotherapy or as psychotherapy at all."[61]

As researchers began to look for biomedical treatments—and some, like Lauretta Bender, found them in strange places—educationalists started to examine ways of teaching children with this new syndrome which presented so many challenges, both for the children themselves and the teachers.

One of the most remarkable pioneers was Belgian-born Jeanne Simons (pronounced Simmons), who started work with a first group of autistic children in Children's House in Washington as early as 1949— just six years after Leo Kanner first introduced the term early infantile autism. This gave her a grounding for her founding of the Linwood Center for autistic children in Ellicott City, Maryland, in 1955. It was one of the first schools specially for pupils with autism anywhere in the world, and she would run it for the next 25 years.

The center developed a national and international reputation, as did the so-called *Linwood Method*, which relied on early, intensive, and prolonged intervention with autistic children.

"Basic to this model is the belief in the worth of the individual in all of his manifestations, and respect for the healthy potential that exists in even the most handicapped human being," Simons wrote, along with Dr. Sabine Oishi, in their 1987 book, *The hidden child: The Linwood Method for reaching the autistic child.*[62]

Simons became aware of autism while working as a psychiatric social worker on a diagnostic team at Children's House. She found her life's purpose after meeting 13-year-old Lee, a colleague's son who had been diagnosed with autism by Leo Kanner and who had been institutionalized for years. "It fell into my lap," she told the *Baltimore Sun* in 1994. "Somebody had to do something. There was no help for the mothers. I was the first one who didn't blame them."[63]

Simons believed that autistic children like Lee desperately needed to be helped, not locked away and perpetually sedated in forbidding, impersonal state institutions. In 1955, she found a dilapidated, 14-room stone mansion on a hill above Ellicott City, managed to make a $500 down payment on the leaky-roofed, three-story house, and transformed it into a welcoming home and school for autistic children.

Hauling in coal for heat and lugging water from a well, she had one assistant and also enjoyed the help of the bus driver who transported the children, 11 of them between the ages of 3 and 5, attending the center from 9 a.m. until 3 p.m. Parents paid tuition fees, but only if they could afford it. To keep her fledgling center going, Simons worked as a therapist at the nearby Taylor Manor Hospital and solicited donations.

Ruth Sullivan, the first elected president of the Autism Society of America and now director of the Autism Services Center in Huntington, West Virginia, said: "She took throwaway children whom nobody else would take and she was able to make progress with them."[64]

Sullivan said the key to Simons's success was that "she had tremendous respect for children, for human beings. She was doing what we now call behavior therapy, and people would come to watch her and just sit in awe."[65]

Jeanne Simons was born in Laeken, Belgium, the second of seven children. She was forced to move with her family to the Netherlands when the German army invaded in 1914. She grew up in The Hague and received a master's degree in education from Teacher's College in The Hague in 1933. She also trained as a Montessori teacher. In 1940, as Hitler's forces were marching across Europe, she was working as a nanny when she helped the young son of an American diplomat posted to the Netherlands escape into Switzerland. She then accompanied the child to the United States on the last ship allowed to depart Italy, leaving her family and a fiancé behind in the Netherlands. A niece, Helene van Oijen, noted that the many children she grew to know over the years became her surrogate family.[66]

During the war years, Jeanne Simons worked with impoverished children in Washington before moving to Boston. In 1949, she received a master's degree in social work from Boston University, with a major in psychiatry, and worked as a psychiatric and family counselor in the Boston area. From 1950 to 1955, she was director of group therapy for Children's House in Washington and also studied at the University of Maryland.

Apart from educating the children, the Linwood Center was involved in a number of research projects. One of the most important was a three-year study (1965–1968) headed by Dr. Charles Ferster, from the Institute of Behavioural Research in Washington. Another key study was carried out by Leo Kanner himself, who undertook to assess all the children attending Linwood during two visits to the school in 1966 and 1968. His conclusions, together with notes by Jeanne Simons, were published in 1973. The findings were extraordinary. Of the 34 children Kanner examined in 1966 and 1968, 10 had attained what Kanner called "a state of near-full or full recovery" by 1973.[67]

This contrasted strikingly with the follow-up cases Kanner and Eisenberg had published in 1956. In that paper, they reported that, of 80 autistic children first described by Kanner, they were able to follow 63 for four years and more, up to an average age of 15 years. Three of these were classified as having a "good" outcome, functioning well academically and socially, and 14 as having a "fair" outcome, being able to attend school at about grade level but distinctly deviant in personality, while 46 (or 73%) had a "poor" outcome characterized by feeble-mindedness and/or psychotic behavior. Thirty-one of the children were non-verbal until the age of 5 and only one of these subsequently used speech for communication and attained a fair adjustment.[68]

One of the most fascinating aspects of the Linwood study was Kanner's decision to divide the children into five nosological categories: "true" autism; schizophrenia; developmental and behavioral manifestations due mainly to organicity (neurological impairments and retardation); or to psychogenecity (disturbances of the emotional environment which produced deviant development and behavior); and dementia infantilis or Heller's disease (now more commonly called childhood disintegrative disorder, in which normal development during the first two and a half years of life is followed by rapid regression).

Simons retired as Linwood's clinical director in 1980 but continued to consult, work on her book, and lecture at schools and conferences around the world. The center she founded nearly a half-century ago continues to provide a full range of services for children with autism and their families. She died on March 8, 2005, at the age of 95.

The other great education pioneer of the 1950s was the child psychologist, Dr. Carl Fenichel, who founded the League Treatment Center, in Brooklyn, New York, in 1953. Fenichel, who always believed that autism had a biological cause, was also convinced that children should remain within the family unit, and that parents should serve as partners in their treatment. At the historic First (and only) Leo Kanner Colloquium on Child Development, Deviations and Treatment, held at Chapel Hill, North Carolina, in 1973, Fenichel declared:

Twenty years ago, when we started the school, we were denounced for having any kind of parental involvement. The assumption was that these kids should be separated from the home. [Bruno] Bettelheim . . . said: "You have a fairly good program, but it's not going to work in a million years because it's a day-school program. These kids are going to be coming home at the end of the day to the very parents who caused the illness. Everything you do is going to be undone by the parents."[69]

When asked how reliable the diagnosis of autism was, at a time when so many of the colloquium speakers appeared to be dividing the condition into subgroups, Fenichel's reply was intriguing:

> We scrapped these labels 18 years ago [in 1955] at our place, after two years of saying we were only going to take the so-called autistic, schizophrenic, psychotic or symbiotic child. We found that all these labels are just meaningless. . . . We learn more about these kids from working with them on a day-to-day basis. Too many people feel that sticking a label on them means that they now know what this kid needs. I think this is a dangerous, misleading and destructive process.[70]

Fenichel added:

> We recognize that we're not going to cure many of these kids. But if we can make it possible for 80% of them to spend the rest of their lives within the community—most of them being productive and taxpayers, instead of a drain on the state—then this has to have economic, as well as humanitarian, value.[71]

One of those who worked with Fenichel at the League School in New York in the late 1950s and early 1960s, Demetrious Haracapos, recalled him as a man with "a warm smile and bushy greying hair who was quite empathetic with the people around him."[72] He remembered Fenichel "arguing vehemently" against Bruno Bettelheim's approach. Haracapos, who now works at the Autism Center in Aarhus, Denmark (see chapter 4), told me he admired Fenichel enormously: "He had a humanistic attitude, combined with a special-education approach, which was very unusual at the time."[73]

# 3

# Blaming the Parents

In the 1950s, professionals were coming to terms with a newly named disorder and largely confusing it with childhood schizophrenia. The 1960s were marked by a baleful influence that continues to hold sway in some parts of the world even today.

When Bruno Bettelheim's 1967 book, *The empty fortress: Infantile autism and the birth of self*, which blamed the parents for their child's autism, became an acclaimed bestseller, there were worldwide repercussions: it was the first book about autism ever to be published in Spanish, for example, leading to years of misconceptions in Spain. About three quarters of French psychiatrists continue to treat autism with psycho-

analytical methods—although, to me at least, most of them claimed not to be admirers of Bettelheim himself. Dr. Sally Ozonoff, a leading autism researcher at the MIND Institute in Sacramento, California, told me that one of the books she was recommended to read while studying in the early 1980s was precisely Bettelheim's *The empty fortress.*[1] In that same decade, it was the only book on autism to be found in any of Denmark's public libraries.[2]

Bettelheim came to America after spending nine months in Nazi concentration camps in 1938 and 1939. His experience in the camps prompted him to

**Figure 12**  Bruno Bettelheim    make a dreadful and damaging mental leap, once he came to America to become director of the Sonia Shankman Orthogenic School in Chicago in 1944. He came to believe that autistic children behaved like the inmates of the Nazi camps and their mothers were like the camp commandants.

The Holocaust had a very different effect on Hans Asperger from Bruno Bettelheim. While Asperger saw the children in his care as potential victims of the Nazis who needed protecting by emphasizing their positive qualities, as well as their oddities, Bettelheim saw a negative equivalence between the camp inmates' reaction to an extreme situation and autistic children's defense mechanism in response to what he considered a similarly extreme situation.

As Bettelheim wrote in *The empty fortress*,

> In the German concentration camps, I witnessed with utter disbelief the non-reacting of certain prisoners to their most cruel experience. . . . I did not know, and would not have believed, that I would observe similar behavior in the most benign of therapeutic environments, because of what children had experienced in the past.[3]

Children with autism, he believed, had an inner reality comparable to the external reality of the prisoners and, like them, directed all their energy into a defensive withdrawal. Their absence of language, he claimed, should be recognized as a "defense against emotional pain or any further depletion of the self," and infantile autism, he concluded, was "a state of mind that develops in reaction to feeling oneself in an extreme situation, entirely without hope."[4]

The disastrously misguided notion of the "refrigerator mother"— one which originated in Leo Kanner's early writings but which was "refined" by Bettelheim—exerted a harmful influence that has clung on obstinately, not just in the United States but throughout the world. How was it, indeed, that one book came to exert such a potent influence over so many professionals and parents?

Like both Hans Asperger and Leo Kanner, Bettelheim was an Austrian. He was born into an upper-middle-class, secularized Jewish family in *fin-de-siècle* Vienna. Although Bettelheim described his mother as an affectionate parent who read fairy tales to him and comforted him when he was ill, his most recent biographer, Richard Pollak, believes his adult behavior reflected hostility towards her and colored his celebrated view that mothers caused their child's autism through their rejection and his comparison of mothers to devouring witches and SS guards.[5] It may also be relevant that Bettelheim's father contracted syphilis which blighted his life until his disturbing death which left a powerful impression on his son. It is interesting to note that one of the first child analysts, Edith Buxbaum, was Bettelheim's cousin and a close friend.

After the First World War, Bettelheim, by his own account, stopped reading escapist literature, preferring texts which "would suggest how the horrors of the world at large could be rectified." His new intellectual heroes were no longer Goethe and Schiller but, as he explained in one of his final essays, "Essential books of one's life," the German philosophers Theodor Lessing, F. A. Lange, and Hans Vaihinger in his youth. Vaihinger, in particular, who was a renowned Kant scholar, argued that, even though fictions should not be mistaken for true propositions, they could work "as if true."[6]

The Nazi *Anschluss* (annexation) of Austria took place in March 1938. On June 2, 1938, Bettelheim was put on a train bound for Dachau concentration camp, where he became prisoner number 15029. He and his fellow inmates were under constant threat of torture or death. On September 23, 1938, he was moved to Buchenwald camp. Here, according to his friend, Ernst Federn, he was fortunate to survive, in part due to the peculiar respect the SS guards showed for Bettelheim's glasses. (Bettelheim denied this, saying that they actually put him at risk because they singled him out as an intellectual.)[7]

On April 20, 1939, to mark his fiftieth birthday, Adolf Hitler announced that he would be freeing a number of inmates as an act of amnesty. Bettelheim was one of those to be released. In fact, the Nazis freed him on April 14, warning him that he faced re-arrest if he failed to leave the country within a week. He later said he had no idea why he had been singled out for release.

Bettelheim sailed to New York, joining the influx of European intellectuals fleeing Nazi persecution and bolstering American academia in the 1940s. Bettelheim received his first academic position teaching art history at Rockford College in Illinois and participating in the Eight-Year Study, which examined art education in American schools. In 1943, he sealed his reputation with the publication of "Individual and mass behaviour in extreme situations," a paper in which he observed that the prisoners in concentration camps were effectively turned into children.[8] He said that rather than fighting their captors, they fought with one another, daydreamed and admired, even emulated, the Nazis. Thus, they were "more or less willing tools of the Gestapo." The paper—the first widely read essay in the United States on the Nazi concentration camps—caused a huge stir. It became required reading across the

56

disciplines and made a great impression on left-wing thinkers such as Theodor Adorno and Max Horkheimer.

A few months later, the University of Chicago asked Bettelheim to take over the Orthogenic School for emotionally disturbed children, which he did in 1944. The term "orthogenic"—which is no longer used in English—was invented in 1896 to refer to something that promotes good health. When the school opened in Chicago during the First World War, the primary focus of its mission was to treat young people with physiological deformities or other similar challenges, though they employed psychologists and others interested in educational testing or mental disorders.

Richard Pollak, his most recent biographer, insists that Bettelheim lied about his qualifications and that his claims that he had lived with two autistic children back in Vienna as part of their treatment was false. In fact, according to Pollak, the only child the Bettelheims took into their home in Vienna was Patricia Lyne, and she could not have been diagnosed as autistic in the 1930s because Hans Asperger and Leo Kanner had not yet introduced the term in its modern sense.[9]

Pollak has strong, and very tragic, personal reasons for wanting to show Bettelheim up as a liar: his own younger brother, Stephen, had been at the Orthogenic School for five years before dying during a family vacation in 1948 when he slipped through a hayloft chute during a game of hide-and-seek. When Pollak approached Bettelheim to tell him about his brother, Bettelheim called Pollak's father a simple-minded *schlemiel* and his mother a false martyr. Then he bluntly announced that the child had committed suicide. And, he added, Pollak's mother was largely to blame, because she had rejected him at birth. "What is it about these Jewish mothers?" Bettelheim apparently exclaimed.[10]

However, in a letter to the *New York Review of Books* in November 2003, Dr. Jacquelyn Seevak Sanders—who was Bettelheim's assistant at the school between 1952 and 1965 and its director between 1973 and 1992—wrote: "I worked very closely, adoringly, with Bettelheim for thirteen years and ran the enterprise after him for twenty years." Sanders said she had reviewed all of the records in the school, including his correspondence—"no longer adoringly, in fact, critically. I found no evidence of his falsifying or exaggerating credentials." Sanders maintained that the distorting documents to which Pollak referred in his biography of Bettelheim were those found in a file at Rockford College, whereas, she said, his real career began at the University of Chicago. At the time, Sanders insisted, there still existed the tradition of not requiring an academic background for faculty appointment. She said Bettelheim had made much of his training in philosophy and aesthetics and that his colleagues at the University of Chicago were well aware of this background. Moreover, she added, in 1944 there were no credentials for running a residential school for disturbed children and "milieu therapy" was too new a concept for any such credentials to have been established.[11]

Bettelheim's approach as soon as he became director of the Orthogenic School was firmly psychoanalytical and it quickly garnered ardent supporters. The time was ripe for a fervently Freudian, psychoanalytical approach.

Throughout the 1930s, new suggestions of how to treat emotionally disturbed children had crossed the Atlantic. The names are legends to this day: Melanie Klein, Anna Freud, Maria Montessori, Jean Piaget. Bettelheim turned to Sigmund Freud, John Dewey, and the psychoanalysts Erik Erikson and August Aichhorn. The historian and sociologist, Chloe Silverman, however, says that Bettelheim also turned to René Spitz's studies of institutionalized children regarding abnormal ego development, as well as Harry Harlow's experiments on infant monkeys.[12]

Richard Pollak quotes Jean O'Leary, a young counselor, as saying: "Bettelheim gave me a religion, which I laugh at now, because psychoanalysis doesn't play a big part in my life any longer. But at the time, it gave me a system, a way to judge things."[13]

Even Eric Schopler, who founded the TEACCH program in North Carolina in 1972 in large part as a reaction against Bruno Bettelheim's teachings, acknowledged Bettelheim's popularity. He recalled that Bettelheim's classes were always huge. "He was teaching personality theory using Freud and psychoanalytical stages of personality, the anal, the phallic."[14]

Schopler remembered that, in one class, a woman in the audience started to knit. "It just bugged the hell out of him and pretty soon, he stopped his lecture and said: 'Miss, don't you realize that your sitting here knitting is an expression of your hostility towards your father? It's probably because you had sexual designs on him as a child and you are now trying to transfer the counter-reaction to me here in the classroom.' The girl was shocked, but she showed up, sat in the same place, a week later, and as soon as he started, out came the knitting again. This time, he said: 'Don't you realize your knitting is nothing but a sublimated form of masturbation? You're sitting in front of the entire class masturbating.' She looked at him indignantly and replied: 'Dr. Bettelheim, when I knit, I knit! And when I masturbate, I masturbate!'"[15]

In the summer of 1955, Bettelheim asked the Ford Foundation for funds specifically to study autism and dynamics or early ego development. He proposed admitting up to 15 autistic children between the ages of 6 and 8 to the Orthogenic School and following them up for seven years. In that grant application, Bettelheim told the Ford Foundation that, quite apart from treating his autistic patients, he intended to explore what their parents might have done "wrong" in raising them. Bettelheim did name Leo Kanner, but did not cite any of the six papers Kanner had published on autism to that time. The Ford grant came through.

The most controversial aspect of the school, of course, was Bettelheim's insistence that the parents, and especially the mothers, were to blame for their child's autism and therefore that the children should be separated from the parents.

It should be recalled that Leo Kanner himself, in his early assessments, had described the parents of autistic children as cold, aloof, intellectual, and obsessive individuals who failed to demonstrate warmth and affection in their interactions with their child. He seemed to be implying that such a social environment would not be conducive to a healthy parent–child attachment. Kanner did not, however, believe that the parents were the sole cause of autism. He saw the probable origin of the disorder as the consequence of the interaction of a biologically based, genetic predisposition for autism, coupled with the unfavorable social conditions provided by the parents.

Bettelheim went much further. He proposed that, in contrast to the parents of non-autistic children, parents of children with autism had a psychological pathology which led them to react abnormally to their infant's normal behaviors. This, he said, set a cycle in motion because, during the process of normal development, the child responded to certain real or imagined threats by withdrawing or becoming less responsive and the mothers of autistic children responded to this unresponsiveness pathologically. The result, he suggested, was an intensification of the withdrawal and a continuation of the cycle until the child retreated into what Bettelheim referred to as "chronic autistic disease." Thus, Bettelheim's concept of autism was very different from Kanner's: while Kanner saw the condition as a unique behavioral syndrome, Bettelheim saw it as a specific disease caused by pathological parenting.

It was a disease, Bettelheim felt, which could be cured only by separating the child from his or her parent—a process for which critics devised a telling, if rather brutal neologism, *parentectomy*. I was told by many of Schopler's colleagues at TEACCH that, when he visited the

Orthogenic School, he heard that Bettelheim often pointed to a large, abstract stone statue representing a mother and told the children: "This is what your mother is like: cold and hard."

**Figure 13** Jacquelyn Sanders

However, Jacquelyn Sanders, who took over from Bettelheim as director of the Orthogenic School in 1973, told me over a drink at a coffee house in Chicago: "What Bruno wrote and said wasn't what he actually believed. I sat with him when he talked to parents and there was no one who could match his empathy. There were some parents who were terrified of him and others who were totally devoted to him."[16]

The issue, Sanders told me, was putting the children in a different environment so that that they could see life could be better. "These children had miserable lives—parents took their kids to the Orthogenic School only if they were desperate. Parents could see they were thriving at the school. The children could stay into their late teens until they could re-enter society and sustain a better relationship with their parents. At the time, there were not a lot of support services. That was the separation issue. It was looked at as though we were taking the children away from the parents—that was not my view of what was going on. Bruno didn't just swoop down and take the children away—it was all done with the parents' permission."[17]

In 1950, Erik Erikson, a German-American developmental psychologist and psychoanalyst, had claimed that the beginnings of autism lay in the mother–child relationship. However, unlike Bettelheim, he attributed it to the mother's reaction to the child's symptoms. Erikson wrote: "These children may very early and subtly fail to return the mother's glance, smile, and touch; an initial reserve which makes the mother, in turn, unwittingly withdraw."[18]

In stark contrast, Bettelheim considered that something preceded the infant's lack of response to the mother. According to one of Bettelheim's former colleagues, Karen Zelan, "he probably would not agree with Erikson's belief that the mother unwittingly withdrew. Although unwitting withdrawal certainly would have happened, Bettelheim was more impressed by the insecure parents' need to defend themselves from their unborn child from the very beginning."[19]

Zelan says that Bettelheim used Piaget's work as a basis for comparing the development of normal infants with 12-year-old Marcia—a preadolescent autistic girl at the Orthogenic School. Bettelheim wrote that, once the developing process was set in motion, autistic children often gained typical infant achievements far more rapidly than the infant normally did. Quoting from Piaget's 1952 observations of his own children, Bettelheim wrote that, in less than six months, Marcia's drawings had moved from infant scribbling to drawing circles, to drawing faces, to drawing the complete human figure—and it would have taken several years for the normal infant to progress this far.[20]

Leo Kanner's colleague, Leon Eisenberg, when I met him in Boston, called Bettelheim 'a sadistic so-and-so,' adding that Kanner shared this view. "I saw Bettelheim humiliate a questioner at a public lecture in a way that was just dreadful to watch."[21]

Pollak claimed that Bettelheim could be cruel, that he often spanked his patients and that one counselor called his training style the "Nazi-Socratic method."[22]

Jacquelyn Sanders admitted that Bettelheim was authoritarian: "He did hit the kids. My criticism was that he never wrote about this. To control the children, other people were using straitjackets, quiet rooms or medication. I found a smack far preferable."[23] She also pointed out that she herself had received her doctorate at UCLA in the 1960s, when Ivar Lovaas was using shock therapy. "There are problems with this, but it is better than the kids cracking their heads open."[24]

In her letter to the *New York Review of Books* in November 2003, Sanders wrote that she had no regrets about hitting a kid who was banging his head hard against the floor and whom she could not control, a child who was throwing ice cubes at another's face, or who had just kicked her hard in the shins. She said it was a very effective method of protecting everyone, including the child. However, she added, she stopped the practice when she realized that it might play into his or her masochistic fantasies.[25]

Sanders did confirm to me that her relationship with Bettelheim was a complicated one and that she had had a falling-out of sorts with him: "He was a typical male chauvinistic professor. He did some marvellous things for me. He was one of the most empathic people I have ever met and he had a remarkable gift for teaching that. On the other hand, he didn't do anything to promote me professionally. Because I didn't want to see him for a while, he was mad at me. He used to say: 'I can't read other people's minds—I have enough trouble reading my own.' "[26]

However, Sanders told me that, away from the school, Bettelheim was "very smart, very cultured, with a great sense of humor. He could be gallant, he could charm everyone. He was a complex human being. He could be very cunning. He was good company. He spent a tremendous amount of time at the school. He came in on Sundays to play chess with the kids, enjoyed birthday presents and gave out presents to the kids. The children felt both affection and fear for him. He sometimes made mistakes, and given his power, this maybe had a big influence."[27]

In 1967, Bruno Bettelheim published *The empty fortress*, which purported to show how three children with severe autism were effectively treated at the Orthogenic School through his application of psychoanalytic theory and milieu therapy. The book received enthusiastic reviews in *The New York Times* and elsewhere. A mental health professional in Connecticut declared: "Bettelheim's lessons are useful for anyone concerned with humanity; they are absolutely essential for all concerned about the present crisis of poverty and inequality in America."[28] Bettelheim's thesis, that the source of autism was the infant's relationship with his or her refrigerator mother, soon became the accepted explanation of the cause of autism in popular circles and in some professional ones.

How did it achieve such popularity? Even before the book's publication, Bettelheim had become a household authority in the 1960s through his articles in a number of publications—for example, the story of "Joey the mechanical boy," one of the case studies in *The empty fortress*, which was originally published in *Scientific American* in 1959. (Bettelheim's hypothesis was that Joey had been driven to his autism by his unfeeling parents, especially his mother, and his attempts to become "human" had failed.) Many of his colleagues, it seems, felt that he had become so well-known and respected by the lay public that, if they criticized him for the shabbiness of his scholarship, they would lay themselves open to accusations of professional jealousy.

In contrast, the American neurologist, Mary Coleman, told me that her anger at the way parents—and especially mothers—were being blamed was one of the primary catalysts for her interest in autism. She described the psychoanalytical approach as extremely "anti-feminine. Leo Kanner was a brilliant man but he was influenced by the anti-feminine element of psychoanalysis."[29]

The lack of scientific rigor in Bettelheim's milieu therapy—as expounded in *The empty fortress*—was probably ignored by much of the psychoanalytic community because of the traditional concept of the patient guiding the treatment and "knowing the other" being contingent on "knowing the self." His Holocaust past also gave him a form of status. In the words of Chloe Silverman:

> As a survivor, Bettelheim enjoyed a unique, almost anthropological authority; as witness, he could speak to the motivations underlying fascism, and authoritarianism, and as a therapist, could claim a theory that transmuted the negative power of the camps into a positive therapeutic insight, just as Lovaas has suggested that witnessing fascism made him realize just how malleable the human psyche might be. . . . Bettelheim's claims about the therapeutic possibilities of a "total environment" and the centrality of the development of human autonomy resonated with a contemporary movement towards milieu therapy, as well as public interest in the role of social environment in the shaping of subjective experience.[30]

Jacquelyn Sanders spoke to Bettelheim about the Nazi camps. "He told me he had seen how the environment could destroy a psyche," she recalled to me during our conversation in Chicago. "But if an environment could destroy a psyche, it could also rebuild it. The issue was how to design it in a way that was the opposite of a Nazi camp."[31]

The French autism authority, Professor Gilbert Lelord, told me that "the biologists were impregnated with psychoanalysis at the time, both here in France and in the United States. They viewed our work [EEG studies on autistic children] with a certain suspicion."[32] Lelord said he had given a talk on his EEG findings at a huge conference on the Tunisian island of Djerba in 1970. "But my research wasn't taken seriously at the time."[33] He said the studies of Ed Ornitz, Ed Ritvo, and Peter Tanguay had contributed a great deal to changing this situation.

Lelord added that it had to be reluctantly conceded that Bettelheim had helped to make the public aware of autism. "Kanner had no idea how to handle the media," Lelord told me. "That was Bettelheim's principal merit. But of course some of his ideas were wrong."[34]

All of this explains why many professionals accepted Bettelheim's work. Not all of them did, however. Dr. Lee Marcus, a psychologist who was a colleague of Eric Schopler and Robert Reichler in the early days of the TEACCH program in North Carolina in the early 1970s, believes that the influence of Bruno Bettelheim was not, in fact, as powerful as is made out today. "He was seen as a brilliant man who wrote well about fairy tales and people listened to him when he talked about autism. People who were already predisposed to that way of thinking found their beliefs reinforced," Marcus told me.[35]

He added that he did not think the Orthogenic School exerted such a strong influence at the time. "But Bettelheim had a kind of Svengali influence on undergraduates. He was a powerful symbolic figure—though his methods were not widely adopted. Professionals blamed the parents for their child's autism, but that was not necessarily because of Bettelheim. The prevailing model was psychodynamic. If you were trained to believe that the problems arose from relationships and that the difficulties came from the parents, you came to that conclusion. Margaret Mahler's writing on symbiosis is every bit as damning, to me—the idea that you cannot separate yourself from your child.

"None of those bizarre theories took into account the possibility that there was something wrong with the child's brain. Of course, the appeal of the notion that autism is an emotional disturbance is that there is a chance that you can undo it. But that is wrong: people who are emotionally disturbed are disturbed for life. It can't be fixed."[36]

What about the parents? Bettelheim's insistence that they were to blame was, of course, supremely hurtful and damaging. An excellent 2002 documentary, called *Refrigerator mothers*, left no doubt about the emotional scars left on women following their child's diagnosis. Many mothers themselves underwent psychoanalysis.[37]

Nevertheless, there was also a perversely contrary way of seeing Bettelheim's message. Donata Vivanti, the Italian president of Autism-Europe, pointed out to me at the organization's 2007 congress in Oslo that many Italian mothers were happy to embrace the notion that they could somehow be to blame for their child's autism because it gave them hope that, by changing, they could improve the child's condition, whereas in contrast, if it were a genetic or neurological disorder, there was far less hope.[38]

Jacquelyn Sanders agrees: "I know there are parents who would much prefer the autism to be due to something they had done, rather than it being a result of something organic, because they could fix it."[39] She also recalled one father telling her that he'd read *The empty fortress* "and it impelled him to bring his son to the school, because it was the first book that had accurately described his boy. But it made his wife feel guilty."[40]

One of the outsiders who was allowed the greatest access to the Orthogenic School and to Bettelheim himself was the French film-maker, Daniel Karlin, The result was a remarkable 1974 TV mini-series, called *Portrait de Bruno Bettelheim* and perhaps an even more remarkable book called *Un autre regard sur la folie (A different look at madness)*.[41]

Bettelheim spoke to Karlin about Marcia, one of the children who features prominently in *The empty fortress*. In that book, Bettelheim claimed that Marcia's intense interest in the weather stemmed in part from her fear that her mother, and later the staff at the Orthogenic School, intended to devour her, as in *we/eat/her*). To Karlin, Bettelheim declared that Marcia's mother

> would have preferred Marcia not to exist, so that she wouldn't be shackled to her husband and child, while the father would have preferred Marcia not to exist so that his wife could devote herself entirely to him. So, from her earliest childhood, Marcia received, unconsciously, through her parents' emotions, the message that everyone would find it better if she didn't exist. Infantile autism is, in fact, the closest way for someone to reach a state of non-existence, while remaining alive, if you can call that living.[42]

In her celebrated 1967 book, *The siege*, about her fight to find help for her autistic daughter, Jessy, in 1960s America, Clara Claiborne Park writes that she understands how some parents might have appeared cold and unfeeling to professionals.

> Refrigerator professionals create professional parents, if the parents are strong enough to keep command of themselves at all. I had gone in a highly emotional state, ready to tremble, to weep, to dissolve in gratitude. Received not even with reproaches, but with no reaction at all, I of course dried up my emotions at once and met professionalism with professionalism.[43]

Park and her husband, David, spent the winter of 1972 in Paris. "We found that everyone there had just discovered Freud and every magazine had a Freudian explanation for everything that happened," David told me. "This was amusing but it had a sombre side. A short time before we arrived, there had been a general strike of television workers. Normal programming was suspended and the industry looked around for something to broadcast. It so happened that Bettelheim was due to give some public lectures on autism and all France listened as he told his fables. While we were there, we met a number of parents who had been unable to get any responsible advice from the psychiatric profession. I don't know how long it was before the profession woke up to the fact that there wasn't at that time, and perhaps still isn't, any case of autism reported in the literature that can be directly traced to abusive parenting."[44]

James T. Fisher has noted that, three years before *The empty fortress* appeared, Virginia Mae Axline published her bestseller, *Dibs: In search of self*, subtitled *Personality development in play therapy*, which tells the story of a little autistic boy, Dibs, who is transformed, through psychotherapy, from a withdrawn, echolalic troubled soul to what Fisher has called "perhaps the most adult-sounding, self-aware six-year-old in the annals of American literature."[45]

As Fisher points out, entire chapters of *Dibs* are devoted to exposing the "extravagant deficiencies of Dibs's mother, an archetypal 'refrigerator mother' who—despite her sophisticated vocabulary—was emotionally more mute than Dibs herself."[46] For Fisher, Virginia Mae Axline was

> Bruno Bettelheim without the baggage, which may explain why this book has transcended the autism wars and continues to be read as a useful guide to the wonders of play therapy. As discrepancies in Bettelheim's biographies—and reports of his abusive treatment of children—gradually began to emerge in the decades following the publication of *The empty fortress*, his stature as visionary leader of autistic children was undermined, but the ideas he had championed remained very much in circulation in the work of Axline and other popularizers.[47]

Fisher feels that Axline's affinity for the more humanistic, person-centered therapeutic model associated with the American psychologist, Carl Rogers, and other post-Freudians helped immunize her from the eventual backlash against Bettelheim and made *Dibs* read like a story that even non-believers in psychotherapeutic categories could embrace. But it is important to remember, Fisher adds, that "even the most militant Freudians on the autism scene were lauded in the 1960s by figures . . . once hostile to the 'irreligion'of psychoanalysis."[48]

Sanders herself accepts that Bettelheim "sometimes took things too far. And he presented it the wrong way, for which he got a lot of stick. But he enjoyed that—he was a great publicist."[49]

Daniel Karlin asked Bettelheim directly for the percentage of children who left the school cured. Bettelheim replied:

> That depends, of course, on the seriousness of the original illness. We have less success with the non-verbal autistic children. No autistic child has true communication, but some of them at least say a few words which they alone can understand. That is not communication. But at least they produce sounds. With the totally non-verbal children, we have success with only about half the cases. If they speak, if they speak well, that goes

up to 70%, and the overall result for all the children, bearing in mind that autism is the most serious mental illness in children, is above 85%.[50]

In *The empty fortress*, Bettelheim compares the results of Leon Eisenberg's long-term study of patients with autism with his own. He claimed that Eisenberg divided the patients into three categories: "poor" (those who had not emerged from their autism at all), "fair" (those who had taken some classes at their appropriate age-level, had meaningful contact with others yet would still be identified as deviant), and "good" (those who were successful socially and academically and who would have been accepted by their peers, even though they might still be considered a little odd). Bettelheim retained what he saw as Eisenberg's three categories, for the sake of argument, and then favorably compared his own treatment results:

> [T]here were eight in our forty for whom the end results of therapy were "poor" because, despite improvement, they failed to make the limited social adjustment needed for maintaining themselves in society. For fifteen, the outcome was "fair" and for seventeen "good." Thus, while Eisenberg reports only 5% good outcome, our experience shows that intensive treatment can raise this figure to 42%. While he reports only 22% fair improvement, we can report 37%. Most important, while he found 73% poor outcome, we had only 20% poor results.[51]

Bettelheim considered the discrepancies between his results and those reported by Eisenberg to provide conclusive evidence that, because the psychoanalytical approach to therapy had been more successful, the ultimate claim of causation for autism was more likely to be psychological than physiological.

However, Eisenberg told me: "Just about everyone active as an investigator in the 1950s reported relatively poor outcomes among autistic children who were reassessed in adolescence. Other than Bettelheim's 'groupies,' no one believed his results. To put it plainly, he was a sadistic monster and doesn't deserve serious treatment as a scientist."[52]

Evidence that autism is in any way related to how parents behave is totally unconvincing. Indeed, by the 1960s, the first studies were being published showing that there was no difference between the parents of autistic children and those of children with other disabilities or those who were not disabled.

But Bettelheim consistently refused to accept any research findings which contradicted his own psychogenic views. As Kenneth Kidd has written:

"For Bettelheim, autism served as a sort of *ur-disorder* from which he could derive his explanation for all sorts of abuse. In doing so, he disregarded much of the clinical literature, which was already cautioning against psychogenic rationales."[53]

In 1972, Dr. Marian DeMyer, an Indiana University psychiatrist, made a careful study of three groups: parents with an autistic child, parents with normal children, and parents with a brain-damaged child. Personality tests showed that the three groups were indistinguishable. The study was published that year in the *Journal of Autism and Childhood Schizophrenia*, but Bettelheim disregarded it entirely.[54]

In fact, as Michael Rutter has pointed out, the psychogenic hypothesis has never actually been disproven. Rutter himself conducted studies in the 1960s indicating that there was no evidence that cold mothers could cause autism, However, he told me, "Many people made a mistake, to my mind, in going from a statement which is undoubtedly true—that there is no convincing evidence that autism has been caused by poor parenting—to the different statement that it has been disproven. It has not actually been disproven. It has faded away simply because, on the one hand, of a lack of convincing evidence and on the other hand, an awareness that autism was a neurodevelopmental disorder of some kind or other. But Bernard Rimland's claim that the hypothesis had been disproven was misleading."[55]

Bernard Rimland, as we shall see in chapter 4, was the father of an autistic son and wrote his own book, *Infantile autism*, in 1964 with the aim of combating the psychogenic argument and showing that autism was biological in origin.

Jacquelyn Sanders told me that Bettelheim had privately acknowledged to her there could be an organic cause for autism. "But the state of the science at the time was such that we couldn't find out. Bettelheim started at the Orthogenic School in 1944, a year after Kanner's study of just 11 kids. There really wasn't much to base it on. What we thought was that our children had no organic component—there was no way of telling. There has been some clear, undisputed evidence, but there certainly wasn't then."[56]

In *The empty fortress*, Bettelheim attacks both Leo Kanner and Bernard Rimland. Bettelheim quite openly claims that Kanner's original error was in viewing autism as a biological disorder. In so doing, Kanner ignored one of Freud's greatest lessons, in Bettelheim's view. By not questioning the underlying motivations driving an individual's behavior, to believe that an individual acts without thinking at least on some level, we easily fall into the trap of attributing cause to an inherent personal defect. Bettelheim argued that Kanner had access to the necessary information to make a more thoughtful conclusion than assuming that autism was an innate disorder. He also criticized Kanner's hypothesis that autism was a disorder existing from birth, noting that most reports finding that autistic symptoms became apparent around the age of 2 were consistent with both his theory and experience.

Bettelheim likewise attacked Bernard Rimland for suggesting that autism was an innate neurological disorder. He wrote: "Since I also believe that autism is basically a disturbance of the ability to reach out to the world, it will tend to become most apparent during the second year of life when more complicated contact with the world would normally take place."[57] Bettelheim argued that, even if a neurological source of autism were to be definitively discovered, this would not preclude a psychological explanation for the disorder, because it could quite easily follow that certain periods existed during which certain neurological systems must be stimulated to maintain normal development. If the child's emotional environment was poor, this could explain why the central nervous system became dysfunctional, he declared.[58]

In *The empty fortress*, Bettelheim does at least agree with Rimland that nothing is to be gained by blaming parents, because their actions were not deliberate. However, his assistant, Jacquelyn Sanders, told me: "He had no compunction about making parents feel guilty if it made them act better."[59]

In fact, even before the publication of *The empty fortress*, Rimland had written to Bettelheim asking him for help in obtaining blood samples of children diagnosed with infantile autism. Bettelheim turned down the request, saying:

> I regret to inform you that I am very critical of the approach that you are using to study infantile autism. In my opinion, your book contains gross errors and mis-statements. I therefore shall give you no help in a study of autistic children which I consider ill-conceived and based on erroneous and biased judgements.[60]

In the same letter to Rimland, Bettelheim wrote:

> Since you seem committed to the conviction that infantile autism is an inborn disease and incurable, no matter what the contrary evidence may be, I see little point in discussing treatment results. Suffice it to say that better than eighty-five percent of our former students have made an

adequate adjustment to life, including some who are your and my colleagues as PhDs in psychology.[61]

Bettelheim also angrily rejected a suggestion by Rimland that they each
write a section in each other's books. Bettelheim wrote:

> Feelings are unimportant to you, and to me they are the most important
> thing in dealing with human beings. But the important reason is that I
> abhor arguments. I firmly believe that scientific progress is best made by
> each man stating his opinions and allowing the present and future gen-
> erations to decide on their merits.[62]

Bettelheim retired from the Orthogenic School—or "Bruno's castle"
as it was sometimes called—in 1973 and moved to California, where
he wrote the work for which, apart from *The empty fortress*, he is best
known, *The uses of enchantment*, in which he argued that such bloody
tales as *Hansel and Gretel* and *Sleeping Beauty* were a necessary outlet
for children's fears and anxieties.

When, in 1985, Anne Donnellan and her editorial panel put together
the first major retrospective on studies in autism (*Classic readings in autism*),
they identified only two articles on autism from the 1950s which they
felt were "classic," that is, which were significant for their time or had
withstood the test of time.[63] One of them was Bruno Bettelheim's
*Scientific American* article, "Joey: A mechanical boy" from 1959.[64]
Bettelheim refused permission for Donnellan to reprint that article. Some
writers have speculated that this was because there had been a number
of attacks on him at around that time and he was stung by the fact that
his reputation had taken a battering. However, Donnellan herself gave
me another version which sheds a much warmer light on Bettelheim's
motives: "He was actually refusing the Autism Society of America (to
whom I gave all the royalties) because they had supported Lovaas (and
others) on the use of shock on the kids."[65]

Bettelheim refused to change his views on autism to the very end of
his life. In the late 1980s, he visited Britain and gave a talk in a huge
hall in Westminster, London. In the audience was the young Francesca
Happé, today among the world's leading autism authorities. "He spoke
about the Orthogenic School in Chicago," Happé told me. "He mentioned that, when the children damaged the walls, the staff would cover
the damaged area with gold leaf, to convey how infinitely precious the
children were—that nothing was too good for them. He said that, after
that, the children never damaged the walls again. It was a beautiful

concept. He didn't actually mention autism at all in his talk. But someone in the audience asked him: 'Haven't you said that mothers are to blame for their child's autism?' Bettelheim replied: 'Yes—and I stand by that.'"[66]

Bettelheim killed himself at the age of 86 on March 13, 1990—52 years to the day after the Nazis marched into his native Austria—by tying a plastic bag over his head. Shortly afterwards, letters began to pour in to newspapers from former students of the Orthogenic School alleging that Bettelheim had physically and emotionally abused the children in his care.

Alida Jatich, a patient for seven years who became a computer programmer in Chicago, published an article in the weekly, *The Chicago Reader*, in which she claimed Bettelheim had once dragged her naked and dripping from a shower and slapped her repeatedly in front of her dorm mates. "In person," she wrote, "he was an evil man who set up his school as a private empire and himself as a demi-god or cult leader." Jatich said Bettelheim had "bullied, awed, and terrorized" the children at his school, their parents, school staff members, his graduate students, and anyone else who came into contact with him.[67] Ronald Angres, another former patient, in a 1990 article for *Commentary*, claimed that Bettelheim had insulted children "just in order to break any self-confidence they might have. I lived in terror of his beatings, in terror of his footsteps in the dorm."[68] Some of the adults Bettelheim had claimed to have "cured" of severe developmental disabilities, including autism, maintained that they had entered the school with nothing more than behavioral problems.

In contrast, one of Bettelheim's closest friends, the Los Angeles psychoanalyst, Dr. Rudolf Ekstein, said:

> He told me that, once you were in a camp, you could never escape the cruelty. He turned it upside down when he started his school for disturbed children. It was a protected, caring environment, the mirror opposite of the camps. The door was locked to the outside, but always open from the inside.[69]

Ekstein added that some people saw Bettelheim "as a sort of god, but you couldn't be a god any more."[70]

Jacquelyn Sanders still remembers Bettelheim fondly—but with reservations: "I think I learnt a lot of good things about teaching autistic children. There are useful things if you take out the idea that autism is engendered by the parents. That caused so much antagonism. And his total rejection of people like Rimland was offensive," she told me.[71]

Other Freudian analysts, as well as scientists who were not psychiatrists, followed Bettelheim in blaming the poor mothers for their child's autism. The psychologist Harry Harlow's research with monkeys who were deprived of their mothers convinced him that autism was caused by "refrigerator mothers."

There was one positive consequence of Bettelheim's misguided teachings. Parents in the United States were driven to a concerted effort to combat his ideas, and in so doing, formed the National Society for Autistic Children, later to become the Autism Society of America. At their first congress in 1969, many of the speakers launched stinging attacks on Bettelheim. And in a witty reference to his cold mothering hypothesis, delegates apparently wore name-tags in the form of little refrigerators.

Laura Schreibman cites a wonderfully energetic and dogged campaign by a mother who found, to her disgust, that the only books on autism stocked by her local library were two Bettelheim books: *The empty fortress* and *Love is not enough*. When the library refused to remove the offending volumes from the shelves, she took them out herself and tossed them away. Each time the library restocked them, she or another parent took them out and threw them away again.[72]

Bettelheim spawned many admirers and supporters around the world. Pre-eminent among the psychoanalysts who were interested in examining Leo Kanner's findings, apart from Bettelheim, were Margaret Mahler in New York and Donald Meltzer in London. We have already seen (see chapter 1) that Kanner had written approvingly of Mahler's division of child psychosis into cases of early infantile autism and cases of symbiotic infantile psychosis.

Donald Meltzer was an influential, New York-born psychoanalyst who moved to London in 1954 to work with Melanie Klein and worked at the Tavistock Institute there. His model of psychoanalytic psychotherapy training was adapted in many parts of France, especially by Wilfred Bion, and in Italy and Argentina. His 1975 book, *Explorations in autism*, documented his experience in treating autistic children.[73] Meltzer postulated that a very early mechanism of normal and psychotic development, the so-called projective identification, did not work in autism. He believed that individuals with autism did not go through the process of "primordial paranoia" and, since they had never created an enemy, they had never been persecuted and, for this same reason, they did not have an ego.

72

Another very significant psychoanalytical thinker—influenced by Bettelheim, Mahler and Meltzer—was Frances Tustin. Tustin began training as a psychotherapist at the Tavistock Clinic in the early 1950s. She first heard about autistic children at a lecture given by Marion Putnam at the invitation of the Tavistock's then director, John Bowlby. In 1953, she did an internship at the James Jackson Putnam Center in Roxbury, Massachusetts, which was treating autistic children psychoanalytically. Back in London, she was keen to apply the Kleinian method of analysis to autistic children. Her view was that children with autism erected defense mechanisms against the anxiety of the traumatic experience of brutal bodily separation from the object. She did not publish her first book, *Autism and childhood psychosis*, until 1972,[74] but this represented the original statement of her views on autistic states of mind and the genesis of varieties of childhood psychosis. (She later regretted her choice of title because she feared it implied that she did not consider autistic children to be psychotic.) Employing Kleinian terminology, she also enlisted concepts from Bettelheim and Mahler, as well as the British pediatrician and psychoanalyst, Donald Winnicott.

Tustin herself enjoyed a great following around the world—and continues to do so to this day, more than a decade after her death in 1994. And yet, even towards the end of her life, Tustin continued her efforts to dispel the notion that autism was congenital and insisted, instead, that it was a neurological disorder caused by cruel treatment by parents who were too busy to love and care for their babies.[75]

Despite these views, however, Tustin appears to have taken a rather different approach in practice. Dame Stephanie Shirley took her autistic son, Giles, to Tustin's house in Tring, Hertfordshire, near London, to be treated. "She never blamed me for Giles's autism," Dame Stephanie recalled. "In fact, she said her aim was to make Giles less aggressive towards me—and she did just that."[76]

The shadow of Bruno Bettelheim continues to loom large around the world. Astonishingly, it was not until 1998 that IACAPAP—the international umbrella association representing some 60 associations of psychiatrists, pediatricians, psychologists, and educationalists—finally announced, at a congress in Venice, Italy, that "parents have absolutely no responsibility for their children's autism." The Italian organizers declared: "This is an historic moment for our country, because the psychogenic theory, long discredited in Anglo-Saxon countries, is still the most fashionable one in Italy. And until now, only the parents' associations have struggled to promote a different approach to the illness."[77]

In Italy, the 2001 edition of the prestigious *Enciclopedia Rizzoli-Larousse* featured the following, shockingly outdated definition:

> Autism is the fundamental nature of the schizoid constitution which can merge into clear schizophrenia. . . . The autistic child, if he receives the appropriate treatment and this is followed up by his relatives (who are often the cause of the syndrome, especially when they overstep the mark and insist on an overperfectionistic upbringing) can be more or less completely cured. Nevertheless, even when the problem is resolved, he will still have difficulties in forging normal connections and calm inter-personal relationships.

Thankfully, the publishers agreed to replace the definition with a new one describing autism as a neurological disorder.

France still largely follows the psychoanalytical tendency. Although, as I will show in a later chapter, a number of truly excellent French professionals are bucking this trend, the same cannot be said for other French-speaking nations. It remains the principal approach in the fran-cophone region of Switzerland.

I recently read of a mother in the former French colony, Morocco, who very articulately described the situation there: "What ever happened to scientific openness? The child psychiatrists here asked me the same old questions: did I reject my pregnancy, did I have emotional blows, how did I respond to my child's handicap? Their suggestion of my imperfect motherhood made me cry for hours on end."[78]

One of France's most vocal supporters today is Dr. Roger Misès, a leading child psychiatrist who drafted the Classification française des troubles mentaux de l'enfant et de l'adolescent (CFTMEA), the French Classification of Child and Adolescent Mental Disorders, in 1993. "Bettelheim's thinking was not really psychoanalytical, but personal," Misès told me. "He believed you could repair the damage done to a child by the environment. At the time he was working at the Orthogenic School, I was calling for everyone to collaborate to help these children. That's exactly what Bettelheim proposed. The research findings, strategies and techniques can complement one another. I was one of the defenders of Bettelheim because he was the first to create an institution where everyone collaborated in the interests of the children with autism. That was a positive move. But his policy of cutting the children off from their parents was totally unacceptable."[79]

Support for Bettelheim's suggestion that an abnormal family envir-onment could play a role in autism also came, rather surprisingly, from

Dr. David Amaral, professor of psychiatry at the University of California, Davis, and since 1998 the research director at the MIND Institute in Sacramento. Maybe, Amaral suggested, there were other ways that the brain systems could be perturbed which were less biological than genetic or immunological factors.

"An impoverished early social environment such as in an orphanage could be one way," he told me. "The lack of social stimulation during a critical period of life may alter the brain regions involved in social behavior. So while it is absolutely true that, in general, what causes autism is not cold, refrigerator mothers, if you look at things in an open way, it may well be that an orphanage-like situation where there is no normal nurturing by a mother to an infant may have a biological impact on the brain which could lead to autism. Behavior affects the brain. So does biology. If the family is not involved, this takes away one of the positive impacts. I obviously don't want to go back to the idea of the refrigerator mother. But to say that it's only biology, not family environment, cannot be true."[80]

Another leading authority, Simon Baron-Cohen, while also not blaming the parents, credits Bettelheim's writings for inspiring him to enter the autism field, as we have seen.[81] After Baron-Cohen graduated, he went to work for a school for autism in 1981, where the adviser was Frances Tustin, a leading British member of the psychoanalytical school of thought on autism—another indication of how long this approach clung on in the UK.

"Here we are in 2009 and they have developed a theory called the Absent Self. It would be interesting to look at the historic links between Bettelheim and Uta Frith's new theory," Baron-Cohen told me. "And after all, theory of mind is all about imagining other people's thoughts and what is going on in other people's minds. This is linked to the concept of self-consciousness. If you're thinking about what other people are thinking about you, about how you appear to others—and theory of mind is very much about self-awareness—that could very well be linked to Bettelheim's idea that people with autism do not have a sense of self."[82]

Nevertheless, Michael Rutter told me he did not have much respect for Bettelheim: "He was a complicated man. But he was not only wrong but less than honest, and that is a more important criticism."[83]

# 4

# The 1960s

## *The Parents Fight Back*

*"Autism is totally unique in all of medicine in that parents have made such major contributions to a particular field." (Mary Coleman, speaking to Adam Feinstein in New York)*

*"I suspect there is more passion behind an organization for people with autism than any other disability in the world." (Ruth Sullivan, speaking to Adam Feinstein in Huntington, West Virginia)*

The years of being told that they were responsible for their child's autism began to take their toll on parents around the world. Undaunted, however, they were determined to fight back and, from the 1960s, they started forming their own associations for the first time to protect the interests of their children and spread awareness of a condition that was becoming a target for serious scientific research but lay mired in misconceptions. According to Britain's National Autistic Society, there were, as of 2009, a total of 90 autism societies spread among 56 countries throughout the world. This chapter seeks to chart the history of some of the principal associations from their very beginnings.

"Those were dark days for families with children who had any kind of autistic disorder [in the UK]," Dr. Lorna Wing, the great British psychiatrist and autism authority, and herself the mother of a daughter with autism, wrote in a personal memoir.

Up to the end of the 1950s, the general public was profoundly ignorant concerning autism and the same was true of most professionals, even psychiatrists and psychologists. Among the few who were interested and aware, many agreed with the theory that the children were potentially normal but had been made to withdraw by cold, distant, overintellectual parents. Diagnosis was difficult or impossible to obtain and there was no help or support for the parents. Children could be excluded from education in school if they had severe learning difficulties or disruptive behaviour and there were virtually no special schools for children with autism.[1]

Wing noted that no one, at the time, knew anything about adults with autism—in fact, they did not even accept that they existed, since the condition was still seen as a childhood disorder. Services were non-existent. "In those days, for most parents of young children with autistic disorders, it was a bleak and lonely existence with no source of information, help or support."[2]

However, the situation began to change in the 1960s, for two main reasons, Wing said.

> One was the development of objective, scientific investigation into autistic disorders, which showed that the children had real disabilities underlying their unusual pattern of behaviour. The approach of the pioneers in research was very different from the armchair theorizing that had gone before. The other was the creation of the National Autistic Society [in the UK].[3]

Also in 1961, the Creak Committee in the UK produced a landmark set of nine points which set the criteria for diagnosis of (or at least screening for) autism. Nevertheless, the condition was still referred to as childhood schizophrenia in this report, which will be discussed in detail in chapter 7.

Mildred Creak herself was an extraordinary figure in the history of child psychiatry—and not just in her native Britain. Born in Manchester in 1898, she qualified as a doctor at University College Hospital in London at the end of the First World War, but there were few posts for women doctors at the time. A Quaker, Creak worked as assistant physician at The Retreat, a mental hospital run by Quakers in York, from 1924 to 1928. However, earlier experience working with children led her to return to London and to a post at the Maudsley Psychiatric Hospital, which in 1929 had just established a Children's Department. Here she helped to lay the clinical and academic foundations for what is now one of Britain's leading centers for the study of child psychiatric disorders.

Shortly after the start of the Second World War, the Maudsley was transferred to Mill Hill Hospital in north London and Creak worked there before joining the Women's Army Corps as a doctor. Part of her war service was in India. At the end of the war, she was offered a post back at the Maudsley, but she wanted to practise in a children's hospital. In 1946, she was offered the first post as physician in psychological medicine at the Hospital for Sick Children, Great Ormond Street, where she had previously worked voluntarily. From 1946 until her retirement in 1963, she played a leading role in establishing the practice of child psychiatry in a pediatric setting.

In the early 1960s, Creak chaired the working party which established the nine-point criteria for the diagnosis of autism. This work was partly based on a series of 100 children she had collected herself. Creak suggested that autism, far from being caused by parental inadequacy—still a widespread view among professionals—was primarily due to genetic or, as she put it, "constitutional" factors.

Creak lectured in Perth, Western Australia, after her retirement and had a unit for autistic children named after her there. She died in the UK in 1993 at the age of 95.

In the 1960s, a remarkable pair of researchers, Neil O'Connor and Beate Hermelin, based at the Medical Research Council in London, began their ground-breaking psychological studies of children with autism (see chapter 6). Also in the 1960s, one of the founders of child psychiatry in the UK, Michael Rutter, became interested in the field of autism and he wrote very clear clinical follow-up studies of children with the condition. He and his colleagues studied the children's psychological profiles and found that they were good at some things and very bad at others. Rutter's views were strictly developmental and neurological and they exerted a great influence on fellow professionals.

In 1965, Rutter discussed the hypothesis that "the basic defect in infantile autism is an impairment in the comprehension of sounds." According to this view, Rutter wrote, the language disorder in autism "is the primary abnormality. Furthermore, it is thought that this abnormality in the development of language is closely similar to other developmental disorders of language involving defects in comprehension—so-called 'developmental receptive aphasia' or 'congenital auditory imperception.' "[4] Rutter's immense contribution to the field will also be examined further below and in chapter 6. As we shall see, he quickly came to the view that there were multiple central deficits in autism.

In 1962, the German psychiatrist, Dr. Gerhard Bosch, published an important book, *Der frühkindliche Autismus*.[5] Bosch was the true pioneer of both autism and Asperger's syndrome in Germany, as we saw in chapter 2, presenting his first cases of autism from the early 1950s.

Bosch's book places a great deal of emphasis on language impairments in autism—although he is careful not to identify this as the core deficit—a few years before this area became a serious target of research in the Anglo-Saxon world.

The book includes some beautifully observed case studies of children with autism and contains a number of illuminating insights. Of particular interest is the appendix written in 1969 for the English edition of the book. In it, Bosch writes that "in the course of the investigation itself I found it necessary to use the term 'autistic' in a wider sense than that permitted by the scope of Kanner syndrome."[6] This is a tantalizing early allusion to what Lorna Wing and Judith Gould would come to call the "autistic spectrum" in 1979.

Even more fascinatingly, Bosch includes a section in this appendix on "The differences between Asperger and Kanner syndromes"—a full 14 years before Lorna Wing officially coined the term *Asperger's syndrome*. In this section, Bosch disagrees with Arn van Krevelen's suggestion that Kanner's syndrome was a process with a pathological development or "a process that has come to a standstill." Bosch expresses doubt that it is possible to draw such clear distinctions between the two conditions, adding that it is his experience that "superior intellectual talents and isolated special talents also occur in cases exhibiting Kanner's syndrome where the general level, of intelligence is usually low."[7]

In an observation strikingly foreshadowing today's misgivings—although written 40 years ago—Bosch declared:

> Asperger's syndrome involves the risk that the concept of autism will be extended to people who are slightly afraid of personal contact, who are unsure of themselves, schizoid and abnormal, and that the concept will be watered down and generalized in a dubious way.[8]

Bosch, who is now over 90 years old, told me from Frankfurt that he believed Asperger's syndrome belonged on the autistic spectrum. "The disturbance, in both cases, is in the same regions of the brain."[9]

The English edition of Bosch's book features a foreword by Bruno Bettelheim and not only frequently quotes, but concurs with, a number of ideas expressed in Bettelheim's *The empty fortress*. (Bettelheim himself had approvingly dedicated a section of the final chapter of *The empty fortress* to Bosch in 1967.) It should be stressed, however, that Bosch does not go so far as to endorse the possibility that the parents might be to be blame for their child's autism. In his 1969 appendix, he writes: "I think it is unlikely that infantile autism is caused exclusively by psycho-social factors. . . . I myself know of only one case in which I think it likely that psychogenetic factors are directly and to a large extent solely responsible."[10]

Indeed, Bosch himself told me that, though he found Bettelheim a very intelligent man and a good teacher, "it was a very bad idea to blame the parents for their child's autism. I found no evidence of this."[11]

In 2004, Bosch and a younger Frankfurt colleague, Dr. Sven Bölte, published a remarkable 40-year follow-up study of two children he had diagnosed with autism and one with Asperger's syndrome. Of particular interest was the Asperger's case, Richard L., who had begun to create an inner fantasy world which he called "Resteten" at the age of 6 and who, in the follow-up in 2001, showed considerable empathy for characters in fiction—notably in the Swiss children's story, *Heidi*—but not for real-life individuals.[12]

In 1966 and 1967, Dr. Victor Lotter, working in the Medical Research Council Social Psychiatry Unit at London's Institute of Psychiatry, published the first paper to give the results of an epidemiological study of autism in a large population of children of all levels of intelligence living in a defined geographical area—the former English county of Middlesex. He used the two criteria modified by Kanner and Eisenberg in their 1956 paper: a profound lack of affective contact and repetitive, ritualistic behavior, which must be of an elaborate kind. (He also used these two features in 1967 to divide autistic children into "nuclear" and "non-nuclear" groups. He did not consider age of onset to be essential.) The 1966 study found a prevalence rate of 4.5 per 10,000.[13]

Lorna Wing knew Lotter well. She told me: "He was a nice man, but rather pedantic. He would stick to his views. When we were doing our 1979 Camberwell study, we sent him our statistics and we found him to be using much stricter criteria than we were doing. But that was his style."[14]

Another of the early epidemiological studies of childhood disorders—though it was not looking specifically at autism—was Michael Rutter and Jack Tizard's Isle of Wight study, also in the 1960s. "We were very interested in the issue of providing services," Rutter told me. "We chose the Isle of Wight because it had a large enough population—around 100,000—but also because the local authorities were very cooperative."[15]

In 1966, Lorna Wing's husband, Dr. John Wing, edited an important collection of essays on autism[16]—he was better-known at the time than Lorna and she had persuaded him to produce it. But it was her own book on the disorder five years later—*Autistic children: a guide for parents*[17]—which was to be seen as a major point of reference not only in the UK but around the globe and provided a much-needed antidote to Bruno Bettelheim's "refrigerator mother" approach.

**Figures 14 and 15** Ed Ornitz (left) and Ed Ritvo

Across the Atlantic, Ed Ornitz had moved to UCLA from the Yale Child Study Center in the early 1960s. Ornitz, Ed Ritvo, and Peter Tanguay collaborated. The two Eds and Tanguay realized that there had to be something neurologically different about the autistic children they saw—despite the continuing powerful psychoanalytical climate in Los Angeles. "Unlike researchers today, I was locked into the idea that you had to start research when the kids were very young," Ornitz told me. "At Yale, I had become fascinated by William Dement's new work on REM sleep and dreaming. I started studying autistic children from this point of view. Ed Ritvo was already here at UCLA. Peter Tanguay came to UCLA shortly thereafter. We lost many nights' sleep putting electrodes on these children and examining their EEGs and event-related potentials. Our subsequent early work on the vestibular system in autism was motivated by some of the findings about the rapid eye movements of REM sleep in these children. We did find significant differences between autistic children and controls, and this was important, to us,

81

because it suggested problems in brain-stem function. Subsequently, I was able to advance the vestibular studies so as to provide neurophysiological evidence for brain-stem dysfunction in autism.[18] However, brain-stem studies fell out of interest, as cognitive issues came to the fore."[19]

Other important evidence began to emerge in the 1960s indicating clear biological abnormalities in autism. As early as 1961, Daniel Freedman at Yale published research showing that levels of the neurotransmitter serotonin were elevated in the blood platelets of individuals with autism.

Bizarre misconceptions remained intact, however. Philip K. Dick's science fiction novel, *Martian time-slip*, first published in 1964, features an autistic boy who slips helplessly backwards and forwards in time.[20]

Some of the most brilliantly vivid insights into what life was like for the family of an autistic child in Britain in the early 1960s can be found in James Copeland's book, *For the love of Ann*.[21] It relates the story of an autistic girl in Salford, in the north of England, whose parents, Jack and Ivy Hodges, were told by a doctor in 1958 when she was 6 that she was a schizophrenic psychopath. Twenty years later, Ann had grown into a young woman "full of chat and charm, devoted to her parents and her brothers, excitedly taking in the world and its challenges." Nevertheless, her autistic traits remained. Not all children with autism, of course, make such good progress, but Ann's story not only gave hope to many across the globe, but it provided invaluable information about a still very misunderstood condition. Similar encouragement to parents came from a Swedish mother's account, Karin Stensland Junker's remarkable 1961 memoir, *De ensamma*,[22] translated into English three years later as *The child in the glass ball*.[23]

Some educationalists were already coming to terms with the challenges of teaching autistic children in the UK by the late 1950s, although autism itself was not the term commonly used for their condition. Dr. Margaret Golding, one of the pioneers in this area, described her journey as reminiscent of Douglas Adams's *The hitch hiker's guide to the galaxy*: "It has been so bizarre and unpredictable that the only consolation seemed to be the words inscribed on the cover of that book—'Don't Panic!'" she told the Second World Autism Congress in South Africa in 2006. "A trip to the galaxy seems almost mundane compared to the fascinating world of autism which has unfolded for me over the past 49 years."[24]

Golding said her journey began in 1957 when, as a young teacher in a London boarding special school for preschool children who had social and learning difficulties, she met a child whose strange character and

82

personality had not been formed by being in an orphanage or various experiences of deprivation like the other children.

> This child seemed to come from a normal caring family and yet he was not a normally developing child. He was a complete mystery to us. He would panic for no apparent reason and perseverated constantly using lots of repetitive language in a loud voice. He was also unable to interact and play with the other children in a normal way but screamed if they came too near him. . . . He was judged to be "very naughty" and "difficult". Staff felt that he was "spoilt" and had been allowed to "get away with things" by his parents and the general attitude towards Paul was punitive and hostile. He was four years old and he got worse.[25]

In 1959, a colleague of Golding, who had become the matron of a small children's hospital for "psychotic" children, invited her to look around the facilities. The hospital was High Wick Hospital in Hertfordshire, north of London, which had been set up because psychiatric social workers had become concerned about the lack of provision for these children. At that time in the UK, such children were considered to be "ineducable," along with mentally handicapped children, and had no rights to education. The Medical Superintendent at High Wick, Dr. George Stroh, was a child psychiatrist and a Freudian psychoanalyst, as were his colleagues: the hospital had links to Anna Freud, and other famous psychoanalytical figures such as Donald Winnicott became involved in parent support and training of staff there.

Golding was offered the post of teacher in charge at High Wick: "I pretty soon found myself unable to go to bed at night," she recalled.

> I well remember picking mushrooms in the early hours of the morning— anything rather than have to get up and face those strange children who did not seem to respond to all my lovely, carefully planned, activities. . . . The general ethos was to keep the children calm and not disturb them further so that hopefully with all the therapy (both for them and their parents) they would emerge from their "psychotic" or "schizophrenic" state.[26]

Golding's successor at High Wick, Lusia Arendt, told Lorna Wing how they tried to return the children there to their infancy so that they could restart their development. One technique was to give them baby-feeding bottles to suck from. Arendt said the children used these to squirt milk at the ceiling.[27]

★ ★ ★

It is generally assumed that the world's first national autism association was established in England in 1962, although the Danish dispute this. When the initial moves began to form a national society for autism in London, there was instant opposition from those who felt that autism should be included under a general disability umbrella and not as a separate classification. One of the principal founders of the National Society for Autistic Children (later to become the National Autistic Society—NAS), was Lorna Wing.

**Figure 16**  Lorna Wing and Adam Feinstein

Wing told me: "One of the founding members of [the society for the mentally handicapped] Mencap, Judy Fryd, thought we should be part of their organization. But Helen Allison and Michael Baron [two other parents] were very keen to get this group of parents of autistic children together as a separate organization. I chatted with a colleague, Neil O'Connor, and he agreed." Wing pointed out that, some time earlier, parents of children with cerebral palsy had left Mencap to form what was then called the Spastics Society. "So we followed their example and formed our society in 1962. . . . There was a lot of hostility on the part of Mencap, with dark mutterings that we wouldn't succeed—but of course we succeeded beyond our wildest dreams."[28]

Michael Baron's position as a solicitor with the National Childbirth Trust meant that the founding parents could use the trust's offices in

London for their initial meetings. Lorna Wing said a lot of parents were very uneasy about the original title of their organization—namely, the Society for Psychotic Children—"particularly as, in many lay people's eyes, the term 'psychotic' was related to psychopathic and the whole ambience of the word was unpleasant. The alternative was 'autistic' but some people felt that was too narrow a term—which is interesting in the light of subsequent developments. . . . We had a meeting when this was discussed with great intensity, with great emotion and finally it was passed that it would be called the Society for Autistic Children—but only after an enormous amount of argument."[29]

Another of the early parents, Peggie Everard, who later became General Secretary of the NAS, recalled that there was some disagreement about aims when they met up informally: some people wanted the money to be spent entirely on research but many others, like Helen Allison, were adamant that the funding should be channeled into practical areas such as education.[30]

In October 1961, Helen Allison appeared on the BBC radio program, *Woman's hour*, which attracted immense public attention to the issue of autism. In November 1962, a feature article on autism, written by Colin Frame, appeared in the London newspaper, the *Evening News*. It bore the rather unfortunate heading, "Children in chains," but once again increased awareness.

Michael Baron, who was to become the NAS's first chairman, told me that it was in that same year that he and Helen Allison—in whose

kitchen some of the very earliest meetings were held—"drew up a very ambitious, wildly optimistic document, which we called The Project, in 1962. It was all about setting up a school and services for adults. A friend of mine said we would never achieve all of that."[31]

Baron added: "I then met two parents of thalidomide children at a Mencap meeting who had been raising money for thalidomide victims. They offered to take me on and run fundraising car competitions. They also funded the TV film, *Child draw nearer* [scripted by the British novelist, Bernice Rubens, and broadcast in 1964] which brought in a lot more parents."[32]

**Figure 17**  Michael Baron

Despite the increasing number of research studies and publications dedicated to autism, Wing recalled an amusing illustration of the continuing ignorance at the time: when she managed to persuade a newspaper to publish their first article in 1962, it appeared under the heading "Problems of *artistic* children." More seriously, in the same year, another planned newspaper article about autism was not published because it was displaced by the Cuban missile crisis.

There were other teething problems. Michael Baron recalled "a disastrous car competition—there was no money for the prizes because it had all been spent. It was all in our name and the writs were beginning to come in! I was chairman of the NAS at the time and I was having sleepless nights. My wife at the time rang a rich uncle in Denmark who paid off the prizes. He then became very interested in autism in Denmark."[33]

The next target was education. In fact, the NAS's Sybil Elgar School may not have been the first school for autistic children set up in Britain. Maggie Golding was involved in an earlier project, although the children were not recognized as autistic at the time—and, as we shall see later in this chapter, there were also claims that Golding was influential in prompting Sybil Elgar's interest in autism, although there were also reservations in some quarters about Golding's psychoanalytical training at High Wick.

As Golding has explained, in the late 1950s there was no contemporary information on autism, no educational programs or conferences, and no one else working in this field of education. In 1961, Golding was visited at High Wick Hospital by Dr. Louis Minski, a child psychiatrist who specialized in working with the deaf. He had been engaged in a project at Belmont Hospital, an institution for the mentally handicapped in Surrey, south of London, to sort out children who were deaf and had been wrongly placed in the hospital. As he carried out this task, he realized that he had another group of children who were not deaf. They were disruptive and difficult in the institution and several of them seemed to have good intelligence although they were functionally retarded.[34]

Dr. Minski approached the Invalid Children's Aid Association (now the ICAN organization)—at the time the richest charity in the UK with Princess Margaret as its patron. The ICAA eventually agreed to open a termly boarding school for these children, named Edith Edwards House, in May 1962 and Golding was appointed its principal. The first pupils came from a halfway house in Belmont Hospital and were soon joined by pupils from all over the south and southwest of England.[35]

"When Edith Edwards House had its initial PR opening for officials and neighbours, the publicity was headlined 'A school for children without love!' I was horrified!" Golding said.

> I had never felt comfortable with the perception of parents as the cause of their children's condition. I noted that many of them had other quite normally developing children and that they suffered greatly from their autistic child's behaviour. . . . At Edith Edwards house, I was able to get close to parents and was full of admiration for the way some of them fought for their children's rights to education.[36]

Nevertheless, the true pioneer in the field of autism education in Britain was undoubtedly Sybil Elgar, who died in 2007 at the age of 92. Lorna Wing said of her: "She was the UK's first autism-specific teacher and an inspiration to those who knew her, at a time when autism was still ill-defined and widely misunderstood."[37]

Born in London, Elgar was the daughter of an engine-driver father and a mother who worked at the Pathé News factory. Her interest in helping children was first sparked during her Montessori training when a visit to a hospital in London for "severely emotionally disturbed children" in 1958 left her deeply shocked. She could not forget how soul-destroying the place was and how miserable the children were. Elgar revisited the hospital in 1960 and, on seeing that nothing had changed, decided to set up her own school, initially in the basement of her home.

**Figure 18** Sybil Elgar (photo courtesy of NAS)

Helen Allison told an interviewer in 1998 that she believed it was Maggie Golding—then called Maggie Chojko—who had "inspired Sybil to do her Montessori course and to get interested in autism, so we owe Maggie a lot."[38]

Lorna Wing is fulsome in her praise for Sybil Elgar: "With patience, instinct and a degree of experimentation, she developed a structured approach to teaching, giving her pupils clear and simple instructions and visual aids to ensure they understood what was required of them. Her methods ran counter to mainstream educational thought at the time. However, all the children in her class made substantial progress."[39]

Shortly afterwards, Helen Allison, Lorna Wing and Peggie Everard interviewed Elgar, who was teaching a group of six learning-disabled children in a basement flat in St. John's Wood, in north London, at the time. "It was perfectly obvious Sybil didn't know anything about autism," Allison recalled in her 1998 interview, "but there was something about her—maybe her practicality, which made us feel she would be valuable."[40]

Allison added that Elgar agreed to change over to teaching autistic children so she began sending her son, Joe, to Elgar's St. John's Wood class: "He started in her basement, alone, and that's where I told her to draw the curtains because I was afraid that he would break the windows; and he proceeded to knock out all the light bulbs. He used to tear paper continuously, and after a fortnight, Sybil wrote: 'There is nothing I can do for this little boy.' Then she decided to try a different approach, making him pick up the paper, then making him use her Montessori materials. Other parents asked me why I was so happy, and I told them about Sybil. . . . She was inspected by the local authorities, and then other children poured in. After that, it was natural that we should invite her to become principal of our first school."[41]

It was Sybil Elgar's husband, Jack, who found the first school building in Florence Road in Ealing, West London—a railway hostel which was being sold. Some remarkable personalities quickly became interested in helping the fundraising campaign, including two of England's leading movie actors, David Tomlinson (a star of *Mary Poppins*), who had a son, Willy, with autism, and Robert Morley (who appeared in *The African Queen*). Morley had no personal connections with the disorder but was a good friend of Tomlinson.

Baron recalled that the building in Florence Road "cost £14,000. The Sembal Trust gave us the money. We knew that the kids could be paid for by the local authorities so we were prepared to borrow the money. Sybil lived on the top floor at 10 Florence Road. We acquired number 12 and, when we formed the Ealing Autistic Trust, we also bought number 8 and that became a sort of boarding arm of the school. So that was the first residential center for autistic children, before Somerset Court."[42]

Sybil Elgar School opened in 1965. Among the most prominent visitors were three members of the Beatles. Gerald de Groot, another of the NAS founding parents, told me that the pop stars had insisted on there being no publicity and they planned to stay for only an hour "but they eventually ended up spending the whole afternoon rolling around with the children on the floor!"[43] Not only did John Lennon give £1,000 to the school—he also persuaded others to donate money.

Another important visitor at this time was Eric Schopler, who had worked briefly with Bruno Bettelheim in Chicago but was appalled at the parent-blaming ethos and had moved to Chapel Hill, North Carolina, where he would shortly found the TEACCH program. In fact, at the invitation of Lorna Wing, Schopler spoke at the first conference of what was to become the National Autistic Society, held at Pontin's Holiday Camp.

The early British pioneers claim that many of the ideas and principles on which TEACCH is based were adopted by Schopler from what he had seen during his trips to London in the 1960s. Indeed, Richard Mills, the National Autistic Society's current Director of Research and Research Director for Research Autism—an independent charity concerned with impartial research into the effectiveness of interventions in autism—said Schopler had told him in Tokyo in 2004 that many of the ideas which inspired TEACCH had come from the Sybil Elgar School, "but that one of the key differences was the decision to embed their program in the university, so as to ensure practice reflected empirical research."[44]

Hugh Morgan, now chief executive of the Welsh charity, Autism Cymru (see chapter 9), told me: "Sybil Elgar showed herself to be an astoundingly perceptive 'reader' of the patterns of thinking and learning of children with autism. Remember that, at this stage, children with autism were simply not being recognized, never mind diagnosed, so there was no autism rule book or guidelines for Sybil to draw upon (as there is today). Sybil therefore constructed her own teaching methodologies which today still pervade many of the approaches used in the education of children with autistic spectrum disorders."[45]

Morgan found Elgar "a formidable and caring woman. She was the individual who set out the basis for the principles for working with people with autism which have become the benchmark for today's practice. I have little doubt that over the years her impact and influence have been greatly undervalued, although I did receive a letter from Eric Schopler in which he conveyed what an inspiration Sybil Elgar had been."[46]

Another of the pioneers in the field of autism education in the UK, Wendy Brown, founding head of Helen Allison and Broomhayes special schools for autism, and the first chairwoman of Britain's

Association of Headteachers for Children with Autism, told me: "Every single one of us climbed on Sybil's shoulders to get where we got. People are not always aware what an enormous debt we owe to her. For people with autism, Asperger's syndrome, a carer or a parent, she was a person who knew where to start and pointed us in the right direction. Her pioneering methodology was widely copied. At a time when people were strict to the point of severity . . . Beate Hermelin told me: 'The great thing about Sybil is that she's a secret cuddler. If you opened a door suddenly, she would be cuddling a child.' "[47]

**Figure 19**  Gerald de Groot

Gerald de Groot is another great admirer of Sybil Elgar, although his son, Mark, came into contact with her later. Mark was diagnosed by Mildred Creak at her clinic at London's Great Ormond Street Hospital in 1962, a year after Creak had published her celebrated Nine Points. Creak took great interest in observing Mark through a two-way mirror and then told de Groot: "He's probably autistic"[48]—a significant choice of word because her committee's report had referred to "childhood schizophrenia," not autism, the previous year.

For a few years, de Groot's son was with Alice Hoffmann in Finsbury Park, north London. Hoffman had founded a school for children who were excluded from mainstream education in 1955. Eventually, this school became a day center for adults with autism. "She was a very strange person," de Groot told me. "Most of the children she was dealing with at the time were autistic. She later got taken over by the Scientologists, so I took Mark out of her class."[49]

By contrast, de Groot remembers Sybil Elgar with enormous admiration: "Sybil had an immense gift. She realized that what autistic children needed was a one-to-one structured approach. TEACCH and all the other systems are really just variants of Sybil's methods. In addition to her technique, there was something about her personality. She was the strongest personality you could wish for. She would not suffer opposition or alternate views on anything at all! But somehow, children who were like wild animals would respond to her, as if by hypnosis. It was quite remarkable. She had a wonderful effect on Helen Allison's son,

Joe—and without Helen, I don't think there would have been a National Autistic Society, Sybil Elgar School, or Somerset Court."[50]

David Tomlinson, who played such a prominent fundraising role in the early days, remembered in his autobiography taking his fellow actor and good friend, Robert Morley, around the Sybil Elgar School for the first time:

> He immediately joined the children at their own level and began crawling around the floor in his best suit. He was as impressed and amazed by Mrs Elgar as I was. When she was talking to us, the children kept coming up demanding a cuddle from her. Autistic children, who actually can shrink from physical contact of any kind, wanted her to cuddle them— which of course she did unhesitatingly, no matter what they interrupted. 'Do you think she hypnotises them?' Robert wondered. . . . Whenever I saw her, the first thing she said was: 'I need money, you know.' . . . Robert had no hesitation in borrowing Mrs Elgar's begging bowl and returning it to her filled up, having of course added some of his own money. It never remained full for long, though. Miracles don't come cheap, and Mrs Elgar was in the business of miracles.[51]

De Groot got to know Tomlinson very well. "I think his role in *Mary Poppins* gives you some idea of what he was like in real life! He was also a wonderful mimic. He once phoned me using Sybil Elgar's voice and I thought I was talking to Sybil—until he started laughing!"[52]

Research took on an increasingly important role for the NAS. "The society was very pleased to find children and adults who could take part in studies," Wing said. "Quite early on, although we started as a parents' group, we very quickly encouraged professionals to join. Very soon, there were almost as many professionals as parents."[53]

Professor Michael Rutter was brought in virtually from the beginning: "As soon as there was a formal admission system to the Sybil Elgar School, I would go regularly to the school to assess the children for admission," Rutter told me.[54] He recalled Sybil Elgar as a "very strong woman" but they worked very well together. "It was a very harmonious and successful period."[55]

Rutter emphasized the courage of the parents at the time: "They behaved very bravely in deciding that they could not control the admissions policy themselves. That had to be done through the local authority. This was a very brave decision because there was a chance that the people who had put so much time and energy into setting up the school might find that their children were not admitted to it."[56]

Another major center of UK activity in the 1960s was Nottingham, in the East Midlands. The Nottinghamshire and District Society for Autistic Children—later to be renamed NoRSACA (the Nottinghamshire Regional Society for Children and Adults with Autism)—was born in 1968 when a number of dissatisfied parents got together with two leading psychologists, John and Elizabeth Newson, who were based at Nottingham University's Child Development Research Unit. The Newsons had a longstanding interest in autism, partly through their professional careers but also because of the difficulties faced by their son, Roger, who is now a highly successful lecturer at the London School of Hygiene and Tropical Medicine.

Two years later, in 1970, NoRSACA opened its school, Sutherland House. Its current principal, Dr. Phil Christie—who is also NoRSACA's Director of Children's Services—told me that the cornerstone of the school's approach was Dr. Elizabeth Newson's conviction that, to make sense of autism, it was vital to understand the "impairment of social empathy." Sutherland House introduced musical interaction, much influenced, Christie told me, by the writings on personal inter-subjectivity of Colwyn Trevarthen and Daniel Stern.[57] Christie told me that Newson was "an early believer in partnership with parents, especially through play-based observation."[58]

Newson attracted a great deal of media attention, both through a controversial study which she claimed proved that violence on television could influence TV viewers but also through her diagnosis of a young girl, Nadia Chomyn, born in Nottingham to Ukrainian parents who began producing remarkable drawings of animals which bore a startling similarity to cave paintings.[59] Nadia stopped drawing at around the time she started to speak, prompting what Christie called the "dangerous romantic notion" in some quarters that we should not be teaching autistic children functional skills because they could lose their artistic talent.[60]

\* \* \*

Professionals were arriving from abroad, as well. Lorna Wing told me that Bernie Rimland visited her at her home in the UK "and he got moving with the autism society in the US," Wing told me. "We had some very good friends in France who had an autistic son. They were keen to get something going, and France did get moving early. But on the whole, they were crazy in France—and the parents knew they were crazy! They've always had this terrible psychoanalytical aspect to deal with. I remember meeting up with the professionals in the field of autism with psychoanalytical views and we simply couldn't talk to each other. The Scandinavians also got going quite early."[61]

Scandinavian parents did indeed start early. Autism Denmark was founded in 1962, shortly after the creation of the British society. Indeed, Bent Vandborg Sørensen, the current president of Denmark's Association of Special Schools and Treatment Centers for Children with Autism and director of the Langagerskolen in Aarhus, told me: "The former president of the Danish association, the late James Gjoel, used to say that leading members of the British and Danish society would discuss which of theirs was the first society, whenever they met. They could never agree. The two national societies had very different views on a number of issues in the early days. The Danish side, unlike the British, was pretty oriented towards what today we would call facilitated communication (it was then known as 'concealed knowledge' here in Denmark)."[62]

One of the most remarkable women in the field of autism in Denmark—indeed worldwide—was Dr. Birte Hoeg Brask, better known as Trille. Her husband, Børge Houmand, was the main organizer of the Resistance movement against the Nazis in Denmark. The couple met in the Resistance in Copenhagen and moved from Copenhagen to Aarhus after the end of the Second World War. Brask eventually became the head of child psychiatry there. In 1972, Brask published one of the first epidemiological studies of autism (see chapter 7).

"As a human being, she was a fascinating person," said Vandborg Sørensen, who worked with Brask for 10 years. "She knew a lot. Trille and Børge had a huge private network in the world of art and literature. Professionally, she was inspirational, because her insight into children with autism was so impressive She listened carefully, but she didn't always accept what you said—and she would tell you so! She was shy and would turn down invitations to give presentations. She was not interested in putting herself forward in that way. But she did have close links with wonderful fellow professionals like Lorna Wing."[63]

Elsa Hansen, another key figure in Danish autism, founded the Sophia School in Copenhagen in 1964. Starting out in a little house, this was the first school for psychotic children anywhere in the Nordic countries, although many of them would be called autistic today. Hansen, the mother of a girl with autism, had been partially inspired by Sophie Madsen, a dressmaker who ran a small home for troubled

93

children, after whom the school was named. But another major inspiration was Carl Fenichel's League School in New York (see chapter 2). Dr. Demetrious Haracopos, a Greek-American who began working with Elsa Hansen at the Sophia School in Copenhagen after arriving there in 1968, told me that Hansen had visited the League School in the 1950s and had been very impressed by what she saw. "Her visit to Brooklyn inspired her to start up the Sophia School," said Haracopos, who is now based at the Autism Center in Aarhus.[64]

Hansen used Mildred Creak's Nine Points as criteria—although Vandborg Sørensen pointed out to me that the last of these was mistranslated in Denmark at the time: "In Danish, it said: 'Islets of ability *occur* in autism' (not 'may occur,' as Creak said)."[65]

The writings of Hans Asperger were known as early as the 1960s in Denmark, since the German-language publications were widely read there. Nevertheless, psychoanalytical thinking remained powerful. "Bruno Bettelheim's influence was strongly felt in most of Denmark, apart from Aarhus. Even as late as the 1980s, the main books on autism in the public libraries were by Bettelheim," Vandborg Sørensen told me.[66]

In the 1970s and 1980s, there was a professional disagreement on the understanding of autism between the two main centers of child psychiatry, Copenhagen and Aarhus. Parts of Copenhagen remained strongly psychoanalytical. "Hansen's ideas were not psychoanalytical, but educational—she believed in a strongly structured environment, as well as in facilitated communication. Brask and her colleagues in Aaarhus were greatly inspired by Lorna Wing and Michael Rutter in the UK," said Vandborg Sørensen.[67]

Vandborg Sørensen recalled a conference organized by the Ministry of Education. "Hansen spoke first and, as she stepped down, she said very clearly to the audience: 'Now I'm going to sit at the back of the hall so I don't have to hear the nonsense spoken by Birte Brask.' It was unbelievably personal. It just shows how difficult collaboration between the leading professionals in the autism field was at that time."[68]

He also recalled a conference in the mid-1970s at which he was talking to Demetrious Haracopos. "Suddenly, someone started tugging at my jacket from behind," Vandborg Sørensen told me. "It was one of my child psychiatry colleagues saying: 'We don't talk to those people.' This again illustrates how difficult it was to collaborate at that time."[69]

94

Vandborg Sørensen emphasized that the situation was very different in Denmark today: "Relations between professionals are very friendly and cooperative now."[70]

After the English and Danish showed the way with their creation of national autistic societies, the world began to follow suit. In 1963, a year after the Danish society was set up, the Irish Society for Autistic Children was born. (It was renamed the Irish Society for Autism in 1992.) Strangely enough, like its later counterpart in Northern Ireland (see chapter 9), the initial burst of enthusiasm subsided and services remained woefully inadequate—especially for adults, who continued to be cared for in totally unsuitable psychiatric hospitals.

In April 1981, nine members of the Irish Society, including parents, staff and two children with autism, visited the La Bourguette farm complex near Aix-en-Provence, in the South of France, and also Somerset Court, Longford Court and Anglesea Lodge in the UK. A national television appeal on behalf of autistic children on the popular children's program, *Youngline*, raised a large sum permitting the society to make a successful bid for Dunfirth House and Farm, near Johnstown Bridge, in North County Kildare, about 25 miles from Dublin. The purchase was completed in July 1982. Residents are involved in farming, as well as pottery, ceramics, woodcraft, crafts and candle-making projects.

Nevertheless, in 2001, an Irish Task Force on Autism came out with a scathing report on the level of provision for autistic children and adults in Ireland. It claimed that parents, who had been marginalized to date, should have a primary role in the decision-making process as soon as their child had been diagnosed. One Irish parent was recorded as saying that she had had to shuttle between the Departments of Health and Education, with neither taking responsibility.

In Scotland, a group of parents formed the Scottish Society for Autistic Children in 1968. At the time, schools based on the spiritual thinking of the Austrian philosopher and educationalist, Rudolf Steiner, were prominent, accepting children with mixed physical and mental disabilities. Such was their worldwide appeal, indeed, that the Scottish child psychiatrist, Fred Stone, told me that, when he was in Israel in the 1950s, he learnt of several Israeli families who had decided to send their autistic child to Scotland to be educated at one of these schools.[71]

Interestingly, Mark Frankland—the award-winning British foreign correspondent who sent his autistic son, Freddie, to one of the new Rudolf Steiner Camphill villages in Scotland in the early 1960s—claimed that

**Figure 20**  Marion Critchley

the superintendent of Camphill Schools at the time, Thomas Weihs, was attracted much less to the communities' Christian spiritual outlook (Weihs was a Viennese Jew) than to its practice of what Camphill called "curative education," which was, Frankland noted, basically an anglicized version of Austria's *Heilpädagogik*, practiced by, among others, Hans Asperger.[72]

Marion Critchley's son, Ian, was diagnosed with autism by Sula Wolff in Edinburgh in 1970 when he was 5. "We were completely in the dark at the time," Critchley told me.[73] Wolff referred her to May Morrison, one of the founders of the autism society in Edinburgh, and to the Camphill Community school in Aberdeen. "It was a very good place and Ian has turned into a very nice man at 42. It wasn't autism-specific. They didn't mention the word 'autism.' But then, they didn't mention the other disabilities, either. There was a cleanliness about the way they looked at the individual. They saw Ian's potential and it came through."[74]

Another couple of the early parents, Bob and Yvonne Phillips, also sent their autistic son, Keith, to the Rudolf Steiner school in Aberdeen but, in contrast, he was not happy there. They told me that the Rudolf Steiner philosophy and that of the Scottish autism society were "poles apart," because the society was a firm believer in schooling specifically for autism.[75]

Critchley remembered that it was very difficult to raise funds in the early days of the autism society "because no one had any idea what autism was. We did get a cheque for £50 from Edinburgh University's rag week— but I think I'd already spent that much on the phone chasing around for money!"[76]

Lack of understanding was widespread. When Chris and Jane Butler-Cole's son, Tommy, showed developmental delays and behavioral problems, they were told he was ineducable. One professional even told them that, when he grew older, was still not toilet-trained, and dribbled from the mouth, "that's when you'll really know who your friends are."[77] Fortunately, they began seeing Sula Wolff who said Tommy had "autistic symptoms" and that led to their becoming involved in the autism

96

**Figure 21**  Ruth Hampton

society. "It was a great relief to meet other parents in a similar situation and to find that they could laugh!"[78]

The Scottish Society for Autism's current chairman, Ruth Hampton, was involved with the autism society right from the beginning. "The parents met in each other's homes and we eventually rented an office in Picardy Place, in Edinburgh," Hampton told me. She recalled that autism was referred to as childhood schizophrenia in Scotland at that time. "It was a battle the whole time for the parents. There were advocates such as Sula Wolff and Fred Stone to help, but even so it was so hard for the parents."[79]

Most parents were pleased to have a label for their child, said Hampton, but some were reluctant because they simply did not understand what autism was. "The professionals were also reluctant to diagnose the condition, as little was known on how to treat it. Lorna Wing and Helen Allison in London were among the pioneers who changed this thinking."[80]

The Scottish Society's first development was Struan House School, which opened in Alloa, central Scotland in March 1977, with just three children. The new school, New Struan. in existence since 1997, caters for 36 children. Balmyre Resource Centre for Adults, also in Alloa, opened in 1983, offering residential and day services.

**Figure 22**  Jim Taylor

Jim Taylor, who became head of Struan School in 1983 and is now director of education at New Struan, recalled that, in the 1980s, the authorities were unwilling to pay for specialized education for autistic children. "So it was very much up to the parents and professionals, in those early days, to push for funding for places," Taylor told me. "For the authorities, autism was almost non-existent. We understood what it was but the world tended not to acknowledge that it was a different condition."[81]

Taylor recalled taking part in a debate on BBC Radio Scotland in the early 1990 at which a prominent member of Strathclyde announced: "We have no one with autism in the Strathclyde authority." As Taylor observed: "We are not talking about ancient history—people were still refusing to recognize autism as a distinct entity here as late as the 1990s."[82]

He said one of the main challenges facing the society, now called the Scottish Society for Autism, was "getting the balance right between the professionals and the parents. In the early days, it was very much parent-led. People like Andrew Lester, as an early chairman of the society, had an outstanding ability to act as both a parent and a professional."[83]

Political devolution in the United Kingdom has led to a number of important initiatives in the autism field in Scotland (as it has in Wales and Northern Ireland, see chapter 9). Jim Taylor, for one, is upbeat. He believes that, despite criticism from some quarters, the level of education for autistic children in Scotland is encouragingly high today. "It is based on the Curriculum for Excellence, which is as good a document as I have seen, even though it was not originally written for autism!"[84]

Andrew Lester, whose daughter, Amy, is autistic, has been involved with the autism society since 1983 and is a past chairman. He recalled that some of the regional autism societies in Scotland were resentful of the Scottish Society and were keen to affiliate with the NAS in London: "It was a clash of personalities, as much as anything, as well as a fear that we would grow and take them over. I didn't see it that way. I saw ourselves as the umbrella organization which would assist the other societies in running services locally."[85]

★ ★ ★

Meanwhile, across the Atlantic, American parents of autistic children, angered by Bruno Bettelheim's accusations against them, rallied to form a united front. In fact, the first local autism association in the US was formed in Albany, New York, as early as 1963.

In 1967, Amy Lettick, a remarkable teacher and mother of an autistic boy, founded Benhaven. Originally a day school, its aim was to serve children with autism whose handicaps were preventing them from receiving an appropriate education in existing public and private schools. As community needs emerged over the next 10 years, residential services, vocational training, and adult day programs were introduced.

Another of the leading members of the US campaign was Ruth Christ Sullivan, now director of the Autism Services Center in

**Figure 23**  Ruth Sullivan

**Figure 24**  Bernard Rimland

Huntington, West Virginia. Her son, Joseph, was diagnosed in 1963 (and would later become one of the two autistic models for Raymond Babbit, the autistic savant played to Oscar-winning effect by Dustin Hoffman in the 1988 movie, *Rain man*).

"When Joe was diagnosed, there was almost nothing known about autism, even among psychiatrists," Sullivan— an extraordinarily youthful-looking and energetic 84-year-old woman—told me. "Joseph was a classic case of autism. Luckily, the young psychiatrist I went to see was an intellectual who read his journals and knew about something called autism. He didn't mention refrigerator mothers."[86]

The move to create a national autism association really began in 1964, after Bernard Rimland published his book. *Infantile autism*, and parents around the US began writing to him. "In my own letter to him. I said I'd like to form a national organization and he wrote back convening a meeting in Teaneck," Sullivan told me.

That first organizing meeting took place in Teaneck, New Jersey, in November 1965. "We met in the living-room of Herb and Roslyn Kahn and it was an amazing occasion," Sullivan recalled. "Arrangements were primitive."[87]

The first full congress of America's National Society for Autistic Children took place at the Sheridan Plaza Hotel in Washington, DC, in July 1969. It was a momentous occasion—not least because the world's eyes were glued to fuzzy black-and-white television screens to see Neil Armstrong take man's first steps on the moon. This was also the meeting where Leo Kanner formally "cleared" parents of responsibility for their child's autism, declaring: "Parents, I acquit you."

"I had been told not to ask him [Kanner] to speak, because one of his colleagues had said he might be too old," Sullivan told me. "So we asked him to come to the banquet informally. In the end, we could have spent the whole night talking to him! He was a very pleasant man. He seemed truly to like parents. In those days, professionals were not cosy with patients. As a nurse, you never even told the patient what his temperature or blood pressure was. For Kanner to come in and be so friendly with the parents was very striking."[88]

It was at the 1969 meeting that Ruth Sullivan was elected the first president of the National Society for Autistic Children. Also at this inaugural congress were Bernard Rimland, who had called them together and organized the meeting from his San Diego office; Eric Schopler, founder of the TEACCH Program in North Carolina, and Ivar Lovaas of UCLA (Schopler and Lovaas would studiously avoid each other over the years to come—see chapter 5), and Clara Claiborne Park, whose 1967 book, *The siege*, about the first eight years in the life of her autistic daughter, Jessy, had made waves throughout America.

Park and her husband, David, edited the new association's newsletter for several years. "My only initiative that I can remember was a fundraising measure called the NSACK, a paper bag kept in the kitchen into which, whenever alcohol was bought, an equal sum was deposited. This had the double merit of supporting the society and discouraging heavy consumption," David Park told me.[89]

Another of the leading participants in the inaugural Washington conference was Dr. Ed Ritvo, the UCLA researcher, who was appointed to the new organization's first advisory group. He told me that not everything ran as smoothly as was sometime made out. The society quickly found itself in conflict with its own founder, Ritvo claimed. "At one point, Rimland even sued his own organization."[90]

The tensions continued for the next two decades, Ritvo said. In the 1980s, Rimland passed a motion at the conference of what had, by then, been renamed the Autism Society of America, laying down that every child diagnosed with autism should automatically be put on a regime of vitamin B12. "I got up and said that this was a parent-led organization, that there was no evidence that vitamin B12 worked and that we didn't want to submit to this regime. To which Rimland replied: 'If you go with Ritvo, then I resign.' When the delegates hesitated, I resigned, but they had another vote, I was reinstated and Rimland was voted off. He was annoyed about that right up to the time of his death."[91]

However, many others I have spoken to praised Rimland wholeheartedly for his energetic battle on behalf of children with autism and their families. He also established the Autism Research Institute in San Diego,

California, in 1967. The Institute conducts and disseminates research into autism and the methods of diagnosing and treating the disorder.

Ruth Sullivan told me: "Bernie was passionate about what he was doing. He was interested in the science. His son is about four years older than my son. We worked well together. I was an organizer and campaigner, but he was the true founder of the Autism Society of America. Bernie was the one who really got the professionals together to speak. I was his cheerleader at the first meeting.

At that first meeting, he said: 'We should weave a cloth so strong that no one can tear us apart.' Of course, the parents can tear each other apart, and that does happen even in autism. There is conflict in all human organizations. But there is more passion behind an organization for people with autism than, I suspect, any other disability in the world."[92]

It was a very difficult time to be autistic in the United States, despite all the efforts the parents were taking to improve their lot. "Even the state institutions did not want them, because they were too hard to handle," Sullivan told me. "They had to stay at home. I wrote two books on what was going on nationwide for children with autism. We didn't want our autistic children in institutions; we wanted them in state schools. We did not want private education. It was not until the Education for All Handicapped Children Law was passed in 1975 that the first special school units opened up."[93]

Just how seriously misunderstood autism continued to be in the United States at the end of the 1960s can be seen in the 1969 release of one of the first feature films ever to deal with the disorder, *Change of habit*, starring Elvis Presley and Mary Tyler Moore. In it, Presley, playing a doctor, suggests that a girl's autism was caused by being rejected by her mother and recommends "rage reduction." This turns out to consist of hugging the screaming, struggling girl tight while Elvis repeats the words "I love you, Amanda, I love you," until she is eventually cured. This is essentially a version of an approach which came to be known as "holding therapy" and continued to be widely used on autistic children for many years around the world (see chapter 6).

The 1960s did see the birth of music therapy specifically for autistic children—far earlier than is generally realized—thanks to the pioneering work of Dr. Paul Nordoff, a graduate of the Philadelphia Conservatory of Music and the Juilliard Graduate School, and Dr. Clive Robbins, a special educator. The two men first met in 1958. They began their American work in 1961 with pilot projects at the Day Care Unit for Autistic Children at the University of Pennsylvania's Department of

Child Psychiatry and the Devereux Foundation. They worked with autistic, emotionally disturbed, developmentally disabled, and multiply handicapped children. As an experienced composer and gifted pianist, Nordoff brought new resources and techniques to meet the special needs of a wide range of disabled children. In 1962, America's National Institute of Mental Health funded the first project to study music therapy with children with autism. In the 1960s, Nordoff and Robbins traveled widely before establishing a base in London in 1974, After Nordoff died three years later, Robbins continued working with his wife, Carol, establishing centers in many countries throughout the world.

★ ★ ★

Australia was another very early starter. Autism Spectrum Australia (Aspect) was founded in New South Wales by a small group of parents in 1966 in response to the lack of existing educational and treatment facilities to meet the specific needs of children and adults with autism and their families. Initially called the Autism Association of New South Wales, its first services were educational—a class of six children in a rented hall. At the time, autism was viewed as a mental health issue in Australia and segregation was the policy most frequently advocated. Behavioralism dominated the educational agenda.

The Association expanded, and more schools were opened: Forestville School in 1971, Annandale in 1974, Newcastle in 1977, and Kingsgrove and Randwick in 1978. Services for adults were introduced in 1982. Parents were early pioneers in other Australian states, as well. Autism Victoria was established in 1967, for example.

New Zealand has an intriguing history as far as the birth of the societies is concerned. The catalyst was the arrival of a celebrity British visitor. Mildred Creak came in 1966 and found a nation where professionals knew little about autism and services were practically non-existent. Creak examined children in Wellington, Christchurch, Palmerston North, and Dunedin, confirmed the diagnosis of autism, and informed families that parents had established autism societies in the Britain, the United States, and parts of Australia.

One of the New Zealand parents, Marion Bruce, met her counterparts in Australia the following year and in 1969, nine families met in Christchurch and agreed to become a sub-committee of IHC (Intellectually Handicapped Children)—a New Zealand non-governmental organization providing support and care for people with intellectual disabilities. The society, now known as Autism New Zealand, has more than 4,000 members—parents and carers, schools, and other professionals—and 15 branches around the country.

★ ★ ★

In continental Europe, the French remained backward in their thinking—parents continue to be held responsible for their child's autism by many professionals and even today, around 75% of autistic children are still cared for in psychiatric hospitals. This explains why so many parents take their children across the border into Belgium.

The first partially autism-related association to be established in France, in the early 1960s, was ASITP (Association au service des inadaptés ayant des troubles de la personnalité, the Association for the Maladjusted with Personality Disorders). In 1963, ASITP established the first day hospital for children, the Santos Dumont Hospital in Paris, the purpose of which was to prevent the separation of children from their families.

One of France's most enlightened autism specialists, Professor Gilbert Lelord, began working in the field in Tours in the 1950s at a time when the psychoanalytical approach was at its strongest. "For some people—thankfully not all—even suggesting that there could be organic causes of autism was a sacrilege. They considered autism to be a psychological and sociological disorder, and should not be tackled with medical language," Lelord—a charming octogenarian with impeccable manners—told me. "They couldn't accept any attempt to examine the autistic child physically."[94]

**Figure 25**   Gilbert Lelord

Lelord appears to have shown intense scientific curiosity from a very early age. As a young child, he asked his parents why no one had invented mint-flavoured cod-liver oil. A true pioneer in the autism field, he was one of the first scientists anywhere in the world to carry out serious EEG tests on autistic children, much to the bewilderment and, at times, ferocious opposition, from the majority of his colleagues at the time. He told me he had been convinced from the beginning that the disorder was organic. As a pupil of the aphasia expert, Alain Joinine, "I was struck by how similar autistic children were to aphasic children."[95]

In 1969, Lelord was joined in Tours by the neurologist, Catherine Barthélemy, who worked directly with the child psychiatrist, Dominique Sauvage. "They made a splendid team," Lelord told me. Lelord and Barthélemy developed a technique called *thérapie d'échange* (exchange therapy) designed to encourage communication through play.

In 1983, parents and professionals urged ASITP members to set up ARAPI (Association pour la recherche sur l'autisme et la prévention des inadaptations, the Association for Research into Autism and the Prevention of Maladjustments). It was, significantly, founded in Tours—center of biological research into autism—rather than in Paris, still highly influenced by psychoanalytical thought. ARAPI differs from ASITP insofar as it brings together parents and professionals and acts on the production of scientific knowledge.

In 1985, two associations—AIDERA (Association Ile-de-France pour le développement de l'éducation et la recherche sur l'autisme) and Pro Aid Autisme—decided to set up institutions oriented towards the TEACCH program. ASITP did not follow suit, however. In 1989, it split into two organizations along ideological lines: Sésame Autisme and Autisme France. The 40 families who established Autisme France condemned the French psychiatrists' definition of autism as a psychosis caused by parents, openly declared that it was a biological disorder, and promoted behavioral interventions. In 1991, Autisme France obtained the financial support of one of France's largest companies, Fondation France Télécom, transforming Autisme France into one of the country's most active parents' associations in any field.[96]

Under pressure from the French parents' associations, three reports were published in 1994 and 1995 at the request of Simone Weil, then Minister for Social Affairs and Health. They led to the Weil Decree (No. 9512) of April 27, 1995, which proposed a five-year plan of action to improve the care of autistic individuals. The reports proposed changes in keeping with the demands of parents' associations and the American model, including the development of early diagnosis, the evaluation of a more rigorous treatment, and the modification of intervention programs by adopting a more educational and behavioral approach involving the parents' collaboration. Again as a result of strong pressure from the parents' associations, autism was officially recognized as a handicap in France by the so-called Chossy Act of December 11, 1996, named after the parliamentarian who introduced it, Jean-François Chossy.

Nevertheless, on November 4, 2003, the Council of Europe's Committee of Social Rights found that France had failed to fulfil its educational obligations to individuals with autism under the European Social Charter. This ruling upheld a complaint that Autism-Europe lodged against France denouncing the non-provision of education to people with autism due to the lack of integration in mainstream education, on the one hand, and the dramatic shortage of specialized educational institutions, on the other hand. Apart from the shortage of places for autistic individuals, the Council of Europe also pointed out that France used a more restrictive definition of autism than that adopted by the World Health Organization.

There are many active parents fighting their corner in France, like Paul and Chantal Tréhin, parents of the talented autistic savant artist, Gilles. Paul has played a leading role in both Autism-Europe and the World Autism Organization, while Chantal has been prominent in opposing the psychoanalytical view in France and encouraging parents' societies there.

One target of the French parents' outrage is the continued use of an approach known as *le packing*, in which autistic children are wrapped for between 30 minutes and an hour in wet sheets which have been kept cool in a refrigerator. The technique—for autism, at least—was pioneered by Pierre Delion, a psychiatrist and psychoanalyst at Lille Regional University Hospital, in northern France, who suggests that the child in the pack undergoes a regression, replaying in a secure environment the relationship between a mother and her new-born child, and that, when used as a therapy for autistic children who self-harm, the treatment allows the child to rid itself progressively of its pathological defense mechanisms.[97]

Remarkably, the French government has sponsored research into this method. Theo Peeters in Belgium also told me that a variant is employed on the French Caribbean island of Martinique, where children with autism are buried up to their necks in sand.[98]

One French mother was prepared to go to the ultimate length in 2000 to force the authorities to provide suitable facilities for her autistic son. Annie Beaufils, who lives in the small village of Barjas, went on hunger strike for more than 30 days in an attempt to convince the powers-that-be that her 15-year-old son, Geoffrey, deserved appropriate treatment. Annie was told categorically by doctors that her son's autism was caused by the fact that—consciously or unconsciously—she had rejected him. Horrified, she looked elsewhere but in vain. In the end, an agreement was reached to offer Geoffrey treatment at an IME (medical educational establishment)—a non-hospital environment. Annie Beaufils opened her mouth and—for the first time in 33 days—nibbled at a biscuit.

Max Artuso, president of Autisme France, said that the case of Geoffrey Beaufils was far from an isolated one. In October 1994, Autisme France drafted a White Book calling on institutions to eliminate "ineffective or harmful" methods in treating autistic children in their care—especially psychoanalytical approaches. Artuso said the French educational system was to blame for France lagging so far behind. If psychiatry still rules the roost, specialized education remains a marginal discipline, he feels, and individuals with autism remain at the mercy of a system which is, if not obsolete, then definitely inadequate.

The historical roots of the psychoanalytical approach in France, as we have seen (p. 34), stem from a fear that any other approach may smack of Nazism. Gilbert Lelord accepts this hypothesis. "And genetics still has this echo of the 'master race'," he told me. "The psychoanalysts who insisted that it was 'all in the mind' bore powerful weapons."[99]

Dr. Bernadette Rogé, a psychologist based at the University of Toulouse, is another internationally respected authority on autism, which she defines as a developmental pathology. She is convinced that autism can take on very different clinical forms depending on the intensity of the symptoms (cognitive and linguistic impairment), the varying etiology, and the presence of a chromosomal abnormality. In 2006, the French Health Ministry asked Rogé to introduce the M-Chat screening measure (see chapter 7) for children from the age of 2.

★ ★ ★

The history of the Spanish parents' associations is a fascinating one. The main organization, APNA (Asociación de padres de niños autistas—Association of Parents of Autistic Children) was founded in the home of Isabel Bayonas in the Calle Añastro in north-eastern Madrid in 1976, and was based there for the first three years of its existence.

106

**Figure 26**  Isabel Bayonas

Bayonas, herself, is an extraordinary woman. She started off as one of Spain's only women bullfighters. In fact, there have only been ten female *rejoneadoras* (the person who fights the bull on horseback) in Spain's history. She told me—sitting in the very room where APNA was born—that her bullfighting career had stood her in good stead, both in dealing with her own autistic son, David, and with her constant battles with the authorities in Spain and around the world as president of the World Autism Organization.

Bayonas's initial struggles were against the dictatorship of General Francisco Franco but also against the vast ignorance—and misconceptions—about autism: Bruno Bettelheim's 1967 parent-blaming book, *The empty fortress*, was the first book on autism translated into Spanish and its influence could be felt long afterwards. There were other, more comical misunderstandings. Bayonas showed me a magazine profile of her which included a photo of a row of cars. "Clearly, they saw the word 'autism' and thought it had something to do with automobiles!" she told me.[100]

Bayonas's son, David, now 40, was diagnosed with autism at the age of 9 by one of Spain's pioneering and most highly respected autism specialists, Dr. Angel Díez-Cuervo. At the time, Bayonas says, she was so desperate to stop her son harming himself and to start him speaking, that "if a doctor told me take him to the Cibeles Fountain [in the center of Madrid] at midnight and dump him in the water to cure him, I would have done just that."[101]

Bayonas was fortunate in that her husband was a pilot working for Spain's national airline, Iberia, which allowed them to travel to both Britain and the United States to see what services were available for autistic children. At the time she founded APNA, many of the parents were told "that they did not understand or love their children, and that was why they were autistic. David himself was originally diagnosed as both 'mad' and 'deaf.' One doctor told me that David was fine and that *I* was the crazy one."[102]

She always says that APNA has been "protected by the Angels." She is referring, first, to Angel Díez-Cuervo, who diagnosed her son;

secondly to her husband's pilot colleagues who donated money to pay for Spanish professionals to train in London, and thirdly to the great Dr. Angel Rivière.

"He [Rivière] didn't know anything about autism at first," Bayonas told me. "I took him on, as a young psychologist, to be APNA's technical adviser, although he was initially reluctant He was a genius—he would have succeeded at whatever he put his hand to."[103]

**Figure 27** Angel Rivière

**Figure 28** Mercedes Belinchón

Without doubt, Rivière is one of the most outstandingly humane and cultured figures in the history of autism worldwide. A talented poet and violinist, Rivière died tragically young at 50 in 2000, but not before he had written a number of illuminating books on autism and encouraged parents with his compassionate and flexible approach to their child's disorder.

A close colleague of his, Dr. Mercedes Belinchón, one of Spain's leading autism experts, told me that Rivière was a theoretical psychologist "who had very original ideas on typical and atypical human development. He was an excellent cognitive researcher who had a profound influence on many generations of investigators and other professionals. It was Angel who introduced the notion into Spain, in 1978, that autism was a developmental disorder."[104]

Belinchón pointed out that Rivière also emphasized the importance of "mentalizing" deficits in understanding autism—in fact, he conducted the first theory of mind study in Spain in 1986. He also stressed that it was essential for professionals to have an extensive knowledge of normal development.[105]

"Intellectually, Angel was supreme," said Belinchón, with whom she wrote a handbook on psycholinguistics. "But he also had an astonishing ability to empathize with everyone. He could communicate, but also create doubts and raise new questions. He was a very seductive man on all levels. He had a vast intellectual curiosity and he wrote marvellously."[106]

She added that Rivière had an enormous personal impact on the families he helped—and even on strangers. A student of Rivière's, Dr. Carmen Nieto, recalled people who had never met him weeping openly on the news of his death.[107]

**Figure 29** Angel Díez-Cuervo

The other Angel, Dr. Díez-Cuervo, has been working in the field since 1961. A delightfully urbane and witty man, he told me that, at the time he began, people still spoke about child psychosis and blamed the mother: "Bruno Bettelheim did more damage than anyone else here in Spain. But when I started, I observed that many of the parents were very warm and friendly. In any case, how could they have damaged one child and not the others?"[108]

He nevertheless recalled going to a conference on child psychiatry in the 1960s "and they were referring to mothers who were 'not good enough.' They carried out a lot of family studies and came to the wrong conclusion, because the mothers often tended to be depressed. That was normal, because she'd spent five or six years with a child who gave her no gratification, who rejected her. It was a *consequence* of the child's coldness, not the cause. It was a tremendous error."[109]

Díez-Cuervo told me that, in Spain in the early 1960s, even though Leo Kanner's paper had appeared 20 years earlier, no one used the term "autism." At that time, he said, "child psychiatry in Spain was limited to mental retardation and Down's syndrome. When they did happen to mention autism, it was considered to be one feature of psychosis. They called autism a symptom of schizophrenia."[110]

He added that he was helped a great deal by the Dutch psychiatrist, Arn van Krevelen. "He was an extroverted, dynamic and very happy man, warm and cultured—and he spoke good Spanish. I met him in Madrid in around 1964 and he taught me about autism."[111]

Díez-Cuervo was involved in the setting up the Spain's first autism-specific center, the Taure Center, in Madrid in 1973. Six years later,

APNA established the Leo Kanner Center in the Spanish capital and held its first International Autism Symposium there in May 1978. This was a glittering occasion attended by more than 1,800 delegates. In his speech to the conference, Ivar Lovaas emphasized the neurological nature of autism, at which some of the more psychodynamically oriented speakers expressed their disagreement, leading to tumult in the audience. The dispute was calmly defused by the chairman of the panel, Angel Rivière, who declared: "In science, not only is controversy not an unpleasant thing—it is necessary." Meanwhile, Bernard Rimland outlined his work on what he claimed were the beneficial effects of vitamins in treating autistic children.

Today, APNA offers a diagnostic service at its Madrid headquarters as well as a roving care service providing treatment for children and adults with autism in their own homes. It runs training courses for teachers, psychologists, pediatricians, and social workers and holds regular conferences.

Another of Spain's major autism organizations is Gautena, founded by Dr. Joaquín Fuentes in San Sebastián, in the Basque country, northwestern Spain, in 1978. Around 400 families in the region use its services and it also has an important research wing.

Speaking in San Sebastián in 2008, Fuentes—who plays a leading part in Autism-Europe and is also coordinator of the Autistic Spectrum Disorders Group at the Carlos III Health Institute in Madrid—told the 14th national conference of AETAPI (the Spanish Association of Autism Professionals—itself celebrating its 25th anniversary that year) that the past decade had produced "fantastic advances" in the elimination of social barriers for autistic children. There had been a fundamental shift, he said, from treating these children as ill to considering them as citizens with a right to the same quality of life as anyone else. The major challenge was posed in adulthood, Fuentes added, because many adults went undiagnosed or were labeled with other disabilities.[112]

Curiously, Cataluña—one of Spain's richest and most sophisticated regions—remains the most backward in terms of understanding autism. Both Angel Díez-Cuervo and Mercedes Belinchón agreed that the reason for this was its geographical proximity to France. Nevertheless, I visited an admirable adult autism center, Mas Casadevall, founded in 1987 about 100 miles from Barcelona, heading towards the French border, and just a couple of miles from Banyoles. The setting is stunning. In the distance rise the Pyrenees, there are rolling hills nearby, and not far away is Figueras, birthplace of the surrealist painter, Salvador Dalí. Wild boar have been seen coming right down next to the main building—they've learnt that this is one place they are unlikely to be shot! The center was set up on the initiative of a group of parents horrified at how little care as available in Cataluña—or any other area of Spain for that matter—for adults with autism. The parents included Manuel Ventura, whose 30-year-old son lives at the center and is both blind and autistic.

I was shown round the impressive workshops, where the residents make paper, beautiful ceramics, and candles. They are not just for show, either: the autistic residents take part in the Banyoles market each week, selling their products. There's also a shop at the center itself and professional artists turn up to buy the paper made here.

The director of Mas Casadevall when I visited, in 2001, was Francesc Pelach i Busom. By his own admission, he was educated in the psychoanalytical tradition. The center's glossy magazine, *L'aixada*, ran an article a few years ago by Pelach in which he felt the need to write: "In the light of the research and and experience which has now been accumulated, it is no longer possible to maintain the view that the mother is guilty of causing her child's autism." Even so, I couldn't help noticing that the full title of the foundation which runs the center is the Foundation of Parents of Psychotics and Autistics.

Spain has seen major advances over the past three decades. Bayonas insists that, today, the country is one of the leaders in Europe in terms of treating children with autism. She also highlights the importance of the Ciudad del Autismo (City of Autism), a vast complex currently being built in Madrid with a vast array of facilities aimed at individuals from all over Spain. She says her only bullfights today are with politicians, adding that the most serious problem in Spain remains the fate of adults with autism and the lack of funding for research.[113]

Mercedes Belinchón agreed that Spanish society was much more sensitized to intellectual disability and developmental problems today. "The stigma no longer exists. But there are still many erroneous ideas," she told me. "For example, that autism is a disease; that autistic children do not show emotions; that a child will always be isolated—the cliché of the child locked within himself."[114]

★ ★ ★

In Italy, there is a north–south divide on autism. In the north, the psychoanalytical ideas remain strong, due to the French influence. In the south, organicist, biological thinking predominates. The head of the main Italian autism organization, Donata Vivanti, mother of twins with autism, told me, during the congress of Autism-Europe, of which she is president, that, in southern Italy, many people were influenced by American thinking due to the major US naval base in Naples. "The south has more problems, in general not in autism."[115]

**Figure 30**   Donata Vivanti

"Recently, the Italian Psychiatrists' Association issued guidelines declaring officially that autism is a neurobiological syndrome. There are many professionals, of course, who claim that the parents are not responsible—but the questions they ask the parents show that they are not entirely convinced," Vivanti said.[116]

Vivanti herself was told that she was to blame for her twins' autism when they were diagnosed in 1990. "I didn't believe it. But the big problem came from my family—my husband's parents, my husband himself. That was very difficult to deal with. I could always change my doctor—but not my family!"[117]

Fortunately, the community spirit is very strong in Italy. Indeed, Vivanti's son, Giacomo, who works in the same field at the MIND Institute in Sacramento, California, has gone so far as to say: "If you're autistic and poor in the US, you're on your own. But the good thing

**Figure 31**   Enrico Micheli

about Italy is that you have a community and friends who help." His mother agrees. "There is a tolerance of disability in Italy because these children are integrated early in schools. That does not mean that the integration is working but at least there is awareness. I had no problem from the general population with my children."[118]

Italy's first autism association, ANGSA—the National Association of Parents of Autistic Children—was founded in the late 1980s. "I was there from the beginning," Vivanti told me. "It was an organization led by parents for parents."[119]

One of the most remarkable Italian autism pioneers was Enrico Micheli, who was among the first to introduce the TEACCH method into Italy. His colleagues were shocked to hear the news that he had died at the age of 58 in 2008 while mountaineering in the Dolomites. As well as writing many books and articles, Micheli and his wife, Cesarina Xais, ran an autism center in Belluno. He always sought to emulate the anti-authoritarian, democratic approach of the TEACCH founder, Eric Schopler, and especially the emphasis on a collaboration between parents and professionals.

What is clear today is that many Italian parents have rebelled so violently against being told they are to blame that they have turned to some of the miracle cures being peddled by charlatans, or at least methods which have not been scientifically proven. "This is a classic reaction to the psychoanalytical culture," Vivanti told me. "Parents say: 'If my son has a neurobiological disorder, then it must be biology which provides the answers.' It's not so simple, of course. But there is a great deal of suspicion in Italy towards psycho-educational care. Parents are looking for medical treatment."[120]

In May 2007, the Italian organization, Genitori contra l'autismo (Parents Against Autism), called for the DAN Protocol—a biomedical approach to autism devised by the Defeat Autism Now movement in the United States—to be debated in Italy, rather than rejected by the scientific community.

★ ★ ★

Switzerland is also split across geographical and cultural lines. The French-speaking part is still very strongly influenced by the psychoanalytical approach to autism. Theo Peeters in Belgium told me a Swiss parent had asked him in all seriousness in the 1980s whether his son's autism could have been due to the fact that his grandfather had slept with a nun, as his psychiatrist had suggested.

Swiss-French parents are demanding that the psychoanalytical methods end once and for all and that specialized schools are created in Geneva. Disillusioned by the blinkered approach of so many professionals, one mother, Marie-Jeanne Accietto, decided to set up a parents' group, with about 25 other families, which is now demanding that autism be recognized as an entirely separate handicap and that autistic children be given specialized care. The parents point to the absence of any real choice in therapeutic and educational approaches in francophone Switzerland. "Psychoanalysis is the only approach used," said Accietto.

113

"It's a true *diktat*. The psychologist at the day center my son is at told me: 'Just have good cry and everything will be all right.' We get the impression of not being listened to. They criticize us for being too anxious. They give us a picture of ourselves which makes us feel that we are to blame."[121]

★ ★ ★

When Theo Peeters, one of the world's leading autism authorities, returned to Belgium after his stays in London and then studying at the TEACCH headquarters in North Carolina, he and the parents decided that the top priority was to set up a strong parents' society in Flanders. "It was important that it was made up with parents inspired by the TEACCH approach," Peeters told me, "because if parents are too divided, this gives politicians too easy an opportunity to say: 'Solve your problems first and then come back to us for help.' "[122]

**Figure 32**  Hilde De Clercq and Theo Peeters

He recalled that when he began working on autism in Belgium "the first professionals were 'idealists' wanting to show the government that it was possible to develop autism-specific education and that people with autism were 'educable.' They gave everything they had, waiting for extra funding from the government which did not really arrive. Today, the best classrooms and services have long waiting-lists—and the ones with the 'easiest' behavior are being selected. It often happens that the 'difficult' ones are once again left at home with their parents."[123]

Belgium is divided in two, not only politically but in terms of approaches to autism. As late as the 1990s, professionals in the French-speaking part of Belgium were still blaming the parents. In Flanders, understanding was more advanced. Theo Peeters' close colleague, Hilde De Clercq—mother of four children, including a son with autism, and now director of the Opleidingszentrum voor Autisme (Training Center for Autism) in Antwerp—told me that there were few links between autism organizations in the two parts of Belgium. When De Clercq's son, Thomas, was diagnosed in 1990, few professionals knew much about autism, although they did not blame the parents.

"There is certainly some rivalry between professionals and parents here in Flanders," said De Clercq, who is also the author of a number of beautifully written and compassionate books on autism. "I think professionals are sometimes afraid of well-informed parents, and parents are not too impressed by professionals who claim to know everything about autism. But the fact was that we got together and discussed the issues, which meant that the correct information was disseminated."[124]

Irène Knodt-Lenfant, a psychologist specialising in autism, is one of the best-known parents of an autistic child with autism in the French-speaking part of Belgium—thanks to her campaigning work on behalf of adults with autism and her book, *Claudin, classé X chez les dinormos*,[125] about her son, whom she adopted in Haiti.

She decided to set up an institution for autistic adults, Le Mistral, in July 1994 after working for several years at a day-care center near Liège. "They had serious behavioral problems, breaking everything, not sleeping at all," Knodt-Lenfant told me. "The government helped out, providing money for the salaries. The premises were paid for by a private association. I didn't meet any opposition from the politicians, at all."[126]

**Figure 33** Irène Knodt-Lenfant

Knodt-Lenfant already had four children—three of her own and one adopted—when she decided to adopt a

115

fifth. "We came across a child in an orphanage in Haiti. He was living in terrible conditions. He was lying on a mattress of sorts. He didn't seem to react to anything. He didn't move. He could have been anywhere between 6 months and 3 years old. He couldn't speak and we were told he couldn't hear, either. My first reaction was: 'We can't take a child like that.' Then I took him in my arms and we both thought we saw him smile at us. I think that's what convinced me to take him. Someone suggested that he could be autistic, but we rejected this idea at the time."

Knodt-Lenfant and her husband returned to Belgium with Claudin in 1990. It turned out that the boy was 3 years old. He was finally diagnosed with autism at the age of 8. But at the center he was attending at the time in Belgium, the professionals told Knodt-Lenfant: "It's you who have invented the diagnosis to justify your theories."[127] This charge is reminiscent of the false accusations of Munchausen's syndrome by proxy (in which parents or carers apparently invent or induce symptoms of a condition in their child) but in this case, it was even more startling, given Knodt-Lenfant's longstanding resistance to imposing a label on her son.

Knodt-Lenfant said that the days when they blamed the parents in any part of Belgium—there is a third, very small German-speaking region—were long gone. But services were saturated. "There was no political desire to create more residential places for people with autism. As a consequence, private institutions started to be created, welcoming French nationals, by preference, because these were 'more profitable.' But they are living far from their families and feel quite lonely. And as the institutions are full, the Belgians stay at home."[128]

Perhaps the last word on the immense role played by parents should go to Dr. Ami Klin, the Yale autism authority, who told me: "I have worked in many different countries: Brazil, France, Israel, Britain. In many of these countries, it was the mothers who really got the ball rolling—I would love to include the fathers, as well! It was the mothers who said: 'There is nothing for my child with autism, so I'm going to create it.' It is what Amy Lettick did in North Haven, for example. In Brazil, I found out that one of the largest schools and agencies serving individuals with autism aged 2 to 40 is in the most impoverished part of the country in the northeastern city of Fortaleza, where a mother—a pediatrician with autistic children—started an absolutely wonderful program. The clinicians and the scientists come afterwards. The catalyst has always been in the hands of mothers."[129]

# 5

# The Two Teaching Pioneers

The history of autism education is marked by some remarkable figures—notably Carl Fenichel and Jeanne Simons, as we saw in chapter 2. Undoubtedly, however, the two names which stand out above all others are Dr. Eric Schopler and Dr. Ivar Lovaas. The two men couldn't stand one another.

**Figure 34**  Eric Schopler

Schopler, who founded the TEACCH (Treatment and Education of Autistic and Related Communication Handicapped Children) program in North Carolina in 1972, was born in the small southern German town of Furth in 1927. He was the second of three children of a Jewish couple, Ernst Schopler, a prominent attorney, and his wife, Erna Oppenheimer.

Under the Nazis, the 11-year-old Eric was not allowed to attend the public swimming-pool and was at one point removed from a public school and transferred to a Catholic school. Some of his Jewish teachers, friends, and acquaintances disappeared suddenly or were imprisoned and even killed.

The Schopler family emigrated to the United States in 1938. On the same boat from Germany was a very young Henry Kissinger. As Schopler recalled in an interview with his TEACCH colleague, Dr. Brenda Denzler, in 2001: "We were at the consulate in Stuttgart—my father, my mother and the three children (my sister, my brother and myself). Kissinger's father taught at the same school where I was and they were sitting across the way from us, in the waiting-room. While we were waiting, my brother noticed a fruit stand, so he conned my mother into giving him a dime to go and get a banana. A little while later, my father noticed that he wasn't anywhere to be seen and he got terribly upset and nervous. 'If we get called in and he's not with us, we can't get our visas and we can't leave at all, so, this is just terrible!' And my mother's sly response was: 'Don't you worry. If he doesn't come in time, we'll take little Henry over there and they'll never know the difference!' But, I don't think he ever had to take little Henry. Unless they did switch them after all!"[1]

Schopler claimed that the anti-Semitic persecution he had witnessed in Germany gave him a sense of solidarity with the handicapped and the marginalized: "I got a sense of being an underdog and I got interested in the underdogs and the handicapped."

Schopler finished high school in Rochester, New York and joined the US Navy. His first wife, Betsy, told me that he had worked as a taxi-driver and was trying to open a restaurant when she met him in Chicago: "His parents wouldn't loan him the money he needed and he was very disappointed."[2]

In fact, it seems Schopler also harboured ambitions of becoming a novelist. His daughter, Susie—one of his three children with Betsy—told

**Figure 35** Betsy Schopler with her and Eric's three children, Susie, Tom, and Bobby

me that his decision to join the Navy was largely inspired by the hope that the experience would provide him with writing material. That ambition was never fulfilled, although Susie told me that he was always an excellent story-teller: "Just before we went to sleep, as children, he would ask us each to think of a noun, and he would make up stories based on those nouns."[3]

In the early 1960s, Schopler attended the University of Chicago, where he ultimately earned a graduate degree in social service administration and his PhD in clinical child psychology in 1964. This was a key stage in his career. It was at the University of Chicago that he worked with Bruno Bettelheim at the Orthogenic School (which was attached to the university's psychology department) and quickly became appalled by Bettelheim's parent-blaming ideas and practices.

It was while he was in graduate school that Schopler became interested in exploring the nature of autism (or "childhood schizophrenia," as it was then called) and the twin questions of how best to treat it and what role parents should play in that process. He became convinced that the prevailing view of autism as a psychological disorder was wrong, that parents had been scapegoated as the cause of their children's condition, and that the best remedy for the prevailing theoretical misinterpretation would come through empirical research.

As a result of his horror at the Bettelheim approach, Schopler saw an urgent need to conduct biological studies of autism. He designed his dissertation as an empirical study of autistic children's receptor preferences. This research, which showed that children with autism tend to rely more on the near-receptor systems of touch and smell than on the distance-receptors of sight and sound, was one of the first studies to establish the neurological basis of the disorder.

During this period, he met many of the leading researchers in the field. "I got to like Mike Rutter. I thought he was exceptionally bright," Schopler said in an 1998 interview with his successor as head of TEACCH, Gary Mesibov. "That was before I learned that, for a British accent you get an extra 20 points!"[4]

Contrary to popular belief, Schopler did not come to Chapel Hill in the 1960s specifically to start up the TEACCH program. One of his closest colleagues at the time was, Dr. Robert Reichler. Today, he looks rather like Robert de Niro. He told me that what actually happened was the following: at the time Reichler moved to Chapel Hill in the mid-1960s, James Anthony was working there. "He was considered one of the wise men by the psychoanalysts. As he talked about autism, he threw up the idea that autistic children had a shattered ego and that, if you put them together in the same room, they might be able to share their ego! It was a bizarre notion and I observed how it worked in practice: every now and then, a therapist would open the door of the room and take a child off into another, invisible room. There was some improvement in a number of children and of course, the psychoanalysts trumpeted their success. But they needed a psychologist to do the research. That was when they recruited Eric Schopler from Chicago to compile the date.

"As it happened, the funding for their program ran out and the program disappeared. But the psychologists, including Eric, stuck around and gained a reputation among parents as some of the few people they could go to to get treatment for their autistic children. Parents started coming to Eric at Chapel Hill. At the time, he was exploring his sensory theories, developed back in Chicago. During one of these meetings with parents, a mother suddenly asked whether she could watch through the one-way mirror. No parent had ever much such a request before. We said: 'Why not?' "[5]

**Figure 36**   Robert Reichler

Thus was founded the Child Research Project, which led to the 1972 establishment of the state-funded TEACCH and its fundamental emphasis on involving parents in the teaching process. The concept of helping parents to interact more effectively with their "psychotic" child ran counter to prevailing theory in the field. Clinical observations of parents far more frequently ascribed to them emotional and intellectual deviations. The primary interpretations of studies in the late 1950s and early to mid-1960s placed the emphasis on parental thought disorder as generating similar impairment in the child. These views were maintained despite reports such as that of Pitfield and Oppenheim in 1964, who found that some of the stereotyped characteristics were not present in their sample of 100 mothers of psychotic children.[6] Schopler himself extended these studies with his research together with Julie Loftin, but most clinicians in the United States persisted in their inappropriate distrust of parents.[7]

120

There was also still a great deal of stigma attached to handicapped children, as highlighted by the recent revelation that the American playwright, Arthur Miller, decided to place his Down's syndrome son in an institution back in 1966.[8]

Reichler recalled the first child they worked with at Chapel Hill: "It was a remarkable case. We saw him at 3 and, by the time he entered first grade, he was speaking and interacting. His mother was a very strong contributor to this process."[9]

Reichler confirmed that TEACCH was quite largely an attempt to rebuff Bruno Bettelheim's thinking. Where Bettelheim recommended "parentectomy"—cutting the child off from his or her parents—Schopler and Reichler wanted to ensure that the parents, on the contrary, were trained to participate as fully as possible in the education process.

In 1964, as we have seen, Bernard Rimland—who was shortly to be one of the founders of the Autism Society of America—published his seminal book, *Infantile autism*, in which he sought, largely successfully, to show that autism had a biological origin. In the ensuing years, a number of methodologically sound studies began to emerge, by Cantwell, Cox, Freeman and Ritvo, and others,[10] demonstrating that parents of autistic children did not differ from parents of normal children or parents of children from other clinical populations (such as developmental aphasia or mental retardation) on measures of personality and social interaction. What was being seen was the effect an autistic child had on the parents, not the other way around. But Bettelheim rejected Rimland's book and the research findings.

**Figure 37** Lee Marcus

"I was once on a panel with Bettelheim," Reichler recalled, "and he started to criticise the parents for their supposed inability to interact with their children. I turned to him, very upset, and said: 'How can you attack parents who are with their autistic children 24 hours a day?' He dismissed my complaint out of hand."[11]

Dr. Lee Marcus, a psychologist who played a leading role in devising the revised version of the Psychoeducational Profile (PEP) with Eric Schopler and

Robert Reichler, said that most professionals in the 1960s "not only had little understanding of autism but did not really care. Remember that the numbers were very low at that time. As a pediatrician, you could go through your entire career and never see a child with autism. They were still using Kanner's restricted definition. When the TEACCH program got going, they started to expand the definition a bit—but when the research project started, there were some children who couldn't get in but did later when the criteria broadened."[12]

Autism, Marcus told me, was still considered an exotic disorder at the time in the United States. "It continued to be seen largely as a psychological and emotionally based disorder. Schopler, from the very beginning, said he did not understand what was going on but it was definitely organic. His views were not generally accepted however—even though Bernie Rimland's book had come out in 1964 and other work was going on at UCLA. Their views took a long time to filter through to practitioners."[13]

The quest for staff to man the TEACCH program began. "We started looking around for therapists," said Reichler, "and at first we thought that it would be best to hire people already in the field of autism. Wrong! They come with preconceptions. You want bright, flexible people. In the end, we were very fortunate in picking people who were very engaged and energetic."[14] Eric's second wife-to-be, Margaret (Miggie), then married to Cornelius Lansing, also got involved at that point.

To start the TEACCH program, Schopler and Reichler and their colleagues also needed a considerable amount of funding from the state of North Carolina. They found an ingenious way of encouraging state legislators to recommend the program. "We set up a breakfast and we had an autistic child sitting next to each legislator so they could see exactly what they were dealing with," Reichler told me. "I gave a talk informing them of what it would cost to keep a child in an institution compared to what it would cost to keep them at home. At the end, each and every legislator stood up and said he or she would do anything possible to help. It was brilliant. . . . The senators themselves were still not entirely sure what autism was, but each one was determined not to be outdone by a senator from another region of North Carolina."[15]

The parents involved in the early days of TEACCH have enormously fond and appreciative memories of Eric Schopler. "When I first met him, he had mud on his boots," one of the first mothers on the TEACCH program, Mary Lou (Bobo) Warren, told me. "I was used to seeing doctors in white coats looking very smart and stiff. I immediately said to myself, with tears in my eyes: 'This is the right place for me. I've finally found someone who wants to help us.' He never made me feel I was responsible for what had happened to my child, as others did, and in around six months, George was talking."[16]

**Figure 38**   Bobo Warren, Brenda Denzler, and Betty Camp

When her son was very young, Warren thought he was extremely bright: he was very inquisitive about lights or the washing-machine. "He had beautiful curls and looked like a Rubens angel! But then he stopped looking at us. He would escape from the yard day and night. He often stayed awake until four in the morning and he didn't seem to hear the loud planes flying overhead—but he could hear the candy wrapper rustling from anywhere in the house."[18] A psychiatrist told her that George had a very severe emotional disturbance and advised her to put him into an institution and forget him.

She did not heed this advice and the family's situation was transformed on meeting Schopler and joining the TEACCH program: "Eric was a was a real maverick," Warren told me, "the equivalent of one of the 'flower children,' challenging what was going on in child psychiatry, challenging the view that the parents were the problem. For the first time, I got the sense that George liked me. Before, he would pull away when I tried to kiss him, or wipe away the patch where I had kissed him. It is so hard to love someone who will not receive your embraces. But one day, when he was 11, I kissed him and he reached round and kissed me on the cheek. It was such a reward after all those years of struggle."[18]

Warren has an even more poignant recollection of that historic fundraising breakfast in Raleigh: "The lieutenant-governor arrived late and had to sit at the table with the autistic children. George proceeded to feed him bread! Later, the governor said he would not stop until he had found a way to help these children."[19]

Another of the TEACCH pioneer mothers from the 1970s, Betty Camp, told me: "You really felt you belonged here at Chapel Hill. I remember Eric telling us that he really wanted both parents to be involved. He was always asking us what we had observed in our children. There was the conviction that the children could do things and that we needed to persuade other people to believe this, too. Once you are dealing with professionals who are not looking down on you, and treat you as another professional, that really empowers you. I've never met anyone with as much respect for parents as Eric had."[20]

Reichler said his many years working with Eric Schopler were wonderful ones. Even before setting up TEACCH, they had been approached with an offer to purchase a tract of land to farm cattle on. They got as far as talks with a bank, who offered them a loan of a million dollars. When they heard that figure, they realized they were out of their depth, especially given Schopler's total impracticality with money. "So, since we couldn't rear cows, we decided to rear children, instead," Reichler told me.[21]

He said he and Schopler were very different characters. "We came from different backgrounds, from different science [Reichler was a psychiatrist and Schopler a psychologist], but it was electrifying. We really liked each other and stimulated one another. We would sometimes have screaming arguments—but then we'd get up and say: 'Let's go and have lunch.' It wasn't personal.

"Eric had an interesting way with people. He was so much himself, so unpretentious. He enjoyed people. And he was also not afraid to ask for help. Chapel Hill is a small town. He would go into a bank, shove the chequebook across the counter, and the teller would balance his account for him. He had never learnt to do it himself! He took it for granted that people would do things for him—and they did. Eric was very open to people, and especially cared about the suffering parents were going through."[22]

Schopler's long-term colleague, Dr. Gary Mesibov, who succeeded him as director of Division TEACCH, agrees with this assessment. A charming man, who generously lent me his driver, Sam, during my stay in Chapel Hill, Mesibov told me that he first met Eric on arriving there in 1974: "I'd read a very favorable article about him in *Newsweek* magazine. He was an impressive guy. I was intimidated by him. The first time I met him was when I gave a talk criticizing the concept of 'normalization.' That got me off to a great start with Eric, because he liked people who criticized things and he didn't like oversimplified concepts like normalization. He was an incredibly courageous and thoughtful man—and he was on my side!

"His wife, Miggie, said that, if there was a small imperfection in a diamond, Eric could find it. That was a great strength, of course, but it could also drive you crazy!"[23]

For Mesibov, Schopler was the ultimate pragmatist. "He needed a diagnostic instrument, so he developed the CARS. He needed an assessment instrument, so he developed the PEP. I believe he was the first real cognitive thinker about autism. He was a bright, broad, reasonable, figure in the field—and it's a field that still lacks that kind of figure.

"The other thing about Eric is that he was creative. He would come up with odd combinations. He could think 'out of the box.' He had an interesting way of connecting disparate elements. That's why TEACCH became so popular around the world: because it means different things to different people. It's an entire philosophy of autism: it's training, manpower, research."[24]

In the course of his 40-year career, Schopler was the author of more than 200 books and articles on autism, his final one being *The TEACCH approach to autism spectrum disorders* (2004). From 1974 until 1997, he was the editor of the *Journal of Autism and Developmental Disorders*, a post he had taken over from Leo Kanner himself. His continued research led to the creation of some of the earliest diagnostic and treatment protocols, such as the CARS and the PEP, which are still widely used today, having been translated into 10 foreign languages for use in autism programs around the world that follow the TEACCH model.

Under Schopler's leadership, the TEACCH program grew from three clinics and 10 special autism classrooms in public schools, to nine clinics and more than 300 TEACCH-affiliated classrooms. The program also developed a comprehensive training division for parents and professionals worldwide, internship and postdoctoral programs for undergraduate, graduate, and postgraduate students, and, in recognition of the fact that children with autism grow up to be adults with autism, a supported employment program.

In 1993, Schopler went into semi-retirement, turning control of the program over to Mesibov, under whose direction it has continued to grow with the inauguration of the program's first residential facility and vocational program.

Schopler received numerous awards for his work, including the North Carolina Award, the state's highest honor, in 1993. Despite his busy professional life, Schopler had an equally full and rewarding personal life. In his spare time, he raised chickens, horses, cows, rabbits, and even catfish with his family at their home outside Mebane, in North Carolina.

When asked what meant most to him in his professional career, he once replied: "If you mean a particular, single event, such as getting a grant or getting awards, or getting things like that, I think it's the parents. When they get genuinely appreciative and excited, and enthusiastic about the progress in their kid, well, that, to me, is probably as important as anything like outcome data. It's unforgettable."[25]

Schopler summed up the humanistic philosophy of TEACCH well when he said: "The long-term goal of the TEACCH program is for the student with autism to fit as well as possible into our society as an adult. We achieve this goal by respecting the differences that the autism creates within each student, and working within his or her culture to teach the skills needed to function within our society."[26]

I myself met Schopler only once—at a conference in Barcelona on bridging the gap between medical and educational approaches. He was very quiet and unassuming, and his lecture was typically shambolic—his papers and slides were deliciously out of order. But what he had to say kept the audience enthralled.

He was indeed a great communicator. Gary Mesibov told me that Schopler loved to travel and wherever he went in the world, he always managed to get his message across, however inadequate the interpreter turned out to be.

Schopler seems to have had no fear for himself—only for others. His close collaborator at TEACCH, Brenda Denzler, told me that they were working one day on a computer looking out on to the garden and an old tree stump covered in foliage. "All of a sudden, the dog, Bingo, started focusing on something in the stump. So Eric picked up a rifle, went outside, poked around in the tree stump and fired his gun. He then calmly picked up a dead snake and tossed it into a bush, before returning to the computer to resume work."[27]

Schopler died on July 7, 2006 at the age of 79. Tributes immediately poured into the TEACCH headquarters from all over the world.

Dr. Cathy Lord, a prominent University of Michigan psychologist who worked with Schopler in Chapel Hill early in her career, said: "He influenced tens of thousands of people. Not only did he develop treatment, he had this understanding about what autism is and how it could be treated in the family and broader context of the community and in the schools. That was unique."[28]

Ruth Sullivan, first elected president of the Autism Society of America, recalled a poignant comment of Schopler's: "He said: 'As a nation, we have three choices with handicapped children: we can dig a ditch, as Hitler did, we can put them in far-away institutions, or we can do the right thing.' "[29]

Shockingly, Eric's widow, Miggie, died shortly after he did, in a car crash.

Michael Rutter, who delivered the memorial address to Eric, told me that, as a passionate advocate of a partnership approach, Schopler had brought the parents on board immediately. "He considered it critical to involve them, because they were in the driving-seat."[30]

Yet even as delightful and popular as man as Eric Schopler had his detractors—and still does, especially among the psychoanalytical community. The French autism specialist, Denys Ribas, probably summing up the nature of the psychoanalysts' opposition to Schopler's approach, wrote, in his book, *Autism: debates and testimonies*:

> Schopler postulated that autism was caused by an organic "handicap" and he therefore thought that there were no psychic defences at work in the child but a permanent incapacity. He considered the child as a handicapped person who needed to be re-educated with the aid of parents, who were permitted to work alongside therapists. Paradoxically, this viewpoint, which ultimately denied any hope to parents—thereby protecting them from the grim wait for the miracle that never came—brought immense relief to parents (with good reason, since they were told what to do and their dignity was restored to them). However, despite its humanistic claims . . . I have strongly criticised this method on the grounds that it abandons any therapeutic ambition, denies the child's suffering and reinforces his failure to emerge as an individual subject.[31]

Professor Gilbert Lelord, the great autism pioneer, who is firmly in the organicist French school, told me that the psychoanalysts had never accepted Schopler's ideas. Lelord recalled a remarkable congress in Paris in 1985 at which Schopler resolutely defended the parents in a country where professionals were still blaming them for their children's autism. "Schopler's message was warmly received by the parents in the audience and when Serge Libovici, the French psychoanalyst, got up to give his own talk and advised Schopler not to generalize, the parents were up in arms, declaring that it was the psychoanalysts who were doing all the generalizing!"[32]

But Eric Schopler's biggest enemy was his main world rival in the field of autism education, Ivar Lovaas.

* * *

Ivar Lovaas was born in 1927 in Lier, Norway, a small agricultural

village outside Oslo. His father was a journalist at the local newspaper, his mother the daughter of a poor tenant farmer. Lovaas is not Jewish but he, too, experienced life under the Nazis—indeed, unlike Schopler, he lived through the whole of the war years under German occupation. When the Nazis invaded Norway in 1940, the family was forced to work as farm laborers. Ivar would cut cabbages and turnips for 10 hours a day until his arms and legs were numb with cold. After the war ended, Lovaas received a violin scholarship to Luther College, a liberal arts school in Decorah, Iowa.

**Figure 39**  Ivar Lovaas

In 1951, he began working on his doctorate in psychology at the University of Washington in Seattle. As part of his predoctoral studies, Lovaas worked as a psychiatric aide at the Pinel Institute, a private mental hospital for the children and grandchildren of Seattle's elite. Most of the patients suffered from schizophrenia. Lovaas would take them for walks through the tree-lined grounds or attempt to comfort them when they became agitated.

One summer, there were two suicides at Pinel, an unusually high number for a small, 20-bed facility. Both patients killed themselves by jumping head-first from the second floor onto the pavement below. "I knew them, and I knew they weren't that crazy," Lovaas recalled later. "The doctors were all medically oriented, so they called it a 'suicide epidemic,' as if it were a contagious disease."[33] This experience appears to mark the beginning of Lovaas's shift away from Freud and towards Skinner and the other behaviorists.

Some have claimed that the allure of behavior therapy was understandable for a man who had lived through the horrors of the Nazi occupation and seen many of its evils at close quarters. The behaviorists seemed to hold the answer to the question of human evil: people were not inherently bad but merely conditioned to act badly by their environments.

In fact, the pioneers in the use of behavioral techniques—especially the use of reinforcement—on children with autism were Charles Ferster and Marian DeMyer at Indiana University Medical Center. In 1961, they reported the findings of an experiment to "develop performances in autistic children in an automatically controlled environment." The experiment involved two vending machines.[34]

In another paper published in 1961, Ferster explained his technique: "The durability and effectiveness of a reinforcer can usually be determined best by reinforcing the behavior intermittently or by providing a strong alternative which could interfere with the behavior in question." The strongest reinforcers, he said, were food or sweets. A parent absorbed in activities such as housecleaning or telephoning might "allow many usually reinforced performances to go unreinforced. . . . Mothers of autistic children often appear to have strong repertoires prepotent over the child. This may be at least a partial reason why mothers of autistic children are so often well-educated, verbal, and at least superficially adequate people."[35]

In 1961, Ivar Lovaas accepted a position as an assistant professor at UCLA. It was the era of Presidents John F. Kennedy and Lyndon Johnson, when the federal government was funneling huge amounts of money into programs designed to combat a whole range of social ills. Lovaas was allocated an entire ward at UCLA's Neuropsychiatric Institute, Franz Hall.

At the time, autism was still being referred to as childhood schizophrenia and, also in spirit with the period, Lovaas believed the "refrigerator mother" theory. If the root cause of autism was a lack of love, psychologists reasoned, then the cure must be an infusion of love. The solution was simple: they would love these children, even when they screamed and scratched and bit. Lovaas believed that Skinner's system of rewards and punishments—or reinforcers and aversives—could be applied to autistic children.

One of his first patients at UCLA was a boy called Billy. "Touch nose," Lovaas would tell him. If Billy touched his nose, Lovaas would give him an M&M sweet and Lovaas would repeat the command. If Billy touched his nose again, he would get another M&M. If Billy touched his ear, or simply ignored the command, Lovaas would let out a loud, angry "No!" Then Lovaas would ask Billy again to touch his nose. In many ways, it looked like a man training a dog.

Of course, by far the most controversial aspect of Lovaas's experiments was his use of aversives. There were the shouts, of course, but there was also corporal punishment for some of the most difficult patients. Staff members would sometimes slap a child; in extreme cases, electric shock treatment was administered.

In 1965, *Life* magazine sent reporters and a photographer to UCLA. The result was a nine-page photo-essay, entitled "Screams, slaps and love," that described Lovaas's work, in a dreadfully tasteless choice of vocabulary, as "a surprising, shocking treatment that helps far-gone mental cripples." The article declared that patients "had turned their homes into hells." The institute was described as an "appalling gallery of madness." Many of the photos accompanying the article were heartbreaking. One showed a staff member slapping a boy in the face for not paying attention to his lesson. Another depicted Pamela, a 9-year-old girl, jerking in pain when a jolt of current from an electrified floor hit her bare feet.[36]

Bernard Rimland, director of the Autism Research Institute in San Diego, was founding the Autism Society of America at the time, traveling around the United States giving talks about the benefits of behavioral therapy. "People in the audience would just sit there waiting for a break," he recalled later, "just so they could say: 'Isn't that the stuff they do at UCLA, where they beat up the children?' "[37]

In fact, in its early days, the Autism Society of America (ASA), founded in Washington DC in 1969, endorsed the use of electric shocks. Ruth Sullivan, who was elected the ASA's first president in 1969, told me in Huntington, West Virginia, where she has established the only cradle-to-grave autism services network: "I always thought Lovaas was a very fine professional, very bright, very committed to what he was doing and committed to the children. One of the things he says is: 'Once you slap a child, you're committed to him for the rest of your life.' "[38]

Sullivan conceded that the ASA accepted Lovaas's use of electric shocks on children at first: "It was a way of gaining their attention and getting them to talk. You don't know what it was like when there was nothing out there. He was the only person at the time who could make a little progress. In the 1960s, cattle-prods were the only thing available. They were quicker. It might take two years to achieve what a cattle-prod could achieve in a week. These days, no one should do it and I can't see how anyone could claim that it was the only thing that worked. Lovaas himself was inquisitive and innovative, and he looked for other, more human approaches with longer-term benefits."[39]

Interestingly, both Schopler and Lovaas (as well as Leo Kanner) were at that first meeting of the Autism Society of America in Washington in 1969. Sullivan told me she thought that the main reason the two men almost came to blows was that they were different personalities.[40]

Lovaas's funding grant from the National Institute of Mental Health stipulated that the treatment for each child would last only one year. Following treatment, some of the children went back to their homes, where Lovaas could help with their continued care, but many stayed at Camarillo, where there were no educational programs. Measured IQ levels plummeted. Many children lost their ability to speak and returned to self-destructive behaviors. Lovaas went to the hospital's director to ask permission to continue treating the children. The director refused.

In the 1960s, Lovaas also assisted in a controversial study on childhood gender problems—dubbed "the sissy boy syndrome" by a co-researcher Richard Green—which sparked protests on the UCLA campus and an article in *The National Enquirer*. (Lovaas has since distanced himself from that work and insists that he took part in the research only to help a colleague.)

In 1970, Lovaas started the Young Autism Project, which stressed early intervention—the kids in the study were between the ages of 2 and 4—and rigorous, eight-hour-a-day training sessions. Over time, Lovaas eliminated the program's use of aversives because of public pressure and the discovery of other, more effective training methods.

Dr. Laura Schreibman, who worked closely with Lovaas at UCLA in the 1970s, told me: "Lovaas was a confident man who really enjoyed having an impact on people. He was very outgoing, with lots of intensity—he was easy to a laugh and easy to anger. He would often say things just to see how people would react, and sometimes these things were totally outrageous. He loved doing that. He was a brilliant and a superb experimentalist.

**Figure 40** Laura Schreibman

He was quite 'brave' in that he tackled very tough problems (such as self-injury) in children with autism and sometimes he used tough methods. But no one else had been really able to help these children. I think he would be the first to agree that we know so much more now that much of the use of aversives would never be necessary now. But he did use them, and a lot of people attacked him for it."[41]

Schreibman said she could not recall ever hearing Lovaas say he felt guilty about having used electric shock aversives. "I don't think the attacks on him bothered him very much, either. I suspect this was because he knew most of these people had nothing better to offer—especially with severely challenging behavior such as self-injury. He could attack with the best of them—and he would. He certainly never backed down from a fight and in fact was just as likely to go after someone (Ed Ritvo is an example). Lovaas could be a real bulldog. He was also quite sexist and at one time was delighted that he won the UCLA 'Male Chauvinist Pig' award."[42]

**Figure 41** Cathy Lord

Dr. Cathy Lord was an undergraduate at UCLA, where she was taught by Lovaas. "He was just finishing his first study where he took the kids out of state hospitals and he was filled with the confidence that, if we just taught these children social skills, everything would be fine," Lord told me. "This, of course, is not exactly true but it was still a great introduction to autism. I joined his team and started working with a couple of kids. That gave me a start, in 1969. He had done shock therapy before I arrived and it hadn't really worked. He was still writing it up and people weren't doing it when I was there. It was more discrete trial, ABA-like things."[43]

By 1974, Lovaas had come to accept that autism had an organic cause and rejected the psychodynamic viewpoint. Interviewed by Paul Chance in that year, Lovaas declared that there was no reason to believe that parents caused autism in their children and that the data strongly suggested that it was present at birth.

However, Lovaas added, many parents still believed that it was somehow their fault. So they went to great lengths to be loving but, faced with the child's even more bizarre behavior—smearing feces on the walls, biting the parents, violent tantrums—the parents were afraid to punish because they had been told that the child behaved this way out of a feeling of being unloved. But he declared that this theory was nonsense, made many parents feel terribly guilty, and sometimes led to the child getting worse, not better.

Then Lovaas continued, oddly echoing the TEACCH philosophy, that instead of blaming the parents, excluding them from treatment, and alienating them from their children, he had brought the parents in on the treatment process, showing them how to reward appropriate behavior and to punish inappropriate behavior. The parents, Lovaas said, "become the principal therapists and we become consultants to the parents. . . . This is great for the kids; without the co-operation of the parents, we could accomplish very little."

However, in the very next part of this interview, another Ivar Lovaas appears to emerge, the one which has come in for a great deal of criticism. He describes the autistic children as "little monsters. . . . All kids have tantrums . . . , but with autistic kids it is extreme." He said that, before you could develop normal social behaviors, you had to eliminate these aberrant behaviors. Asked how he got rid of these behaviors, Lovaas replied: "Spank them, and spank them good." He claimed that this technique was very successful.

Lovaas freely admitted that one method of controlling the children was through the use of electric shocks. "We know the shocks are painful; we have tried them on ourselves and we know that they hurt. . . . But then when you shock him and you see the self-destructive behavior stop, it is tremendously rewarding."[44]

Eric Schopler's children, Susie, Bobby, and Tom, told me that their father rarely discussed autism at home, but they did recall him strongly condemning Lovaas's use of electric shock aversives. Mischievously, however, Schopler did bring a cattle-prod home one day—but he used it only on the cows outside.[45]

In 1981, Lovaas published *Teaching developmentally disabled children: The ME book*, which in essence was a training manual consisting of seven units laying out the principles of behavior therapy.[46] The considerable publicity this book received was as nothing when compared with the uproar following his 1987 decision, after 17 years of testing and research, to publish the highly controversial results of his study, claiming that 47% of the autistic patients achieved "normal functioning" and were able to attend mainstream schools. Children who participated in the program for two years made average IQ gains of

30 points, he insisted, and many of the children maintained their gains into adolescence. His claims represented a marked contrast from comments he had made at the second ASA conference in San Francisco in 1970, when he declared that his program "does not turn out normal children, and should a child become normal as we treat him, then that no doubt is based on the fact that he had a lot going for him when we first started treatment." But in that sentence lay the seeds of the criticisms that have come his way ever since the 1987 study was published.

Some psychologists hailed the study, while others fiercely attacked its inadequacies. Dr. Bryna Siegel, of the University of California, San Francisco, fell into the first camp, Eric Schopler very much into the second. Siegel declared: "It was our first breakthrough where kids could be brought back to normal function."[47]

Schopler, as Gary Mesibov told me, maintained that the 1987 study had "methodological deficiencies: the way Lovaas calculated IQ, did not measure social interpersonal aspects at all. It really wasn't fair to the parents to set up that expectation."[48]

For his part, Michael Rutter told me that he had been very unhappy at Lovaas's use of aversives, "especially electric cattle-prods to induce social behavior" and highly critical of the claims that the children were behaving normally after the treatment. Rutter also recalled Schopler's hostility to Lovaas: "He was offended by Lovaas's willingness to use very abusive measures and also criticized the study in that it was not a randomized controlled study and Lovaas's claims outstripped the findings. Lovaas also made sweeping demands of the parents, especially expecting mothers to give up work. Schopler might have accepted this if there was any evidence that the treatment worked."[49]

Lovaas's former colleague, Cathy Lord, also dismisses the conclusions of his 1987 study. "Randomized, blind controls were not applicable then. They didn't even want to test the kids. Lovaas tried to structure things in a way that, even in the 1980s, did not reflect what really happened and certainly cannot be used as scientific evidence. I don't think there's a cure for autism and I don't think it [ABA] makes a difference with that high a proportion of children. On the other hand, you can change the trajectory by getting the children engaged early on."[50]

Parental expectation was a very real problem after the publication of Lovaas's 1987 study. Dr. Ed Ritvo, who was researching autism at UCLA at the time but definitely not with Lovaas—he described Lovaas's use of electric shocks with cattle-prods as "sadistic"—told me: "People were calling UCLA all the time asking for a cure for their child's autism. But we at the Medical School Neuropsychiatric Institute weren't promising a cure—Ivar Lovaas in the Department of Psychology was promising a cure."[51]

The 1987 study was also criticized for the high treatment costs and the biased selection of patients. However, Dr. Peter Tanguay, who was also working at UCLA at the time and who described Lovaas to me as "a very intense, smart, ambitious guy," told me: "They rightly took high-functioning kids, because they could at least show they could make progress. But I still think they put far too much emphasis on the rote learning of language."[52]

One of the most persistent criticisms was that Lovaas's 40-hour-a-week treatments and repetitive trials did not allow children to learn in a natural setting. Gary Mesibov and others have also pointed out that the 1987 study—and its 1992 follow-up—have not been replicated.

Lovaas's former colleague, Laura Schreibman, has not seen him for many years but she suspects he still believes the 1987 study is the only scientifically proven method of teaching autistic children. "Being wrong is not something he admits very easily!" she told me.[53]

The controversy was reignited in 1993 with the publication of Catherine Maurice's book, *Let me hear your voice: A family's triumph over autism.*[54] In it, Maurice claimed that, using a behavioral program based on Lovaas's principles, her two autistic children had recovered from autism.

Schopler fell out with Lovaas on numerous occasions—not merely over the 1987 study. As Gary Mesibov told me: "They got into many heated battles. The most heated was when Eric wrote in one of our books that the behaviorists didn't do assessments. Lovaas went through the roof. He threatened to sue us. But I think a lot of that was down to a different use of the term 'assessment.' If you read Ivar's *ME book*, there *is* no individualization in it. Everyone goes through the same sequence—they just go through it at different speeds. So assessment, for Lovaas, meant knowing whether the child was ready to move on to the next stage. But he never does what the PEP does—which is to look at developmental skills, not levels. Eric and Ivar got into tremendous battles because I don't think Eric ever understood how Ivar used the term 'assessment.' Lovaas would probably have said: 'You're selling out to the autism, giving into it.' And Eric would probably have responded: 'That's ridiculous.'"[55]

**Figure 42** Gary Mesibov

Mesibov told me the TEACCH system had developed partly on the basis of criticisms that ABA–Lovaas did not encourage a generalization of skills: "I think there are two important differences between the two approaches. One is philosophical: ABA, Lovaas or discrete trial training works on the basis that, with some form of intensive, systematic teaching, you can acquire a 'normal' or neurotypical model. We at TEACCH try to enhance the children's strengths and develop around some of their interests, to help them function more comfortably. ABA–Lovaas is teaching the more 'normal' model of development and functioning, while we at TEACCH are trying to expand around the differences. Both are looking for development and progress but the emphases are different.

"The other big difference between us—and it's not talked about as frequently as the philosophical difference—is that the major concept behind ABA and discrete trial training is that reinforcement is the main trigger for development and learning. They believe that, if something positive follows a behavior which is very systematically and precisely taught, then that behavior is going to increase. Whereas I think that the TEACCH system comes more out of the *Gestalt* tradition, which focuses on meaningfulness and understanding. My argument is that, if a thing makes sense to someone, if they understand it, then it is going to promote their learning more effectively. It's a real challenge for anyone—especially someone with autism. If you put me up against Dr. Lovaas or any ABA person, and said: 'You have one chance to work with this child, and whoever works the most effectively wins the battle,' what they would try and find is the most powerful reinforcement, whereas I would try and get a concept to make sense to a child, to communicate understanding."[56]

I asked Mesibov whether he thought some of the people who had shifted away from the original UCLA approach to Lovaas's methods were moving closer to the TEACCH model in some ways. I was specifically referring to Lynn and Robert Koegel's emphasis on motivation and pivotal response. Mesibov replied: "Absolutely. I look at their pivotal response concept, and I would probably interpret it in a different way—but I agree entirely that the notion of motivation brings in much more the person's understanding and the personal connection to what you are teaching. . . . I'll let you into a secret here! You can come into our program and you'll see people using reinforcements. After all, reinforcement works. We get paid to work. If we don't get paid, we don't work as well. The world operates on that principle. And the ABA people are focusing more on interests and things that are meaningful. But there is still a legitimate distinction between TEACCH and ABA–Lovaas: we would look first at meaningfulness, whereas they would look first at reinforcement."[57]

Nevertheless, ABA has become enormously popular all over the world. It is the preferred educational method in China. Tian Huiping (Hope), who founded the first autism school on mainland China, defended ABA in the strongest terms when I met her in Beijing (see chapter 9). American-trained ABA therapists arrive on a regular basis in the United Kingdom and elsewhere seeking work with families.

But the critics of the method remain just as loud as the advocates. Lorna Wing told me she thought Lovaas was "too rigid with his behavioral approaches: you get rewarded or you get punished. You need more flexibility and human warmth than that. They've stopped electric shocks by law, of course, but consistency is very important. So are other things, like visual strategies. You should work up from things that fascinate the children to wider aspects. Some teachers have an instinctive understanding and others don't."[58]

Wing added that she much preferred the TEACCH approach, "because it is based on human understanding of autistic children. Bits and pieces of the ABA approach are reasonable."[59] Nevertheless, Wing recalled that Lovaas had visited her daughter, Susie, at their house when she was around 8 or 9 years old. "He showed us how to teach her color names by using the fact that she was already able to understand the concept of 'large' and 'small,'" Wing told me. "Susie was amazingly cooperative, gazing at him instead of avoiding eye contact. At one point, he looked away from her to show that she had made an error—and she pulled at his hand to get back his attention! It is sad that, having such a magical effect on a very autistic child like Susie, Lovaas spread ideas that led to a very mechanical approach to the children. Maybe it was because he could not pass on his personal magic, only the rather mechanical rules of behavior modification."[60]

Dr. Peter Tanguay in Louisville said that it was difficult to generalize about ABA but the problem he had with it was that "some of the practitioners do not have a good understanding of normative development."[61] Isabel Bayonas in Spain, although she likes Lovaas personally, complains that the cost of ABA is exorbitant for families already suffering from a tremendous burden. Many people (including Ed Ritvo) protested that the insistence on 40 hours a week was simply too strenuous for most young children and that there was no evidence that it was any better than two or three hours a day, two or three times a week. This incurred the personal animosity of Ivar Lovaas as a result.

Many schools around the world insist that they are adopting an eclectic approach, picking elements of a particular educational method to suit the needs of a particular autistic child. Many professionals agree that this is the most enlightened approach and one which reflects a greater understanding of autism than those who advocate a one-method-fits-all program.

There have been few studies comparing the merits of the various educational approaches to autism. As a linguist, Helen Tager-Flusberg in Boston feels that TEACCH has more of a curriculum and is more or less developmentally based. "ABA is a technique, a method. Many children with autism need the methods of ABA. But I don't like the curriculum so much," she told me. "Of course, that depends on how developmentally informed the therapist is. But why bother drilling a child to learn ten color words? They are not the most important words to learn, which is why there are some languages with only two color words."[62]

Yet the fact is that education often seems to have what the British autism expert, Rita Jordan, has called a "Cinderella role" in the treatment of individuals with autism—largely because education is often not recognized as having a therapeutic role in autistic spectrum disorders as well as being an entitlement. But, as Jordan adds: "Biological research, while exciting, is a long way from offering a 'cure' for autism, and education remains the one treatment approach with the best track record for dealing with the difficulties associated with autism."[63]

# 6

# The 1970s

## Major Steps Forward

If the 1960s was the decade of the first parents' associations, the 1970s were marked by huge leaps forward in understanding the nature of autism—and its treatment. We have already examined the genesis of the TEACCH program in North Carolina and the beginnings of behavioral treatment of autistic children. But this was the decade that saw the first study clearly delineating autism and childhood schizophrenia, the first major twin study, the introduction of the concept of an autistic spectrum (and by extension, the broader phenotype), and the Triad of Impairments. It could also be said that it was in the 1970s that researchers began to work systematically on the cognitive aspects of autism, in stark contrast to Leo Kanner's emphasis on the affective and social deficits in this syndrome.

By the beginning of the 1970s, there was a great deal of interest and investigation into the condition worldwide. In Australia, for instance, the cause of the child with autism had been taken up by a service organization which organized a walk around the huge country. Much of the money raised was directed to research and some valuable papers came out of this enterprise—the most significant being a 1969 study by Helen Clancy and her team who undertook a comprehensive program of observation of autistic and other groups of children and produced a new list of points based on descriptions of behavior.[1]

The year 1971 saw the publication of a landmark work, Lorna Wing's book, *Autistic children: A guide for parents and professionals*. In many parts of the world, this work acted as a powerful counter to Bruno Bettelheim's 1967 book, *The empty fortress*, although, as we have seen, I was told by Dr. Sally Ozonoff at the MIND Institute in Sacramento, California, that Bettelheim's book was still considered required reading when she started working in the field as late as the 1980s.[2]

By the beginning of the 1970s, it was started to be more broadly accepted—in some circles—that parents had nothing to do with causing their child's autism. But understanding and acceptance of autism in society were still very basic. There was a revealing exchange of views in the letters pages of the *British Medical Journal* in March 1970, in which a correspondent wrote: " 'Autistic' has taken over from 'spastic' as the currently fashionable euphemism to embrace all non-communicating children functioning at a mentally subnormal level, whatever their level of intelligence and whatever the cause of the condition."[3]

That year, 1970, saw the publication of Dr. Beate Hermelin and Dr. Neil O'Connor's classic text, *Psychological experiments with autistic children*,[4] in which the London-based researchers described experiments designed to demonstrate a distinctive cognitive profile in autism (see below).

Through the 1960s, the British psychiatrist, Michael Rutter and his colleagues began their series of studies on typical autism. They described in detail the clinical features of the disorder, they investigated the children's profiles on intelligence tests, and they followed them up into adolescence and adult life.

**Figure 43** Michael Rutter

Michael Rutter's contribution to the study of autism has been immense. He is a larger-than-life character whose many research papers are constantly cited throughout the world. He was actually born in the Lebanese capital, Beirut, in 1933. In his early years, he spoke as much Arabic as he did English, and he told me that he had never spent more than a few years in one city at a time, which was why, in his words, his accent was difficult to place.[5]

In the brilliant 1971 paper, "Causes of infantile autism: Some considerations from recent research," Rutter and the Australian child psychologist, Lawrence Bartak, assessed the prevailing notions of autism at the time. They found little to back up some of them. Discussing Gerald O'Gorman's suggestion that autism was a defense mechanism and that the autistic syndrome was merely an exaggeration of normal phenomena, they wrote:

140

That autistic children are seriously impaired in their social relationships in early childhood is obviously true, but O'Gorman's suggestion that this is the same type of selective withdrawal found at times in normal people has no empirical support. The hypothesis fails to account for the other features of the syndrome, it does not explain why autism is four times as common in boys as in girls, and it by-passes the evidence of organic impairment in autistic children.[6]

Rutter and Bartak also examined the proposal, by Kit Ounsted and the Hutts at Oxford, that autism might consist of a genetically determined extreme degree of introversion associated with high arousal in social situations. They pointed out that, if Ounsted's view were correct, the parents of autistic children should be markedly more introverted than normal. But this had been shown not to be the case. "Mothers of autistic children are actually slightly (but not significantly) more extroverted than the general population," they noted, adding that, again, the Oxford theory could not account for the heavy male preponderance among autistic children.[7]

Rutter and Bartak called attention to the fact that another study they had conducted had disproved the psychogenic causation theory of autism by showing that the parents of autistic children did not differ in the characteristics from the parents of children with other language disorders.[8]

They also declared that it was "most unlikely" that social deprivation was a cause of autism, because autistic children did not usually have a history of depriving experiences and there was usually little effect on language comprehension in socially deprived children, whereas this was almost always seriously impaired in autistic children.[9] In 1972, in his book, *Maternal deprivation reassessed*, Rutter argued that, where perceptual and linguistic stimulation was inadequate or disorganized, cognitive development was likely to be retarded.[10] Rutter would return to this theme nearly two decades later in his study of children in Romanian orphanages (see chapter 8).

One of the most significant aspects of the 1971 paper was the emphasis Rutter and Bartak laid on the cognitive deficits in autism— an element which, it will be recalled, Leo Kanner himself entirely neglected in his 1943 paper, concentrating instead on affective deficits. They allude to Rutter's 1967 study with David Greenfeld and Linda Lockyer[11] which had demonstrated that autistic children, even after they ceased to be withdrawn might still remain retarded in language, have a low IQ and show obsessive-like symptoms. In a 1968 paper, Rutter had concluded that autistic children had a central disorder of language involving both the comprehension of language and the utilisation of

141

language or conceptual skills in thinking.[12] Three years later, in 1971, Rutter and Bartak said that this view had largely been confirmed by work by Uta Frith, and by Beate Hermelin and Neil O'Connor, adding that these researchers "have also shown that the cognitive defect is rather wider than suggested in 1968."[13]

Rutter and Bartak were at pains to stress that

> the fact of the matter is that autistic children usually exhibit multiple central defects. At the present time, it is uncertain which of these are *necessary* and *sufficient* causes of the disorder. We have suggested that a central defect in the processing of symbolic or sequence information is likely to prove the basic defect, but the evidence is not yet available to decide conclusively between the different types of cognitive or sensory disorders which have been *postulated* for autism.[14]

The authors pointed to "the probability of neurological disorder in some autistic children." But they are cautious about ascribing possible specific causes. They said the high rates of fits in intellectually retarded autistic children "suggests the existence of some kind of organic brain damage or disorder. In the few cases where some specific brain disease has been found, the type of disease has been far from uniform." They added that the rate of genetic factors "remains quite uncertain."[15] That would change just six years afterwards, as we will see later in this chapter, with Rutter's landmark twin study with Susan Folstein.

In what turned out to be a very important year for autism research, 1971, Stella Chess brought out her key paper showing that mothers who contracted rubella in pregnancy gave birth to children who went on to develop autism.[16] Leo Kanner's colleague, Leon Eisenberg, told me that it was this study which actually convinced Kanner that there could be a specific organic cause for autism.[17] Nevertheless, the Swedish psychiatrist, Christopher Gillberg, pointed out to me that, despite its importance, Chess's study had never really been replicated.[18]

**Figure 44** Israel Kolvin (courtesy of *British Medical Journal*)

Again in 1971, Dr. Israel Kolvin published his landmark study of 33 British children, outlining what he saw as the differences between autistic and schizophrenic children. One of the chief distinctions, he said, was the age of onset. Still using the term "psychosis," he noted that children developed psychosis in two waves: In the first wave, he said, symptoms were evident before the age of 3 and in the second, they showed up between the ages of 5 and 15. The children in the first wave typically had the characteristics of autism, Kolvin claimed, and would probably receive this diagnosis. Whereas children of the second wave more closely resembled schizophrenic adults in symptomatology, he said, and would probably be diagnosed as having childhood schizophrenia.[19]

This paper certainly appears to have convinced Leo Kanner once and for all that autism and childhood schizophrenia were two distinct conditions. In 1973, he published a book, *Childhood psychosis: Initial studies and new insights*,[20] in which he declared that there had been a definite shift away from a 1968 paper by Ed Ornitz and Ed Ritvo stating that early infantile autism, atypical development, symbiotic psychosis, and certain cases of childhood schizophrenia were, in Kanner's words, "essentially variants of the same disease."

Ornitz himself told me that his 1968 paper[21] was "simply speculation and not to be taken seriously today. The paper, particularly its case histories, described the similarities and the differences in symptomatology amongst cases that received these different labels. In the 1960s, when not much was known about autism, there was speculation that it might be related to schizophrenia. But with increasing experience, it became clear that, with a few rare exceptions, autistic children did not become schizophrenic and that there was no obvious relationship between the two conditions. Eventually, the different labels lost any importance that they once might have had. The terms 'atypical development' and 'symbiotic psychosis' are long forgotten. And childhood schizophrenia, which has persisted, is now considered an early developmental manifestation of schizophrenia, and distinct from autism. So, Kanner's reference is correct, but now moot."[22]

Israel Kolvin, affectionately known as Issy, was an engaging and fascinating character. Born in 1929 to immigrant Polish-Jewish parents in Johannesburg, South Africa, he had a harsh upbringing. He first studied psychology and philosophy and chose child psychiatry as a career after witnessing at first hand the deprivation and malnutrition suffered by children at the Baragwanath Hospital in Soweto. He came to Britain in 1958 to train, first in Edinburgh and then in Oxford. It was with the encouragement of Kit Ounsted, a well-known child psychiatrist, that Kolvin embarked on the autism and childhood schizophrenia study, his first important piece of research and the one which would make his name. It is still quoted to this day.[23]

After being appointed to a personal chair in child psychiatry at Newcastle University, he oversaw a scientifically rigorous 1981 project to evaluate the effectiveness of psychotherapeutic interventions in schools with emotionally disturbed youths. The study, published as *Help Starts Here*, showed that psychotherapy could contribute to schoolchildren's well-being.[24] In 1990, Kolvin was appointed to the newly established Bowlby chair in child and family mental health at the Tavistock Clinic and Royal Free Hospital Medical School in London. He died in 2002 at the age of 72.

One of those who knew Kolvin well while he was at the Royal Free Hospital and the Tavistock Institute in the early 1990s is Dr. Ann Le Couteur. Now based at the University of Newcastle, Le Couteur told me that Kolvin's 1971 paper demonstrating the differences between autism and childhood schizophrenia was "absolutely crucial. But he had a whole tranche of different research projects. He was a very persuasive, thoughtful, supportive and conscientious man and it was very hard to say no to him. When he was dying, he called me in from his hospital bed at the Royal Free and, even though he was desperately ill, I took dictation from him at his bedside."[25]

The other important article to be published in 1971 was Leo Kanner's follow-up paper of his 11 original cases in the *Journal of Autism and Childhood Schizophrenia*. The first of the 11, Donald T, had demonstrated a remarkable memory when Kanner saw him from 1938 onwards but, Kanner reported, seemed to draw into his shell and live within himself and had destructive temper tantrums. In the 1971 follow-up, Kanner repeated his original allusion to the odd detachment of Donald's parents. In 1970, when Donald was 36, his mother wrote to Kanner to tell him that her son was still living at home and working as a bank teller. He showed no interest in the opposite sex but played a lot of golf, for which he won trophies. "While Don is not completely normal he has taken his place in society . . . so much better than we ever hoped."[26]

Of the other original 11 cases Kanner followed up in 1971, he seems to be referring to a case of regression when he quotes Richard M's mother as saying that he had "gone backward mentally."[27]

Other children in the original 1943 group maintained their stereotypical behaviors. What is most interesting about Kanner's 1971 paper, perhaps, is that he is quite happy—two years after he had publically "acquitted" parents of blame for autism at the first conference of the

National Association of Autistic Children in Washington DC—to reiterate his reference to the "frosty atmosphere" in which one of the children, Virginia, had lived at home.[28] Nevertheless, Kanner also attempts to clarify this issue in his conclusion to the 1971 paper. He says he stands by his original 1943 assumption that the children had been born with an innate disability.[29]

Indeed, he added that this was now a certainty. However, he complained, some people still believed him to be an advocate of the theory that autism was caused by "post-natal 'psychogenicity,'" mainly because all 11 children studied had highly intelligent parents. "It was noticed that many of the parents, grandparents, and collaterals were . . . strongly preoccupied with abstractions of a scientific, literary, or artistic nature and limited in genuine interest in people. But at no time was this . . . phenomenon oversimplified as warranting the postulate of a direct cause-and-effect connection. To the contrary, it was stated expressly that the aloneness from the beginning of life makes it difficult to attribute the whole picture one-sidedly to the manner of early parent–child relationship."[30]

Important pharmacological studies began in the 1970s. One of the pioneers in the field was Dr. Magda Campbell, who started work at the Bellevue Hospital in New York in the early 1960s. Campbell's younger colleague, Dr. Richard Perry, told me that, although everyone seemed still to be referring to childhood schizophrenia in the US, "it was clear to Dr. Campbell that there was a difference between schizophrenic and autistic children."[31]

The two major studies Campbell was working on in the 1970s concerned the effects of haloperidol on children with autism. "This reflected her interest in finding a medication that would calm the kids down but also make them better learners," her colleague, Perry, told me. Despite Dr. Campbell's studies, "there is still no specific medication for autism," he said. "The important thing is to try and make the children more amenable to special therapies."[32]

Magda Campbell was one of the many outstanding participants in the historic first (and, as it turned out, only) Leo Kanner Symposium on Child Development, Deviations and Treatment, held at Chapel Hill in North Carolina in 1973. Among the other speakers were Kanner himself, Eric Schopler (who had founded TEACCH the year before), Stella Chess, Ivar Lovaas, Marian DeMyer, Laura Schreibman, and Robert Reichler.

Dr. Marian DeMyer, who was conducting pioneering experiments on children with autism at the University of Indiana, told the 1973 symposium that her research showed four main points: that the intelligence

145

of autistic children could be measured reliably; that the IQ had a good predictive power about the child's eventual functioning; that most autistic children had below-average intelligence (different from what Leo Kanner—who was sitting in the audience at the time of DeMyer's talk—might have expected); and in only a few children with autism did the verbal IQ reach normal levels, "no matter how intense the treatment and education."[33]
DeMyer added:

> While these IQ studies of large numbers of autistic children revealed that their IQs were related to important features of their illness, they told us little about the reason for low measured IQ of 94% of the children. While the most socially withdrawn autistic children had the lowest IQs, we did not learn if the withdrawal caused the low IQs or if the low IQs were the cause of the withdrawal.[34]

Importantly, in view of the lack of brain-scanning equipment at the time and the continuing doubts in many quarters over the nature and causes of autism, DeMyer said she had found that the autistic children had significantly more signs of neurological dysfunction than the normal control group and nearly as many as the "non-psychotic subnormal" children.[35]
In 1976, the American neurologist, Dr. Mary Coleman, published the results of a 1974 study suggesting that autism should be divided up into

**Figure 45**   Mary Coleman with her husband, Jay Gonen

a number of subtypes. Prior to this study, Coleman had considered autism as three general subgroups: classic Kanner's autism, childhood schizophrenia, and neurological impairment with autistic features. In her 1974 study, Coleman examined 78 autistic children with a median age of 9 at the Children's Brain Research Clinic in Washington DC, each accompanied by a developmentally normal child of the same age and sex.[36]

"As a result of this study, I came to realize that autism is like mental retardation—it's a final common pathway in the brain affected by many different underlying causes, many different disease entities," Coleman told me.[37]

**Figure 46** Susan Folstein

The concept of a broader phenotype of the central disorder was first given a serious boost by one of the greatest studies of the 1970s—indeed, one of the most significant in the history of autism. In 1977, Dr. Susan Folstein and Professor Michael Rutter carried out the first systematic study of twins with autism, showing conclusively that the genetic component in the disorder was a significant one. It was a study of 21 pairs of British twins. For 10 pairs of fraternal (dizygotic) twins in which at least one twin was diagnosed as autistic using strict criteria, not a single co-twin was diagnosed as autistic: concordance for fraternal twin pairs was zero. Previous studies had also found a lack of resemblance for non-twin siblings. Because heritable disorders are expected to run in families, this was one of the reasons the possibility of genetic influence on autism had not been given serious consideration. The startling result from the Folstein and Rutter study came from 11 pairs of identical (monozygotic) twins, who are genetically identical. Of the 11 pairs, four were concordant for strictly diagnosed autism.[38]

In the 1960s, Rutter himself—by his own admission—was among those who thought a genetic etiology for autism was unlikely. "People paid attention, as I did at first, to the low rate of autism in siblings rather than focusing on the very high relative rate," Rutter told me. "I then put it right. I think you need to be open when you make mistakes—we all make mistakes!"[39]

Folstein told me in her comfortable Baltimore apartment which she shares with her husband, Marshall, inventor of the Mini-Mental States for assessing Alzheimer's disease, that when she started in the field she knew autism existed but knew nothing about the condition. "I always presumed it was organic—I don't know why."[40]

Her first meeting in London with Michael Rutter was "very friendly," she said. "He was already a professor and I had written a proposal which had a million different projects in it. He smiled—he knew I was naïve. He made two suggestions: one was a psychology project, which didn't interest me. But he also said he had accumulated a list of twins from the widow of a Dr. Carter. I liked that one—genetics had always interested me from the time I was at medical school.

"Mike himself had written an earlier paper in which had pointed out that, although the prevalence of autism was 4 to 5 per 10,000—given the criteria at the time—the rate in siblings was about 3%. So he made the hypothesis that autism could be a genetic disorder. I'm sure that's why he suggested our project."[41]

Folstein said that, although the twin study was Rutter's idea, it was she who conducted all the interviews and examinations. "Mike asked me to read a little book called *The study of twins*. It included several pitfalls in twin studies. One is that, if you ask for volunteers, you get more identical, monozygotic twins and more twins where both are affected. Rutter went to great trouble to write letters to every child psychiatrist, pediatrician and doctor specializing in developmental disorders, as well as subnormality hospitals (which were quite full in those days) and asked for all the twins who had autism—whether or not they were identical or fraternal. That took a while. There were also two twin registries in London— one at the Maudsley Hospital and the other at Great Ormond Street Hospital. We began to write letters to the families asking permission to access their records. At that time in the UK, they really did send you big packets of case notes. We decided that we wanted only same-sex twins. We thought male–female twins would be more likely to be discordant."[42]

Michael Rutter told me that the much lower rate of autism in females as compared with males "meant that we were bound to have completely inadequate statistical power to look at opposite-sex pairs. In terms of what we know now, it would be informative to study opposite-sex pairs but, even now, I doubt that there are any available twin samples with the power to make use of such a comparison. I think it was the right decision to exclude them, in that the numbers would have been inadequate to make any sense of the findings."[43]

148

Folstein said that, at the time, it wasn't considered good manners to call people up in Britain. "I thought this was wrong. So I decided to call them if they didn't respond to the letters. I don't think Mike wanted me to do that—but I did it anyway! I took trains, I drove, I even flew once, to interview the mothers and examine the children."[44]

She discussed their two main findings. "The first, which we expected, was that the monozygotic pairs were more likely to be both affected than the dizygotic twins. We didn't have any dizygotic pairs who were concordant. There are dizygotic pairs who are concordant—just as siblings are affected—but in our sample, we didn't find any. So that was strong evidence of a genetic mechanism of some kind.

"The other thing I noticed—and this was something for which we hadn't designed the study—was that, even though there were quite a lot of monozygotic co-twins who did not meet the criteria for autism, there was something wrong with them which was reminiscent of autism. They had language problems, they were socially awkward, and some were cognitively impaired. So when you added those in, it brought the concordance up to about 90% among the identical twins. That put us on the path of defining the broader phenotype—but that was a different study."[45]

Folstein said that other scientists began to conduct genetic research in autism very soon after her study. "But the techniques were very basic at the time. There were really no ways of looking at genes. A couple of people replicated our twin study. One was Christopher Gillberg [in Sweden]. He tends to use looser criteria. His concordance for identical twins was 100%. Somewhat later, Mike Rutter followed up my twins and added new ones. He came up with concordance rate of 40 to 50%. We usually combine the three studies to produce a concordance rate of around 60%."[46]

Folstein told me her twin study was "a true cultural experience—traveling on British trains which had no door-handles on the inside. I actually went past my stop once because I didn't realize I had to open the door from the outside! I remember once going to a gypsy camp where one of the families had two children with autism. That was fun—they were gorgeous people with wonderful red hair. There was a little girl with a mentally retarded twin sister and the mother said to me: 'How did you find us?' I replied: 'The doctor you were seeing wrote me a letter.' She said: 'Oh, so there *is* something to this writing after all!' They disparaged book-learning, even though they were clearly intelligent."[47]

In some ways, the Folstein–Rutter twin study could be seen as the forerunner of Wing and Gould's landmark concept of an autistic spectrum two years later—although Folstein praised Wing's concept as original and unique. Folstein said the thinking changed "after our descriptions of the co-twins who had milder features. I remember talking to [the late] Donald Cohen [at Yale] and he said to me: 'These criteria are too narrow—I see so many kids who I feel ought to be called autistic and they don't make it.'"[48]

In fact, Folstein and Rutter concluded—as they stated in their 1977 paper and Rutter reiterated six years later[49]—that the evidence suggested that it was probably not autism, as such, which was inherited, but rather some broader predisposition to language and cognitive abnormalities of which autism constituted only one part. Folstein told me: "We thought that at the time, because family members had some of the language and cognitive features but not autism. If you think about it, that is what you would expect if several genes were required, which is certainly true in many cases, perhaps most. Any given gene would not cause the whole phenotype. I like to think of autism as a 'compound' phenotype—one which could cause one or more of its components."[50]

The criteria they used for defining autism were Michael Rutter's four criteria, which he formally introduced the year after the twin study, in 1978 (see also chapter 7). These were: impaired social development which has a number of special characteristics out of keeping with the child's intellectual level; delayed and deviant language development that also has certain defined features and is out of keeping with the child's intellectual level; "insistence on sameness" as shown by stereotyped play patterns, abnormal preoccupations, or resistance to change; and onset before 30 months of age.

Then came Wing and Gould's research, published in 1979, which was indeed pioneering. The findings of their Camberwell study had repercussions which—as we shall see—are still felt around the world.[51]

Lorna Wing and Judith Gould were both based at the Maudsley Hospital in south London when they began working on their study in Camberwell, in the south of the British capital, in 1977. Ironically, in view of its revolutionary findings, one of Wing's original aims in conducting the study was to prove Kanner's restricted criteria for autism correct.

"Leo Kanner would have found it very difficult to accept the idea of an autistic spectrum, because he was so wedded to his idea of a unique syndrome," Wing told me.[52] "The funny thing is that our daughter, Susie, fitted Kanner's syndrome to a T. I filled in Bernie Rimland's questionnaire and he said Susie got the highest score for Kanner's autism of any person he'd ever seen!

**Figure 47**   Lorna Wing (right) and Judith Gould

"In fact, I myself started off quite convinced that Kanner was right. One of the reasons I embarked on my study of children in Camberwell with my colleague, Judy Gould, was that I wanted to show evidence that Kanner's view was correct, but meeting the children—working, to start with, through a thousand children in a very brief screening process and then picking out 173 children who either had some sort of autistic features or had an IQ of under 50, or both—meeting the families, seeing them at school and at home, showed me that the idea of a neat barrier between Kanner's autism and the others was rubbish. And slowly, my view was changed. I had to accept the experience in front of my very eyes."[53]

Wing said there were certainly some children who beautifully fitted Kanner's criteria, "but there was a huge collection in the middle who could not be put into either category. Very few fitted Asperger's syndrome, because they virtually all had an IQ of under 70 and none were mainstreamed."[54]

She added that, since the 1979 study, "we've seen that the best way to look at and describe these children is on the dimensional system. You look at all the different dimensions of social skills, motor skill comprehension and use of language, etc., and describe where they are on each. That gives you a meaningful profile in terms of helping that child. You don't say he fits this or that group."[55]

151

Lorna Wing's co-author on the historic 1979 Camberwell study, Judith Gould, told me: "Camberwell had a whole cross-section of occupations and ability levels. We showed there was no bias whatsoever on a socio-economic basis. That differed from Kanner's early view that autism was a middle-class disorder.

"What made us different was that all the diagnostic systems referred to social and communication difficulties and rigidity. They were the three aspects. We referred to imagination as a separate deficit. The Triad of Impairments we introduced was social, communication, and imagination. People misquote the triad as social communication and rigidity. We weren't saying anything new in that sense. But we *were* saying that you could have manifestations in different ways.

"We accepted the Kanner group but also the children who were passive, who were very happy to go along with someone else if they led but if the person went away, they became solitary. Then the third group was the active but odd group—they come along and talk at you on their terms but do not modify their behavior depending on how you interact with them. Under the narrow definition, the children making contact would not have been called autistic."[56]

For her part, Lorna Wing told me: "If you look at all the different criteria—Mike Rutter's and lots of other individuals' suggestions—all of them emphasize the social impairment, the communication impairment, and perhaps language. We do agree with Isabelle Rapin that it is the *way* language is used that is impaired in autism. Judy [Gould] and I thought that imagination was very important—it was the development of imagination in the non-autistic children which enabled them to think and feel what other people were thinking and feeling. That is what imagination and pretend play are for. That is the root of the social skill— and that is why we put imagination in the Triad. We now emphasize that it is *social* skills, communication, and imagination which are impaired. Autistic children *do* have imagination, but it is not social."[57]

Wing insists that she and Gould did not emphasize the social impairment in autism strongly enough at first. She cites the case of the highly articulate British autistic woman, Ros Blackburn, who gives insightful talks around the UK and further afield: "Ros speaks wonderfully well. But she still has a social communication problem. She says she does not care much for people. She knows the social rules, like Temple Grandin."[58]

Both Wing and Gould stressed that, although their findings also came to the conclusion that there was a broader autism phenotype, their research was conducted independently from the 1977 twin study. "We knew about Folstein and Rutter's twin study, of course," Gould told me. "And they were talking about a similar thing to us. In fact, we first called it the 'autistic *continuum*' and then we realized that the word continuum had an implication of discrete descriptions along a line, whereas that was not really what it was. It was not a question of moving in severity from very severe to mild. That was not what we were trying to get across. The concept of a spectrum is more like a spectrum of light, with blurring."[59]

Wing recalled that one of the children in the Camberwell study, Joseph—an 8-year-old boy who was the only son of parents from the Caribbean—had never been able to walk. "He could feed himself with a spoon but had no other self-care or schoolwork skills. He had no speech at all but laughed and cried and made sounds to attract attention from others. When he was approached, his face lit up with the delight the social encounter gave him. This made him a great favorite with the staff at his special school."[60]

Another of the Camberwell children—Anne, aged 9, the daughter of English parents—was fully mobile and energetic and had no idea of possible danger. She could feed herself and cooperated in self-care, though she needed help with this. She had some speech but had echolalia and she mixed up pronouns. She loved music, which was her main interest and source of pleasure. "Opera was her special favorite and she could name the opera from which any piece was played after hearing one or two opening bars. She would instantly know if a record was played at the wrong speed," Wing told me. "However, she was socially aloof and indifferent to others, and had poor eye contact. She showed no pleasure in response to social approaches."[61]

I will return to the Camberwell study in the following chapter, when I discuss the evolution of diagnostic criteria.

The recognition of the need for a wider definition of autism quickly spread across the Atlantic. The American psychiatrist, Dr. Theodore Shapiro, told me that he had found no choice but to accept the existence of a broader phenotype. "We saw so many children who didn't fit Kanner's original three criteria. You had to include them somewhere. But even so, we had to be restrained."[62]

This dual view—full acceptance of the validity and value of the concept of the autistic spectrum and caution over its overextension—seems to be very widely shared by professionals throughout the world. Leo Kanner himself, in the last years of his life, lamented the way the term "autism" had become a "pseudo-diagnostic wastebasket."[63]

153

Dr. Fred Volkmar, one of the world's leading autism authorities, told me: "The concept of an autistic spectrum was a really interesting idea. But it does risk becoming so diffuse that it inhibits research—because in some cases, you need to focus on a specific condition."[64]

\* \* \*

Research continued in other areas, as well. Dr. Ed Ornitz told me that, when he was a Fellow in Child Psychiatry at the Yale Child Study Center, he became aware of two additional symptom clusters—apart from the Wing–Gould Triad of Impairments—which, he said, were also a striking manifestation of autistic behavior during the preschool years. "These disturbances of sensory modulation and motility usually wane after the age of 5. In the 1970s and 1980s, I studied these behaviors, observing that the disturbances of sensory modulation were characterized by under- and overreactivity to sensory stimuli, including the seeking out of sensory stimulation. The underreactivity included ignoring auditory or painful stimuli. The overreactivity included distraction by background stimuli, distress from stimulation, and, paradoxically, behavior that provides repetitive sensory input. The motility disturbances are stereotypical behaviors that provide such sensory input. The disturbances of sensory modulation occur in response to visual, auditory, tactile, and vestibular input, and input in all of these modalities evokes either severe distress or, paradoxically, the seeking out of such stimulation."[65]

Ornitz said that, to study these behaviors, he developed an inventory of 21 specific behaviors which exemplified these disturbances, along with 18 specific behaviors that exemplified the autistic disturbances of relating to people and objects.

In a 1978 study, the parents of 74 preschool autistic children and 38 normal control children filled out the inventory on a scale of behavior ranging from "never occurred" to "almost always occurred." "Depending on the specific behavior, up to 71% of the autistic children showed disturbances of sensory modulation," Ornitz told me.[66] "None of the normal children showed the behavior."[67]

Ten years later, Ornitz conducted a similar study on which parents of 242 young autistic children, almost all younger than 6 years of age, filled out the inventory.[68] "The inventories had data which could be used to compare the disturbances of sensory modulation with the disturbance of autistic relating. The frequencies of occurrence of the two types of behavior correlated strongly. But these disturbances of sensory modulation, while such a prominent manifestation of autism during the preschool period of development, did not become part of the diagnostic criteria for autistic disorder in DSM-IV. I suspect that this may be because most clinicians have studied autism cross-sectionally and after the preschool period, when these behaviors are less frequent and may not be seen. It is clearly very important to study autism developmentally."[69]

Also in the 1970s, the first serious studies into language abnormalities in autism began. The delay may have been partly caused by Kanner and Eisenberg's mysterious 1956 decision to remove language deficits from their three basic criteria for autism.

Marian DeMyer and colleagues, in her 1974 study, claimed to have found "a profound language dysfunction in every autistic child. This language dysfunction was manifest in symbolic aspects, even if the mechanism of speech were present."[70]

In 1975, Michael Rutter, Lawrie Bartak, and colleagues published a comparative study of infantile autism and specific developmental receptive language disorder. The researchers took a sample of boys aged between 5 and 10 years with no demonstrable neurological dysfunction, hearing loss, or mental retardation but who had a severe developmental disorder of the understanding of spoken language and showed that, within this group, children diagnosed as autistic had a more deviant language development than non-autistic children, had a more severe comprehension defect, had a more extensive language disability, and also showed a defect in the social usage of the language they possessed. They concluded that a language disability was "probably necessary for the development of the behavioral syndrome of autism."[71]

Today, Bartak believes that the primary deficit in autism "seems to lie in processing information to do with people, emotions and social situations," as he told me. "Handling that kind of information is probably done automatically by anyone who is not on the autistic spectrum. There is probably a brain system which mediates this process. My hypothesis is that this mechanism is not working for some people. They therefore have to learn it, through cognition."[72]

Another area of great activity in autism research around the world in the 1970s was the issue of prevalence. Victor Lotter's 1966 study in Middlesex, England, was, as we have seen, the first such study. The first prevalence study in the following decade was published in 1970 by Darold Treffert—better known today as the world's leading authority on the autistic savant syndrome (he was one of the principal advisors on the film *Rain man)*—in the US state of Wisconsin. This study—and a whole range of prevalence studies which appeared in Japan, Denmark and France later in the 1970s—are examined in more detail in chapter 7.

**Figure 48** Uta Frith

One of the key players who began researching autism in earnest in the 1970s was Dr. Uta Frith. Now an emeritus professor at University College London and best-known today for her role in the development of theory of mind and weak central coherence as applied to autism, Frith was born Uta Aurnhammer in Rockenhausen, Germany, in 1941. She originally planned to study history of art at the University of Saarbrücken before discovering psychology as an experimental science and being struck by the realization that the study of the mind could be researched using empirical methods.

She arrived in London in 1964 to do an internship at the Institute of Psychiatry and stayed there to begin a course in clinical psychology. During this course, she came across her first cases of so-called "childhood psychosis"—now autism. She was instantly fascinated by the contrast between the children's attractive appearance and apparent intelligence, on the one hand, and their profound level of handicap on the other. Despite the fact that the climate in the late 1960s was still dominated by psychogenic theories, and only a minority of experts were prepared to countenance the idea that autism might be an "organic" condition, Frith became convinced that it must indeed be a biological disorder.

Frith has described the first autistic children she encountered as "remote, beautiful and mysterious," reminding her of the children in John Wyndham's science fiction novel, *The Midwich cuckoos*. She told me: "I was captivated. There is something so fascinating about autism. It poses us fundamental questions about ourselves, our consciousness, our relationship to other people. I started to be introduced to autistic children here in London by Professor Michel Rutter who was at the Maudsley Hospital at the time, in the mid-1960s, while I was training as a clinical psychologist. At the same time, I found my future PhD supervisors and mentors, Beate Hermelin and Neil O'Connor."[73]

**Figure 49**   Neil O'Connor and Beate Hermelin, pictured in the late 1970s (photo courtesy of Uta Frith)

The studies of the Berlin-born Beate (Ati) Hermelin and the Australian Neil O'Connor were unique at the time, because they were designed from the perspective of experimental psychology. Frith has compared this celebrated duo of researchers to the principal characters in

*The Avengers*, the fashionable British TV series in the adventure/spy genre running in the 1960s. Uta Frith told me. "They were so *glamorous* and so unusual. They had such radical and original ideas."[74]

Frith is far from alone in her admiration for Hermelin and O'Connor. Frith's colleague, Dr. Francesca Happé, who worked with her on the weak central coherence theory of autism, also began working in the field thanks to these two crucial players in the field of early autism research. Happé recalled that she went to see Hermelin and O'Connor after reading Clara Claiborne Park's book, *The siege*, to see if they trusted her to collect data,

**Figure 50**   Francesca Happé    since they usually did this themselves.[75]

"I met Neil first and went with him to Sybil Elgar School and Springhallow School, both in Ealing. Neil was a fantastic person. He had infinite time for people. He sat with me while I spent time with a low-functioning autistic young man. Neil probably thought I was going to give up."[76]

But he and Hermelin asked Happé to collect data from people with special memory skills and a control group. "I went all around the country testing them. It was an astonishing experience to see what autism really was."

She recalled O'Connor as "a remarkably brilliant man with a dry wit and always beautifully dressed. He drove a sports car and in those early days, he would put the car in the tramlines, take his hands off the steering-wheel and read his mail on the way from home to work!" Hermelin, she remembered, was equally larger than life—"a tough but enormously generous woman."[77]

Uta Frith has frequently acknowledged her debt to Hermelin and O'Connor but Frith's own PhD students include some of the biggest names in the field, like Simon Baron-Cohen, Tony Attwood, and Digby Tantam. As Dorothy Bishop correctly writes in her 2006 tribute to Frith's many contributions: "It is important to realise that autism research in the 1960s and 1970s was a very different enterprise from how it is today. The concept of 'high-functioning autism' was not recognised, and the children who were the topic of study had severe cognitive limitations."[78]

Frith told one interviewer: "In the 1960s, the burden of blame was put on the mother. This was terribly wrong."[79] She emphasized this same point to me: "I felt incredibly sorry for the families, I felt very strongly that they needed to be told as often as possible they weren't responsible."[80]

Instead, Frith and her colleagues believed that there must be a very specific fault in the brain that was responsible for "derailing" mental development. "We believed that the mind is not a big bowl of spaghetti tangles, but more like a building with different floors and rooms," she told an interviewer. "In other words, we began to think of the mind as developing in different ways for different cognitive capacities. This brought us closer to thinking about the brain basis of cognitive functions. It was the phenomenon of autism that encouraged us to think in this way. We found that autistic children had both stark deficits in some cognitive components, and outstanding talents in others. For instance, like normally developing children, they had the ability to form associations and to learn by rote. At the same time, they were extremely poor at finding meaning and at reciprocating social overtures."[81]

Frith said the experiments she carried out on perception and memory were some of the first applications of information processing theory to autism. "Hermelin and O'Connor had the brilliant insight to compare and contrast autistic children with learning-disabled children who did not have a specific diagnosis, and with younger normally developing children who were matched in terms of mental age on a variety of cognitive functions. This approach is now standard in the study of developmental delays."[82]

Frith recalled that there was a great deal of pressure, at that time in London, to conduct intervention-based, rather than cognitive, approaches—an emphasis heightened by the visits of prominent educationalists like Eric Schopler.[83] At around this time, in the late 1960s, behavior modification was making its first appearance on the scene in the UK. Now called ABA, it was then referred to as Skinnerian conditioning.

"The Maudsley Hospital was one of the places they tried it and quite successfully," Frith told me. "I was really quite impressed—but also horrified. Did the ends justify the means? It seemed very strict. There was a lot of shouting to get a child to do something at all costs. It appeared to be brutal and without any refinement. But it seemed promising at the time. Children could be prevented from doing really destructive things—especially self-injury—which were extremely distressing."[84]

One of the behaviorists working at the Maudsley who both impressed and horrified Frith was Dr. Irene Kassorla. Today, Kassorla is much better known as a glamorous Los Angeles psychologist dubbed the "shrink to the stars" because of her prominent Hollywood patients and she appears regularly as herself on the soap opera, *General Hospital*. She began working with autistic children at the Maudsley in 1968 and the BBC made a TV documentary called *The broken bridge* about two autistic children, Philip Morrall and Iris Faith, treated by Kassorla. It is believed to be one of the first programs ever shown about autism on British television—although it frequently referred to the children as psychotic. Kassorla had already published a paper in 1965 and she also featured in the unflattering *Life* magazine article a couple of years later about Lovaas's work, "Screams, slaps and love" (see p. 130).

★ ★ ★

Pseudo-scientific approaches to autism continued to emerge during the 1970s.

Nikolaas Tinbergen, the Dutch ethologist who shared the 1973 Nobel Prize in Physiology or Medicine with Karl von Frisch and Konrad Lorenz, misguidedly turned his attention to autism—and indeed devoted his Nobel acceptance lecture on December 12 that year to the disorder, following much of the thinking of "holding therapy." He declared that most experts in autism believed that it was due either to a genetic defect or to congenital factors, for instance, brain damage caused by a difficult birth.

> Some of the specialists are certainly emphatic in their assertion that autism is "not caused by the personalities of the parents, nor by their child-rearing practices." If this were true, the outlook for a real cure for such children would of course be bleak. . . . But there are also a few experts who are inclined to ascribe at least some cases of autism to damaging environmental causes—either traumatizing events in early childhood, or a sustained failure in the parent–infant interaction. If this were even partially correct, the prospect for a real cure would be brighter.[85]

Tinbergen went on to speak about the therapy he and his wife, Elizabeth, had recently introduced to help autistic children, which involved "cautiously touching the child's hand with one's own" and "by the continuation of contact, by touch and by indirect vocalization," to "begin to cement a bond." He referred to this approach with severely autistic children as "taming procedure" and said he had succeeded in "drawing them out of their shells." He claimed that the Australian therapist, Helen Clancy, had been treating autistic children in a similar way, using a form of operant conditioning for speeding up the child's

response to a change in the mother's behavior. "In other words, she tries to elicit a mutual emotional bond between mother and child, and refrains, at least at first, from the piecemeal teaching of particular skills."[86]

Tinbergen claimed that many young psychiatrists "are sympathetic to our views, or even share them and begin to act on them."[87] He also wrote a book on this subject, which received an extremely critical review from Uta Frith.[88]

One of Italy's leading autism authorities, the Siena-based Professor Michele

**Figure 51**  Michele Zappella     Zappella, worked with Tinbergen in the

late 1970s. He later rejected Tinbergen's approach to autism and holding therapy, but at the time he was convinced: "His idea was that you
had to relate very cautiously to autistic children," Zappella told me. "When
I came to study holding therapy, I realized that what was happening
was that the mother was interacting with the child. The child initially
reacted with rage but then he or she calmed down. The second part of
the session was happy play. In a short period of time, I changed this
approach and I introduced a method which was essentially based on
physical play, which was a different kind of intense interaction, but
without rage. I found that physical play was very useful in changing
autistic behavior. I also found there were rapid improvements in
children with Tourette's syndrome using this approach."[89]

Zappella described this approach as "a very atypical one, compared
to other methods. Intervention is usually seen either in terms of
intended structuring or in terms of intense conditioning. These are two
very different approaches. Structuring is very important for autistic
children, in my experience, especially the severe ones. You should
certainly motivate the child, but not through conditioning."[90]

Holding therapy itself was introduced by, among others, Martha
Welch in the United States and then adopted in Germany by Jirina
Prekop, who still uses it to this day, calling it *Festhaltetherapie* and
insisting that autism is simply an inability to love.

Claire Sainsbury, a well-known writer with Asperger's syndrome, has
described holding therapy as "sensory rape." Another autistic writer,
Therese Jolliffe, actually underwent the therapy. She said: "To me, the
suffering was terrible and it achieved nothing."[91]

There is, indeed, no scientific evidence to show that holding therapy
is effective. The most extreme form today can be found in France—in
the form of *le packing* (see p. 105).

Another spurious approach to autism—which took almost as firm a
grip for a while as holding therapy in some parts of the world—was
Doman–Delacato. In 1974, Carl Delacato published a book, *The ultimate stranger: The autistic child*, in which he expounded his view that the
cause of autism lay in a specific brain injury and recommended treatment by neurological rehabilitation using sensory integration therapy,
taking advantage of the brain's natural plasticity and the ability to
create new learning connections via new neural pathways.[92] The concept
of neural plasticity is a valid and important one, but the therapies which
Delacato, his son David, and a colleague, Glenn Doman, introduced to
"repair" the brain injury—and what proponents claim are the associated

sensory abnormalities—have not been rigorously tested in scientific trials. The major virtue of Delacato's writings was his rejection of the psychoanalytical approach to autism.

⋆ ⋆ ⋆

Amid the burgeoning, and increasingly solid research—and the sometimes decidedly misguided approaches—there were a number of positive stories to tell around the world on other fronts. One of these was certainly the opening of Britain's—and Europe's—first autism-specific residential school, Somerset Court, in Brent Knoll, southwest England, in 1974, although, as we have seen (see chapter 4), the Sybil Elgar School in Ealing, West London, had a number of boarders as early as the 1960s.

Among the key players in the Somerset Court operation was Gerald de Groot. "Our children were coming up to 14 or 15 and we realized that they were going to regress if they did not have somewhere else to go," De Groot told me. "The idea we had was for a center for autistic adults."[93] The majority wanted Sybil Elgar to run. She agreed, but on the understanding that it would be somewhere in the West Country, in southwestern England. De Groot told me this was because Elgar's husband had been transferred there by the company for which he worked, British Rail.

"We spent around 18 months traveling up and down from London looking for suitable premises. That was before the M4 motorway was joined to the M5 and the journey took ages," de Groot told me. "The building we eventually chose was owned by a millionaire suitably named Cashman who hated the house. We bought it for a bargain price. The parents lent money interest-free. I keep reminding people that Somerset Court is perhaps the only place bought by parents with their own money. I then negotiated a sale to the National Autistic Society."[94]

Somerset Court opened its doors in 1974. Within weeks of Sybil Elgar's retirement as head in 1979 and her replacement by Bob Reynolds, it was turned into a 52-week residential facility, de Groot told me. "In a way, Bob saved Somerset Court. He set up a proper organization with a qualified staff and it has never looked back."[95]

Another parent, the actor, David Tomlinson (see chapter 4), was also fulsome in his praise of Reynolds. In his autobiography, he described him as "a worthy successor" to Sybil Elgar.[96]

Meanwhile, new legislation was enacted in the UK in 1975 which opened up education to all children, regardless of disability. Expectations had changed and appropriate curricula began to be developed for children then called "subnormal" who had previously been denied education. At around this time, Margaret Walker and her colleagues developed a multimodal communication system called Makaton which used signs and symbols together with normal speech to assist communication in people with learning difficulties.

Despite its later huge significance in the UK and abroad, Britain's National Autistic Society was not relevant to the majority of people working in the learning disabilities field in the 1970s. Hugh Morgan OBE, now chief executive of Autism Cymru, Wales's National Charity for Autism, was working in long-stay hospitals in Oxfordshire, North Wales, and Wiltshire during this period. "Through [the actor] Brian Rix's leadership and profile, we tended to take notice of Mencap, and I recall specifically a training film produced by Mencap which was shown to hospital staff at Bradwell Grove back in 1975." Morgan told me. "On the ground, we did not know about the existence of the NAS, which looking back and with the benefit of hindsight is somewhat ironic as probably around half of the 66 adults I worked with on a locked long-stay ward would today be diagnosed as autistic."[97]

Much was happening elsewhere in the field of autism education around the world, as well. Maggie Golding had left London for Northern Rhodesia—soon to become Zambia—to start married life. Two years later, she and her husband moved again to South Africa and it was there, in 1969, that she received a letter from Dr. Vera Buhrmann, a child psychiatrist and Jungian analyst, also living in Cape Town.

"She had read the one and only paper I had written where I compared children with autism in the classroom to normally developing children," Golding recalled in her talk to the World Autism Congress in Cape Town in 2006.

> Dr. Buhrmann had a small group of children with autism as patients at the Red Cross Children's Hospital and she and the parents hoped to set up a school. The letter had traveled from Cape Town to London, from London to Zambia and from Zambia to Cape Town where it finally reached me. The inevitable happened and the first school for children with autism in South Africa, which developed into the present Vera and Alpha Schools, opened in Cape Town in 1970 with myself as its principal.[98]

Golding said the story of the development of education for learners with autism during apartheid in South Africa was a strange and challenging one. Initially as a private school run by the Cape Town Autistic Society, we took children of all races referred from the Red Cross Children's Hospital. . . . In those days of racial segregation, we were aware that this was a situation which was not secure. However, the change came from an unexpected source. In those days, every race group had its own department of education and the parents of learners from the Cape Coloured community and one teacher of the same racial group decided that they should apply for a subsidy to the Department of Coloured Affairs. While ensuring that teachers' salaries were paid. this meant a separate school. Even a sympathetic Minister of National Education could not overrule this, as he had oversight only over white schools. . . . In the end, we had to respect the parents' wishes and the two schools worked as sister schools until South Africa became a rainbow nation."[99]

Meanwhile, in the United States, President Gerald Ford signed the Disabilities Act on October 6, 1975. Reporting the news with great excitement in its newsletter, *The Advocate*, the National Society for Autistic Children (later to become the Autism Society of America) declared: "As expected, autism is specifically included in the definition. In brief, we are definitely in!"[100]

On a more sombre note, the same edition of *The Advocate* informed its readers of the death of the teaching pioneer, Dr. Carl Fenichel (see chapter 2), on September 25, 1975, at the age of 69: "He did what his peers said could not be done: he learned how to break through the barrier of autism, find the child inside and lead him out."[101]

# 7

# Definition, Diagnosis, and Assessment

## *The History of the Tool*

Ever since Leo Kanner first identified the syndrome he called early infantile autism in 1943, controversy has raged among professionals over the precise nature of the condition. In general, clinicians have appeared to diagnose children according to those aspects of the disorder which they consider important or in which they have a particular knowledge or skill.

In 1943, as we have seen, Kanner declared that early infantile autism "differs. markedly and uniquely from anything reported so far." In fact, however, he did not attempt to specify strictly defined diagnostic criteria for his syndrome, but rather presented meticulously and admirably detailed case histories of eight boys and three girls, noting the following characteristic features:

- inability to relate to people, including members of the child's own family, from the beginning of life;
- failure to develop speech or—in those children who did speak—abnormal, largely non-communicative use of language (he observed pronoun reversal in all eight children who could speak and echolalia, obsessive questioning, and ritualistic use of language in several of the children);
- abnormal responses to environmental objects and events, such as food, loud noises and moving objects, which Kanner saw as reflecting an anxiously obsessive desire for the maintenance of sameness, which led to a limitation in the variety of spontaneous activity;
- good cognitive potential with excellent rote memory; and, finally, good fine muscle coordination but occasionally clumsiness in gait.

Progress in documenting and understanding autism did not follow smoothly in the years following the publication of Kanner's first paper. In 1965 Kanner himself complained of two related trends in child psychiatry: some child psychiatrists did not accept that autism was a distinctive syndrome, and suggested it was fruitless to draw sharp dividing boundaries between autism and other types of atypical development, while other professionals accepted that autism was a syndrome, but applied this fashionable diagnosis far too widely.

Lorna Wing has also pointed out that there was another trap into which a number of professionals fell: interpreting Kanner's summary of the features of his syndrome far too narrowly, so that autism would not be diagnosed unless the child showed no sign of awareness of other people, despite the fact that none of Kanner's own cases was this severely impaired.[1]

There were other confusions as we have seen. Lauretta Bender used the term "childhood schizophrenia" from 1947 onwards, and it was adopted by child psychiatrists and psychoanalysts around the world until at least the 1960s. Some of the stereotypes about autism and schizophrenia can be traced back to DSM-I (1952). It specifically claimed that the primary manifestation of childhood schizophrenia was autism:

> Here will be classified those schizophrenic reactions occurring before puberty. The clinical picture may differ from schizophrenic reactions occurring in other age periods because of the immaturity and plasticity of the patient at the time of onset of the reaction. Psychotic reactions in children, manifesting primarily autism, will be classified here. Special symptomatology may be added to the diagnosis as manifestations.[2]

Although Israel Kolvin and colleague's pioneering 1971 paper (see chapter 6) appeared to disprove the long-held notion that autism was "the earliest form of schizophrenia," the study was not universally accepted and research continued into the 1980s into the differences between the two conditions. In 1984, a study at UCLA reported three case histories of children who originally had many of the features of autism (aloofness, lack of eye contact, echolalia, resistance to change, ritualistic behavior, peculiar attachments to objects, and stereotypical movements) but later developed characteristics of schizophrenia, including hallucinations, delusions, altered perception, and illogical speech.[3]

In contrast, a 1986 study led by Judith Rumsey at the National Institute of Mental Health in Bethesda, Maryland, tested 14 adults with documented childhood histories of autism and 14 adults with schizophrenia. They found that, while some symptoms overlapped, several fundamental

166

features—such as the autistic subjects' "poverty" of language and the schizophrenic subjects' "thought derailment" and illogicality—were not common to both groups. All of the adult subjects who had been diagnosed as autistic in childhood still met the criteria for autism and none met the criteria for schizophrenia.[4]

Nevertheless, a year later, in 1987, Dr. Fred Volkmar, at Yale University's Child Study Center, declared: "There is no reason to suspect that having autism acts to *protect* an individual from schizophrenia—i.e., at least some autistic people might be expected to suffer from a superimposed schizophrenic illness."[5]

The Polish-born Freudian psychoanalyst, Dr. Beate Rank, who emigrated to the United States, referred to "atypical ego development" and "atypical autism" in 1949 and this, again, became common usage. In 1952, the Hungarian-born psychoanalyst, Margaret Mahler, who was preoccupied with mother–child pathology, introduced the diagnostic term "symbiotic psychosis." Four years later, Dr. Stanislav Szurek was writing: "We are beginning to consider it clinically fruitless, or even unnecessary, to draw any sharp dividing lines between a condition that one could call psychoneurotic and another that one could call psychosis, autism, atypical development; or schizophrenia."[6]

In 1949, the World Health Organization published ICD-6, the sixth revision of the *International statistical classification of diseases,* which included a section on mental disorders for the first time. Three years later, the American Psychiatric Association published DSM-I, the first edition of the *Diagnostic and statistical manual of mental disorders.* Both DSM-I and DSM-II (published in 1968) reflected the predominant psychodynamic sprit governing psychiatry at the time, although they also included biological perspectives and concepts from Emil Kraepelin's system of classification. Symptoms were not specified in detail for specific disorders. Many were seen as reflections of broad underlying conflicts or maladaptive reactions to life problems, rooted in a distinction between neurosis and psychosis. Meanwhile, astonishingly, ICD-7, published in 1958 and still in use in the 1960s, referred to terms like "idiocy" and "imbecility" as official diagnoses.

In 1956, Leo Kanner and his colleague, Leon Eisenberg, discussed Kanner's original conception of autism and the five features he considered to be diagnostic. These were:

• a profound lack of affective contact with other people;
• an anxiously obsessive desire for the preservation of sameness in the child's routines and environment;

- a fascination for objects, which are handled with skill in fine motor movements;
- mutism or a kind of language which does not seem intended for interpersonal communication; and
- good cognitive potential shown in feats of memory or skills on performance tests.

Kanner also emphasized the importance of onset from birth or before 30 months. In this 1956 paper, Kanner and Eisenberg modified the diagnostic criteria by selecting two as essential. These were: a profound lack of affective contact and repetitive, ritualistic behavior, which must be of an elaborate kind. They considered that, if these two features were present, the rest of the typical clinical picture would also be found. As we have seen (see chapter 2), it remains puzzling that they decided to drop the original language abnormality criterion. More precisely, as they noted in the 1956 paper, they considered that the language peculiarities could be seen "as derivates of the basic disturbance in human relatedness."[7]

In the 1950s, some professionals continued to insist on what they considered to be similarities between autism and childhood schizophrenia. In 1961, a group of British experts formed a working party under the chairmanship of Dr. Mildred Creak, a child psychiatrist at Great Ormond Street Children's Hospital in London. The aim of the working party was to try and get to grips with the problem of definition of this peculiar syndrome. The terminology was still confused. Creak called the condition "the schizophrenic syndrome in childhood"— although she also used the terms "childhood psychosis" and "infantile autism" in the titles of other writings.

The British working party proposed nine points for the diagnosis of "childhood schizophrenia" (including autism). They are:

1 gross and sustained impairment of emotional relationships with people;
2 apparent unawareness of his own personal identity to a degree inappropriate to his age;
3 pathological preoccupation with particular objects or certain characteristics of them, without regard to their accepted functions;
4 sustained resistance to change in the environment and a striving to maintain or restore sameness;
5 abnormal perceptual experience (in the absence of discernible organic abnormality);

6   acute, excessive and seemingly illogical anxiety as a frequent phenomenon;
7   speech either lost, or never acquired, or showing failure to develop beyond a level appropriate to an earlier age;
8   distortion in motility patterns;
9   a background of serious retardation in which islets of normal, near normal, or exceptional intellectual function or skill may appear.

One of the members of the historic Creak Committee, the Scottish psychiatrist, Dr. Fred Stone, told me: "I was very proud of one contribution I made to the discussion, which I had great difficulty putting across. I said: 'We don't know enough about early brain function to understand what is going wrong. But I do understand one thing: the child has found, by trial and error, a way of persisting in a state of sameness, because it is only where there is sameness that these children can begin to feel more relaxed.' I tried to put across this notion that, although there is such a diffuse picture of clinical signs, the child's brain devises a way of maintaining sameness."[8]

Significantly, one of the Creak Committee's nine points reinstates the criterion which Kanner and Eisenberg dropped five years earlier, in 1956: abnormalities of language. The committee also recognized the children's impaired intellectual functioning, unlike Kanner. It is also telling that the committee made no reference to the parents of autistic children as a possible factor in the diagnosis or etiology of the disorder. This is surprising, perhaps, given the prevailing psychoanalytical climate and the fact that at least two members of the committee—Fred Stone and Gerald O'Gorman—were psychoanalytically oriented.

Diagnostic confusion impeded research, because the inconsistent and contradictory use of diagnostic terms made it difficult to interpret studies. Some investigators proposed a distinction between "primary" and "secondary" autism, depending on whether associated medical conditions—for example congenital rubella—could be demonstrated, whereas others continued to emphasize possible psychogenic etiologies. It also became clear that many behaviors commonly observed in autism—for instance, stereotypies—were also present in mentally retarded, non-autistic individuals, which suggested that, at least for purposes of definition, such behaviors could not be considered unique to autism.

Psychological evaluation of children has traditionally involved a battery of tests designed to assess functioning in a variety of areas. These tests assess the child's social maturation, intellectual abilities, expressive and receptive language, physical development and developmental milestones, family intervention and parental behavior, and emotional responses. For disorders like autism, for which there is still no physical or biological marker, assessment and diagnosis generally depend on determining the presence of behavioral characteristics associated with the disorder.

As early as 1959, C. G. Polan and B. L. Spencer devised a 30-item inventory designed to allow the respondent to note whether a child exhibited certain deviant characteristics which, the writers believed, were indicative of autism. The five symptom categories within the checklist were:

- social detachment;
- language deviance;
- disintegrative motor activities;
- obsessiveness and disruptive nervousness; and
- family nervousness.

This questionnaire served as the prototype for similar inventories that followed.[9]

Key research by Neil O'Connor and Beate Hermelin and by Michael Rutter in London in the 1960s demonstrated that autistic individuals could be tested. In contrast to Kanner's surprising insistence that autistic youngsters were endowed with normal cognitive abilities, Rutter and Lockyer showed in 1967 that autism and mental retardation frequently co-occurred.[10]

In 1964, Bernard Rimland devised a Diagnostic Checklist for Behaviour-Disturbed Children (Form E-1)—a questionnaire for parents about their child's behavior and development. He later revised the form to include questions applying to a child five years and older. The checklist contains 80 questions about the child's birth history, social responsiveness, speech, and other aspects. Scoring consisted of a plus for each response consistent with a diagnosis of autism and a minus for each response indicating behavior not characteristic of autism. The aim was to differentiate Kanner's 1943 classical autism from the more diverse population of youngsters considered to be "autistic-like."

In 1966, the American child psychiatrist, Dr. Bertram Ruttenberg, designed the Behaviour Rating Instrument for Autistic and Atypical Children (BRIAAC). Unlike Rimland's E-2 form, the BRIAAC constructed a developmental scale for describing a child's current behaviors during the clinical evaluation. It consisted of eight sub-scales.

Observations of autistic children enrolled in a day-care program provided the content base for preparing the items. When Donald Cohen used BRIAAC in 1978 to study 27 children who had been categorized variously as having primary childhood autism, secondary autism, aphasia, psychoses, and mental retardation, the composite scores failed to differentiate autistic children from the other disabled groups. However, teachers and therapists did continue to use the instrument to formulate goals and to predict future developmental levels for "atypical" children.

As we have seen (see chapter 4), the British epidemiologist, Victor Lotter, based at the Medical Research Council Social Psychiatry Unit at the London Institute of Psychiatry, published the first papers, in 1966 and 1967, concerning prevalence in a complete, large population of children of all levels of intelligence living in a defined geographical area (the former English county of Middlesex).[11] At about the same time, but independently, Birte Hoeg Brask was identifying children with "childhood psychosis" in touch with psychiatric and mental retardation services in Aarhus, Denmark. Both studies came up with a prevalence of around 4.5 per 10,000.[12]

**Figure 52** Darold Treffert

Across the Atlantic, Dr. Darold Treffert was also conducting an important early state-wide, epidemiological study in Wisconsin.[13] Treffert, a charming, bespectacled man, told me that he had been prompted to initiate his study by reading Bernard Rimland's writings vociferously condemning the unfairness of the "refrigerator mother" theory.

"The media were still describing autism as an emotional disorder. I looked at the mothers in my unit in Winnebago and they looked the same as any mothers to me. So I thought of doing a state-wide study in looking at the mothers of autistic kids in terms of their educational levels and medical history. I examined 270 cases between 1962 and 1967. The children were actually diagnosed with childhood schizophrenia—we still weren't actually using the diagnostic term 'autism' at that point. I divided the children into three groups: those with classic Kanner autism, those who were probably psychotic but not autistic, and a third group who had with a degree of 'organicity' [some known medical condition]."

171

"I found that the mothers of autistic children were no different from those of other developmentally disabled kids. But to my surprise, it turns out that the educational levels of the mothers and fathers were higher. Kanner had described this phenomenon, but I thought this was because his sample had been biased."[14]

Treffert found a prevalence rate of about 4.5 per 10,000 in his study, which was published in 1970. "That was roughly the same as Victor Lotter's study. The only difference was that only 25% of my sample had classic infantile autism," Treffert said.[15]

In 1969, Helen Clancy, Alan Dugdale, and John Rendle-Short enlarged the 1961 Creak Committee's nine diagnostic points to 14 major categories, developing a 54-item questionnaire to identify children manifesting symptoms of early childhood autism. Based on parental responses, the researchers reported that 25 autistic children could be distinguished from 32 normal ones, 25 mentally retarded, 25 deaf, and 15 with cerebral palsy. No attempt was made in this study to match the groups for either mental or chronological age. The researchers concluded that autism was an ill-defined cluster of behaviors which might exist even among normal children and that age was an important parameter in the evaluation of these atypical children.[16]

In 1971, Marian DeMyer, of the University of Indiana, led a study comparing five diagnostic systems designed to differentiate infantile autism and early childhood schizophrenia. In the categorical system designed by DeMyer with her colleague, Don Churchill, disorders were divided up into early schizophrenia, primary autism, secondary autism, and non-psychotic subnormal. DeMyer said that "primary autism" most resembled Bernard Rimland's concept of infantile autism as measured by his E-1 version. Under the DeMyer–Churchill system, developed throughout the 1960s, the four criteria for infantile autism were:

- emotional withdrawal from people before the age of three;
- lack of speech for communication;
- non-functional, repetitive use of objects; and
- failure to engage in role play alone or with other children.

In order to be diagnosed as autistic, a child had to manifest all of these four criteria.[17]

Interestingly, nearly a decade before Lorna Wing's introduction of an autistic spectrum, DeMyer felt that, if a such a child had perceptual-motor performances which were approximate to his chronological age

172

or some which were markedly above other aspects of his performance, then that child should be classified as having primary or "higher-functioning" autism. DeMyer does not seem to have been aware of Hans Asperger's work at this point in 1971.

DeMyer–Churchill's criteria for diagnosing early childhood schizophrenia were:

- islands of more normal relatedness or emotional dependency in a background of emotional withdrawal and flat affect;
- some speech for communication with speech abnormalities such as echolalia, stereotypy, dysemphasis, bizarre fantasies and failure to answer questions.[18]

In a paper published in 1978, Michael Rutter usefully documented the chaos that reigned for some years after Kanner's 1943 report, with various terms—infantile autism, childhood psychosis, childhood schizophrenia—being applied inconsistently to children who had some or all of the clinical features of Kanner's early cases.[19] Rutter discussed the question of how far autism could be regarded as a syndrome and how it related to other conditions and then suggested four criteria for defining childhood autism. These were:

- impaired social development which has a number of special characteristics out of keeping with the child's intellectual level;
- delayed and deviant language development which also has certain defined features and is out of keeping with the child's intellectual level;
- "insistence on sameness" as shown by stereotyped play patterns, abnormal preoccupations, or resistance to change; and
- onset before 30 months.

Rutter provided many examples of the above behaviors, based on his own research and clinical experience and on Kanner's descriptions. Unlike Kanner, who made a clear distinction between intellectual retardation and autism, Rutter argued that these were not mutually exclusive diagnoses. Using conventional IQ tests to classify children, it was found that most children who fitted the criteria of autism were also intellectually retarded.[20]

In fact, as Rutter told me, his four criteria for autism had derived from a systematic study he had conducted with Linda Lockyer in the

1960s.[21] They were formalized at the International Symposium on Autism in St. Gallen, Switzerland, in July 1976, which in turn gave rise to a book he edited with Eric Schopler two years later.[22] Rutter said there was a serious need for criteria "because diagnostic confusion was the order of the day at that time."[23]

In the 1978 paper, Rutter noted that his four diagnostic criteria left many unresolved issues, in particular the question of whether there were distinct subtypes of autism, and how to classify children who showed some but not all of the features of autism. However, on the basis of a review of research, he made a strong case for supporting the proposed criteria as the best available for defining the syndrome of autism in a valid and meaningful way. His diagnostic criteria have been widely adopted and formed the basis for the third edition of the *Diagnostic and statistical manual of mental disorders* (DSM-III) published in 1980, and revised as DSM-III-R in 1987.[24]

In a significant and influential observation for educationalists, Rutter also pointed out that it was not helpful to adopt a rigid response to diagnostic labels which assumed that, because a child was diagnosed as autistic, the only suitable educational placement was in a unit for autistic children. He argued for a flexible approach: it was important, he said, to consider the level and pattern of handicaps when deciding educational placement: some children may do well in a unit for language-impaired or mentally handicapped children or, with appropriate support, in a normal school.[25]

In 1978, Lorna Wing and Judith Gould introduced their Handicap, Behaviour and Skills (HBS) Schedule—one of the first attempts to develop a systematic method of collecting and recording information on development and behavior needed for diagnosis (rather than one based solely on questionnaires or clinical impressions). The following year they published their landmark Camberwell study and introduced the concept of the "autistic spectrum," broadening the definition of autism considerably. They studied children in the former London borough of Camberwell who were known to have any kind of special educational need. They chose to limit their study to this group because Lotter had found that the children he diagnosed as autistic were of this kind. From among this group, they selected for special study all those with an IQ of under 50, or who had any of the features of autism, or both of these criteria. They identified all children who were impaired in their capacity for reciprocal social interaction and found that this kind of abnormality of social interaction was closely associated with impairment of communication and imagination, the latter resulting in a narrow, repetitive pattern of activities. They referred to this as the Triad of Impairments.[26]

Wing and Gould found that there were many more children who had the Triad but who did not precisely fit Kanner's descriptions of his syndrome. The important point, as Wing has written, was that

> there were no clear-cut borderlines between typical autism, atypical autism and other manifestations of the Triad. Many children with the Triad were severely, even profoundly mentally retarded but others were in the normal range of intelligence. Some of the latter fitted Asperger's description of his syndrome.[27]

Wing noted that the real problem for any system of diagnosis was

> the lack of any clear boundaries between "classic autism"—whichever of the existing definitions is used—and the rest of the autistic spectrum. All those with the Triad of Social Impairments share the features that are regarded by all systems as crucial to autism, the only differences being the ways in which the features are manifested. For example, most workers would classify insistence on doing nothing but lining up toy cars in a precise sequence as an elaborate repetitive routine, but some would not recognise insistence on verbally retailing facts about cars, regardless of the social situation, as another manifestation of the same phenomenon.[28]

Wing said there was still no answer to the issue of whether there was any value in defining a particular "core autism," as distinct from the rest of the continuum. Further research was needed, she said, to define subgroups of the spectrum that had some external validity apart from aspects of their observable behavior.

> It is possible that Kanner's criteria happen to be found mainly in those who are mildly to moderately retarded and aged between 4 and 12 years of age, not because the criteria define a separate syndrome but because the level of cognitive ability determines the way in which the triad of social impairments is manifested. All those with the Triad share a common need for a structured and organised daily programme to help them cope with the demands of life. . . . Considering the wide variety of possible behavioural manifestations of the Triad of Impairments and the changes over time, it is not surprising that there is difficulty in achieving consistency in diagnosis among workers in different areas.[29]

In 1979, the World Health Organization finally recognized autism officially for the first time when it published ICD-9. It referred to "infantile autism" (Kanner's autism) and explicitly excluded childhood schizophrenia. Interestingly, ICD-9 also refers to the condition described by Hans Asperger—although he is not named. It appears under the new category of "Other specified pervasive developmental disorders" and is defined as follows:

> A childhood disorder predominately affecting boys and similar to autism. . . . It is characterised by severe, sustained, clinically significant impairment of social interaction, and restricted repetitive and stereotyped patterns of behaviour. In contrast to autism, there are no clinically significant delays in language or cognitive development.[30]

Despite the rapid rise in research, when Dr. Betty Jo Freeman joined the Division of Child Psychiatry at the University of California, Los Angeles, in the late 1970s, there was still no objective way to document and compare specific behavioral symptoms in autistic children. Together with her UCLA colleague, Ed Ritvo, she developed observational methods and statistical models which resulted in the publication of the Behavioral Observation Scale (BOS) in 1980.[31] This scale was widely accepted as a tool both for diagnosis and for rating changes in subjects due to educational and medical interventions, and is often cited in the literature. That same year, Freeman and Ritvo established the Registry for Genetic Studies in Autism at ULCA to test the hypothesis—raised by the Susan Folstein–Michael Rutter 1977 twin study—that genetic factors were etiologically significant in autism.

Also on the West Coast, and at around this same time, the Autism Behavior Checklist (ABC) was being developed at Portland State University in Oregon by David Krug—the father of a boy with autism—and his colleagues.[32] Published in 1980, it was a component of a broader tool, the Autism Screening Instrument for Educational Planning (ASIEP), which they had published two years earlier. The ABC is designed to be completed independently by a parent or a teacher familiar with the child who then returns it to a trained professional for scoring and interpretation. Although it is primarily designed to identify children with autism within a population of school-age children with severe disabilities, the ABC has been used with children as young as 3 years of age. The ABC has 57 questions divided into five categories:

1   sensory;
2   relating;

3  body and object use;
4  language; and
5  social and self-help.

Meanwhile, on the East Coast, Eric Schopler and his TEACCH colleague at Chapel Hill, Robert Reichler, were developing the Childhood Autism Rating Scale (CARS). Just like the BOS, CARS was designed to help to differentiate children with autism from those with other developmental disorders and mental retardation. It is the most widely used standardized instrument specifically designed to aid in the diagnosis of autism for use with children as young as 2 years of age.

When work began on CARS in the early 1970s, it incorporated the criteria of both Kanner's original three criteria and the Creak Committee's Nine Points. One of its inventors, Robert Reichler, told me: "We benefited enormously from research by Mike Rutter, especially the studies showing that you could test the autistic children. And we felt that, even if you couldn't test the kids, you could test the parents! Like all the best scales, it was simple."[33]

Published in 1980, the CARS was intended to be a direct observational tool used by a trained clinician. The 15 items of the CARS include:

* relationships with people;
* imitation;
* affect;
* use of body;
* relation to non-human objects;
* verbal communication;
* non-verbal communication;
* intellectual functioning; and
* the clinician's general impression.[34]

The current director of Division TEACCH, Gary Mesibov, told me: "Eric developed the CARS to demystify autism, to remove it from the shrouds of psychoanalysis. It was based on all the prevailing definitions of autism, including Leo Kanner's and the Creak Committee's Nine Points. Eric and Bob felt strongly that these were objective criteria which anyone could be trained in. But I don't think they realized that CARS would become so widely used."[35]

In 1989, Mesibov suggested that the CARS was a good screening instrument for adolescents and adults, as well as children. However, since the mean age of the group in this study was only 15.9 years, it failed to demonstrate the ability of the CARS to diagnosis autism in adults. The CARS has been used with adults in clinical settings, but researchers have yet to verify its diagnostic ability with this population.

At the same time as they were working on the CARS as a diagnostic tool, Schopler and Reichler were also developing the Psychoeducational Profile (PEP) for assessment purposes. The PEP assesses skills and behaviors of children with autism and graphically represents uneven development, emerging skills, and autistic behavioral characteristics, evaluating their learning difficulties and providing data which can be used to plan behavioral interventions and educational programs.

First published in 1980, it was revised by Schopler and Reichler in 1990 and, like the CARS, is now used by educationalists in schools all over the world. "The idea was to look at skills acquired developmentally," Reichler told me. "We carried out a systematic, scientific assessment of both normal and autistic children and we also consulted the parents. The idea that there was a scattered pattern of abilities made a significant contribution to the field. Showing that the kids had different skills at different levels made PEP a very useful model."[36]

PEP meshed well with the CARS. As Mesibov put it to me: "Eric Schopler always made a distinction. He said there was diagnosis and assessment. If you think about autism as a group of characteristics that people have in common, within that group they all have their own individual learning styles. So diagnosis is the process of grouping, while assessment is the process of identifying unique learning styles. Eric thought you had to identify that style to teach a child effectively."[37]

In 1980, the third edition of the *Diagnostic and statistical manual of mental disorders* (DSM-III) was published by the American Psychiatric Association. More than 500 pages long, it transformed mental health, especially clinical trials and psychiatric epidemiology. For the first time, it introduced the term "pervasive developmental disorder" (PDD) for the general category of autism and related conditions. A subgroup labeled "infantile autism" was defined by five factors:

- lack of responsiveness to others;
- language absence or abnormalities;
- resistance to change or attachment to objects;
- the absence of schizophrenic features;
- onset before 30 months.

DSM-III also included categories for childhood onset (after 30 months and before 12 years) and for atypical pervasive developmental disorder.

Dr. Theodore Schapiro, one of the psychiatrists on the international task force working on DSM-III, told me that one of the main issues was "how to include autism under Axis II, rather than Axis I, which got us into trouble here in the US."[38] Many hospitals, clinics, and insurance companies require a "five-axis" DSM diagnosis of the patients who are seen. Under Axis I fall clinical disorders, including major mental disorders, as well as developmental and learning disorders, whereas Axis II includes underlying pervasive or personality conditions, as well as mental retardation.

**Figure 53**  Theodore Schapiro

DSM-III was revolutionary in many ways. Unlike its predecessors, it was based on scientific evidence. Its reliability was improved with the addition of explicit diagnostic criteria and structured interviews. The inclusion in DSM-III of the item "absence of schizophrenic features" was discussed by Cialdella and Mamelle in 1989.[39] They considered that listening attitudes, formal thought disorders (undefined by the authors), and incongruent laughing and crying were "schizophrenic features." When they excluded the children with these types of behavior, which are common in autism, the rates of autism they found in the Rhône region of France dropped by half.

In 1981, Lorna Wing coined the term "Asperger's syndrome."[40] She did not believe it was a separate condition from autism, unlike Hans Asperger himself, but rather that it lay on the autistic continuum. They discussed the matter together when Asperger visited London in the late 1970s, and agreed to differ.

Although Wing's paper brought the condition to the broader English-speaking world for the first time, Asperger's syndrome was not yet taken seriously as a diagnostic label. It did not appear, for example, in DSM-III-R—the revised form of the third edition, which was published in 1987. That manual consisted of the deliberations of a workshop on the diagnosis of autism and related disorders. The participants agreed that the essential features of autism were social impairment, delayed or deviant language (communication), and repetitive, stereotyped, or ritualistic behavior. These were the familiar features appearing in all systems of definition. The difference was the recognition—in agreement with Wing and Gould's 1979 paper—that all these features could occur in widely varying degrees of severity and in many different manifestations. For example, it was no longer felt that autism was diagnosable only if the child was (or had been) aloof and indifferent to other people. Passive acceptance of social approaches without any spontaneous initiation of contact, or active but inappropriate, one-sided approaches should also be included as forms of social impairment. This shift of emphasis would permit the inclusion of children with the most subtle, as well as those with the most obvious, features of autism.

Age of onset was considered to be difficult to establish and not to be regarded as an essential criterion. Significantly, however, the term "infantile autism" was replaced by "autistic disorder," in recognition both of the fact that some autistic disorders first appear in childhood and that, as autistic individuals matured into adulthood, the term "infantile autism" was increasingly inappropriate. It was also accepted that the diagnosis of autism or related conditions should be made independently of intelligence, etiology, or any associated conditions but that the clinical picture should be evaluated in the light of the developmental age.

DSM-III-R redefined pervasive developmental disorder with only two subtypes: autistic disorder and PDD-NOS (pervasive developmental disorder—not otherwise specified). Theodore Schapiro was involved in the revision of DSM-III: "We did a whole bunch of studies and we found that all we were doing was shifting the criteria towards autism and away from PDD," he told me.

**Figure 54** Elizabeth Newson (photo courtesy of Sutherland House)

At around this time, the early 1980s, Professor Elizabeth Newson, at the University of Nottingham's Child Development Research Unit in the UK, found there were children referred with a possible diagnosis of autism who did not seem typical in that they shared some of the features but displayed other very different behaviors and characteristics. There were also more girls affected than boys.

As Newson's colleague, Dr. Phil Christie, explained, she and her colleagues began to feel increasingly dissatisfied with the description of atypical autism and felt that it was not particularly helpful in removing the confusion that was often felt by parents and teachers who were struggling to gain greater insight into the child's behavior.

> Over time, Newson began to notice that, while these children were atypical of the clinical picture of autism or Asperger's syndrome, they were typical of each other in some very important ways. The central feature that was characteristic of all the children was "an obsessional avoidance of the ordinary demands of everyday life." This was combined with sufficient social understanding and sociability to enable the child to be "socially manipulative" in their avoidance. It was this level of social understanding, along with a capacity for imaginative play, which most strongly countered a diagnosis of autism.[41]

After several years of careful note-taking and interviews with parents, Newson felt that there was sufficient evidence to create a new syndrome or diagnostic description within the category of pervasive developmental disorders. She named this "pathological demand avoidance syndrome" (PDA) and first brought it to public attention in the 1980s. Since that time, there has been much debate between professionals as to whether this is indeed a separate condition or whether the behaviors found in PDA can be explained within other disorders such as attachment disorder or personality disorder or a female form of autism.

Lorna Wing, for one, told me: "Judy Gould and I have always seen PDA as part of the autism spectrum. The features listed by Elizabeth as typical of PDA are, in fact, scattered among those in the spectrum—the number present varying widely among the whole autism spectrum."[42] Wing added that she and Gould had collected data on this but had not got round to analyzing it.

In some other parts of the world, at this time, researchers were attempting to establish their own diagnostic criteria for autism. In Toyota, Japan, in 1983, Ishii and Takahashi published a paper in which they considered essential for a diagnosis:

- disturbed interpersonal relationships (defined by a list of clinical examples comprising nine items);
- absence or deviance in speech and language development (eight items);
- insistence on the preservation of sameness or resistance to change (six items); and

- abnormal responses to sensory stimuli or motility disturbance (10 items).

Age of onset, intelligence level, and organic etiology were not mentioned among these diagnostic criteria. The English summary did not specify how many items were needed for a diagnosis of autism, nor whether the autistic subjects were subgrouped.[43]

In 1986, Betty Jo Freeman and Ed Ritvo, at UCLA, devised the Real Life Rating Scale.[44] Ritvo told me that they had developed the scale while administering fenfluramine to assess clinical changes. "The scale was used by many other professionals in their research on medications and behavioral treatments," he said.[45]

The world's first international Asperger's syndrome conference took place in London in 1988. One of the results of this meeting was the publication of the first diagnostic criteria the following year, drawn up by Christopher Gillberg and Peter Szatmari.[46] Gillberg told me that his six criteria were "based on Hans Asperger's own descriptions—unlike the other criteria which exist." They were:

- severe impairment in reciprocal social interaction;
- all-absorbing narrow interests;
- imposition of routines and interests;
- speech and language problems;
- non-verbal communication problems; and
- motor clumsiness: poor performance on neurodevelopmental examination.

All six criteria had to be met for a confirmation of diagnosis.[47]

In 1991, Hans Asperger's 1944 paper was finally translated into English by Uta Frith[48] and the next year, the World Health Organization published ICD-10, officially recognizing Asperger's syndrome for the first time. The American Psychiatric Association followed suit when DSM-IV appeared in 1994. (Both definitions have been heavily criticized, as discussed below.) Among the essential features of autistic disorder, according to DSM-IV, were trouble interacting with others and a tendency to have narrowly focused and odd interests. Most researchers accept that these traits are the hallmarks of autism, but they also claim that this does not help a great deal when attempting to diagnose autism in children younger than the age of 2 or 3.

**Figure 55** Ami Klin

One of those involved in drawing up the section on autism in DSM-IV was Dr. Ami Klin, of the Yale Child Study Center in New Haven. "For the first time, it was based on empirical research," Klin told me. "We had 19 centers around the world and all sorts of tentative criteria. We asked clinicians—who had documented proof of experience in the field—to see their patients and lay down their criteria. There was then a complicated statistical process of evaluating which criteria were valid and which were not. Then there was a form of 'smoothing-out'—I don't know whether it was a political or a practical process because neither I nor Fred Volkmar were involved in it. The question of Asperger's syndrome was very peripheral. We had no idea that this would become such an issue, but now it needs to be addressed very seriously indeed."[49]

Diagnosis of autism remains difficult because the best early indicators involve the absence of consistent social and communication behaviors, rather than the presence of an abnormality. As Dr. Wendy Stone, of Vanderbilt University School of Medicine in Tennessee, has put it: "There could be lots of reasons you're not seeing a behavior—because it's not developing, or it could be that the child is not showing it to you at that time."[50]

With this in mind, two diagnostic tools were developed in the late 1980s—the Autism Diagnostic Interview (ADI) and the Autism Diagnostic Observation Schedule (ADOS)—which are extensively used throughout the world to this day.[51] The ADI (devised by Ann Le Couteur, Michael Rutter, and Cathy Lord)—like its revised version, ADI-R—is an interview given to parents or other care-givers about how the child acts in typical situations, in terms of social reciprocity, communication, and repetitive behaviors and also what the child was like during preschool years. The ADOS creates situations designed to elicit certain behaviors in children such as pointing or requesting something. Autistic children often fail to draw the attention of others to objects by pointing and tend not to ask for things in the same way as other children.

Among the strengths of both instruments is that they quantify separately the three domains that define autism spectrum disorders: social reciprocity, communication, and restricted, repetitive behaviors and interests. This can be very helpful in increasing parents' understanding of their children's disabilities and in setting goals. ADI relied on developmental history and ADOS on physical, activity-based assessment and they worked together.

One of those involved in setting up both tools, Dr. Ann Le Couteur—now at the University of Newcastle in the UK—told me that they were developed "as a semi-structured package with a focus underpinned by the research at the time, especially Susan Folstein and Michael Rutter's 1977 twin study. In fact, we developed them specifically for the twin and family studies at the Institute of Psychiatry in London." The two had to be used together, Le Couteur said: "No diagnostic tool should be used in isolation."[52] Le Couteur also noted that the original ADI and ADOS—published in 1989—did not cover the broader autistic phenotype.[53]

Dr. Susan Folstein confirmed that she was using a precursor to the ADI in her 1977 twin study which had been developed by Michael Rutter in a previous study together with Dr. Linda Lockyer. "I had Mike Rutter's four criteria for autism in my head. The phrase everyone was using at the time was 'Kanner's criteria, as operationalized by Rutter' [see above] and I picked the most salient features of each item," Folstein told me. "It never occurred to me that I had created the first ADI algorithm, but Cathy Lord [also involved in developing ADI and ADOS] told me I had done just that!"[54]

Rutter said he wanted to develop an instrument that was "sensitive to the unexpected." What he meant by that, as he told me, was that many measures which ended up with "yes" and "no" answers "don't end up telling you anything that wasn't in your mind to begin with. Highly structured instruments have their value, but a standardized instrument which generates descriptions will throw up new findings."[55]

Dr. Cathy Lord, now based at the University of Michigan, Ann Arbor, said: "We're working on a cognitive version of ADOS. I think we can say that, if a child gets a high score at 12 months, this should give major cause for concern. But it's a bit like high blood pressure: it doesn't mean you're going to have a stroke, but it does mean you should take some action."[56]

Not everyone is enamored of the ADI, or its revised form now commonly in use, ADI-R. At IMFAR (the International Meeting for

Autism Research) in London in May 2008—and then at the Autism Neuroscience conference, also in London, in September that same year—critics lambasted the tool for either missing many cases of autism or overdiagnosing it, but mainly for the fact that, in many parts of the world, professionals—especially those in research laboratories rather than clinics—were forced to use an expensive and "ineffective" instrument.

One leading critic is Dr. Dorothy Bishop, professor of developmental neuropsychology at the University of Oxford. "To my mind, the main problem with ADI-R [as a tool for research] is not just the financial cost (though that is certainly prohibitive for many) but also the cost in time: time for training, time for administration, and time for scoring and consensus coding," Bishop told me. "If it could be shown that there were real benefits in accuracy of diagnosis from adopting this lengthy procedure, then I'd be happy to say: 'OK, this is the best way forward and we just have to find a way to do it.' But the originators of the instrument have never demonstrated that you actually need such a long process—it is really more an article of faith with them."[57]

Bishop added: "Part of the problem is that criteria for autism keep changing, and cut-offs are entirely arbitrary. I personally think we'd be better off with a dimensional, rather than categorical, conceptualization of autism—that is, one with a measure that gave a quantitative index of level of autism symptoms on different dimensions."[58]

Bishop accepts that it is recommended practice for ADI to be combined with ADOS, but she insists that this "compounds the problem for those researchers with limited time or finances. I think there is some empirical evidence for improved diagnostic efficiency if you use both, but there are still plenty of children who come out as meeting criteria on one instrument only, and there seem no sensible guidelines as to how you then proceed, other than to seek expert clinical opinion."[59]

The bottom line, she told me, was that those devising the diagnostic instruments for autism "should be doing studies to see what is the minimum set of items you can have to get reasonable diagnostic accuracy. I doubt that [as researchers], we really need a three-hour interview for each case, but this has not been put to empirical test."[60]

Michael Rutter accepted some of the criticism: "I acknowledge that ADI-R is not a perfect instrument and is not always applied as one might wish," he told me. "But a lot of the criticism is very emotive—I don't know why. I don't feel the need to defend ADI-R and ADOS, because I accept they need improvement."[61]

185

The 1994 edition of DSM-IV underwent a text revision in 2000. Among the errors corrected in the DSM-IV-TR was a seemingly minor error—the word "and" had appeared in a checklist, instead of "or," in the original version. In fact, this was by no means as trivial a typographical mistake as it may have seemed: it resulted in a broadening of the definition of autism. The DSM-IV wording had allowed the diagnosis of PDD-NOS in the absence of social impairment. DSM-IV-TR makes it clear that PDD-NOS is, foremost, a disorder of "reciprocal social interaction that is associated with" impairments in "either verbal or non-verbal communication," and with repetitive behaviors and/or restricted interests. The 2000 text revision restored the intended, narrower definition. (Nevertheless, the guidelines for PDD-NOS in DSM-IV-TR continue to be problematic, in the opinion of many professionals, because they are vaguely worded and difficult to translate into clear definitions or explicit operational criteria. By definition, individuals with PDD-NOS present with fewer or less severe symptoms than those who have autism or Asperger's syndrome and do not meet criteria for Rett's syndrome or childhood disintegrative disorder.)

While DSM-IV and ICD-10 are used almost universally around the world, in France—as we have seen—the psychoanalytically trained professionals prefer to use the French classification, CFTMEA R-2000—the Classification française des troubles mentaux de l'enfant et de l'adolescent (French Classification of Childhood and Adolescent Mental Disorders), last revised in 2000—according to which autism is still considered a rare and severe psychosis. The terms "pervasive developmental disorder" and Asperger's syndrome were not introduced until the 2000 version and many psychiatrists in France consider the diagnosis of Asperger's syndrome to be an Anglo-American construction.

The man who devised the French classification, Dr. Roger Misès, defends it staunchly to this day. When I asked him for his response to critics' complaints that the classification was based on a psychodynamic approach, Misès said: "That's true—it is. It certainly takes those elements into account, which does not mean that I ignore the organic factors. But by 'psychodynamic,' I mean that I take account of the person, with his entire history."[62]

Denys Ribas, a Paris clinician who, although he represents the psychoanalytical tendency, has written several intelligent books on autism, stood by the French definition of the disorder as a psychosis: "Psychosis means a withdrawal from reality. No one could say that autistic individuals have an excellent relationship with reality. Clearly, people with autism are psychotic. For the Americans, in DSM-III, autism was considered an illness. But in psychiatric terms, it is reasonable to say that autism is one of the psychoses."[63]

# Screening Instruments

In the late 1980s, Professor Simon Baron-Cohen and his Cambridge team designed the CHAT (Checklist for Autism in Toddlers), intended to diagnose autism in children as young as 18 months old. The genesis of the new tool was the 1987 publication of Baron-Cohen's studies of pretend play in autism—one of the first carefully designed such studies—and, two years later, his first demonstration of a dissociation between protoimperative and protodeclarative pointing in autism (the latter requiring joint attention, the former not).[64] As Baron-Cohen told me, "since both of these behaviors are normally present by 18 months old, were absent or delayed in autism, and were plausible candidate cognitive precursors to a theory of mind, it seemed a valuable next step to see if we could use these results to create a practical screening instrument to detect autism at 18 months old on the basis of the *absence* of behaviors that should be present if a child was developing normally. The CHAT was therefore our attempt to use basic (cognitive) research in an applied way."[65]

In 1992, Baron-Cohen's team conducted a study of high-risk siblings. In it, he concluded that absence of pretend play and joint attention successfully predicted which infants would go on to receive a diagnosis of autism.[66] Four years later, he completed a population study of 16,000 toddlers which again indicated that absence of these key behaviors successfully predicted autism. (Eleven out of 12 children who lacked these behaviors at 18 months old went on to develop autism.) However, by Baron-Cohen's own admission, the population study also showed that the CHAT had a high rate of false negatives—in other words, it missed many cases.[67]

"We suspect it missed the high-functioning autism or Asperger's syndrome cases because the CHAT asks 'Has your child *ever* done x?' and therefore only detects children who have *never* done x (for example, never shown any pretence or joint attention). While this severe phenotype might be true of classic autism, it is unlikely to be true of the broader spectrum."[68]

To counter the deficits of the original CHAT, Baron-Cohen's team is now evaluating the so-called Q-CHAT which asks questions of a more dimensional (not categorical) type—for example, "How often has your child shown x?"

In 2006, researchers in the Netherlands developed the 14-Item Early Screening of Autistic Traits Questionnaire (ESAT). Children with three or more negative scores are considered to be at high risk of developing autistic spectrum disorders and are invited for further systematic psychological examinations. Interestingly, a number of Dutch researchers, like Dr. Rutger-Jan van der Gaag and Dr. Herman van Engeland, are convinced that what they call "multiple-complex developmental disorder" (MCDD) represents a distinct group within the autistic spectrum based on symptomatology, because—they claim—unlike autistic children, some MCDD children develop schizophrenia in adult life.

Dr. Sally Rogers told me: "I have certainly known higher-functioning children with ASD [autistic spectrum disorder] who develop schizophrenia later in life. I have never thought that ASD was somehow immune from schizophrenia or any other type of psychiatric disorder. I personally don't feel that one needs a special subtype to account for development of schizophrenia in ASD."[69]

One of the most detailed clinical instruments is the Diagnostic Interview for Social and Communication Disorders devised by Lorna Wing and Dr. Judith Gould (and better known under its slightly inaccurate acronym of DISCO, following a suggestion by Sweden's Christopher Gillberg). It built on Wing and Gould's own semi-structured Handicap, Behaviour, and Skills (HBS) schedule (see above). Unlike ADI, DISCO was designed to ask: what problems, advantages, and skills the individual had, rather than whether he or she had autism. It attempts to examine the person's history from infancy onwards and to trace the ways in which different aspects of development have gone right, wrong, or differently. In clinical work, the primary purpose is to facilitate an understanding of the pattern over time of the skills and impairments that underlie the overt behavior. Wing and Gould are convinced that adopting a dimensional approach to clinical description is far more helpful for prescribing how to help each individual than assigning a diagnostic category. They consider that this dimensional approach is one of the main aspects which distinguishes DISCO from other diagnostic schedules.

Gould explained the genesis of DISCO to me: "When Lorna and I set up Elliot House [the Centre for Social and Communication Disorders, a diagnostic and assessment center run under the auspices of Britain's National Autistic Society] in 1991, together with Carole Murray, we needed something which was more clinically rather than research-based for diagnosis. So we added infancy sections, repetitive play, and other aspects which emerged from the research and incorporated these into the DISCO."[70]

They realized that the HBS, which they had designed for research with children, was not detailed enough for the clinical diagnostic work of Elliot House, concerned with diagnosis of individuals of all ages. Wing and Gould therefore expanded the areas covered by the HBS to include sections on infancy, developmental domains, the Triad of Impairments, repetitive routines, emotional difficulties, and challenging behavior. The HBS schedule—renamed DISCO—was adapted to cover all ages, all levels of ability, and conditions on the borderlines of autism.

From the experience of training professionals to use the DISCO, it became clear that a separate section for recording clinical judgment was necessary. This had to be based on all the information obtained from the rest of the schedule, psychological assessment, observation, and any other sources of reliable information. This section of DISCO asks the interviewer to make a judgment concerning the quality of the social interaction, social communication, social imagination, and pattern of activities.

Gould told me that the DISCO was now on version 11 and that the model had been adopted in many parts of the world, including Japan and Singapore. "It's not set in stone. We add and modify things in the light of new research. It is a very comprehensive tool for diagnosing children and adults of any level of ability, and that's what makes it unique."[71] It can also assist in identifying conditions often associated with the autistic spectrum, such as ADHD, tics, dyspraxia, and catatonia-like disorders.

Another tool, the 3Di (Developmental, Dimensional and Diagnostic Interview), was developed in 2004 by Professor David Skuse, head of the Behavioural and Brain Sciences Unit at the Institute of Child Health, University College London. Skuse was drawn into the autism field through his work on Turner's syndrome, a rare genetic condition occurring only in females where there is a partial or complete absence of one of the two X chromosomes found in normal females. Some of the girls in the study were exhibiting what he thought were autistic traits.

# Early Diagnosis

In the late 1970s, H. N. Massie pioneered the use of home videos to observe the relations between infants who were later diagnosed with some

189

type of childhood psychosis—which for Massie included autism—and their mothers.[72] He focused mainly on the mother's behaviors and the presence of "psychotic" behaviors in the infant. He found differences with a control group in mother–infant eye contact, touch, and attachment behaviors. Later, he used home videos to examine Piagetian sensori-motor development in 14 children who were subsequently diagnosed with childhood psychosis, six of whom had a diagnosis of autism. Compared with a control group of normally developing children, the psychotic group exhibited fewer age-appropriate behaviors.[73]

The earliest that anyone has proposed a definite diagnosis of autism is in infants of just a few months old, but the research of Dr. Philip Teitelbaum at the University of Florida at Gainsville, working with his colleague, Dr. Ralph Maurer—better known for his association with the neurologist, Antonio Damasio—remains highly controversial. Teitelbaum has viewed hundreds of videotapes of infants who went on to develop autism and became convinced that it was possible to detect specific movement differences in these children at just a few months old and that these could represent a potential diagnostic measurement. In particular, he pointed to the way a child would not hold out his or her arms when tumbling over from stomach to back in a cot.[74]

One of the pioneers in the field of inter-subjectivity and autism, Dr. Colwyn Trevarthen, agrees that there is some evidence that "children who develop autism demonstrate abnormal patterns of movement at four to six months old. It is also reported that they show a general developmental delay, poor facial expression and failure to make eye contact at six months old."[75]

Trevarthen urged prudence, however:

> The particular findings of research are not always supported by experience of parents and professionals and they should be treated with caution, as not one of these features, taken individually, is unique to autism. Normal infants, too, show periods of gaze avoidance and withdrawal from intimate face-to-face communication as their motives for engagement with people and for mastery of objects change and become integrated. These early signs, then, taken alone, cannot reliably identify a child with autism, and the answer may lie in taking a more systemic approach—one that looks not only at how the child behaves, but at the whole-life situation, including the behaviour of people who live with the child.[76]

Trevarthen maintains that, in the 1970s, a revolution took place in recognition by psychologists of the innate and developing capacities of infants for communicating with the intentions, interests and emotions of other persons. . . . Biologists, paediatricians, developmental psychologists and psychiatrists and linguists reported new detailed observations, comparing the evidence in an attempt to repair decades of neglect of the communicative capacities of children before they can speak.[77]

Trevarthen told me that "it is commonly observed that first signs of any neurodevelopmental condition are disturbances in movement. I think it is important that motor processes, and their timing, set the stage for the syntax and strategies of all more elaborate developments in cognition, language and thinking (or 'theory of mind')."[78]

A 2003 study by Dr. Eric Courchesne at the University of California, San Diego, demonstrated dramatic head growth in infants who went on to develop autism.[79] Courchesne told me that his study—if replicated— could lead to a simple tape-measure diagnosis of autism.[80] Others were less optimistic. But in 2008, a multicenter team led by Dr. Lonnie Zwaigenbaum at the University of Alberta in Canada measured head circumference prospectively on a total of 761 high-risk and 400 low-risk infants from 11 sites across North America and supplemented by data from health records. They also found that infants who were later diagnosed with autism did have a more rapid rate of head growth in the first two years of life than infants who did not develop autism. They concluded that "rapid head growth may help health professionals identify infants at increase risk of autism."[81] Indeed, Zwaigenbaum told IMFAR 2008 in London: "Head circumference is one of the most consistently replicated and promising biological markers for autism," adding that roughly 20% of children with autism had a head circumference above the 97th percentile.

In 2007, Dr. Rebecca Landa at the Kennedy Krieger Institute in Baltimore published a study showing that it may now be possible to diagnose autism at the age of 1 year old. She told me: "The things we found are not so off base from the DSM: specific social abnormalities which, when you see them in a cluster, are going to signal an autism spectrum disorder.

**Figure 56** Rebecca Landa

These would include social orienting, social initiation, as well as diversity of behavior that is used for functional interaction."[82]

That same year, Dr. Sally Rogers carried out research showing that deferred imitation was impaired in autism.[83] She told me that deferred imitation had "a very privileged place in cognitive theories. I would now argue that imitation is the most important primary criterion for autism—more than almost any other symptom."[84]

**Figures 57 and 58**   Sally Rogers (left) and Sally Ozonoff

However, Rogers' MIND colleague, Dr. Sally Ozonoff, disagrees that imitation is a core deficit in autism: "In our study, we didn't find any differences at 34 months, let alone at 23 months, so I think it is a more a primitive cognitive mechanism, rather than imitation or mirroring. Babies don't spontaneously imitate at six months."[85]

Cathy Lord, at the University of Michigan, told me that there could be "signs" as early as 6 months of age. "But I think it would be difficult to determine which signs were really meaningful. It gets easier at 12 months and at 18 months we're ready to go. The only caveat is that we're ready to go with the more severe cases, but we don't know what's going on with the milder cases. After all, we can spend a lot of time with a 14-year-old asking whether he or she has Asperger's syndrome or ADHD with autistic features, so you can imagine that, with an 18-month-child, it's really hard—there's still so much room for change."[86]

Most researchers hope they will find biological or genetic markers for autism that could accurately diagnose autism at birth and would bolster the behavioral measures. In one of the latest pieces of research, Judith Miles at the University of Missouri is using three-dimensional imaging to reveal correlations in the facial features and brain structures of children with autism with a view to developing a formula for the early detection of the disorder. The facial and brain-imaging work will focus on the two ASD groups suggested by Miles, a professor of pediatrics and pathology. She claims that children with a tendency toward more physical and brain abnormalities and smaller heads have "complex autism." Only about 20% of affected children fit into this group. The other 80% are classified as having "essential autism."[87]

Dr. Wendy Stone at Vanderbilt University is developing a screening tool that she hopes will allow clinicians to check for autism in children aged 2 and possibly younger. She has identified three specific skill areas, all in the realm of social and communication skills, which appear to be deficient in autism: reciprocal or functional play, motor imitation, and joint attention.

## The Reason for the Increase in Diagnoses

As we have seen in previous chapters, the increase in prevalence of autism has been dramatic—from around 4.5 per 10,000 in Victor Lotter's 1966 study to the 2007 figure of the Centers for Disease Control and Prevention of 1 in 150. The general feeling among professionals I have spoken to around the world is that, far from there being an "epidemic" of autism, the increase in diagnoses is mostly due to the broadening of the spectrum and the improvement in diagnostic tools.

A 2008 study funded by Britain's Wellcome Trust and led by Dorothy Bishop appeared to support this theory. It revisited 38 adults, aged 15 to 31, who had been diagnosed with having developmental language disorders, but not autism, as children. Bishop and her colleagues looked at whether they now met current diagnostic criteria for autistic spectrum disorders, either through reports of their childhood behavior or on the basis of their current behavior. When reassessed by Bishop and her colleagues using current criteria, around a quarter were identified as having an autistic spectrum disorder.[88]

"Our study shows pretty direct evidence to support the theory that changes in diagnosis may contribute towards the rise in autism," said Bishop.

These were children that people were saying were not autistic in the 1980s, but when we talk to their parents now about what they were like as children, it's clear that they would be classified as autistic now. Criteria for diagnosing autism were much more stringent in the 1980s than nowadays and a child wouldn't be classed as autistic unless he or she was very severe. Now, children are being identified who have more subtle characteristics and who could in the past easily have been missed.[89]

## Autism as a Medical Condition

Dr. Mary Coleman, the pioneering New York neurologist, continues to be convinced that autism will eventually be found to consist of dozens—possibly hundreds—of different subtypes, each the result of a specific medical condition. She told me: "I'm not talking about co-morbidity. I'm talking about the basic disease which causes the autistic symptoms."[90]

**Figure 59**  Isabelle Rapin

However, the Swiss-born autism authority, Professor Isabelle Rapin—who received a lifetime achievement award at IMFAR in London in 2008—told me: "Autism is a behavioral, not a medical diagnosis. Because it is behavioral, it is dimensional and has a broad range of severity. We have cut it into slices and somehow these slices have taken on lives of their own, like Asperger's syndrome. I agree entirely with the concept of autism as a disorder of the developing brain. What I emphasize is that autism is defined behaviorally, in the same sense that dementia is behaviorally defined (on the basis of behavioral tests and/or observations) but is, of course, medically caused. There is no single cause, but many. I disagree with the idea that autism is a 'disease'—in the sense that it has one defined cause. I have always believed it reflects dysfunction of particular circuitry in the brain, whatever the biological cause of the dysfunction."[91]

Rapin added: "That does not mean that there are not groups within the syndrome. Dementia was thought for years to be either normal aging or some kind of disease, when it is entirely behaviorally defined, based on Mini-mental Status or some other measure or the family's awareness that the person cannot function in the real world. There are dozens of different types of dementia, depending on its medical cause in the individual and which parts of the central nervous system are most severely affected. I have no problem in saying that Asperger's is on the milder end of the autism spectrum in children who did not speak late. But I think that the concept that autism is not a specific disease is not widely understood, and this surprises me."[92]

Dr. David Amaral, research director the MIND Institute in Sacramento, California, and head of the Autism Phenome Project, is hoping that his work and that of his collaborators will lead to a biomedical test for at least some types of autism. But such a test is still some way off. He told me: "I think we're within a decade of doing this for some forms of autism. We used to think there might be a blood test. That's clearly not the case. Immune factors and others, when taken together, might produce indications that a person has autism. We're really interested not in the big brain itself but *why* an individual had a big brain. We now have 110 families in the Autism Phenome Project. If we looked at the big brains but also at the cytokine levels, we might find linkages—or disprove them."[93]

**Figure 60**   David Amaral

## The Controversy over Asperger's Syndrome

"What a waste of time," was how Judith Gould described the definition of Asperger's syndrome in ICD-10 and DSM-IV to me. "Hans Asperger never said you had to have normal self-help skills, adaptive behavior, and curiosity by the age of three or earlier," Gould told me. "It is more likely that, if someone is social and chatty and functioning at a higher level cognitively, he or she will be diagnosed with Asperger's. In clinical practice, professionals rarely ask whether he or she was doing all those things before the age of three."[94]

**Figure 61** Christopher Gillberg

Christopher Gillberg, who first defined Asperger's syndrome in 1989, agreed: "The DSM-IV and ICD-10 criteria are very artificial. They just say: if there is no problem with language or early development, then we call it Asperger's. I think there is a huge problem with DSM-IV: there is no good evidence that the majority of people with Asperger's syndrome have had perfectly normal development in the first three years of life. And you need very little in terms of symptoms to qualify for a diagnosis of Asperger's under DSM: you need only three symptoms. So quite a lot of people in the general population would qualify for them."[95]

ICD-10 and DSM-IV-both state that, for a diagnosis of Asperger syndrome, spoken language development must be normal. In contrast, children with high-functioning autism may have had significant language delay. But Hans Asperger's original descriptions of the condition stated that speech and language peculiarities were a key feature.

Dr. Patricia Howlin, a leading world autism authority who worked at

**Figure 62** Patricia Howlin

St George's Hospital in Tooting, South London, when my son Johnny was diagnosed there, but who is now based at London's Institute of Psychiatry, conducted a study in 2003 indicating that individuals with Asperger's syndrome did indeed have considerable language abnormalities. She is equally scathing in her criticism of the DSM-IV criteria: "One of the problems is that DSM-IV says that, if you have a diagnosis of autism, you cannot have a diagnosis of Asperger's syndrome. That is just silly," Howlin told me. "It is probably the exclusionary criteria that are problematic rather than the actual behaviors."[96]

In fact, a diagnosis of high-functioning autism and one of Asperger's syndrome can be made in the same individual at different stages of development. Occasionally, a child has been diagnosed with high-functioning autism in early childhood and this diagnosis has been changed to Asperger's syndrome when they started school. Some diagnosticians still do believe that Asperger's syndrome cannot be diagnosed before a child begins school. However, this is largely because areas such as social skills deficits may not become apparent until a child spends a lot of time in social settings.

**Figure 63**   Fred Volkmar

Dr. Fred Volkmar, of Yale University, agreed that Hans Asperger himself would not have recognized the definition of his syndrome which appears in DSM-IV, even though Volkmar himself was on the committee drafting the classification. "You have to realize that in general, at the time, there was an argument saying that you should avoid precipitous change in nomenclature and be very careful about pulling in new categories," Volkmar told me. "Another problem with Asperger's and DSM-IV, in addition to the unwillingness to accept change, is that there is probably more than a usual reluctance to accept child disorders. I often say that the trouble with those devising DSM is that they were never children themselves! I think they would prefer not to have a child section at all. The DSM criteria were—and remain—problematic. But even so, including Asperger's syndrome in DSM-IV was better than not including it."[97]

Volkmar added that Lorna Wing's coining of the term Asperger's syndrome was helpful from a research point of view. "Hans Asperger was talking about the problems the children had despite their good linguistic skills. In autism, language is not usually a strength early on. Whereas in Asperger's, you often hear it said about a child that 'he talked before he walked.' The other important point about the invention of the term 'Asperger's syndrome' is that it helps us to talk about treatment, and about the various different routes towards social disability."[98]

Debate continues to rage over whether there is any clinically valuable difference between Asperger's syndrome and high-functioning autism.

197

There have been suggestions that some individuals with Asperger's syndrome might have a stronger impulse to make friends, although their inability to do so, in many cases, could lead to severe depression. When I put this notion to one of the world's leading authorities on Asperger's syndrome, Dr. Tony Attwood, in Melbourne, Australia, he said he had seen individuals who were diagnosed with classic autism when they were younger—exhibiting major problems with communication, socialization, and play—and later progressed to a level where they were viewed as an enormous success, and saw themselves in that light, as well.

So they are happy by what they compare themselves with. But those with Asperger's syndrome who compare themselves with the neurotypical will have more depression and dejection. Quite often, therefore, those with classic autism who have progressed to high-functioning autism and success are happier, and people will see them as a success.[99]

**Figure 64**  Tony Attwood

However, Attwood added:

My view is that, if we are not careful, we are going to have an "autistic" view of autism. We are going to overfocus on the tiny details and miss the big picture. There may well be academic studies which suggest that there could be differences between the two groups on some aspects. However, I think that this is more of academic than practical interest, because when it comes to socializing, communicating, community integration, etc., there are more similarities than differences.[100]

Attwood said that, when looking at the drive for friendship in high-functioning autism and Asperger's, it also depended on the individual's personality. "Some with very limited skills are desperate to relate to others. While others who have remarkable communication and social skills choose isolation, by their character. So we must look at the personality, as much as the diagnostic expression."[101]

Sally Rogers in Sacramento agrees: "I have found variations across the board. There are many different levels on which to evaluate an individual's desire for social relations. I don't perceive people with autism as disliking social contact. They generally like to be interacted with. What happens is that people have been pestering them so much that it is easier to be left alone. That has been my experience. I wonder whether the depression felt by individuals with Asperger's syndrome over their lack of friends might be due to the fact that they tend to live in more typical environments and so feel more lonely, whereas people with autism live in more disabled environments where the carers give them more support. Perhaps the people with Asperger's have less support because they are seen as less disabled."[102]

In a study Rogers conducted with Sally Ozonoff and Bruce Pennington in 1991, she compared the neuropsychological profiles of individuals with high-functioning autism and Asperger's syndrome. In comparison with matched controls, both groups were impaired on executive function tests.[103] Only the high-functioning autistic group demonstrated deficits in theory of mind and verbal memory, performing more poorly than both controls and Asperger's subjects. The researchers said their results suggested that high-functioning autism and Asperger's syndrome were empirically distinguishable on measures independent of diagnostic criteria.

Rogers told me she was not sure the concept of Asperger's syndrome was a necessary one. "The situation we have right now, with the multiple categories, is very confusing for parents. The diagnosis of autism gets far more services than that of Asperger's syndrome, because Asperger's is seen in the US as a mental health disability."[104]

Dr. Francesca Happé, who is on the committee (headed by Sue Swedo at America's National Institutes of Health) developing the new definitions of autism and Asperger's syndrome in DSM-V, told me that the current criteria for Asperger's "do not work, either theoretically or practically, especially on language. Would it be better to include it on the spectrum but refer to the particular pattern of 'active but odd'?"[105]

Meanwhile, the latest "craze" is to diagnose famous personalities in history with Asperger's syndrome retrospectively, The leader in this field is the respected professor of psychiatry at Trinity College, Dublin, Dr. Michael Fitzgerald. Fitzgerald, who claims that Beethoven, Swift, and Mozart, among many others, would have been labeled Asperger's, told me that his work in this area was actually removing the stigma from the condition. "I'm showing what a positive contribution people with Asperger's syndrome have made to the world."[106]

That is certainly a view shared by many well-known advocates with Asperger's syndrome, who refer to their condition as a difference, not a disability. One of these, the Australian writer, Wendy Lawson, has coined the term "diffability."

It is true that, in some parts of the world, the stigma attached to autism remains so potent that parents are reluctant to admit that their child has the condition. But in general, the label is seen as essential in order to receive the appropriate services. As Leo Kanner's colleague, Leon Eisenberg, told me: "Autism has spread well beyond the restrictive venue that Kanner had in mind. Maybe we never saw the children with mental retardation that are now seen as autism. Autism is a preferred diagnosis among parents today. Mental retardation is a stigmatized disorder. Autism, while hardly something you're proud of, is at least a more legitimate diagnosis for your child. Furthermore, you are entitled to services that go beyond the special classroom. Since there are no indisputable biochemical or pathological findings, restricting the diagnosis becomes a matter of judgment."[107]

**Figure 65**  Helen Tager-Flusberg

Dr. Helen Tager-Flusberg, the world's leading expert on language abnormalities in autism, ruled out the possibility that these linguistic deficits were so specific as to provide hope for a diagnostic profile— at least for the time being. "The approach which I think we'll need is that we apply to cardiovascular disease," she told me. "The field of medicine has been completely transformed because we have learnt all about risk factors. Nowadays, someone with hypertension has a form of cardiovascular disease. We won't have a gene test for that disease, and nor will we for autism. Some sort of score will determine that you are at high risk. My goal would be to work on infants at risk with other groups to come up with what the risk factors are: none of them will be diagnostic on its own. I absolutely believe that we have the potential, before the onset of symptoms—let's say by twelve months—of developing a risk profile. My hope is that we will have a pretty good set of risk factors a decade from now."[108]

Tager-Flusberg said that, right now, the risk factors for autism would include delays in speech and language development—both expressive and receptive—and other behavioral features, combined with biological markers.[109]

At the time of writing, in 2010, some professionals believe that the weight of evidence supports the hypothesis that autism is a quantitative or dimensional spectrum, with no clear qualitative distinction between traits found among individuals with the disorder and the general population. A 2001 autism review by London's Medical Research Council—in which I myself took part—decided that the majority of individuals with autism probably have IQ scores in the normal range, although autistic behaviors may be proportionately more common among those with learning disabilities.[110]

This does not, of course, mark a return to Leo Kanner's 1943 failure to find cognitive deficits in autistic children but, instead, represents a recognition that the broadening of the spectrum means that previous— and longstanding—suggestions that around 75% of people with autism were mentally retarded was a major over-estimate. Professor Laurent Mottron in Montreal and his autistic colleague, Michelle Dawson, have thrown their own weight behind this adjustment of IQ profile by suggesting that most autistic individuals with autism would score far higher if clinicians used the non-verbal Raven's Matrices test rather than the verbal Wechsler Scale. Others, like Christopher Gillberg in Sweden, strongly disagree with this latest proposal. He pointed out to me that the Wechsler was based on the Stanford-Binet test, which had been a universal test of intelligence for decades.[111]

For many years, it was thought that "you either had autism or you didn't." Dr. John Constantino, of the Washington University School of Medicine in St. Louis, Missouri, is among those respected professionals who continues to believe that autism is unidimensional. But many others disagree, providing evidence that social and language deficits in autistic disorders were not closely correlated with stereotyped and repetitive behaviors. Very recently, Dr. Francesca Happé published a study suggesting that Lorna Wing and Judith Gould's Triad of Impairments may have "fractionable" causes, at the genetic, neurological, and cognitive levels.[112] "I believe there has been a slippage between Lorna's triad— of social, communication and imagination—and DSM-IV and ICD-10's notion of repetitive behavior as the third element," Happé told me. "I think the Wing–Gould version does indeed form a true unitary triad. But when you change the third part from imagination to repetitive behavior, that is no longer tied in with social and communicative impairments."[113]

Happé herself conceded that her concept of a fractionable triad did not imply an attack on the validity of the diagnosis:

> It is quite compatible to assert that ASD [autistic spectrum disorder] results when a number of independent impairments co-occur and to assert that

the resulting mix has a special quality, distinct prognosis and response to intervention and is therefore worthy of a distinct diagnostic label. Similarly, when the cognitive characteristics of impaired theory of mind, executive dysfunction and detail-focused bias co-occur (as they do above chance), many possible compensatory mechanisms are stripped away and interactive effects occur.[114]

She does feel that her concept may have implications in terms of current diagnostic categories. The DSM-V workgroups—of which she is a member—are currently considering whether a dimensional, as well as categorical, approach should be taken to the diagnosis of autism. "The question arises whether one should conceptualize autism and related disorders as lying on one spectrum, or whether each individual should be mapped in a three-dimensional space along three, perhaps orthogonal, dimensions: social interaction, communication and RRBIs [restrictive and repetitive behaviors and interests]."[115] Happé believes that mapping individuals, or diagnostic subgroups, within a three-dimensional space would, at least, help to clarify the meaning of the currently vague PDD-NOS label. As she points out, under current DSM-IV criteria, this label can be applied to a child who shows all aspects of the Triad of Impairments but who is "sub-threshold" for a full diagnosis of autism, or to a child who shows only one aspect of the Triad. This problem, she says, compounds problems of heterogeneity in autistic spectrum disorders and renders the PDD-NOS label largely uninformative.[116]

# 8

# The 1980s and 1990s

## *Theories and Concepts*

Despite the continuing misconceptions about autism, there was a growing acceptance in the 1980s—a decade which saw the deaths of the two great pioneers in the field—that it was a biological disorder, probably caused by neurological abnormalities. As more researchers abandoned the debate over whether the impairments in autism were cognitive or social and sought, instead, to understand how both social and cognitive deficits could be conceptualized as emerging from one primary dysfunction, a number of significant breakthroughs were made.

Hans Asperger and Leo Kanner died within a year of each other. Asperger, though 10 years younger than Kanner, died first. He never lived to see the condition he identified given its due attention in the English-speaking world, because Lorna Wing's paper on the subject—in which she coined the term "Asperger's syndrome"—did not appear until 1981, a year after his death on October 21, 1980, at the age of 74. Nor did he live to see the first international conference on Asperger's syndrome, held in London in 1988, or the official acknowledgment of the existence of the condition in DSM-IV in 1994, three years after Uta Frith translated his 1944 paper into English. It has frequently been suggested that he would have found it difficult to recognize the American Psychiatric Association's definition of his children. However, his daughter, Dr. Maria Asperger Felder, told me that this was not the case: "There are many elements in the DSM-IV definition—the linguistic peculiarities, the motor difficulties—which my father would have accepted."[1]

In a moving tribute to Asperger at his funeral in Vienna on October 30, 1980, one of his pupils, Dr. Franz Wurst, declared: "With ambition and humanity, he dedicated himself to the questions of handicapped children at a time when they scarcely received any public attention."[2]

Asperger's close colleague, Dr. Elizabeth Wurst (no relation to Franz) recalled that he had a very lively sense of humor and he used to love driving up into the mountains with his colleagues, singing much of the time.[3]

Lorna Wing referred to her landmark 1981 paper describing and naming Asperger's syndrome for the first time as "opening Pandora's box"—meaning she was introducing an extra element to the autistic spectrum, already potentially fraught with danger—and she is not convinced today that her coinage was altogether a positive development.

In fact, Wing told me: "I wish I hadn't done it. I would like to throw all labels away today, including Asperger's syndrome, and move towards the dimensional approach. Labels don't mean anything, because you can get such a wide variety of profiles—some people are brilliant at mathematics but get pleasure rocking back and forth twiddling their hands. The trouble is that, it would be very hard to make an international system based on profiles. Human beings seem to need categories."[4]

Judy Gould recalled those early, historic moments in London as her colleague was coming to an understanding about Asperger's syndrome. Gould told me: "When we were doing our research at the Maudsley Hospital, we were also seeing young adults who were referred there. Many of them were suffering from depression, but we started to see a link with autistic behaviors. That set Lorna off on the track. Although we had been talking about the Triad of Impairments, the autistic spectrum and the different manifestations for a couple of years, the idea hadn't really caught on yet.

"But how could someone who was severely disabled with Kanner's description be the same as an individual Asperger was describing? What core difficulties could they have in common? So from a clinical and practical point of view, it was a good idea to call them something different. Asperger used the term 'autistic psychopathy,' but since *Psychopathie* has negative connotations in English (though not in German), Lorna chose the term Asperger's syndrome in her 1981 paper. Then, as time went by, an obsession arose of separating Asperger's syndrome from high-functioning autism. We were saying all along: they're not different, they're different manifestations of the same core problem, the social instinct. That's why she regrets coining the term."[5]

Leo Kanner died in Sykesville, Maryland on April 3, 1981. He was 86 and had achieved worldwide recognition. He was delighted, for example, to find, during a visit to Brazil in 1969, that a village had been named after him. Asked whether it was a little frightening at 75 to be turning into an institution, Kanner replied: "No. I've been in and out of institutions for a long time."[6]

In a tribute to his close colleague, Leon Eisenberg wrote:

> We shall not see his like again. As much as any one man can be so credited, he was the father of child psychiatry in the Americas. He was a man with a passion for social justice: a great teacher, a loving father, grandfather and great-grandfather and a scholar of great learning. Most astonishing of all was his capacity for entering the world of the child . . . he was a veritable Pied Piper whom no child could resist. He cared for children; they trusted him and told him what they chose to reveal to no other.[7]

One former neighbor of Kanner's wrote to the *Baltimore Sun* (April 15, 1981) to say:

> Our paths crossed many times and we visited. The memoir of those *savoir vivre* visits were titillating, because this chronological octogenarian was physiologically cerebrally agile and sparkling—be it scholarship, or retelling his many voluminous experiences and encounters, or chanting German or Hebrew folk songs.

The most painful personal event in Leo Kanner's adult life was the premature death from cancer of his married daughter, Anita Gilbert, at the age of just 42. She was a talented social worker who had contributed to child psychiatric research.

Kanner and his wife, June Lewin, whom he described as his "guardian angel,"—and to whom he remained married for 60 years until his death—opened their home to many of the European refugees he had personally helped to reach American soil safely. In his unpublished autobiography, he wrote:

> I made many lifelong friends among the newcomers who, in unforgettable gatherings in my house, while trying to adjust to a new environment, revelled in the best that European culture had to offer. The memory of unspeakable tortures and the mourning for murdered relatives were attenuated by lively discussions of music, art, literature, and science.[8]

The fact that many of the refugees whom Kanner welcomed into his Baltimore home had arrived from Austria and Germany makes it all the more puzzling that he never cited the work of Hans Asperger. Even if, during and shortly after the Second World War, papers out of Nazi Germany and Nazi-annexed Austria would not generally have been viewed in a positive light in the United States—assuming they reached American shores at all—it seems very likely that at least some of these refugees would have read Asperger's writings and that they might have mentioned them to Kanner in Baltimore over the subsequent years. Perhaps they did not discuss autism socially. After all, Kanner's son, Albert, told me he recalled his father frequently protesting: 'Why does everyone only talk about my work in autism? I've done plenty of other things in my career.'[9] Kanner's colleague, Leon Eisenberg, suggested that it was by no means a foregone conclusion that the refugees would have discussed Asperger's work with him at all.

## Neuropathological Findings

Since it was known that epilepsy was common in autism—two of Kanner's original 11 cases had seizures—researchers stepped up their quest for the source of the neurological impairments involved. They remained hampered by a lack of brains to study or equipment with which to examine them.

Both the left and right sides of the brain came under serious consideration. The left hemisphere was of interest because it was known that as many as 50% of all individuals with autism, as defined by Kanner, remained mute—and in most adults who are right-handed, linguistic analysis is performed in left-brain structures. But the alternative possibility of right-brain dysfunction in autism was also of interest because this appears to be the site of non-verbal communication such as gestures and patterns of emphasis which express emotion (prosody, etc.), and this is an area which poses major problems for children with autism.

In 1983, a study by Christopher Gillberg at the University of Gothenburg in Sweden suggested there was evidence of prenatal brain damage in autism. Gillberg told me this was a population study of all children with autism who had been born in a maternity ward on the same day. "The autism group had many more problems in pregnancy and during birth. At the time, we interpreted this as meaning brain damage at the time of birth or late in pregnancy. That is still a reasonable interpretation but it could also be interpreted to mean that, if you have an inborn problem as a fetus, you're more likely to produce problems in the mother during pregnancy. If you have poor muscle tone and that is a genetic problem, you will almost invariably have more problems when you are born: difficulties in starting to breathe, labor could be prolonged if you are a late maturer in various brain systems or all your organs. That chain of events might explain why these children have reduced optimality."[10]

**Figure 66**   Thomas Kemper and Margaret Bauman

By far most important—and far-reaching—study in the history of neurological research into autism was that of Dr. Margaret Bauman and Dr. Thomas Kemper at Boston University, published in 1985, which reported on the brain of a 29-year-old autistic man who had died from drowning. For the first time, their study demonstrated specific neurological abnormalities associated with autism: cells in the hippocampus, subiculum, and amygdala were found to be more tightly packed and reduced in size. The study suggested that abnormalities occur at the cellular level and date from very early in development. These and other findings of neurological abnormalities opened the way to treating autism as a biological disorder.[11]

Bauman told me that they started working on this study in 1983. "We didn't have any preconceptions. We didn't look at the cerebellum because, at that time, the law in neurology was that, if you had an abnormality

207

in the cerebellum you went around as though you were drunk and at that point, children with autism were said to have very good motor skills."[12]

The significance of their study went beyond the solid scientific findings. Parents felt reassured and wrote to Bauman and Kemper to thank them for clearing them of blame. But not everyone was convinced. Bruno Bettelheim telephoned Kemper when the news of their finding was released and told him: "There must be two kinds of autism, yours and mine!"[13]

Bauman and Kemper felt the miswiring in the brain of the 29-year-old man in their study must have occurred prior to 28 weeks' gestation because of the connectivity between the Purkinje cells and the olive. (Purkinje cells send inhibitory projections to the deep cerebellar nuclei and constitute the sole output of all motor coordination in the cerebellar cortex.) "Since we found decreased numbers of Purkinje cells but the olive looked fine, we decided that whatever happened to the Purkinje cells had to have occurred before the connection was made. Otherwise there would not have been preserved cells in the brain stem. It seemed reasonable—based on the state we had at that point—that this was prenatal and before 28 weeks." Bauman told me.[14]

Other investigators, such as Andrea and Roland Ciaranello at Harvard and Professor Anthony Bailey at Oxford University (the latter recently established an impressive state-of-the-art brain-imaging center outside Oxford)—have argued that the changes seen in postmortem autistic brain tissue (and in autistic brain anatomy as assessed by *in vivo* measurements as well) are too subtle to have occurred so early and that the findings more likely imply a late gestational or early postnatal onset. Some researchers have claimed that Purkinje cell vulnerability to metabolic stressors such as excitotoxicity could be a potential basis for postnatal loss of such cells. Although Dr. Ed Ritvo at UCLA conducted a study in 1986 in which he also showed a decreased number of Purkinje cells in the cerebellar hemisphere and vermis, Bauman and Kemper themselves recently reported a postmortem study which had failed to replicate their 1985 Purkinje cell and brain-stem findings.

Research into a prenatal "insult" to the brain which might cause autism intensified in the 1990s. In 1994, two pediatric ophthalmologists—Marilyn T. Miller of the University of Illinois at Chicago, and Kerstin Strömland of Gothenborg University in Sweden—described a surprising outcome from a study investigating eye motility problems in people affected by thalidomide, the morning-sickness drug that caused an epidemic of birth defects in the 1960s. The study's subjects were adults who had been exposed to the drug while still in the womb. Miller and Strömland made an observation that had mysteriously eluded previous researchers: about 5% of the thalidomide-impaired subjects had autism, which is about 30 times higher than the rate among the general population.[15] Dr. Patricia Rodier, professor of obstetrics and gynecology at the University of Rochester in New York, says she "became dizzy and began to hyperventilate" with excitement when she learnt of this finding. The connection with thalidomide, she noted, suddenly threw a brilliant new light on the subject, suggesting that autism might originate in the early weeks of pregnancy, when the embryo's brain and the rest of the nervous system were just beginning to develop. What made the new study so thrilling to Rodier was Miller and Strömland's discovery that most of the thalidomide-impaired people with autism had anomalies in the external part of their ears but no malformations of the arms or legs. This pattern indicated that the subjects had been injured very early in gestation—20 to 24 days after conception—before many women even knew they were pregnant.

Head size has attracted increasing attention. A 1998 study led by Anthony Bailey—then at the Institute of Psychiatry's MRC Child Psychiatry Unit in London—of brain tissue from six mentally handicapped

**Figure 67** Manuel Casanova (photo courtesy of Manuel Casanova)

individuals with autism reported that four of the six brains were unusually large and heavy.[16] As noted in chapter 7 (p. 191), Dr. Eric Courchesne reported that he had found evidence that infants who go on to develop autism had rapid brain overgrowth in the first year of their lives.[17]

Much interest has been aroused by the research of Dr. Manuel Casanova, a neuroscientist at the University of Louisville, Kentucky, who has discovered increased numbers of mini-columns of neurons in the neocortex of autistic individuals.[18] Casanova believes he may have found a vital clue to the pathology of autism. Mini-columns are the smallest unit of cells capable of processing information. According to Casanova, they are smaller and more numerous in people with

209

autism. In addition, the neurons within each mini-column are reduced in size. He believes his findings may explain the hypersensitivity of some individuals with autism, as well as the high rate of seizures.

Casanova told me that he was now beginning to test the possibility of treating the problem through transcranial magnetic stimulation and said the preliminary findings were encouraging.[19] He and his team placed a coil, which created a magnetic field, near the scalps of 13 people with autism. They then reversed the magnetic field's polarity. After receiving a 20-minute treatment twice a week for three weeks, the patients were reported to have shown fewer instances of hyperactivity, sensory overload, and repetitive behaviors.

Many of the neurotransmitters in the brain have been implicated in autism by various teams of researchers, although these studies are largely awaiting replication. A number of teams have reported imbalances between the glutamate (excitory) and GABA (inhibitory) brain mechanisms.[20]

The fact is that, while many regions of the brain have been implicated in the genesis of autism, the neurobiological basis of the disorder remains unknown. Both Bauman and Kemper accepted that, despite the huge advances in brain-imaging techniques a vast amount of research remained to be done: "In any case, there is not going to be one cause of autism or one treatment," said Kemper. "There's not necessarily a consistent pattern in the change in the brain. People are paying more and more attention to the variability—structurally, chemically, clinically, and genetically."[21]

Bauman agreed that these differences exist, but was at pains to add: "I still think there is a unifying feature or group of features about children with autism: the way they use language, the way they interact socially, their play skills. There is a key group of features. I accept that it is a spectrum. But we should still be hunting for what is similar, for the unifying characteristic. Even if Mary Coleman refers to 70 different kinds of autism, she's still calling it autism. There may be different ways of getting there, but I'm not ready to give up on the hunt for some core, unifying feature of the brains of children with autism."[22]

Bauman told me she was particularly interested in the possibility of abnormalities in the structure or composition of the myelin—the fatty coating of the neurons in the brain—which would explain the information-processing problems. "I also like the idea of looking at the neurochemistry of the brain. Functional imaging studies are useful, but I don't know how much structural studies can show us."[23]

## Neuropsychological Theories

As we have seen, the non-social features of individuals with autism include a sometimes dramatically uneven pattern of intelligence—strengths as well as weaknesses. By the 1980s and 1990s, researchers had begun to explain these non-social features of autism by two major cognitive theories and their variants.

### *Theory of mind (TOM)*

The hypothesis that children with autism lack an ability to understand that other people have minds was first tested by Uta Frith, Simon Baron-Cohen, and Alan Leslie at the Medical Research Council's Cognitive Development Unit in London at the beginning of the 1980s.

Professor Uta Frith herself finds the term *theory of mind* "cumbersome and misleading" because—as she told me—"people think it is a consciously held theory. But it is not."[24] Frith prefers the term "mentalizing." She says that thinking about what others think, rather than what is going on in the physical world outside, is essential for engaging in complex social activity

> because it underpins our ability to cooperate and to learn from each other. Our research has shown that theory of mind is either absent or severely delayed in autistic individuals and that this can explain their difficulties in social communication. It may be present in chimpanzees and bonobos, and maybe even in other species, but it's not there in monkeys. In humans this network is active all the time; reputation management and political spin are only possible because of this feature of the human brain. The ability to mentalize is hugely important for social interaction and in communication, and we believe it is impaired in autistic people.[25]

Theory of mind was a revolutionary idea for autism studies in 1985 when Frith, Simon Baron-Cohen, and Alan Leslie published their study.[26] Nevertheless, as Frith told me, "It started from animal studies and evolutionary stories. Even much further back, philosophers talked about our capacity to reflect on ourselves and to distinguish between appearance and reality."[27]

The 1985 study, which was part of Simon Baron-Cohen's PhD thesis, showed that children with autism had impairments in understanding false beliefs. This result was skeptically received, at first, but after it

211

had been replicated it had a profoundly positive impact on subsequent scientific progress in the field of autism.

The most direct influence on the idea was Premack and Woodruff's 1978 study examining whether chimpanzees or other primates could think about others' minds.[28] "Then Heinz Wimmer and Josef Perner published their paper in 1983 which basically provided a methodology for studying theory of mind in children 3 to 4 years old. We adapted that with the Sally–Anne test," Simon Baron-Cohen told me. "In the original test, the characters had Austrian names!"[29]

In the Sally–Anne test, "Sally" and "Anne" are two dolls in a room with an experimenter and a child. The child is shown Sally placing a marble in her basket and leaving the room. While she is out of the room, Anne is seen to take the marble from Sally's basket and put it in her own basket. The child, who has been observing all this, is then asked where Sally will look for the marble when she comes back into the room. Children who have theory of mind say that Sally will look in her own box, because that is where she last saw her marble. These children realize that Sally can have a "false belief" and that her belief is true, as far as she is concerned. Children with no theory of mind say that Sally will look for the marble in Anne's box, because they cannot imagine Sally's belief about the marble being any different from their own, and they saw the marble being put into Anne's box.

Much has been written about TOM in autism, so this is not the place to go into detail.[30] Perhaps the most intriguing development is the use of brain scans designed to detect which regions of the brain may be involved in "mentalizing." Researchers have found a specific pattern of activation associated with theory of mind and these brain regions showed reduced activation in autism.[31]

### Weak central coherence

A second concept developed by Uta Frith and her colleagues has been labeled "weak central coherence"—a tendency to process incoming information at the expense of contextual meaning and in favor of piece-meal processing, or "failing to see the wood for the trees." An example is the block design test found in both the child and adult versions of the Wechsler intelligence scale (as illustrated in a study by Uta Frith and her PhD student, Amitta Shah, in 1993).[32]

Once again, Frith does not like the name commonly given to her theory. "People have said my choice of term 'weak central coherence' implies negative connotations," she told me. "This is so ironic, because I use it to celebrate the children's strengths. It's not good always to be taken in by the whole: this means you have prejudices and it weakens independent thought."[33]

Simon Baron-Cohen agrees: "I don't go along with the term 'weak' in weak central coherence. It implies something which is underdeveloped, whereas if you look at the tests Uta does, the individuals often shows strengths in the embedded figure test, for example," he told me. "The block design test also involves figuring out a rule by manipulating patterns. Children with autism are often very good at seeing patterns."[34]

Intriguingly, Leo Kanner alluded to weak central coherence in his 1943 paper when he referred to the children's "inability to experience wholes without full attention to the constituent parts."[35]

### Executive dysfunction

The third main cognitive theory that appeared in the 1990s with the aim of explaining the non-social aspects of autism is executive dysfunction. Poor performance has been demonstrated in autism on many tasks of executive function—a set of cognitive abilities which are necessary for goal-directed behavior and include the capacity to initiate and stop actions, to monitor and change behavior as needed, and to plan future behavior when faced with novel tasks and situations. Using a variety of tasks, children with autism have been shown to have deficits in planning. One typical task is the Tower of Hanoi, or the related Tower of London, in which individuals must move discs from a prearranged sequence in three different pegs to match a goal state determined by the examiner in as few moves as possible. In the 1990s, Sally Ozonoff and others showed children with autism were impaired on such tasks.[36]

In 2006, Rebecca Landa at the Kennedy Krieger Institute in Baltimore surprisingly found that the relationship between executive function, language, and social performance was weak to non-existent in high-functioning schoolchildren with autism. Landa told me that it would make sense to see executive dysfunction as being at the root of some of the communication problems we see in autism. "But that does not seem to be the case. Even though we understand that all these 'deficits' we observe in autism contribute to the overall phenotype of what we see behaviorally, it's complicated to see them as a cause-and-effect relationship. What this means from an intervention perspective is that we have to treat multiple aspects of developments."[37]

213

## Responses

Michael Rutter told me that TOM had been a very influential hypothesis. "It took off from Hermelin and O'Connor's work showing cognitive ability but social deficits. However, Hermelin and O'Connor's studies were not sufficiently focused to provide a clear mechanism about how this might work. Theory of mind was also important in that it brought in a much broader range of cognitive psychology. A much wider group of people came into the picture—people who had nothing to do with autism. There remains the question of whether a single modular deficit explains autism."[38]

Not everyone is enamored of TOM or the other cognitive theories as a means of understanding the deficits involved in autism—and even some who appreciate its value believe it can also be misleading. Professor Rita Jordan, of the University of Birmingham in the UK, one of the world's leading autism authorities, says that TOM has undoubtedly been a wonderfully revealing insight into one of the factors affecting behavior in autistic spectrum disorders.

> But in what sense does it explain those differences in behaviour? How is our understanding advanced by being told that the reason people with ASD/C have difficulty understanding and using mental states (the evidential data for the theory) is that they lack a Theory of Mind Module, a construct used to explain the ability to understand and use mental states? In other words, does the theory take us beyond the data?[39]

**Figure 68**  Simon Baron-Cohen

Jordan added: "In general, therefore, the decades of grand psychological theories have increased data about autism but have not come near to any unifying explanation."[40]

Simon Baron-Cohen conceded that his TOM test had come under attack at the time it was introduced. "One frequent criticism was that, because we used dolls instead of real people, it wasn't fair. So we did the test again with real people and produced similar results."[41]

Other critics claimed that individuals with higher-functioning autism might be able to solve the false belief task intellectually. "But the field also changed in terms of who got diagnosed," Baron-Cohen told me. "In the 1980s, we thought that even the high-functioning children had below-average IQ. We didn't know much about Asperger's syndrome at that point."[42] In a sense, this is surprising since, by coincidence, two men who would go on to become world authorities on Asperger's syndrome—Digby Tantam and Tony Attwood—were being supervised for their PhDs by Uta Frith at the time. Indeed, Tantam was already working on Asperger's syndrome in the early 1980s.

## *Joint attention*

In the late 1980s and early 1990s, Dr. Marian Sigman at UCLA and Dr. Peter Mundy at the University of Miami did a great deal of research into joint attention deficits in individuals with autism. Joint attention skills refer to the capacity to coordinate attention with a social partner in relation to some object or event. This capacity begins to emerge by at least 6 months of age and is a critical milestone of early development and social learning. It also involves the capacity to understand that the other person has a "point of view"—and in that sense, the deficit is linked to theory of mind. Indeed, Simon Baron-Cohen and others have interpreted the joint attention deficit as a deficit in the activation of a specific Shared Attention Module (SAM), a module which, they proposed, would normally have preceded the Theory of Mind Module (TOMM).

Sigman, a key figure in autism research in the 1970s and 1980s, started off looking at typical child development. When she arrived at UCLA, the two Eds—Ed Ornitz and Ed Ritvo—were already conducting autism research, as was Betty Jo Freeman (better known as B. J. Freeman).[43] "We started out with a study on sensorimotor development in normal children and another on the development of play, and then we started looking at these in autistic kids," Sigman told me.[44]

**Figure 69**   Marian Sigman

When Judy Ungerer joined her team, they began doing cross-sectional studies, moving on to longitudinal studies following autistic children from 3 to 5 years all the way up to their twenties. "We identified problems with sensorimotor and symbolic play. Then we started looking at parent–child interaction in more depth."[45]

Sigman's landmark study with Judy Ungerer in 1984 showed that autistic children were just as likely to be upset when separated from their parents as children without autism. "There is not much interest in attachment disorders today." Sigman told me. "There should be more."[46]

Also starting in the 1980s, Dr. Peter Hobson, of the Tavistock Institute in London, attempted to depict autism as an impairment of innate mechanisms of affective relations and in the failure to distinguish between "you" and "me." Hobson's model is a single-deficit model and, like Leo Kanner's, 40 years earlier, it maintains that the primary deficit in autism consists of the difficulty in organizing normal affective contact with others. For Hobson, this difficulty may be the expression of a specific brain pathology, acquired through blindness, for example, or severe sensory deprivation. Hobson is positioning himself on the affective end of the admittedly artificial divide of affective–cognitive approaches to autism, as opposed to the cognitive theories such as theory of mind.

One of the latest theories which has been exciting neurologists and psychologists alike is the mirror neuron system, which some studies have shown to be defective in autism. Mirror neurons are brain cells which light up both when a person carries out an action *and* when he or she is observing someone else performing that action. If these are not functioning properly in autism, this might explain problems in socializing and empathizing.

Dr. Sally Rogers at the MIND Institute in Sacramento told me that this was very important area which, she believed, also related to joint attention and other capacities known to be impaired in autism. "It opened up the importance of the role imitation has in autism. In my 2007 paper, I examined whether this was a representational problem in autism or a general imitation deficit. This is significant, because it may be that the problem is not necessarily the shift into symbolic thought. We are saying that pretend play and language difficulties—which Piaget claimed were linked to representational difficulties—could be related to the general imitation deficit in autism, with its own specific brain region. I want to understand why symbolic play, language, imitation, and joint attention are also so impaired in autism. We think they are linked."[47]

Rogers added that she believed imitation deficits were present from the beginning of life in autism. "In the same way that Kanner was talking about affective deficits, the mirror neuron theory talks about inability to connect with other people's feelings, as well—the inability to mirror back people's expressions and affect. This is not theory of mind—this is a more immediate capacity. He couldn't talk about the causes, because he didn't have any models other than the Freudian one to explain how people relate to one another. Now we *do* have a model, the mirror neuron one."[48]

Rogers's colleague at the MIND Institute, Dr. Sally Ozonoff, says she is not a firm believer in core deficits. "In the 1980s, we did indeed think of it in that way," she told me. "We asked: what is the core psychological (not biological) construct that leads to all the other symptoms? I was studying executive function, and I realized within a decade that I didn't believe this was a core deficit. I have maintained my skepticism. I don't think there will be one psychological construct which will explain everything. I no longer do research pitting one aspect against another. I used to compare executive function with theory of mind—but I don't think that's helpful any more. And most people are no longer enamored of a single deficit. The social aspect is what distinguishes autism from other disorders, but getting at what construct that is, is not very useful."[49]

Marian Sigman told me: "I don't think you can separate the social and cognitive aspects. I think it is social cognition that is affected, not just cognitive development."[50]

One of the most recent theories is Simon Baron-Cohen's notion that autism is an extreme manifestation of the male brain. In some senses, he is harking back to a comment precisely to this effect made by Hans Asperger in his 1944 paper. Indeed, he told me he developed his hypothesis to test Asperger's statement.[51] But Baron-Cohen believes he has biological evidence to support his thesis: namely, his studies showing increased levels of the male hormone, testosterone, in the serum of fetuses who later turn out to have autistic traits such as skills at performing the embedded figure task.[52] He regretted that some sections of the media had wrongly suggested that his study demonstrated that elevated fetal testosterone was associated with a clinical diagnosis of autism or Asperger's syndrome. His study had not yet shown this, he stressed. The number of autistic traits was not necessarily indicative of autism: all the children in his study were developing "typically"—that is, they did not have autism. He also emphasized that his research was not a screening study and was conducted purely to understand the basic neurobiological mechanisms underlying individual differences in autistic traits.[53]

Baron-Cohen also maintains that in general, males are better at systemizing—and he points to the large numbers of computer programmers with Asperger's syndrome and the large numbers of mathematicians in families with an autistic member—while females are, by and large, better at empathizing. Of course, this theory has met with resistance from a number of quarters. I pointed out to Baron-Cohen that many people with Asperger's syndrome could actually be said to have *too much* empathy. (Indeed, Carol Gray, the author of the Social Stories, which she developed in 1991 to help individuals with autistic spectrum disorders develop greater social understanding, told me in 2007 that she had devised a new social curiosity spectrum, to reflect the wide variations in this area.)[54]

Baron-Cohen conceded: "People with autism I have met are not unkind or uncaring. But it looks as though, on some of these tests, they have difficulty in picking up on other people's cues. If someone is upset or bored, they may not notice it. Or they may say something which upsets someone, when they did not intend it to happen. If they have difficulties with empathy, this does not mean that they do not care about other people. They may just have difficulty in recognizing the emotions in other people. They often have a very strong moral conscience. They care about the environment. They care about people not breaking rules."[55]

## Language abnormalities

There is still debate over whether the language impairment is a core deficit in autism. For a while, when this was believed to be the case, it reinforced the assumption that autism was a left-hemisphere disorder. But as Professor Isabelle Rapin pointed out to me in New York: "That's too simplistic. The brain works as a whole. In any case, one of my many pet peeves is that researchers have studied individuals who can speak, rather than those who can't, because they thought they were irrelevant or untestable."[56]

Rapin said her close colleague at the Albert Einstein College of Medicine in the Bronx, New York, the late Dr. Doris Allen, "taught me about language and I taught her about neurology. She taught me you could study language in people who don't speak, because there are other methods of communication besides what you do with your mouth and your ears. So we developed a very simplistic categorization of language disorders—for clinicians, not researchers. I learnt that, if you pay attention to how well children produce speech sounds and make them into sentences and how well they comprehend—so that what they say to you is relevant to what you have said to them—you can learn a lot. For example, you can have a child who doesn't speak but who understands well, and that is not common in autism."[57]

In 1983, Rapin and Allen wrote that one subtype of developmental language disorder—which they called "semantic-pragmatic syndrome" and has since been renamed "semantic-pragmatic disorder" by Dr. Dorothy Bishop in Oxford—was frequently seen, in a severe form, in verbal children with autism.[58] In children with this syndrome, Rapin and Allen wrote, the onset of language use was delayed and, when language emerged, it was accompanied by echolalia, jargon and auditory inattention. When they were older, such children used superficially complex language with clear articulation but had difficulty with the use and understanding of language, interpreting overliterally and using language inappropriately in conversation. Whether semantic-pragmatic language disorder forms part of the autistic spectrum remains a subject of debate.

In 1977, Christiane Baltaxe at UCLA had published a study exploring the pragmatic deficits that are apparent in conversations and other discourse contexts, identifying those features that distinguish communication problems in autism from those found in other clinical groups.[59] At a theoretical level, these communicative impairments have been related to deficits in understanding other minds (theory of mind) and to other features of the disorder, particularly in social functioning.

However, as the world's leading authority on language deficits in autism, Dr. Helen Tager-Flusberg, with her colleague Margaret Kjelgaard at Boston University School of Medicine, have emphasized, in contrast to the universal nature of these communicative deficits, "language functioning in autism is much more variable. At one end, there are children with autism whose vocabulary, grammatical knowledge, and articulation skills are within the normal range of functioning, while at the other end a significant proportion of the population remains essentially non-verbal."[60]

In one of her studies, about one quarter of the autism group showed essentially normal language skills, indicating, said Tager-Flusberg, that

deficits in language skills are not universal in autism, although they are found in the majority of children with this disorder. This contrasts with the universal impairments that are found in communication skills in this population, and which are among the defining features of this disorder. . . . The profile of language performance found among the children with autism who have borderline or impaired language abilities mirrors what has been reported in the literature on SLI [specific language impairment].

... Autism and SLI are complex genetic disorders that have very high heritability estimates, based on family and twin studies. . . . The cumulative evidence from both family and genetic linkage studies suggests that autism and SLI may involve one or more shared genes, arguing strongly for biological overlap between these disorders.[61]

# Social Deprivation

After the fall of the Ceaușescu regime in Romania in 1989, Michael Rutter carried out a study of children in orphanages in that country. In 1999, he published a paper describing a sample of 144 children adopted from Romania by British families. Rutter and his colleagues reported that children adopted before their second birthday had "quasi-autistic features," include rocking, self-injury, unusual and exaggerated sensory responses, and problems chewing and swallowing. This study found that, with the exception of unusual sensory responses, the rate of difficult behaviors in most cases steadily declined after the child entered the adoptive family. In a number of cases, the difficulties remained despite quality care in the new home.[62] In another report on this same study, published in 2001, Rutter wrote that he had examined 165 children adopted from Romania before the age of 4. They were examined at 4 years and 6 years and compared with 52 children of the same age and gender adopted in infancy in the United Kingdom. The researchers found that 12% of the Romanian adoptees had "quasi-autistic features," whereas none in the UK sample did.[63]

"When we started our study, it did not cross our minds that autism could be caused by the situation in which the children found themselves," Rutter told me. "But by coincidence, as we started the pilot study, a couple of children were referred to me who had been in Romanian orphanages. Autism is strongly associated with institutional deprivation. Does this take us back to the notion that poor parenting causes autism? We concluded that it did not. It is unusual for children with autism to have a background of institutional care. We found the pattern of behavior to be different in the Romanian orphans, which is why we preferred to talk about 'quasi-autism.'"[64]

Rutter said the parallel was more with the work of researchers like Peter Hobson and Rachel Brown on congenital blindness. "The autistic-like features could be caused by problems processing incoming sensory stimuli. In the profound conditions the children were living under, there could be extrinsic interferences with sensory stimuli," Rutter told me. "But this does not take us back to poor parenting, I am a dispassionate scientist, and if it had done, I would have said so."[65]

## Other Research

A number of important studies were being conducted in the 1980s in Scandinavia, notably by Christopher Gillberg in Gothenburg. In 1980, Gillberg found that both maternal and paternal age could increase the risk of having a child with autism—research that has been replicated far more recently. When I asked Gillberg about the possible significance of these findings, he told me that there were various theories: "One is that, as an older parent, you face more difficulties during pregnancy and also in the interpartal period. But there is also a case to be made for some genetic change taking place."

In 1987, Gillberg conducted a study showing that children with autism often had immigrant parents. He told me that he had been inspired to carry out this research after Lorna Wing's observations that there were more immigrants in her autistic population. "Lorna felt at the time, in the early 1980s, that this was probably caused by viral infections during pregnancy in mothers moving from one area of the world to another, and that where she had come from she was immune to various agents but she was not immune to things like rubella—against which most people nowadays are vaccinated. We knew that viral infections in pregnancy could cause autism because of the studies of Stella Chess [in the 1970s] and others. My wife, Carina, did a study in subgroups of immigrants and we found—as Victor Lotter had observed back in the 1970s—that if people had migrated over long distances, there was an increased risk for autism. That seemed to support Lorna's view that it could be due to a viral infection.

"But then Carina started to look at where the parents came from and found that it was almost invariably the mothers who were the migrants. The fathers were Swedish, but they had Asperger's syndrome. So one explanation, in Sweden at least, was that fathers with Asperger's syndrome could not find anyone to marry them and have a child by, because they were perceived as socially odd. Whereas, in this period of globalization, if they go to the other side of the world, the man will be seen as a typical Swedish reserved guy! We do still see quite a number of these cases in Sweden today."[66]

Gillberg said he had conducted another study showing a huge increase of cases of autism in the Somali population of Stockholm. "We have no idea why this is. It's very non-politically correct to be doing studies like this—but if you observe it in your clinic, you can't really just close your eyes to it. And if you're seeing it, you have to report it."[67]

In 2008, the Minnesota Department of Health in the United States announced that it was conducting an epidemiological survey, in consultation with the federal Centers for Disease Control and Prevention, to examine reports of high rates of autism among Somali immigrants in Minneapolis (see chapter 9).

Meanwhile, Mary Coleman—a co-author of the book, *The biology of the autistic syndromes*—continued to expound her view that autism would be found to be many dozen subtypes, each associated with a medical condition.[68] Others disagreed with this assessment. In 1994, Michael Rutter conducted a study with his colleagues, Anthony Bailey, Patrick Bolton, and Ann Le Couteur, in which they concluded that the strength of the association with medical conditions was strongly dependent on IQ level: "It is greatest when autism is accompanied by profound mental retardation . . . it is still substantial in the presence of severe retardation but it is rather lower when autism occurs in mildly retarded individuals or those of normal intelligence."[69]

Rutter and his team added that known medical conditions seemed to be more frequent in the case of atypical autism than autism diagnosed according to ICD-10 criteria. More detailed studies of Fragile X and Rett's syndrome subjects had shown that, although they often showed some autistic features, the overall clinical picture was "usually rather different from autism. The findings support the value of differentiating autism, atypical autism and other subcategories of pervasive developmental disorders."[70]

## Autism Treatment

By the 1980s, the two main educational approaches to autism, TEACCH in North Carolina and Ivar Lovaas's behavioral methods, were well-established and beginning to expand across the globe. However, as Sally Rogers told me, "there were no cohesive models at the time." Rogers, who has been working in this area since 1981, said: "It was a good challenge for a developmental psychologist, because not much had been written on treatment other than those from Ivar Lovaas and the old ones from psychoanalytical treatment. But I'd been diagnosing young children for enough time to know that the children didn't fit any of the models you read about: there were far more negative than positive symptoms, hugely disruptive problems, delays in play and communication skills. We used affect as the basis for teaching communication skills. Thirty years later, we have brought all this together in a developmental model which fuses developmental processes and relationship-based work. We now have data to support developmental theories of autism which didn't exist in the 1980s."[71]

As we have seen, up until the 1970s, many psychiatrists took the view that although the autistic child failed to communicate, underlying language competence was intact. So long as autism was seen as a purely affective disorder, speech therapy was seen as largely irrelevant, because the child was assumed to have normal language competence, even though this might not be expressed. Once the true severity of the language deficits in autistic children was appreciated, the position changed dramatically, and there was a massive drive for language training, with the hope that if the verbal difficulties could be overcome, other problems would be resolved.

As Dorothy Bishop has pointed out, the position today is that there is a recognition that, although autistic children clearly have difficulties with language, traditional approaches emphasizing mastery of the formal properties of language are largely inappropriate. As Bishop puts it:

Training children to speak is not going to bring about a transformation of their behaviour. The autistic child needs to learn not so much how to speak as how to use language socially to communicate. One still encounters those who regard speech therapy as inappropriate for children with a diagnosis of autism, but this attitude usually derives from a mistaken belief that speech therapists are concerned only with articulation training and grammatical drills.[72]

One highly respected professional, Dr. Robert DeLong, of Duke University in Durham, North Carolina, believes that

**Figure 70**   Robert DeLong

quite a number of children with autism

223

also suffer from bipolar disorder (manic depression). He told me that he had recommended the use of electric convulsive therapy (ECT) for two youths with autism, aged 18 and 14. "In both cases, it was helpful," said DeLong. "They both had bipolar disorder, I believe. One, a high-functioning boy, was tremendously obsessive about killing his parents. It was a desperate situation. He was relieved of all that by shock therapy and did very well indeed. The other one was low-functioning. His maternal grandmother had been hospitalized, his father had episodes of bipolar disease. But he was unusually brilliant. We treated the youngster with risperidone and that managed to control him for a while. But then he had severe rage episodes almost constantly, despite all the medication. At that point, they started to do shock treatment, which I recommended. His behavior stabilized. I don't know whether he did much better intellectually, but he was manageable. There was no doubt that it made a tremendous difference."[73]

# Prevalence

The 1980s saw more prevalence studies in Japan (by Tanoue and others), in Sweden (by Bohman and colleagues and by Gillberg), in Ireland (by McCarthy and colleagues), in West Germany (Steinhausen), in France (Ciadella and Mamelle) and in the United States (Ritvo).[74] Most studies reported prevalence rates of between 4 and 7 per 10,000, although one Japanese study reported a rate of 16 per 10,000.

The very latest report—from the Centers for Disease Control and Prevention (CDC) in the United States in October 2009—puts the prevalence rate at far higher. It estimates that roughly 1 in 90 children aged 3 to 17 were given a diagnosis of autistic spectrum disorder in 2007.[75] Whether there has been a genuine increase in incidence of autism, or whether the increase in diagnoses is due to the broadening of the spectrum and improved diagnostic tools, was a topic of heated debate in the 1990s, and remains so today.

Christopher Gillberg told me: "I don't think there has been a major increase. I certainly don't believe in the idea of an autism 'epidemic'. But there could be a rise in some subgroups where infections might be a contributory cause. You would expect this type of autism to be more common in nations where these infections are more common. We have seen much higher rates of autism in children with ataxia—cerebellar problems. We published studies showing that herpes encephalitis can lead to autism. So if you have an agent which hits either the cerebellum or the fronto-temporal regions, you're much more likely to have autism."[76]

Those who do believe in a steep rise in cases of autism have pointed to a number of possible environmental agents. There is very little evidence to support these claims. Some of them—like the suggestion that heavy metal poisoning is causing the disorder—have proved to be dangerous: at least two autistic children have died while undergoing a process called chelation to remove these metals from their bodies (see below).

In the mid-1980s, researchers at UCLA and the University of Utah carried out one of the largest population-based autism studies to date. The goal of the study was to identify every person born with autism between 1960 and 1984 and who lived in the state of Utah during the four-year survey. The study, led by Ed Ritvo and B. J. Freeman at UCLA, was published in 1989 and found that autism "was not associated with parental education, occupation, racial origin or religion. . . . Twenty (9.7%) of 207 families had more than one autistic sibling, which supports the authors' previous finding that there may be a familial subtype of autism."[77]

Ritvo told me about one mother in the 1989 study who was herself autistic and had two children with autism and one without. "She got lost on the way to the hospital. At one point, she got off her bus with the kids and called us from a payphone right by a hamburger store. We drove to meet them, took them all inside, bought them burgers, fries and milkshakes—and conducted the research interviews while they ate their fast-food 'research lunch.'"[78]

A follow-up study of 41 of the original Utah participants was published in March 2009—by the same two universities—and appeared to indicate that they had a higher social outcome than in similar studies. The researchers had no explanation as to why the Utah group fared better overall in living independently, developing social relationships, and in some cases even showing higher IQs than 20 years ago. The first author of the follow-up study, Megan Farley, said that the positive outcomes might be related to intensive early intervention and strong social and family networks.[79] A number of commentators pointed out that many of the families in the study were Mormons who traditionally had strong family networks. But Ed Ritvo told me: "Based on my 40 years' experience in the field, good family support—love, receiving the proper early intervention—are helpful no matter what the religion or ethnic background of the person with autism."[80]

# The MMR Story

The best-known hypothesis of an external causative agent—though since rejected by many large-scale studies—is the 1998 proposal by the British gastroenterologist, Dr. Andrew Wakefield, in the medical journal, *The Lancet*, that the triple MMR (measles, mumps, rubella) vaccine could be bringing about autism in children.[81] The story began in February that year when the Royal Free Hospital in London called a press conference at which Wakefield took the microphone and announced that he and his colleagues had discovered that eight of 12 children in their study had developed a serious intestinal inflammation—which he called "autistic enterocolitis"—an average of six days after receiving the MMR jab. Wakefield suggested that the virus—especially the measles component—might damage the intestine, permitting harmful proteins to enter the bloodstream and then cross the blood–brain barrier into the brain. However, other scientists claimed that their own intestinal biopsies of autistic children had found no traces of the measles virus after administration of the MMR. Nevertheless, alarmed British parents decided not to give their children the triple jab and the take-up plummeted from 92 to 80%.

In May of 1998, Finnish researchers at Helsinki University Central Hospital published their own study, after following up three million doses of the combined vaccine. They found that the dose had not caused a single case of autism or the inflammatory bowel disease, Crohn's disease. Every hospital and health center in Finland was asked to report any adverse effects of the MMR vaccination between 1982 and 1996 when 1.8 million children were inoculated.[82] Critics complained, however, that this study was funded by Merck, the pharmaceutical company which makes the triple vaccine.

Even the British Prime Minister at the time, Tony Blair, found himself caught up in the controversy when he refused to say whether his 19-month-old son, Leo, had received the MMR jab, calling such questions an invasion of privacy. Blair said he believed the advice given to the government—that there was "overwhelming" evidence that the vaccine was safe.

In 2002, a huge British Medical Association study once again cleared the MMR vaccine. Scientists examined research into MMR from 180 countries around the world and found no evidence that MMR or single measles vaccines were associated with autism or inflammatory bowel disease. But they did find strong evidence that both MMR and single measles vaccination virtually eliminated risk of measles and measles complications. Opponents were not convinced. JABS, a British-based support group for parents who believe their children have been damaged by the MMR vaccine, called this "old evidence rehashed" and demanded fresh research.

Despite assurances by the British government and many scientists around the world that the MMR vaccine was safe, a number of researchers came forward with studies which initially appeared to support Wakefield's hypothesis. In 2002, the Irish pathologist, John O'Leary, of Coombe Women's Hospital in Dublin, announced that he had found DNA from the measles virus in 7% of the normal child population but in 82% of autistic children. That same year, Vijendra Singh and his colleagues at Utah State University reported the discovery of high levels of antibodies to the measles virus in the blood and spinal fluid of children with autism, leading him to postulate that the MMR had provoked a hyperimmune response which attacked the brain.[83]

A celebrated figure in the history of autism leapt into the fray to support the anti-MMR campaign in 2002. Bernard Rimland, founder of the Autism Research of America and the San Diego-based Autism Institute—who, as we have seen, wrote the first book, in 1964, to show that the disorder was biological and not caused by parents—said there had not been adequate, unbiased research to determine whether the combined vaccine could trigger autism in some cases. "The link is probably very real," Rimland said. "The vaccine industry and drug companies need to deal with it."

In 2003, the American gastroenterologist, Arthur Krigsman, of New York University, announced that he had found a serious intestinal inflammation in 40 children with autism.

The following year, after families on both sides of the Atlantic decided to take legal action against the manufacturers of the MMR vaccine, the High Court in the UK asked a London-based molecular biologist, Professor Stephen Bustin, to inspect the O'Leary laboratory in Dublin. Bustin identified several problems, ranging from the quality of the preparations used to the conduct of the testing, the use of controls, and the analysis and interpretation of data. He said the results were positive for DNA—confirming contamination, because measles is an RNA virus. Bustin declared that it was "a scientific certainty" that the O'Leary lab had failed reliably to identify measles virus RNA in any child.

227

Michael Rutter told me that the evidence of a link between the MMR vaccine and autism was "resoundingly negative."[84] Yet despite the fact that research in Denmark, Finland, the UK, and elsewhere has disproved any link between the combined jab and autism, many parents have become too alarmed to give their children the vaccine—or have chosen to space the components out in separate jabs—and this has led to several outbreaks of measles around the world.

In 2004, a public inquiry was demanded after questions were raised about Andrew Wakefield's credibility. *The Lancet*—the British medical journal which published Wakefield's paper in 1998—claimed that Wakefield had been carrying out studies both for the Royal Free Hospital and for the Legal Aid Board, which created the risk of a conflict of interest. Dr. Richard Horton, editor of *The Lancet*, said:

> If we knew then what we know now, we certainly would not have published the part of the paper that related to MMR, although I do believe there was, and remains, validity to the connection between bowel disease and autism, which does need further investigation—but I believe the MMR element of that is invalid.[85]

By 2004, 10 of Wakefield's 12 co-authors on the original 1998 paper had disowned that study and on February 2, 2010, *The Lancet* announced that it was retracting the 1998 paper. The previous week, Britain's General Medical Council had ruled that Wakefield had been "dishonest, irresponsible and showed callous disregard for the distress and pain of children." In one instance described, Wakefield took blood samples from children at his son's birthday party without the appropriate ethical committee approval and in an "inappropriate social setting." The GMC panel said he had abused his trust as a medical practitioner and brought the medical profession into disrepute.[86]

Wakefield, who lost his gastroenterologist's post at London's Royal Free Hospital after the publication of his 1998 paper, moved to the United States and founded a research and treatment center called Thoughtful House in Texas, from which he resigned on February 19, 2010. He continues to be seen as a hero by many parents around the world, convinced that their child did undergo a severe reaction at the time of the combined jab and became autistic afterwards. The problem is that symptoms of autism tend to begin to emerge at around the same time—18 months of age—that the vaccine is normally administered, so a temporal association appears, to most health professionals' eyes, to have been misconstrued as a cause.

Wakefield told the British newspaper, *The Times*, in 2009 that the link between the MMR vaccine and autism was "under investigation. I would absolutely agree it's not proven. Nor have I ever claimed that it's proven."[87] In the same interview, he said

> the suggestion that parents should have the option of single vaccines was based on a review of all of the safety studies which had been conducted on all of the vaccines, from the single vaccine through to the MMR, and was not based on a case report of 12 children with a possible new syndrome. Based upon my review of the literature, the safety studies were totally inadequate.[88]

Dr. Wakefield added: "The re-emergence of measles is not the consequence of a hypothesis. We did not cause a scare. We responded to parents' legitimate concerns. . . . Not to have done so would have been negligent."[89]

Meanwhile, in 2007, across the Atlantic, a trial involving nearly 5,000 families opened before the United States Court of Federal Claims in Washington in which the claimants hoped to show that their children had been harmed by vaccination. The parents' argument was that the mercury-based preservative, thimerosal—used in many vaccines, although in not the MMR—could be causing autism. Proponents of this view pointed to a number of similarities between the symptoms of mercury poisoning and autism, but once again, the scientific evidence for any such link appears to be lacking. Indeed, just as in Japan—where the MMR has been withdrawn but the number of cases of autism is still rising—so around the world, thimerosal has been taken out of most childhood vaccines, yet the prevalence of autism continues to increase.

On February 12, 2009, the US court ruled that there was no evidence that vaccines caused autism. Some attorneys representing the petitioning families expressed their intention to appeal against the ruling. Barbara Loe Fisher of the National Vaccine Information Center was quoted as saying: "I think it is a mistake to conclude that, because these few test cases were denied compensation, it's been decided vaccines don't play any role in regressive autism."[90]

## Facilitated Communication

As in the 1970s, dubious methods of treating and teaching autistic individuals continued to emerge during the 1980s and 1990s. One of the most prominent—which continues to arouse heated debate today—is facilitated communication (FC), a process in which a facilitator supports the hand or arm of a communicatively impaired individual while using a keyboard or other devices in order, it is hoped, to help the individual to communicate.

FC first emerged in Australia in 1977, when Rosemary Crossley claimed to have produced communication from 12 children diagnosed with cerebral palsy and other handicaps and argued that they possessed normal intelligence. These findings were disputed by the hospital where she worked—St. Nicholas Hospital in Melbourne—as well as the Health Commission of Victoria. Undaunted, Crossley wrote a book about one of her students, Anne McDonald, called *Annie's coming out* in 1982.[91] FC gained further exposure when the Nobel laureate, Arthur Schawlow, used it with his autistic son in the early 1980s and felt that it was helpful.

In 1989, Dr. Douglas Biklen, a sociologist and professor of special education at Syracuse University, in New York State, investigated Rosemary Crossley's work in Australia and went on himself to popularize FC in the United States, creating the Facilitated Communication Institute at Syracuse University. He began reporting cases in which students with severe autism and no spoken language were said to be producing entire paragraphs of clarity and intellect on computer keyboards.

However, serious questions about the method quickly emerged. Some of the autistic subjects employed vocabulary which was apparently beyond their years and level of education; many, indeed, produced complex poetry. Another serious concern arose when some of the typed messages accused parents of children with autism of severe sexual or physical abuse. Although not all such allegations were proven true, some sexual abuse allegations made via FC have been found to be valid.

In late 1993, PBS in the United States screened a *Frontline* documentary highlighting these concerns. At about this same, controlled studies were conducted on this method, most of which reported that it was the facilitator who was unconsciously producing the communication. By the late 1990s, FC had been discredited in the eyes of most scientists and professional organizations, including the American Psychiatric Association.

Nevertheless, proponents of FC suggest that some people with autism and moderate and profound mental retardation may have "undisclosed literacy," or the capacity for other symbolic communication, consistent with higher intellectual functioning than has been generally presumed.

Sue Rubin, an American autistic FC user initially diagnosed as mentally retarded but who now attends college and types without physical support, has described her own experience with facilitator influence as a contributing author to the book *Autism and the myth of the person alone*, edited by Douglas Biklen, which features accounts by a number of functionally non-verbal published authors with autism, including Tito Mukhopadhay and Lucy Blackman.[92] Rubin was also the subject of the 2004 Oscar-nominated documentary, *Autism is a world*.

A few controlled studies since 1995 have reported instances of genuine authorship by FC users. In contrast, the Norwegian psychologist, Dr. Stephen von Tetzchner, the author of a leading textbook on augmentative and alternative communication,[93] has carried out theoretical research about facilitated communication. He believes the existing evidence "clearly demonstrates that facilitating techniques usually led to automatic writing, displaying the thoughts and the attitudes of the facilitators."[94]

One country where FC remains popular to this day is Germany. In 1992, a young man of 19, Birger Sellin, became the first functionally non-verbal person with autism to be a published author in that country. His book, largely consisting of poetry, was entitled *Ich will kein inmich mehr sein* (translated into English in 1995 as *I don't want to be inside me anymore*).[95] It was supposedly typed by Sellin independently on a computer. Although critics maintain that his mother contributed considerably to the writing, some German autism specialists I have spoken to, such as Klaus Brause claim that Sellin's 1992 book showed German society conclusively, for the first time, that individuals with autism were educable.[96]

## Greater Awareness

The 1980s was the decade when a mass audience were made aware of autism through the release of the 1988 movie, *Rain man*, starring Dustin Hoffman as an autistic savant, Raymond Babbitt, and Tom Cruise as his brother, Charlie. Although Hoffman won an Oscar for his performance, honed after closely observing individuals with autism, including Ruth Sullivan's son, Joe (see chapter 4) there were complaints in some circles that the film presented a misleading picture of the disorder: only 10% of autistic individuals, the critics pointed out, had the kind of savant skills Raymond displayed.

One of the principal advisers on *Rain man*, Dr. Darold Treffert, acknowledges that "there is a danger of walking away from the movie with the impression that all autistic persons are savants and that all savants are autistic. Neither of course is true."

However, Treffert told me, this danger was offset by the fact that the movie "did more to bring autism and savant syndrome to the public attention than any other public-education effort had done up until then. Moreover, the movie is not a documentary. It is entertainment, yet informative. Were it not for the savant skills (toothpick counting, square roots, calendar calculating, card counting), there would have been no screenplay or movie. Indeed, it was the savant skills of Kim Peek (who was not autistic) that inspired Barry Morrow to write the screenplay. Later, a conscious decision was taken to portray the underlying disability as autism, rather than mental retardation—hence the rituals, sensory sensitivity, flatness, need for sameness on which the savant skills are superimposed."[97]

Treffert added: "The main messages of the movie—that there is no six-day cure for autism and that it is really Charlie who changes, not Raymond—overshadow any caveats. Charlie's accommodation with, acceptance of, and appreciation for his brother at the end of the movie—rather than the stereotypical rejection and ridicule—that change in Charlie—is a message for all of society. We need to make those same changes—and we are really beginning to do just that."[98]

# 9

# Autism in the Developing Nations

In 1984, the Egyptian-born Jewish psychologist, Victor Sanua, published a study claiming that infantile autism "appears to be an illness of Western civilization, and appears in countries of high technology, where the nuclear family dominates. . . . We also saw that the illness [sic] seems to be quite infrequent in Latin American countries, Africa and India, while the rate is high in Japan, but only in Westernized families."[1] In other studies, Sanua also suggested that autism was more common in families with higher socio-economic status—echoing Leo Kanner's observations in his original 1943 paper.

Sanua's conclusions have generally been rejected. It is now widely accepted that autism recognizes no geographical or social boundaries. The prevalence rates are virtually identical in most parts of the world. There have been some recent reports of isolated anomalies. In 2008, the Minnesota Department of Health in the United States announced that it was conducting an epidemiological survey, in consultation with the federal Centers for Disease Control and Prevention, to examine claims of high rates of autism among Somali immigrants in Minneapolis. Increased prevalence of autism among the Somali community in Sweden has also been reported.

Dr. Michael Cuccaro, a clinical psychologist at the Miami Institute for Human Genomics, has conducted genetic studies comparing African-American and Caucasian children with autism. He says it is possible that different ethnic groups have genetic differences which lead to an increased susceptibility to autism. "People in autism [research] tend to suggest the same rate regardless of culture or country. But when you look at other diseases, that's not necessarily the case," Cuccaro says, pointing out that Alzheimer's disease and multiple sclerosis have different prevalence rates in Africa than in the United States or Europe.[2] But the fact remains that previous studies on autism prevalence among ethnic groups have found few differences. What is clearly true, however, is that the cultural attitude to autism is dramatically different in the developing nations, where in some cases the condition was not acknowledged until the early 1990s.

The Chinese have two expressions for autism. On the mainland, they say *gudu zheng*, meaning "lonely disease." In Hong Kong, Taiwan, and among the Chinese communities in Malaysia and Singapore, they use *zhibi zheng*, meaning "being closed off." Neither expression is particularly enlightened and they both illustrate just why the sense of stigma remains so potent in China today, just as it does in most of the other developing nations.

People first began talking about autism in China in 1982, when a Nanjing child psychiatrist, Professor Tao Guotai, who is now 93 years old, published the first paper on the disorder in Chinese. A further 30 cases were discussed in 1984. Before that, there was no official recognition of autism whatsoever. When the French psychiatrist, Georges Heuyer, visited China in the 1960s, he was told that there had been no cases of autism in the country since Mao came to power.[3]

One of China's leading autism experts, Professor Jia Meixiang, who has been working in the field for almost 30 years, told me over dinner in Beijing that she and her colleagues realized before 1980 "that these children had special problems and special abilities, even if we didn't understand what was wrong with them. Those with language and intellectual problems were generally put into institutions."[4]

There seems to have been an instinctive understanding, however, that autism was not an emotional disorder. Chinese professionals, by and large, did not fall into the trap of blaming the parents. Perhaps this was because psychiatrists in China

**Figure 71**  Jia Meixiang

were not as strongly influenced as their European and American colleagues by the need to shun echoes of the Nazi eugenic laws and notions that genes could control behavior.

**Figure 72**   Guo Yanqing (second left), with Professor Liu Jing (far left)

"I think most Chinese professionals did not make the parents feel responsible," one of Beijing's leading child psychiatrists, Dr. Guo Yanqing, told me. "However, they misled them in other ways, by suggesting that the children were mentally retarded or simply speech-delayed. Most professionals here tend to feel sorry for parents who have a child with medical problems. They try their best to help or understand, rather than apportion blame. Not all doctors here are like that, of course. But the overall culture and history of the traditional Chinese doctor–patient relationship is based on trust. Until recently, that is, when this relationship hit a series of problems and the trust has started to fade."[5]

Perhaps one of the most moving accounts of what life was like for the mother of an autistic child in 1980s China comes from Tian Huiping, the outspoken woman who eventually came to set up the first private autism school in mainland China, Stars and Rain.

I met Tian at her small but comfortable apartment on the outskirts of Beijing.

**Figure 73**   Tian Huiping

She is an attractive, bubbly 50-year-old with a contagious laugh and excellent English and German. She is very much a maverick and an independent spirit.

Tian—who is better known as Hope—was one of the first Chinese students to be sent to West Germany (where she studied public administration) rather than East Germany after the Cultural Revolution. That was in 1986. The year after her return to China in 1988, her son was diagnosed with autism. She told me that, as soon as she heard the diagnosis, "I wanted to die. I couldn't find any reason to be alive. I didn't tell my husband that our son was autistic. I don't think that he would have been any help, in any case."[6]

Hope said that there was a serious cultural problem facing disabled children and their families in China: "Here in China, everyone believes that, if a child is disabled, it is the child's fault, not the fault of the system or society. Our government is the luckiest government in the world. Nobody expects them to help. But it is their job to help! The problem is that you have to be very patient with the Chinese government because it is like an autistic child—it is developmentally disabled."[7]

She added: "Parents go to different centers—there are more and more of them. But I don't think many of these centers really work in the autistic children's interest. They work for society, for other values. They think: 'We must change this child to make him or her as normal as possible.' They don't think about changing society to fit the child's needs."[8]

Despite this rather bleak appraisal, she regained her hope (hence her nickname) and love for life and set up Stars and Rain in 1993. The school now has 50 children and 18 students. The lovely name comes from a Taiwanese allusion to autistic children as "children of the stars" and from the 1988 film, *Rain man.* It quickly became a huge success, attracting pupils from all over China. Its only major crisis occurred during the SARS (Severe Acute Respiratory Syndrome) epidemic which killed more than 300 people in 1993, when she had to close the school for a term.

Hope says that, despite the vast problems remaining, she is very optimistic for the future. And above all, she says her son has given her a mission in life.[9]

The main autism organization in China is BARAC, the Beijing Association for the Rehabilitation of Autistic Children. Set up in 1993, it now works closely with parents, runs an advice hotline for parents to consult, and publishes magazines for the association's members four times a year as well as books and other journals to increase awareness.

236

BARAC's status is a little confusing. Its members insist it is a non-profit-making public organization, but independent of the government. However, many of the professional members are doctors working for Beijing's Sixth Hospital which is affiliated to Beijing University and is therefore, of course, a state-run institution. It receives no government funding—all the income is from members' fees and private donations.

BARAC also runs two autism-specific schools in Beijing. I visited one, a large, impressively equipped center with the evocative name of Colorful Deer, situated in the east of the Chinese capital, near the international airport. It was set up four years ago by Sun Menglin, a law graduate who studied in Canada, and now has 100 pupils.

**Figure 74**   Sun Menglin (right) and Professor Sun Dunke

"When I returned to China in 2004, I was shocked to meet some autistic children," she told me. "They were cute, mostly boys, and I was touched but also hurt. It was the first time I heard the word 'autism.' I decided I wanted to help so I set up what was then a small center. The money came from parents and friends. There was no government help at all."[10]

Sun said that she had a Canadian passport and many contacts in North America, from where she received valuable assistance, but there was still a need for more funds and more training for her teachers.[11] The

237

school's director, Griffin Wang, told me he used a mixture of educational approaches, but ABA was the favorite method.[12]

Dr. Guo Yanqing, a prominent member of BARAC who acted as my excellent interpreter during my visit, told me: "At the time BARAC was founded, only a few professionals knew what autism was. That's why we delegated some of the tasks to the parents, and parents are a major component of our association. As the years passed, we learnt a lot of other support strategies: for example, early diagnosis, other assessment tools. We led campaigns to broaden awareness of autism throughout China. We invited experts from the USA, UK, Japan, and elsewhere and we sent our professionals abroad."[13]

The Chinese government does now officially include autism as a disability. "Autistic children have the same rights as all other disabled children," Dr. Guo told me: "And in addition, the one-child policy does not apply to couples who have an autistic or other disabled child—they can have another child. In Beijing and Shanghai, the government gives couples 400 yuan [about $58] a month if they have a child with autism. Recently, autism was written into the eleventh national Five-Year Plan, in China, so every one of the country's 31 provinces is being asked to establish a center to help children with autism."[14]

However, Tian Huiping is highly skeptical about the Chinese government's promises. Hope told me that society did not understand autism there, adding: "It doesn't make any difference that people with autism are recognized as disabled. Even if they are in a group of disabled people, that doesn't give them legal protection. It just means they are different. Believe me, it just provides another reason for them to be discriminated against."[15]

Dr. Guo agreed that the stigma attached to autism remained strong—and surprisingly, more so in the big cities: "In the rural areas of China, they do not have the same awareness about autism and people are treated as mentally retarded or special. But they are not taken away to be interviewed by specialists. Whereas they are in the cities, and many parents who have children with autism don't want this known. My classmate from university has a child with autism. She brought him to me for an interview when he was 5. I found out later that she had already received a diagnosis at 3 and had rejected it. Even after I confirmed the diagnosis, she picked up the phone and called me: 'Don't tell my cousins that I have a child with autism.' "[16]

Professor Jia Meixiang is also pessimistic about the future facing adults with autism in China: "Few of them can find employment here in China or take care of themselves."[17]

The authorities claim that the official number of individuals with autism in China is 540,000. This estimate is clearly ludicrously low in a nation of 1.3 billion: the number of autistic people in the United Kingdom, with a population of just 60 million, is also said to be half a million. I raised this issue in Beijing, and I was told by Professor Liu Jing, another leading child psychiatrist and also a vice-president of BARAC, that the discrepancies could be due to the fact that the screening process was inadequate in China and many professionals still used non-Western diagnostic tools.[18]

Professor Sun Dunke, an unfailingly courteous grandfather of a boy with autism and a leading light in BARAC, told me, in excellent English (as befits a university English teacher): "When I got the news of the diagnosis, my reaction was the same as anywhere else. I felt sad, even guilty. In January 1995, few professionals knew anything about autism. It was not officially recognized in China at the time. It has been a long, hard road for me."[19]

The main problem today, he said, was how to educate the parents. "We mustn't lose hope. It is the government's duty to provide facilities. But this is impossible without the joint effort of the parents and the professionals. At the moment, people are having to travel thousands of miles to Beijing for services. We need to win society's respect for autistic children. That is my hope."[20]

Elsewhere in Asia, awareness of autism generally began even later than in China. In India, articles have appeared in medical journals and books since the 1950s in which the authors describe cases of pervasive developmental disorder, using the terminology of the day. However, there is a tantalizing report in 1944—just a year after Leo Kanner's landmark paper—by a Viennese pediatrician, Dr. A. Ronald, based at the time in Darjeeling, presenting an overview of the detection, causes, types, and treatment of what he termed "abnormal children"—an echo, actually, of Hans Asperger's terminology. The report, which appeared in the *Indian Journal of Pediatrics*, refers to several types of "difficult" child, including the "precocious" child who, to our ears, sounds like an autistic savant: "Such children are no longer child-like, they do not play and are not cheerful. Partial precociousness shows itself in the development of a particular sense, for example, musical sense, calculations, mechanical handling, and so on. In this group is included the so called prodigy."[21] Whether or not Ronald was referring to autism in 1944, in the decades that followed autistic children were dismissed as idiots or insane.

**Figure 75** Merry Barua

No one knows more about the situation in India than Merry Barua, the hugely energetic and delightful director of Action for Autism who has an adult son, Neeraj, with autism. An elegant lady with an engaging sense of humor and a ready laugh, Barua met me at her office in New Delhi. "There was the occasional doctor who diagnosed autism for the past 25 years, but as a generally recognized disability, it is only over the past five to 10 years that it been properly understood," she said.[22]

The media had played a major role in this increase in awareness, she told me, and the stigma which used to be attached to the disorder was waning: "The entire disability sector has been very active over the past five to six years. General perceptions of disability have changed. For instance, Indian films used to be limited to physical disabilities—now people are looking at mental disabilities, including autism. Of course, the handling is still often very inappropriate and inept. But they are achieving some commercial success."[23]

Modestly, she did not point out that it was her organization, Action for Autism, that had done more than any other to raise awareness, improve education, and liaise with the government on legal and other issues. Its school, Open Doors, is a model of its kind. Indeed, it was the very first autism-specific school in India. Of the 3,000 special-needs schools in the whole of India, only 25 are autism-specific, although the latest estimates suggest that there could be 1.7 million people affected by autism in the country. Action for Autism also runs a program working with parents who come not only from all over India but also from Pakistan and Bangladesh to learn more about how to handle their children.

Even when discussions first began about including autism as a disability in legislation, as recently as 1994, few people had even heard of the term in India. And the battle to persuade the authorities to bracket autism in with other disabilities has been a tough one, largely led by Barua and Action for Autism. The problem, as Barua explained, is that the situation "is skewed towards physical disabilities. For example, if you had one arm and leg but high intellectual capacity, you would still

240

be considered far more severely impaired than someone with autism. People do not really understand disability in India."[24]

A recent example of this occurred in 2006, when the autistic son of the Tamil actor, Prithviraj, and his wife Beena, was prevented from boarding a flight at Bangalore airport. Ahed and his parents were stopped at the security gate and a CISF (security forces) inspector told them that Ahed could not board the Air Deccan flight to Chennai because he looked different. This was not the first time Prithviraj has had to deal with such insensitive remarks about his son. An official at Delhi airport once asked Prithviraj whether his son was mad.

The actor said he had once tried to get an autism certificate for his son from a medical authority in Delhi. "But autism has not been classified as a disability under the Disability Act. The authorities asked me if I could accept a certificate that labeled him mentally retarded . . . Autism is a disability and not a disease. Nor is it retardation. Treat an autistic child with sensitivity."[25]

Barua told me: "I still remember trying to explain to senior professionals in India that autism was not a rare condition. But one of them told me that it was so rare we should not be bothering with it. In fact, he said it did not occur at all in the sub-continent—and that was as late as 1995! They said it was a Western disorder."[26]

Despite the considerable improvements, some professionals prefer to blame the parents: "Even now, people say things like: 'Both parents are working, so what do you expect?'" Barua told me. "Of course that's

ridiculous. Even if the child may not get the appropriate amount of attention, this does not cause autism. But unfortunately, the belief that parents are the cause still persists here in India."[27]

Barua admitted that there still a huge stigma attached to autism in India. Nevertheless, one major battle has been won. Although autism is not included in the Persons with Disabilities Act, the disorder is now enshrined in the so-called National Trust for Autism and Cerebral Palsy Act.

In Pakistan, as in India, full awareness of autism has emerged only over the past few years. A key year was 2006 when Qazi

**Figure 76**  Qazi Fazli Azeem  Fazli Azeem became the first person in a

241

country of 160 million people to come out openly on television and admit he had Asperger's syndrome. (In fact, he believes 11 other members of his family also have the condition, although they have not been officially diagnosed.)

A charming man with an excellent understanding of computers, Qazi told me: "Things are moving slowly. The Disability Act does not include autism. There are still few doctors able to diagnose autism. And there are no autism-specific schools whatsoever."[28]

Qazi has set up his own autism organization in Karachi, the Pakistan Autism Meetup Group, and feels there is a pressing need for more awareness in services: "In a few years' time, there will be more people with autistic spectrum disorders than without," he said. This was a reference not only to the increase in diagnoses but to the broadening of the spectrum to include other conditions.[29]

The stigma attached to autism remains strikingly potent in Pakistan. In 2001, in an unprecedented ruling, Chicago immigration officials granted political asylum to a 10-year-old autistic boy, Umair Choudhry, whose mother had claimed his disability was so misunderstood in Pakistan— their homeland—that he would be tortured and persecuted if they returned there. In her application for asylum, Farah Choudhry said her son was subjected to discrimination and persecution because of his autism, which in Umair's case includes compulsive behavior and mystifyingly violent, self-abusive outbursts. Today the boy routinely wears a hockey helmet and mittens for his own protection.

"He was forced to undergo various degrading and dangerous mystical treatments consistent with the 'curse of Allah,' which is how the Islamic majority in Pakistan view his condition," Choudhry wrote in her asylum application.[30] Among the treatments was making the boy drink dirty water meant for crows. At the time, Islamic experts warned against confusing traditional cultural mores with religious beliefs. Although the notion of God's will was consistent with Islam, there was nothing in the religion that ascribed a physical or mental limitation to a curse from God, they said.

Bangladesh is even further behind than Pakistan. The chairman of SWAC (Society of the Welfare of Autistic Children) there, Anwar Hossain, told me: "The concept of autism started in 1995 or 1996. Before that, these children were labeled as insane or idiots. After 1996, when a small school of five or six students was opened up, people started talking about autism. But that was only in the capital, Dhaka."[31]

The center is part-residential and the funding comes largely from the fees charged to parents. Since Bangladesh is one of the poorest nations on earth, it seems surprising that parents are able to pay these fees, but Hossain told me: "Funnily enough, most of the autistic children come from rich, intellectual parents."[32] This observation struck an odd echo of Leo Kanner's comment in his 1943 paper about such parents predominating.

As elsewhere, the social stigma remains powerful in Bangladesh: "We must fight this. That's why we take our children to parties. Let people stare at them, so at least they learn what autism is," said Hossain.[33]

There remains no legal protection for individuals with autism in Bangladesh, where the condition is not recognized as a disability. And people with Asperger's condition are routinely bullied. Sadly, this is true in even the most advanced of nations.

The situation in Vietnam is an interesting one. One of the world's leading autism authorities, Professor Margot Prior, of the University of Melbourne, Australia, spent three weeks in Hanoi in October 2001. At the Institute of Psychology in Hanoi she found that many of the 24 social scientists had received their basic degrees in Russia, and their postgraduate training in France. Prior wrote

> The demand for clinical psychology services in Vietnam is very high, with virtually no services available for the population unless they suffer from a florid psychiatric condition. The courage, enthusiasm, dedication, and keen desire for learning in these predominantly young research psychologists in the Institute of Psychology was truly remarkable. The conditions in which they work can only be described as Spartan; they lack access to books, journals and up-to-date research information, which we take for granted.[34]

Prior said that services and special education opportunities for autistic children in Vietnam were minimal and the families were in a desperate plight. "Their situation is parallel to that obtaining in the 1960s in Australia, when autism was first recognized and the first services were developed."[35] During her stay in Vietnam, Prior helped in the formation of an Autistic Childrens' Parents Association to lobby for services for their children.

The Public Medicine Association estimates that of Vietnam's 83 million population, 160,000 people are autistic. Dr. Do Thuy Lan of the association said in 2007 that parents who sought help from the Vietnam Association for Handicapped Children in Hanoi admitted they did not know what to do when faced with their child's developmental problems. Many also said they were embarrassed to let other people know their children were not developing or behaving normally. "Some don't even want to acknowledge the doctor's diagnosis that their child is autistic and keep going for behavior and development check-ups at different places. When they finally decide to cooperate [for therapy], it is too late for effective intervention."[36]

This process of intervention required cooperation between pediatricians, psychologists, and educators but this was especially difficult because there was no special educational model for them in Vietnam, Lan said.[37]

One Asian country stands out in terms of how early it began to talk about autism and approach the disorder seriously: Japan. This was because some of its leading professionals actually worked with either Leo Kanner or Hans Asperger. Dr. K. Makita studied with Kanner at Johns Hopkins in Baltimore. Dr. Nobuyoshi Hirai met Asperger in Vienna in 1962 and invited him to give a talk on "Probleme des Autismus im Kindesalter" (Problems of Autism in Childhood) to the newly formed Japanese Society for Child and Adolescent Psychiatry (JSCAP) three years later.

Dr. Tokio Uchiyama, one of Japan's leading child psychiatrists and autism authorities, told me that, throughout the 1960s, a fascinating debate took place between Makita and Hirai over which constituted the "true autism"—Kanner's or Asperger's.[38]

In Japan, the health services have traditionally been excellent and on the whole this has permitted early recognition and diagnosis of autism. Some of the earliest prevalence studies took place here. Nevertheless, there are still serious misconceptions. A 2005 poll conducted by the Tokyo-based Autism Society Japan showed that about 30% of Japanese believe that autism is an emotional disorder or is caused by poor parenting. The same poll found that about 20% of parents were uneasy about their children playing with autistic children. Culturally, there is a powerful drive in Japan to conform to the norm, which explains why it is still difficult for parents to come to grips with having a child who is "different."

A particular educational approach to autism has its origins in Japan. The Higashi (Japanese for "hope") or Seikatsu Ryouhou (Daily Life Therapy) method was developed in Tokyo in 1964 by Dr. Kiyo Kitahara, who said it had reduced the symptoms of autism in more than 3,000 children. It was based on Dr. Kitahara's experience of teaching autistic children and normal children in the Musashino Higashi Kindergarten. Higashi is based on a strong belief that physical education and vigorous

244

exercise should play an essential role in teaching autistic children. A school based on Higashi principles opened in Boston, in the United States, in 1987, with much of the funding coming from Kitahara. Prior's Court School, established in the United Kingdom by Dame Stephanie Shirley in the 1990s, also largely used Higashi principles, although it now adopts a more eclectic approach.

In South Korea, many professionals continue to view autism as an emotional condition. As Roy Grinker has pointed out,[39] it is frequently misdiagnosed as reactive attachment disorder. But the situation is improving and parents are fighting to improve understanding. On January 12, 2006, a new group, the Love Autism Society of Korea, held its inaugural meeting in the capital, Seoul. Its president, Kim Yong-jik, 51, himself the father of a 22-year-old son with autism, told reporters that awareness of autism had increased in South Korea—notably after the 2005 release of Jeong Yun-Cheol's movie, *Marathon*, based on the real-life story of an autistic youth training to become a marathon runner—but most of the burden was still left on the shoulders of parents.

In Thailand, public awareness was boosted for tragic reasons in December 2004 when Poomi Jensen, the 21-year-old autistic grandson of one of the world's longest reigning monarchs, King Bhumibol Adulyadej of Thailand, was killed in the huge tsunami of December 26, 2004, while jet-skiing at a Khao Lak beach resort in the Phang Nga province of southern Thailand. Poomi Jensen had actually been brought up in San Diego, California, the son of a Thai princess and an American businessman. He went to live in Thailand with his mother a few years ago, after his parents waged a custody battle over him in a bitter divorce. The prince often accompanied his mother, Princess Ubolratana, to official and social functions. In a departure from Thai tradition, the princess was open about her son's disability, discussing his special needs in interviews and lending her name to fundraising drives for autism.

★ ★ ★

Interest in autism in Africa is longer-standing than is generally realized. In 1978, Victor Lotter—who, it will be recalled, carried out the world's very first epidemiological study of autism in 1966, in the English county of Middlesex—published what was, in geographical terms, at least, a far more ambitious piece of research. Over a two-year period, he visited institutions for the mentally handicapped in nine cities in six

245

nations in Africa—South Africa, Zimbabwe, Zambia, Kenya, Nigeria, and Ghana. Lotter was surprised by what he found. The number of autistic children in the institutions was far lower than he had expected: only nine of the 1,312 mentally handicapped children he saw were autistic. Lotter also discovered—as Kanner had in his 1943 paper—that the parents of the children tended to be professionals, or as he called them, from the "elite" class.[40]

At around this same time, in the late 1970s, clinicians in Nigeria and later in Kenya confirmed that autism indeed was present among African children but found it extremely rare. The three Kenyan children's parents included a medical doctor, an engineer and the "chairman of a parastatal organization." The reason for this bias was probably similar to the Kanner imbalance: it was the more "sophisticated" parents who were more likely to refer their child to a clinic for a diagnosis. (In the same way, a parent in Vietnam recently reported that her therapist did not see any children when she visited schools in poorer neighborhoods: it was only children of middle-class families, those that could afford Western-style health care, who were affected.)

Today, autism rates are recognized to be the same in Africa as elsewhere in the world—but the levels of ignorance about the disorder remain startling and frightening. Many autistic children are kept locked away. In Nigeria—and even in South Africa—many parents take their autistic children to witch doctors to expel the "evil demon." Many countries are only now coming to grips with understanding the disorder: Cameroon held its first-ever autism conference in 2007.

Parents are playing a key role in the battle against ignorance against autism. In Ethiopia, most mothers of autistic children "are single-handedly crying in the dark, and most do not feel at ease to talk about them openly," says Zemi Yenus, founder and director of the Joy Center for Children with Autism and Related Developmental Disorders (J-CCARDD) in the capital, Addis Ababa. "Instead, they feel guilty and are ashamed of their autistic children, due to the pressure and misunderstanding of society."[41] Many people in Ethiopia still believe that autism is related to evil spirits or is caused by close-kin intermarriage.

The Joy Center was established in May 2002 by Yenus, herself the mother of an autistic child. She noted:

> Thousands of children with autism in Ethiopia are confined to their homes with no access to sunlight, education or rehabilitation. These children desperately need our help. We are the ones who can help unlock the doors.

Being the mother of an autistic child, I had faced overwhelming senses of confusion, denial and frustration.[42]

A telling example of the continuing lack of understanding of autism in Africa is the case of a severely autistic young Nigerian boy, Great Agbonlahor, deported from Ireland in 2006, who is now virtually a prisoner in his own home in Accra, Ghana, because neighbors consider him to be a "wicked" child or possessed by voodoo spirits.

★ ★ ★

Parents' associations have taken almost as long to take shape in the Middle East. The exception is Israel, where ALUT was established in 1974 and now provides educational, residential, vocational, and leisure-time services to people with autism and works to advance their rights and to improve the services available to them and their families. At the time ALUT was founded, the only treatment available to autistic children and adults was admission to psychiatric hospitals. Indeed, when the then Israeli Prime Minister, Yitzhak Rabin, visited the United States in 1976, his wife, Leah, spent a morning at the Linwood Children's Center in Ellicot City, Maryland (run by Jeanne Simons—see chapter 2), and met Leo Kanner there. After her visit, Mrs Rabin declared: "I can't believe it. We have nothing like this."[43]

In a sense, this was a surprising statement, because Israel at that time was the only country in the Middle East with any resources for autism—and Leah Rabin herself had been instrumental in establishing these services.

Another of the founders of ALUT was the remarkable Edna Mishori. When her son, Dror, was 2½ years old, she was told he was a "later bloomer" and had "special sensitivities." As Mishori told me: "Back then, in the late 1960s and early 1970s, one would hardly ever hear the word 'autism' in Israel, and when you did, it was always related to a psychiatric diagnosis and a form of failure on the part of us, the parents."[44]

After Dror was eventually given the correct diagnosis of autism by an American-trained pediatric neurologist, Mishori realised there were no facilities geared toward kids with autism, nor was there any professional guidance. "My son was referred to a psychiatric day programme at the Tel Hashomer hospital. It was in that waiting-room that we met other parents and realized we were not alone. That is how ALUT started up in 1974. We were around three or four families at first, all of us

247

determined to convince the authorities that our kids deserved special services."[45]

Personal connections really helped. Haim Tzadok, the Israeli Justice Minister, had a niece who was autistic. Leah Rabin—who happened to be a relative of Mishori's—agreed to serve as chairwoman of ALUT's Board of Directors.

"Once ALUT was formed, we started scouting the country for other kids and families. We were often horrified to find many of them institutionalized in psychiatric wards," Mishori told me. "This was not the future we wanted to see for our children. We felt deeply that we had to alter how people viewed autism and how autistic children were being understood and treated. The psychiatric approach had to be changed into an educational approach. At the core was a belief in each child's potential to function within the community to the best of his or her ability. Some of us had the opportunity to travel to the US and see, at first hand, what services were provided to autistic kids over there. We were impressed and knew we wanted the same for our kids."[46]

Mishori said that, along the way, they encountered many bitter disagreements with the medical community in Israel, which was not used to responding to parents' demands. "Finally, in 1977, the first school opened in Tel Aviv—Yachdav [meaning *together* in Hebrew]. It was an old, decrepit building: three rooms, and no yard to speak of. The teachers we hired, however, were all quite enthusiastic. The first class consisted of nine children. It was our first victory, and the beginning of the long road ahead. The school grew quickly and attracted children from far south and far north. I became its principal in 1980. A point of pride at the school was the way we incorporated the arts and music into our curriculum. We had started an orchestra—kids who could not read were suddenly reading music and playing together. We also had a unique arts program and were amazed to discover the hidden artistic talents of many of our students."[47]

After 10 years of hard work, they were able to open the first residential home for young adults in in 1988—Kfar Ofarim (Ofarim Village).

Thanks to ALUT, there are now special nurseries and several centers in Kfar Ofarim, Ramat Hasharon, Jerusalem, Holon, and Netanya. ALUT has also established 15 Homes for Life throughout Israel. The homes are located in residential areas, with daily life resembling normal family life as much as possible. Israel also has a number of respected autism specialists, including Nurit Yirmiya and Nurit Bauminger.

In the Arab world, a number of very well-equipped associations now exist—but they took much longer to be established. The first to be formed was the Kuwait Center for Autism (KCA). As elsewhere in the Arab world, the organization requires official approval by the government so it sacrifices a certain degree of independence. The Kuwaiti Ministry of Education has supplied the center with a number of teachers.

The founder and current director of the KCA, Dr. Samir al-Saad, told my monthly international autism newsletter, *Looking Up*, that the first moves to create the center actually began in 1989, as a classroom in her home. Dr. al-Saad has a daughter with autism. One of the KCA's most prestigious events was its first conference on autism and communication deficits, held in February 2000. The KCA has also cooperated with the University of London in launching an autism diploma course for teachers and other professionals. In addition, the KCAS runs a diagnostic service for families, both inside and outside Kuwait, offering psychological, medical, genetic, and clinical advice.[48]

There is a particular poignancy about the situation in Saudi Arabia because a prominent member of the Saudi royal family has autism. Dr. Talat al-Wazna, the secretary-general of the Saudi Autistic Society, told me that some stigma remained. Some parents, he said, argued: "We don't want our child to be labeled autistic. That's a psychiatric condition. Why not put us under the umbrella of cerebral palsy?"[49]

He added that the major challenge in Saudi Arabia was those individuals "in the middle, who do not achieve higher education but do not need 24-hour residential care, either. There are also very few services for adults with autism. We need vocational programs for adults. We still miss some of them, but at least it will be a start."[50]

I brought up with Dr. al-Wazna the unusual phenomenon of arranged marriages involving men with autism in Saudi Arabia. He told me that there were three preconditions for this to happen: the possibility of sterilization should be considered, care had to be ensured, and the religious authorities had to agree to the marriage. "There are certainly some women who accept the idea of marrying an autistic man to care for him, and she expects to have a healthy child. But is not easy to discover a woman in this position."[51]

The Kingdom's first international symposium on autism and related development disorders was held in Riyadh in October 2003. A positive sign of tolerance of difference is the fact that Saudi Arabian Airlines became the first airline in the world to provide special care for autistic passengers. It has also developed special casein- and gluten-free meals for autistic passengers.

Dr. al-Wazna told me that his organization had launched a concerted awareness campaign, which, he said, enjoyed the personal support of the King because of autism in the royal family. "We have been placing information in the print and electronic media—and religious leaders have even been persuaded to talk about autism during Friday prayer meetings."[52]

In war-ravaged Iraq, some 40 children who range in age from 4 to 15 attend the Rami Institute for Autistic and Handicapped Children in the Mansour district of the western part of the capital, Baghdad. The center appears to be the only one of its kind in the country, although there may be at least 3,000 autistic children in Iraq, Sabah Sadik, national adviser to the Iraqi Ministry of Health, told the IRIN news agency in 2004. However, many of the country's health records have been destroyed.

The Rami Center was established in 2002 by Nebrass Saadoun Reda and named after a 10-year-old autistic boy, Rami Saba. The non-profit-making Iraqi organization, Iraq Foundation, donated a computer, educational software, sketchbooks, colored pens and pencils, and cleaning products to the center. In 2004, Enfants du monde, a French-based children's aid agency, furnished a special speech therapy room with colorful puppets and other tools of the trade.

The center could teach the children only until they reach the age of 12, said Saadoun. After that, their families had to find another way to teach them and take care of them. "Our society doesn't know anything about disabled and handicapped children. We need more education to teach them," he added.[53]

★ ★ ★

In post-communist Eastern Europe, the understanding of autism is very uneven. Take the former Yugoslavia. In Serbia, a small group of parents and professionals founded the Autism Society as early as 1977. The society has fought, successfully, to ensure that people with autism have access to specialized education, health care and social security. A paper published in the Zagreb-based *Croatian Medical Journal* in 2003 claimed to have found significant differences in ridge counts on the fingers and palms of individuals with autism and their family members.[54]

In 2004, J. K. Rowling, the best-selling author of the *Harry Potter* novels, was so shocked by the newspaper photograph of a small autistic boy, Vasek Knotek, staring out from his caged bed in a care home in the Czech Republic that she launched a multimillion-pound campaign to transform his and other children's lives across Eastern Europe. Vasek is no longer caged and is making progress at a new institution, the Raby Social Care Home near the Czech capital, Prague.

Liuba Iacoblev, president of the Autism Society in Romania, told me that the situation remained bleak there—and had not really improved much in the 10 years she had been working in the field. "There are no autism-specific public services except for a couple of day centers for children in the whole country and there is nothing at all for young people or adults over the age of 18. Until 2007, autistic spectrum disorders did not even appear as a category in our legislation granting special services to the disabled. Autistic individuals were included in the category of psychosis."[55] She said parents, in general, had not acquired the habit of advocacy in Romania. "Recently, we launched an online campaign for the introduction for specific legislation on special education."[56]

The situation in neighboring Hungary is more encouraging. The Hungarian Autism Foundation, a non-governmental organization, was founded in 1989 by Dr. Anna Balázs, one of the best-informed autism specialists in Central Europe. It now runs a school, a research group, an outpatient clinic, and a therapy center. The Autism Foundation's school in Budapest, which has around 30 pupils, adopts a TEACCH-based approach. The Foundation also runs the HANDS (Helping Autism-diagnosed Teenagers Navigate and Develop Socially) Project, in collaboration with international partners, which develops new software to help teenagers and adults cope better with their autism. Balázs is a firm believer in a partnership between pupil, teacher, and technology.

She also directs a publishing house, Kapocs, which in 2005 published *Autismussal onmagamba zarva* (*Closed into myself with Autism*) by the remarkable Hungarian autistic savant, Henriett Seth-F, a highly accomplished writer, poet, and artist who also learnt the gypsies' Romany language in just two months. Henriett's story is a salutary reminder of how difficult life has been, and remains, for even the most gifted of individuals with autism. In 1987, she was refused admission to all the primary schools in her town because of her communication problems— even though, at the age of 8 she was playing the flute and a year later writing poetry. She went on to study at Eszterházy Károly College of Psychology and Sociology in Eger, northern Hungary, but her behavioral problems forced her to leave in 2002. Since then, she has written two books and appeared in a documentary.

251

The plight of autistic children in the former Soviet Union remains bleak. The main autism organization in Russia itself is called Dobro (the Russian word for "goodness"). It was founded by the child psychiatrist, Dr. Klara Samuilovna Lebedinskaya, in 1989 and is run today from its Moscow headquarters by a father-and-daughter team, Sergey Morozov and Svetlana Morozova. Svetlana, Dobro's leading psychologist, is the author of two books: *Autism: The treatment of severe and combined forms* and *The principles for creating individual treatment programs for children with autism*. Svetlana's mother, Tatiana, is a special-education teacher, one of Russia's most experienced and best-known professionals in the field, who has been working with children with autism for the past 28 years.

Most of Dobro's funding comes in the form of grants or donations. According to Sergey and Svetlana, the final years of the USSR's existence were crucial for the birth of organizations like Dobro. However, they say that the problem of autism still resembles a mirage in Russia: it exists in that there are so many children, adolescents, and adults with autism who need qualified teachers, psychologists, and doctors. At the same time, it is as if autism does not officially exist: it is still not included among the developmental disorders which require special treatment in Russia, not is it enshrined in any legislation.

Sergey and Svetlana point out that this situation is ludicrous, since autism has been known about for more than 60 years in Russia: it was described by a child psychiatrist from Leningrad, Samuil Mnukhin, in 1947, independently of Leo Kanner.

From the 1940s to the 1960s, Soviet psychiatry lent special weight to schizophrenia, and many other disorders—including autism—were viewed as specific types of schizophrenia. As a practical consequence, individuals with autism were treated with drugs in psychiatric hospitals and clinics. According to Sergey and Svetlana, it took more than 30 years for there to be an acceptance that such practices were ineffective, that autism was first and foremost a developmental disorder, and that autistic children needed a complex range of psychological and educational assistance. "Parents are growing more informed every year in Russia," Svetlana told me. "Before, they had no idea what autism meant. But the problem remains that they do not receive sufficient support from the education department. They do not know where to turn for help."[57] According to Svetlana and her father, more than 70 years of totalitarian regime produced a tendency in most Russian citizens—including the parents of autistic children—to rely entirely on the state and not fight actively for the rights of their offspring to education and an acceptable quality of life. Sergey said: "We have no legislation specifically for autism here in Russia. We have some laws referring to deafness and blindness."[58]

Svetlana gave me a graphic illustration of the continuing misconceptions about autism: "We tried to establish a special center earlier. They built a beautiful building in northern Moscow and we were on the point of opening, with about 30 staff. Then suddenly, they decided to change the whole program: each teacher, they said, should work with the same programs as children with mental retardation and normal children. We couldn't come to an agreement with them."[59]

Sergey told me that diagnosis remained a big problem in Russia "because we have different traditions from Western countries. First of all, there is the question of links between autism and mental retardation, and autism and schizophrenia. The average age children are diagnosed is 3 to 5, but the problem is the older range, because the traditional thinking here in Russia is that it is impossible to diagnose autism above the age of 15. But that is not true. ICD-10 [the World Health Organization's classification dating from 1992] does not make any such distinction."[60]

There is absolutely no information about autism outside Moscow, according to Svetlana. "No one works with the kids. They just stay at home. Sometimes, they are accepted at ordinary kindergartens, but they just sit in a corner and nobody knows what to do with them. Even here in Moscow, some of our parents are told by their doctors to put their child into an institution, because they don't have any future. It's very sad. For some reason, the Russian government does not want to do anything for them—for the more difficult children, that is. For the easier ones, the government wants to integrate them into mainstream schools."[61]

In 1994, Dobro urged the Moscow government to create the first special school for children with autism. Five years later, Russia saw the establishment of its first school for children with severe forms of autism (using applied behavioral analysis). This school existed until 2002.

Sergey said he knew of only two state-run autism schools in the whole of Russia today—one in Moscow and the other in St Petersburg. "But no one could call themselves satisfied with either school—the quality of the teaching is so low."[62] There are no private autism-specific schools at all, despite the new capitalist climate in Russia following the collapse of communism.

Unfortunately, although the best teachers use an eclectic method, there is a Russian variation of the psychodynamic approach which remains a powerful one in the country today. "It has been going on for the past

30 years," Svetlana told me. "It is called the 'emotional behavioral approach.' It is based on a very complicated theory of five levels of emotional relations. They believe that some of these levels are damaged in autism and that these can be repaired through play therapy."[63]

Another instance of how autism continues to be misunderstood in Russia is that of Rozagy, a talented musician and artist who has been diagnosed with Asperger's syndrome. She recalls that she was subjected to an exorcism before deciding to leave for the UK, where she now lives with her son, who is also on the autistic spectrum.[64]

In Ukraine, the diagnosis and treatment of autism was still lagging three to four decades behind the situation in the West until recently. Olga Bogdashina was instrumental in setting up the Ukrainian Autism Society—although she was born in Siberia and now lives with her autistic son in the UK, where she is a well-known speaker and author of several books on autism.

> For many decades, the totalitarian regime in the former USSR forced psychiatrists to be occupied with questions which were unrelated to medical treatment. . . . Some psychiatrists thought that, if a child was hyperactive. he could not be autistic. Other specialists considered autism to be synonymous with "childhood schizophrenia" or "mental retardation" and they insisted that these children were imbeciles and, therefore, ineducable.[65]

In the eastern Ukrainian region of Donetsk, there were no children officially recognized as having autism until 1995. The situation is improving, according to Bogdashina. She told me that a group of dedicated parents founded Ukraine's first autism society (poignantly known as "From Despair to Hope") in Gorlovka, in July 1994, and she is its president. In March the following year, the first school for autistic children opened in the same town. "They have achieved quite a lot," Bogdashina told me in 2009. "Autism is now being diagnosed. More and more people are becoming aware of autism in the country. As in so many other countries, the parents do not wait for the professionals to catch up with developments—they educate themselves about the condition and urge the authorities to recognize their children's needs."[66]

★ ★ ★

In Latin America, the influence of the psychoanalytical model of autism has been very powerful, and remains so in some nations. The Brazilian-born Professor Ami Klin, of the Yale Child Study Center in New Haven, knows the region well. He told me that psychogenic thinking was still strong in Argentina due to the influence of French (particularly Lacanian) ideas, as well as those of the Austrian-born psychoanalyst, Melanie Klein. Even in Brazil, where things are changing for the better, "just 10 years ago, an autistic child would be given a place in a school only on condition that the mother received psychoanalytical therapy."[67]

Some truly harrowing accounts have emerged from the region in recent years.

In El Salvador, an autistic boy, Oscar Nosta, was taken to an institution and then moved around the country without his parents' knowledge. At the age of 12, Oscar was put away behind a cold steel door, while rats nibbled at his feet and insects crawled all over his skin. His mother, Adelina, whose husband and brother had been murdered, finally tracked him down and took over his care in 2003. Now in his early twenties, Oscar is able to recount his horrific experiences.[68]

In 2003, Mental Disability Rights International (MDRI)—a human rights group with a focus on the rights of disabled people throughout the world—traveled to Paraguay where they found two young boys with autism, Jorge and Julio, locked away behind bars at a state-run neuropsychiatric hospital. The two boys were naked and had been detained in an isolation cell for five years. MDRI reported: "Lacking toilets, Jorge had been forced to urinate and defecate in the very space where he was to sleep, eat, and reside." MDRI immediately filed a report with the Inter-American Commission on Human Rights (IACHR) and on December 31, 2003, Paraguay's President, Nicanor Duarte Frutos, dismissed the institution's director. Jorge was released but Julio was less fortunate: he still remains in a cell at times.[69]

Governments have not generally been helpful in assisting parents in their efforts to campaign concertedly on behalf of autistic children. In any case, the autism associations have been formed much later than in Europe—sometimes as long as three decades later.

One of the continent's oldest is Domus, in Mexico. Its president, Judith Martínez de Vaillard—mother of five children, the youngest of whom, Fabián,

**Figure** 77 Judith Martínez de Vaillard

is autistic—founded the organization in 1980, along with two other families. This part of the world has very particular problems to deal with, as Martínez de Vaillard—also the new president of the Latin American Autism Federation (FELAC)—explained to me in Mexico City: "We rented a house for the premises but the building was badly damaged in the 1985 earthquake, so we quickly had to find a new place. We started training teachers, we knocked on doors to break down ignorance about autism, and we now have 78 children and adults here at Domus."[70]

Edna García de Martínez, former president of FELAC and the founder-director of the Castello autism center in the Mexican city of Monterrey, has a 17-year son, David, with autism. In 1993, she began her search to understand why his development was so different from that of his brothers. "I ended up diagnosing him myself. At that time, I knew as much about autism as I know about astronomy today—in other words, almost nothing."[71]

She said a number of articles by Bernard Rimland had given her the first clues to David's condition. "It was not easy to find books on autism in Mexico at that time, but information began to appear on the internet: articles from the European and American autism associations and others. Most people seemed to accept that the right methods were behavioral modification (ABA), speech therapy, and the famous vitamin B6 and magnesium.

"Ten years ago in Mexico, the word 'autism' caused considerable fear among professionals here. They preferred to give you any other label. Above all, they talked about the immaturity of the child. The diagnostic confusion exists to this day because of the various myths which cling on and also due to the lack of up-to-date information available to the professionals—and that includes doctors and neurologists."[72]

She told me that the initiative to spread information about autism had come largely from parents. "Although the professionals didn't necessarily blame the parents, they did often suggest that the autism could have been caused by some deterioration in the child's emotional environment, some family event or trauma which could have affected him or her in the early years."[73]

What influence could Mexico's geographical position have, pincered as it is between the United States to the north and the rest of Latin America to the south? In other words, could there be a tension in the way the concept of autism has evolved between the more "organicist" notions in the US and the old "Bettelheimian" approach still powerful in some Latin American nations? "Mexico adopts everything that comes from the United States. It is as if to say that, if it comes from there, it has to be good!" García de Martínez told me. "But Bettelheim is generally rejected because of his idea of cold parenting. Some Mexican professionals, however, especially child psychologists and some psychiatrists, continue to insist that we are talking about child-hood schizophrenia and that there is a need to build up the 'ego' in these individuals. That is, they continue to see autism as a problem of emotional development."[74]

The biggest advances in understanding of autism have been seen in the Mexican states with greatest access to information (Nuevo León, Jalisco, Mexico City), and those who share a border with the United States (Tamaulipas, Baja California).

García de Martínez emphasized that it was the parents who had played the key role in increasing awareness and understanding of autism in Mexico. "Economic problems mean that the government is not able to integrate a strategy for autistic individuals across the nation, so it was left to the parents to spread information and start up services."[75] She recalled that, when she first announced plans to set up a center for *autistas* (autistic individuals), people were confused and constantly referred to *artistas* (artists) and even to *bautistas* (Baptists).

Mexico City is also the headquarters of FELAC, which represents the interests of individuals with autism throughout Latin America. Made up of parents, professionals, and autism-related institutions and associations, it was founded in 2000 by the World Autism Organization (itself set up in 1988 with its base in Luxembourg).

According to García de Martínez, almost every Latin American country has at least one autism association, but Mexico and Argentina are the best-informed nations (in Mexico, there are three parents' associations in Monterrey alone and at least five specialized centers). And yet even in Mexico, the stigma associated with having an autistic child remains powerful: "Much of the population lives in poverty, with no access to education or information, and so they believe in all the myths. There are some parents who are so desperate that they accept anything they are offered, from magic potions to hypnosis. I even had a child who had been taken to an exorcist," García de Martínez told me.[76]

Elsewhere in Central America, we find one of the "babies" among autism associations throughout Latin America. Intégrame (Integrate Me) was launched in Guatemala by mothers of children with autistic spectrum disorders in April 2007, with the aim of providing services and increasing awareness. One of the first children helped by the new organization was an 8-year-old boy, Henry, who had been abandoned by his father and now lives with his mother and 2-year-old sister. Intégrame offered the family both financial and moral support, as well as medication to decrease Henry's disruptive behavior. Nevertheless, there are few professionals capable of diagnosing autism in Guatemala or places offering appropriate treatment at affordable prices. Intégrame is looking at the possibility of buying land to build a center offering a wide range of therapies, as well as opening a school.

In contrast to Intégrame, one of the veterans among Latin America's autism associations is ASPAUT in Chile. It was born in 1983 when a group of parents got together to attempt to create a care center for their autistic children who, until then, were not accepted in any of the country's schools, either state-run or private. It now runs two special schools, Aspaut San Miguel and Aspaut Maipú, and a specialized center called Aspaut Cordillera with more than 270 children with autism.

The stigma attached to autism remains strong in Chile—especially outside the capital, Santiago—due to lack of understanding. One mother of a boy with autism told me in Temuco, southern Chile, that when she took her son out and he delved into strangers' handbags looking for sweets, the owner of the handbag frequently turned round and angrily accused the mother of training her son to be a thief.

The desperate lengths to which some Chilean parents are willing to go was illustrated in 2001 when Pedro Pinto Cortés—the father of an 11-year-old boy with autism—was shot dead in the center of the capital, Santiago, after trying to rob a bank to raise money to care for his son.

Argentina—with its longstanding tradition of psychoanalysis and where many professionals remain rooted in the thinking of Melanie Klein and Jacques Lacan—is one of the Latin American countries where there remain pockets in which parents are still blamed for their child's autism. But the situation is improving—especially with the creation of organizations such as APADeA—Asociación Argentina de Padres de Autistas (Argentine Association of Parents of Autistic Children)—which was founded on August 25, 1994. Its members largely accept that autism is a neurological condition.

APADeA played a key role in breaking away from the psychoanalytical standpoint and opting for other methods—notably behavioral modification or ABA. APADeA's president, Dr. Horacio Joffre Galibert, whose son, Ignacio, is autistic, said: "Today, we know that the educational aspects are much more important than the medical ones. It is not the doctors' job to treat autistic children, but the teachers.' "[77]

Parents in Argentina, as elsewhere in the world, have been instrumental in forcing the authorities to introduce legislation offering protection to individuals with autism. The woman behind the pioneering Autism Law 13380—which came into force in Buenos Aires province in October 2005—is the deputy for the district of Matanzas, Karina Rocca, the mother of a boy with autism. She said the legislation was very important. "It's difficult to get treatment at the appropriate age, which is around a year and a half. Generally, it starts at 4 or 5 years of age at the moment. The children with autism who live in well-off families generally have access to special schools," she said, "but many children live in more modest areas and do not receive any form of special care whatsoever."[78]

The new law is multidisciplinary. It involves aspects of health, education, development, and employment. Rocca said that a special committee of parents of autistic children had been set up to ensure that the law functions successfully. She pointed out that other Argentine provinces were now looking to introduce autism laws, following the Buenos Aires model. She also said that she had received invitations from Brazil and even from as far afield as Australia to explain how such a law could be applicable in those countries. (Indeed, in March 2007, legislators in the Brazilian state of Bahía approved their own autism law.)

Much work still needs to be done in Argentina. As late as August 2008, a conference was still being held there on "autism and infantile psychosis"—as if the two conditions ran parallel with one another or were even equivalents.

The striking differences between Latin American and European methods were highlighted by Theo Peeters who, during one visit to Buenos Aires at the invitation of APADeA to talk about the TEACCH approach, informed his hosts that he would need to consult the parents first "because they were the experts. I will never forget that one of the parents started crying when we asked for her advice. This was the first time, she said, that any professional had asked to speak to a parent. That was extraordinary, because talking to the parents should always be the first stage."[79]

Economic well-being is no guarantee whatsoever of better conditions. Venezuela is one of the most prosperous nations in Latin America, thanks to its oil reserves. But few of these funds have been channelled into autism. The leading parents' association is Sovenia (Sociedad Venezolana para Niños y Adultos Autistas). Its director, Lilia Negrón, told me: "I began in the field of autism in 1975. I couldn't find any help in Venezuela so I sought it in the United States where I met Eric Schopler and the TEACCH group, who gave us a huge amount of assistance, as well as Bernard Rimland, who was our guide. We are leading a quixotic battle here in Venezuela because many neurologists and psychiatrists do not accept what we are doing. And some who claim to be 'autism experts' don't read the latest research or go to conferences, and this is disastrous for our children. Add to that the political problems here in Venezuela, where we're governed by an authoritarian military leader who has closed doors and money to us. This makes our task even harder."[80]

Negrón's reference to criticism of her organization was an allusion to those who do not accept the emphasis she places on the latest biomedical approaches to autism. This pioneer of the TEACCH method in Venezuela is, she told me, "a fervent believer that biological treatments are going to help our children. I'm a doctor, and as such, I know that there are few things that medicine can actually cure. But we are now beginning to demonstrate scientifically what had previously been in the realm of parental anecdote."[81]

The history of Brazil's leading autism association, Asociacão de Amigos do Autista (AMA), began in 1983. There was virtually total ignorance about the disorder in Brazil at the time. A group of parents decided to create the new society and within a year, they had a school which functioned in the backyard of a Baptist church, thanks to the local pastor, whose son, César, has Asperger's syndrome. AMA has won a number of awards, including Unesco's 1998 Human Rights Prize which was presented personally by Brazil's then-President Fernando Henrique Cardoso.

Unfortunately, the country as a whole has shortcomings. Indeed, Brazil risks being internationally condemned for failing to offer adequate care conditions for people with autism. On August 23, 2007, the Defensoria Pública (Public Defence Institution) for Rio de Janeiro presented a document to the Organization of American States (OAS) criticizing the country. If the condemnation is upheld, Brazil will be called to defend itself and it could be warned or suffer various types of sanctions—even economic ones.

Cuba has some excellent autism teachers. The Dora Alonso Special School for Children with Autism was inaugurated in Havana by Fidel Castro himself on January 4, 2002 to mark the fortieth anniversary of special education on the island. The school has 55 pupils—44 boys and 11 girls—from all over Havana, aged between 2 and 18 years old.

Its director is Imilla Cecilia Campos Valdés, 35, a special-education graduate. She said the school included speech, music, and therapy, as well as a library and a workshop where the children make fans. Campos Valdés added that the family's collaboration was crucial. One of the unusual features of the school is the so-called circle of "pioneers"—known as Hombres del Futuro (People of the Future). These are fellow children trained in autism who look after the school pupils and encourage them to relate to others.[82]

Elsewhere in the Caribbean, Teresina Sieunarine told my international autism newsletter, *Looking Up*, that she had decided to set up the Autistic Society of Trinidad and Tobago (ASTT) in 1990 out of a sense of helplessness after her son, Kester, was diagnosed with autism in Florida and, on her return to Trinidad, she found that most autistic children were either in a mental hospital or living at home. There was still a stigma attached to having a child with a disability on the island: when Kester was featured in a newspaper article, his mother told me, "some people called and expressed surprise that we should do such an unusual thing" as to reveal the existence of an autistic son.[83]

★ ★ ★

Devolution in the United Kingdom has produced some very positive results in the autism field in the regions which have become more politically independent—particularly in bilingual Wales. Autism Cymru—

**Figure 78** Hugh Morgan (photo courtesy of Autism Cymru)

Wales' National Charity for Autism—was set up by Dame Stephanie Shirley in 2001 to improve the lives of people in Wales with an autistic spectrum disorder and their families.

Autism Cymru's chief executive, Hugh Morgan, told me: "Political devolution in the UK gave us in Wales a golden opportunity to inspire our national government to accept ownership of autism. We gave the government a different handle on the situation, showing them how public finance was being haphazardly used and emphasizing the need to develop specific policies for people with autism and we asked ministers to develop a ground-breaking national strategy for autism. We also cut out the usual emotion contained in autism lobbying and were quickly seen as providing an authoritative message and as an organization with which the government could work."[84]

Morgan added: "The world's first strategic action plan for autistic spectrum disorders developed by a national government was implemented in Wales from April 2008. This is underpinned by the identification of 'Local ASD Leads' for autism in each of the 22 authority areas throughout Wales; the appointment of regional support officers to getting regional planning and sharing of costs in place, and national direction by the Welsh Assembly Government (WAG). The Welsh Assembly Government is also working with various groups to develop a mass of awareness-raising materials."[85] In 2008, Morgan was appointed the Welsh Assembly Government's implementation manager of the ASD strategic action plan.

Autism Cymru also set up a pioneering bilingual website, www.awares.org and from this runs an annual international autism online conference—the largest of its kind in the world—run by myself and attracting more than 60 of the world's leading autism experts and thousands of delegates. This small charity also runs the biennial Wales International Autism Conference, which attracts delegates and speakers from across the world. It has also delivered training on autism throughout hundreds of primary and secondary schools in Wales and has a partnership with each of Wales's four police forces to raise awareness of autism.

Morgan told me that he thought one of Autism Cymru's greatest achievements to date was the partnership it had formed with Cardiff University and Autism Speaks UK—the British arm of the US charity of the same name.[86] This partnership led to the establishment of the chair in autism research in the School of Psychology at Cardiff University. Morgan feels that "the world's first national government approach to autism also requires a world-class research capability." The first occupant of the chair was Professor Susan Leekam, formerly at Durham University, who took up the Cardiff post in April 2009.

The situation in Northern Ireland is virtually unique, due to the decades of political violence and sectarian strife. Arlene Cassidy, Chief Executive of

**Figure 79** Arlene Cassidy (photo courtesy of Autism Northern Ireland)

Autism Northern Ireland, pointed out to me that there was an autism society back in the 1970s. Some of its members, like Betty Peters, were also involved in the NAS on the British mainland. "But it folded up. Our society, then called PAPA (Parents and Professionals and Autism) was formed in 1990."[87]

At the time, as Cassidy recalled, there was no interest in autism in Northern Ireland either from across the border in the Republic of Ireland or in England. "But what TEACCH was doing in England seemed very impressive to us. Holding therapy was the therapy method of choice in Northern Ireland at the time In fact, there was only one book on autism in the public libraries in Northern Ireland in the early 1990s and that was Niko Tinbergen's book on holding therapy! We were unsuccessful in our request for the book to be taken off the shelves, so in the end we had to dedicate scarce funds to donating supplies of Simon Baron-Cohen's *Autism: The facts.*"[88]

Cassidy agreed that the lengthy absence of a parents' association between the 1970s and 1990 was specifically due to the political problems in Northern Ireland: "Communication, travel and funding in social care were curtailed. Until the 1986 Education Order, children with autism were considered to be 'ineducable.' And yet despite the Troubles, the 1990s were a creative time. We were starting to learn things. The problem was that there was not a lot of information about autism coming in and we felt very isolated. It was only when parents and pioneering professionals got together in an innovative partnership that things got started. So it is a fact that the mechanism for awareness and social change regarding autism in Northern Ireland was the creation of PAPA. But when PAPA was founded, the government was still saying that autism did not exist or was a rare condition."[89]

# Worldwide Collaboration

The worldwide collaborative drive is illustrated by the establishment of organizations like Autism-Europe, a network of associations of parents of individuals with autism in 30 European nations, and the Latin American Autism Foundation (2000). This spirit was further highlighted by the founding of the Celtic Nations Autism Partnership (CNAP) in 2006. The partnership—comprising Autism Cymru, Autism Northern Ireland, the Scottish Society for Autism, and the Irish Society for

Autism—also signed a Memorandum of Understanding with the United States Congress during a visit to Washington, DC, in September 2007. The CNAP is committed to the exchange of information and political action across the devolved nations of the UK, and Ireland.

# 10

# Where the Future Lies

In my voyage of discovery across the globe, I have witnessed howls of despair from some parents, desperately seeking a cure for their child's autism, and smiles of pride from others, indignantly insisting that they would not accept a magic bullet even if it would rid their child of his or her condition. I have received equally mixed messages from professionals, when asked to glimpse into the future as we enter the second decade of the twenty-first century. For some, that future is rosy, full of optimistic prospects for major advances on the research and treatment front. For others, we have not moved very far in our understanding of autism since the 1940s.

In general, the consensus has been that the notion of autism has undergone a dramatic metamorphosis since Hans Asperger and Leo Kanner first described the symptoms in the 1930s and 1940s. What was initially seen as a specific and extremely rare syndrome has evolved into a condition which, with its many different manifestations, is considered among the most common childhood disorders. Kanner, as we have shown, initially recognized social and affective impairments in autism, but not cognitive ones. From the 1960s onwards, researchers like Michael Rutter, Beate Hermelin, Neil O'Connor, and Uta Frith were demonstrating that cognitive deficits were considerable. Today, the issue is more how the affective and social impairments interact.

Nevertheless, Sally Ozonoff, at the MIND Institute in Sacramento, California, reread Kanner's original 1943 paper on a paragraph-by-paragraph basis for a book she was writing and found, she told me, that "almost everything Kanner said was exactly right. He was full of great insights—even in the sense of foreshadowing the head circumference findings." She did not mean that we had not made huge progress—she is remarkably hopeful for the future—and she accepts that there were a couple of areas Kanner got wrong, notably his failure to recognize cognitive impairments in the children.[1]

What would Kanner himself have said if asked what the future held for autism? The closest we can get to an answer is from his colleague, Professor Leon Eisenberg. He told me: "The failure to find a single cause that shows up in autistic children suggests there are multiple causes. I am sure that there will be progress as a result of the MRI brain scans and the haplotyping of the human genome. But we are making the problem of the genetic researchers worse by extending the clinical characteristics of the disorder further and further, so that in a thousand autistic children diagnosed today, there are more different subtypes—some of whom Kanner would never have called autistic—than there would have been if you took Kanner's first 50 patients and the geneticists worked on them."[2]

Hans Asperger, for his part, would have been thrilled to find out what was happening today—or at least, that was what his daughter, Dr. Maria Asperger Felder, told me. "He was a very inquisitive man, and he would have been very interested in all the discussions and research taking place today."[3]

The New York-based neurologist, Mary Coleman, as we have seen, is one of those who has expanded the clinical features of autism. She believes that scientists will discover dozens, even hundreds, of "autisms"—not mere subtypes but specific biological "diseases."[4] Professor Jeremy Turk, the child psychiatrist who diagnosed my son, Johnny, with autism at St George's Hospital in London, with his colleagues published a very recent study of autism spectrum disorder in children with and without epilepsy and concluded:

> Our data add to the growing number of publications that support the notion that autism is not just one condition, but a wide range of social and communicatory disturbances that are influenced in their clinical presentations by etiology, level of intellectual functioning, presence or absence of epilepsy and a range of other factors that affect socialization and language development.[5]

In contrast, the pioneering UCLA researcher, Ed Ritvo, told me: "Autism spectrum disorders—primary autism, Asperger's disorder, and PDD-NOS [pervasive developmental disorder—not otherwise specified]—all have similar symptoms. They differ only in their degree of severity. It is the abnormal rates and sequences of brain development which cause the symptoms of autism spectrum disorders. In turn, it is abnormal micro RNA—non-coding genes—that regulates the timing and sequencing of brain development and cause the clinical symptoms of autism. The abnormal micro RNA that causes autism spectrum disorders is genetically transmitted—but as yet, we do not understand what the exact mode of transmission is nor what turns it on in certain individuals."[6]

Peter Hobson, at the Tavistock Institute in London declared:

> How do we reconcile the heterogeneity of autism (in neurological and genetic terms) and its homogeneity (as Kanner recognized)? What is common in all the autisms? There may be nothing—but I claim there will be something. If we're going to grasp how this particular constellation of behaviours occurs, we're going to need a multilevel approach on a psychological level which will connect particular impairments in interpersonal relationships and repetitive behaviours."[7]

For parents, of course, a theoretical concept of autism as well as the abstract—and sometimes abstruse—debate surrounding it, may all seem irrelevant. What they want to see is research which will guide appropriate and effective treatment in the future—and as near a future as possible. Some researchers, like Dr. Sally Rogers at the MIND Institute in Sacramento, do indeed share this concern and conduct research directed not only at early diagnosis but also at ascertaining the most effective treatment for children already diagnosed with autism.

Dr. Sula Wolff, the German-born psychiatrist, told me that there would definitely be a breakthrough in the search for the causes of autism, "but whether that will help us prevent or treat autism, I don't know. Parents are always going to clutch at straws, and what is really worrying is that they are going to be seduced by people who sell them methods which are of no proven value—additives, nutrients, diets, etc."[8]

As yet unscientifically unproven methods of treating autistic children earn a great deal of money for their practitioners. It has been estimated that American parents spend an average of $50,000 each on treatments for their children with autism. Some, like the gluten- and casein-free diet, are now undergoing controlled trials because parental anecdotes are occasionally very promising. Other treatments can be dangerous. One of these is chelation (pronounced *key-lation*), which is based on still undemonstrated claims by some researchers that the bodies of autistic children are overloaded with heavy metals. Chelation is a process involving the administration of an agent designed to bind with these metals, which are then excreted from the body. In at least one case, that of a 5-year-old boy, Abubakar Tariq Nadama, it proved fatal during a treatment in Pittsburgh in 2005. The National Institutes of Health in the US announced in 2008 that it was abandoning plans to carry out a study of the safety and effectiveness of chelation specifically for autism.

The bizarre recent adventures of "the Horse Boy," Rowan Isaacson, who was taken by his parents, Rupert and Kristin, to live with wild horses and shamans (traditional healers) in one of the world's most hostile environments in northern Mongolia and experienced rituals including whippings with reindeer thongs, were recounted by his father in a best-selling book.[9] Rupert Isaacson insists Rowan's tantrums stopped, he became toilet-trained, joined in games, and described objects, rather than simply repeating learned phrases, and having since taken his son to see the Bushmen in Namibia Isaacson now says he wants Rowan to meet Aboriginal and Maori healers in the Antipodes.

The secretin story is particularly instructive. This hormone was given to a 3-year-old American autistic boy, Parker Beck, in 1998 during a regular endoscopy to try to help his chronic diarrhoea. Soon afterwards, not only did his bowel movements normalize but his autistic features improved: he had more eye contact, language, and sociability. Word quickly spread—Bernard Rimland, among others, professed great excitement—and for a few years, secretin was touted as the new "magic bullet." Parents around the world paid vast sums of money—usually with few results. In 2002, a study by the Universities of Washington and Colorado, believed to be the first to measure the effectiveness of both natural porcine secretin and a synthetic form of the hormone, and a placebo, found that neither form of secretin reduced the symptoms of autism beyond the effects noted for the placebo. The study's co-author, Dr. Geraldine Dawson, then director of the University of Washington's Autism Center, said: "With autism, we know there is a very large placebo effect, so you have to show a bigger effect to say a treatment worked." As Dawson told me at the time: "The placebo effect can be really startling, at times."[10]

One rather strange treatment has recently gained a limited measure of credibility thanks to a new randomized, double-blind controlled study which showed that autistic children who received 40 hours of treatment in a hyperbaric oxygen chamber over a month were less irritable, more responsive when people spoke to them, made more eye contact, and were more sociable than those children who did not receive the treatment.[11] The study's co-author, Dan Rossignol, a family physician at the International Child Development Resource Center in Melbourne, Florida, said the pressure applied during the treatment might reduce inflammation believed by some researchers to restrict blood flow to regions of autistic children's brains. Other studies have shown no useful results, however.

Another possible biological mechanism leading to autism has been proposed by Eric Hollander at the Mount Sinai School of Medicine in New York. He suggests that levels of oxytocin—a hormone which plays a role in a variety of behaviors, including parent–child and adult-to-adult pair bonding, social memory, social cognition, anxiety reduction, and repetitive behaviors—could be reduced in autism. Hollander has even suggested a treatment involving an intravenous infusion of pitocin—the synthetic form of oxytocin. In a test, he claimed to have found that the infusion produced a rapid reduction of repetitive behaviors. He has also experimented with nasal delivery of pitocin. Although he claims his findings are promising, Hollander remains cautious:

> Our findings will need to be replicated in large-scale, placebo controlled trials to fully explore treatment potential. And, though both intravenous and intranasal approaches have been well tolerated, we need to understand more about the safety of these potential treatments, particularly before these effects are explored in autistic children.[12]

Intriguingly, there could be a link between oxytocin and another hormone, testosterone. Unrelated to Simon Baron-Cohen's testosterone findings (see chapter 8), it is known that testosterone down-regulates oxytocin receptors in the brain. This down-regulation may, following Hollander's hypothesis, lead to the reduction in social behavior seen in autism.

\* \* \*

Sula Wolff told me that, thanks to the work of Uta Frith, Simon Baron-Cohen, Francesca Happé, and others, "we can now be more precise about the psychological functioning of people with autism. But it is terribly important to understand that it is not man-made, that it has a constitutional basis."[13]

This message—that mothers do not cause autism—has finally been accepted by professionals in most parts of the world, although the psychoanalytical approach remains strong in France and parts of Spain, Italy, and Latin America, as we have seen. (Manuel Ventura, father of a blind adult son with severe autism, recalled in Barcelona that the head of an autism center in the south of France had recently decided that a young autistic girl had acquired a fear of swimming because the girl's mother kept affectionately calling her "Mon petit sucre"—my little sugar—and the daughter was afraid of dissolving in the water.[14])

Most people who meet a child with autism would, I hope, find Bruno Bettelheim's choice of title for his 1967 book, *The empty fortress*, profoundly misguided. There is nothing remotely fortress-like about autism, which can so often be marked by fragility. And we now know, from the first-hand accounts of articulate autistic individuals like Temple Grandin and Donna Williams, that their minds are anything but empty.

While the acceptance of an organic etiology has become firmly entrenched, another danger has arisen: the conviction, among parents and some professionals, that there must be a biological solution to what is perceived as a medical problem. It is, of course, very useful, from a practical point of view, to present autism as a medical condition because it means that it can be included under medical insurance cover—as is being mandated in more and more US states, for example. But as yet there are no biomedical biomarkers for autism, despite claims to the contrary.

Dr. David Amaral, research director of the MIND Institute in Sacramento, is optimistic: "I think we're within a decade of doing this for some forms of autism. We used to think there might be a blood test. That's clearly not the case. Immune factors and others, when taken together, might produce indications that a person has autism. We're really interested not in the big brain itself but why that particular autistic individual had a big brain. We now have 110 families in our Autism Phenome Project. If you looked at the big brains and also looked at the cytokine levels, you might find linkages or disprove them."[15]

There is an increasingly active campaign on both sides of the Atlantic seeking to present autism and Asperger's syndrome as positive differences, rather than disabilities. Aspies for Freedom holds an Autistic Pride day every June 18—along the lines of the civil rights and gay rights movements—and in the United States and Europe advocates organize annual gatherings called, respectively, Autreat and Autscape.

The search for a cure for autism is sure to continue unabated but it will be hampered by the fact that the causes remain unknown for the majority of so-called idiopathic or non-syndromic cases where there is no known associated medical condition—which is true for an estimated 90% of cases. Examples of known medical conditions associated with autism include Fragile X, tuberous sclerosis, and phenylketonuria (PKU). The hunt for a cure—and even more so, prevention—is also beset with ethical dangers. But it is ironic that, after decades of ultimately successful battles in many parts of the world to persuade governments to accept autism as a disability, many vocal advocates with the condition are now claiming that it should not be referred to as such.

Sally Ozonoff is extremely optimistic about very early identification and prevention. "I think that, not just within my lifetime but maybe within the next decade, we will be able to determine which babies are at risk for autism. And I don't think it is pie in the sky to use treatment to prevent autism so early that we don't even know whether we were right about the diagnosis. I think if you could treat children between 9 and 15 months, I really feel you could pull them out of that trajectory."[16]

Not long ago, a team of doctors at one of Britain's leading hospitals, University College Hospital, in London, announced that they were preparing an application to the country's fertility watchdog which would allow them to screen out male embryos. As boys are four times more likely to be born with autism than girls, the reasoning went, couples with a family history of the condition would want to ensure they had only girls. Although such sex selection is not permitted, at present, the technique, called preimplantation genetic diagnosis (PGD), has been used to create babies free from life-threatening illnesses such as Duchenne muscular dystrophy and hemophilia.

Clearly, screening embryos to prevent babies being born with autism would prove hugely controversial. Joy Delhanty, professor of human genetics at University College London Medical School, was quoted as saying that couples would undergo the treatment only if autism had inflicted severe suffering on the family. "Normally, we would not consider this unless there were at least two boys affected in the immediate family. We would be reducing the risk of autism. Couples are not going to undertake this lightly when we explain what they are going to need to go through."[17] But Simone Aspis, parliamentary and campaigns worker for the British Council of Disabled People, said: "Screening out autism would breed a fear that anyone who is different in any way will not be accepted. Screening for autism would create a society where only perfection is valued."[18]

As we have seen, there is a very vocal lobby of high-functioning individuals with autism—loosely known as the "neurodiversity movement"—who consider talk of a cure or prevention to be insulting because it suggests that autistic individuals are damaged and need to be "fixed." They view their condition as a difference and an essential part of their identity, rather than a disability, and view the idea of being able to "remove" autism from the world with horror and disgust.

271

Dr. Temple Grandin, the world's most famous woman with the disorder, told me: "There would be a horrible price to pay if we got rid of all the mild autism and Asperger's. There would be no sciences, no arts. I don't think social people invent things."[19]

Rita Jordan told me she was very unhappy about the idea of "getting rid" of autism. "The idea of curing autism implies that people with autism are somehow more 'diseased' than people without autism. That is not my experience."[20]

Sally Ozonoff agrees to a certain extent with those who claim their autism is a valuable difference, not a disability: "A lot of them are incredibly interesting and fun people to be around. But if you can't tell who those 30% or 40%—let's say—will be, and yet you can prevent someone from having something really difficult . . . I'm not talking about curing autism but preventing them from having the really disabling versions. It is very hard to predict even as late as 3 whether a child will have the kind of autism which will be valued as an important contribution to society, or whether it will be the kind that makes life very hard and is a disability."[21]

One of the greatest living authorities on the genetics of autism, Dr. Susan Folstein, told me: "There are pros and cons to prenatal testing. If we could predict who would be very severely affected, some families might want to know that. If there were an effective treatment that worked only if— or better, if it were started earlier than—a certain diagnosis could be made, that would be an excellent reason to do it. But note all the *ifs*."[22]

Dr. Mary Coleman is forthright on this issue: "If a genetic finding could help them, we must continue to think of them as being on the medical continuum, rather than outside of it—even if they themselves don't like it and they feel insulted! We must think about the children of the future."[23]

Simon Baron-Cohen told me: "The autistic spectrum involves areas of disability (social skills and communication) but often areas of strength (for example, attention to detail) that in some individuals can blossom into talents. I am horrified by the idea that biological research might be used for prenatal screening for autism: we would risk screening out talents as well as disabilities; we would be discriminating against those with disabilities; and we would be implying that people with autism are of less value."[24]

## Genetic Findings

In the first years of the twenty-first century, genetic research on autism accelerated at an extraordinary pace and continues to do so—but I found caution virtually ubiquitous across the globe. As the great French autism pioneer, Professor Gilbert Lelord, put it to me: "Genetics is a great source of hope. But we need much more time."[25] For her part, Marian Sigman at UCLA said: "I'm a little skeptical that the genetic phenotypes will explain everything—but don't say that too loudly!"[26]

There are likely to be dozens of genes involved in autism. Virtually every chromosome has been implicated, but not convincingly. And we still do not know the significance of the preponderance of males over females in autism. Some recent research suggests that the ratio could be lower than the frequently cited figure of four males to one female, because females may be being under-diagnosed (their interests may be apparently more social, for example). The preponderance is not specific to autism: it is true of other developmental disorders, as well, such as attention-deficit hyperactivity disorder (ADHD), reading disability and developmental language disorder. As Susan Folstein told me: "There are no really strong candidate genes on the X chromosome to suggest an X-linked recessive expression, as in Fragile X. There could be genes on the Y chromosome or on any other genes that cause sex-limited expression."[27]

There have been some exciting recent developments. In February 2008, US researchers identified two separate genetic defects linked to autism, one which directly causes the disorder in about 1% of cases and a second that may play a role in a much larger percentage of patients by increasing their susceptibility to environmental or other genetic influences. The findings offer hope that it may be possible to identify vulnerable children early in life and begin treatment to mitigate autism. In the first study, led by Dr. Mark J. Daly of Massachusetts General Hospital, a multicenter team called the Autism Consortium reported that deletions or duplications of a specific segment of chromosome 16 increase the risk of autism 100-fold. The genetic defect was found in children with autism but not in their parents, indicating that it was a spontaneous mutation that occurred at some point after fertilization. The location, called 16p11.2, on the short arm of chromosome 16, is what is known as a *genetic hotspot*, meaning it is unusually susceptible to such mutations. The deletions or repetitions were found in 24 of 2,252 people in families with at least one autistic member but in only two out of 18,834 people without the disorder. The team is now trying to identify the specific gene involved.[28]

The second defect was originally identified in 2006 in four Amish children. Three groups of researchers independently reported that they had

273

identified the same defect in much larger groups of subjects. The gene they found is called contactin-associated protein-like 2, or CNTNAP2, which produces a protein that allows brain cells to communicate with one another. One of the researchers, Dr. Daniel Geschwind of UCLA's David Geffen School of Medicine, said: "This gene may not only predispose children to autism. It may also influence the development of brain structures involved in language, providing a tangible link between genes, the brain and behavior."[29]

Another very important genetic study, in 2007, found compelling evidence suggesting that most cases of autism could be due to errors in human DNA that are random and spontaneous, rather than inherited. Technically known as *copy number variations* or CNVs, these errors are changes in the human genetic code, or genome, involving the loss or addition of fairly large sequences of DNA. Though not a newly recognized phenomenon, it is only recently that scientists have started looking at CNVs as a potential cause of disease in general. The new study found that missing segments of DNA, which can be several genes in length, may confer increased risk of autism in families with no history of the disorder. This study could have a wider, more practical scope. It could allow scientists to scan the human genome as a whole and look for those CNVs which could flag unstable regions and which might be risk factors in patients without a family history of autism.[30] Geraldine Dawson, former director of the University of Washington's Autism Center and now Autism Speaks' research director, said such progress would allow clinicians to diagnose infants at risk from autism and begin treatment as early as possible. "The goal," she said, "is eventually to be able to identify infants at risk for autism at birth so we can begin treatment as soon as possible."[31]

The discovery by Scottish scientists in 2007 that the symptoms of Rett's syndrome could be reversed in mice was also greeted with excitement by professionals in the autism field, some of whom consider this condition to lie on the autistic spectrum. Rett's syndrome, which affects mainly girls, often leaving them wheelchair-bound, unable to speak, and suffering from breathing difficulties, had been considered an untreatable neurological disorder. But the Edinburgh and Glasgow University teams were able to make symptoms disappear in mice by activating the MECP2 gene that causes the syndrome to develop. They found that, when this gene was activated in mice which had been born with it switched off, symptoms such as breathing and mobility difficulties ceased. Over a four-week period, the mice often became undistinguishable from their healthy counterparts. Professor Adrian Bird, director of the Wellcome Trust Centre for Cell Biology at the University of Edinburgh, who led the research and first discovered the MECP2 gene in 1990, said that the unexpected reversibility finding "gives a major boost to the search for treatments or a potential cure."[32]

Another 2007 study by researchers at the Picower Institute for Learning and Memory at the Massachusetts Institute of Technology found that blocking a key brain chemical could reverse many of the symptoms of Fragile X syndrome—an inherited form of mental retardation and the most common genetic cause of autism—in mice that had been genetically manipulated to have the disease.

"We already know that genes play a huge role, although I'm not convinced that we will be able to predict the level of risk of autism in individual families," Mary Coleman's Swedish colleague, Christopher Gillberg, told me. "It is going to be more complicated than that, because there are going to be gene–gene interactions and gene–environment interactions. . . . In fact, our 1983 optimality study might well be taken to mean that there is a combination of genetic and perinatal factors. If you have something that predisposes you to perinatal problems, this can become a vicious circle. We all know of families where the child has autism and there are Asperger's traits in the father or mother."[33]

Gillberg, who devised the first diagnostic criteria for Asperger's syndrome in 1989, believes that more fruitful than seeking a gene for Asperger's will be a quest for various factors that contribute to the autistic-type features: "I think what is inherited in Asperger's syndrome is the social communication 'style' which is different in the sense that an individual with Asperger's can communicate with others and has some social skills, but they are very unusual. They seem to be less aware of the perspective of the other person during the actual interplay. Afterwards, they are very well able to think back to what happened.

"I think there may be just a few genes that predispose people to this phenotype, but when they interact with other genes you get autism. So our neuroligin gene findings in 2003 with Thomas Bourgeron [of the Institut Pasteur in Paris][34] seemed clear, because all those who had the gene also had autism and all those who didn't have the gene did not have autism. The correct conclusion appeared to be that this gene can cause autism. But they have discovered that a few cases can have mental retardation with autistic features."[35]

275

Gillberg thinks there could be different genes involved in each of the domains of autistic symptomatology. "I'm inclined to believe that the ritualistic repetitive behavior is genetically based. We need studies to show that."[36]

For her part, Susan Folstein believes that, as scientists grow closer to detecting specific etiologies, these cases will be investigated to see whether there are particular clinical features that define them. "Sometimes, as with Rett's syndrome, we expand the phenotype to include cases that did not meet the original criteria. Sometimes, it works the opposite way," Folstein told me. "For example, cases with advanced paternal age are more likely to have a single-gene defect that is sufficient to cause autism. These cases may be a sub-phenotype, depending on how many different single genes can be sufficient. This is of course iterative—once you have a sub-phenotype, you look at cases like that to see how many have the etiology you have uncovered. In this way, the concept of autism will become more etiology-specific over time. My guess is that the ones with severe mental retardation will have different causes from the ones with little cognitive impairment."[37]

## Environmental Factors

On the environmental front, a 2008 study led by Irma Hertz-Picciotto at the University of California Davis and using participants from the CHARGE (Childhood Autism Risks from Genetics and the Environment) study—a large population-based control study in California—showed that mothers of autistic children were twice as likely to report using pet shampoos for fleas or ticks during the exposure period, as compared with control mothers.

Another University of California team believes that chemicals known as PCBs (polychlorinated biphenyls) disrupt the auditory cortex, a part of the brain that is impaired in autistic children. A third West Coast team found that women who live near California farm fields sprayed with organochlorine pesticides may be more likely to give birth to children with autism. Yet another California team of researchers discovered that men and women who wait to have babies later in life may increase their children's risk for autism.

The scare that the combined MMR (measles, mumps, rubella) vaccine could cause autism—which started when the British gastro-enterologist, Dr. Andrew Wakefield, published a paper about 12 autistic children in *The Lancet* in 1998 (see p. 226)—has not only led to many parents refusing to vaccinate their children, or giving them separate jabs years apart, creating a serious risk of a measles epidemic.[38] It has also introduced a new "blame game." For many years, Bruno Bettelheim and his acolytes induced guilt in mothers for what they had supposedly done to their child; now, once again, parents are being made to feel responsible for causing their offspring's autism. Despite the fact that many studies have since cleared the triple vaccine of any such link, a survey carried out in the US in 2008 indicated that one in four Americans continues to believe that the MMR can cause autism.

Other scientists are investigating reported intestinal difficulties in children with autism. Researchers at Vanderbilt University in Nashville, Tennessee, are focusing on a gene called MET, which is involved in brain development before birth and in connections between brain cells after birth, as well as in the process through which the gastrointestinal system repairs itself. In March 2009, they claimed to have discovered that a variation in this gene was associated with both autism and gastrointestinal problems in 118 of 214 families.[39] But researchers found no link to the genetic variation in autistic patients who did not have gastrointestinal problems. The study met with caution and skepticism in many quarters.

The mother's age has long been implicated in neurodevelopmental problems in children. A 2006 study indicated that fathers over 40 also had a significantly increased risk of having a child with autism. The researchers, from the Institute of Psychiatry in London and Mount Sinai School of Medicine in New York, looked at data on 132,271 Jewish children born in Israel during the 1980s. All men, and three quarters of women, born in these years were assessed by the draft board at the age of 17 for eligibility to serve in the Israeli military, during which time any disorders were recorded. Among them, 110 had been diagnosed earlier with autism or related disorders, including Asperger's syndrome. Among those whose fathers were between 15 and 29 when they were born, the rate of autism was six in every 10,000, rising to nine in every 10,000 when fathers were aged 30 to 39. In the group whose fathers were aged 40 to 49, the rate rose to 32 in 10,000. The mother's age, surprisingly, did not seem to have any influence.[40] The researchers suggested there might be a genetic fault which was more common with age. This could be spontaneous mutations in sperm-producing cells or alterations in genetic "imprinting," which affects gene expression.

## Gene–Environment Interaction

Many professionals believe that there are likely to be at least some types of autism which are caused by an interaction of genetic make-up and environmental agents. They point out that subtle differences in genetic factors cause people to respond differently to the same environmental exposure.

Susan Folstein, for one, disagrees. "I don't think this is going to be very important," she told me. "Autism is a highly heritable condition. When you look at the twin data, the heritability is 100%."[41]

An interesting 2004 study led by Wendy Kates, of SUNY Upstate Medical University in Syracuse, New York, indicated that, even in identical twins, there were neurological differences.[42] But Folstein told me: "More and more data suggest that, while monozygotic twins are genetically identical, their level of gene expression can vary for any given gene. That is one reason that there would be neuroanatomical variation which, not surprisingly, is correlated with clinical variation."[43]

## Brain Research

Brain studies are another hopeful avenue of research—especially with the development of more sophisticated scanning equipment. But here again, the professionals retain their reservations. "Non-evasive brain exploration has made huge leaps forward," said Gilbert Lelord. "But it still won't help us to determine prognosis, which remains uncertain."[44] One of Lelord's colleagues, Dr. Monica Zilbovocius, at the University of Tours, echoed his caution over the advances in understanding: "We still don't know what happens neurologically in autism, which is a highly complex condition, but I am optimistic about brain research in general. If you take the amount of knowledge on brain functioning and mechanisms over the past 30 years, the increase has been enormous. What we need to do is to transfer this knowledge of the normal brain to those whose brain is not so normal."[45]

Ever since the 1980s, researchers like Leslie Brothers at UCLA have attempted to identify the "social brain"—specific affected brain areas—in an effort to construct a neurological basis for the social deficits observed in autism. Candidate regions cited in the two decades since then include the amygdala—which processes emotions—and the fusiform gyrus—which is normally activated in face recognition but is underactive in autism.

278

A 2008 brain-imaging study from the Baylor College of Medicine in Houston, Texas, which Professor Uta Frith called "an exciting advance," indicated that individuals with Asperger's syndrome lack a particular brain signal linked to a sense of self. Dr. Read Montague, Dr. Pearl Chiu, and their colleagues scanned the brains of adolescents with Asperger's syndrome while they played an interactive trust game. They found that these adolescents played the game just as a non-autistic person would but they lacked the characteristic "self" signal in the brain. Normal people lacked the signal only when they believed that they were playing against a computer, suggesting that high-functioning autistic people viewed interactions with other people similarly to the way that non-autistic people thought about interacting with a computer.[46] Montague and his team ultimately hope to develop the brain-imaging results into a diagnostic test. They have converted the activity signal from the cingulate cortex into a simple numerical score, which they claim correlates well with a clinical test for the severity of autism.

Professor Nancy Minshew and colleagues at the University of Pittsburgh have done important work showing that there are problems in underconnectivity between different regions of the brain of autistic individuals.[47] And more recently, in the first study of its kind, researchers in North Carolina discovered that in autistic individuals, connections between brain cells may be deficient within single regions, and not just between regions.[48] Dr. Tony Wilson, lead researcher and assistant professor of neurology at Wake Forest University School of Medicine, said he hoped this study would eventually lead to earlier diagnosis and more targeted medications for autism.

The newest brain imaging technology, diffusion tensor imaging (DTI)—a magnetic resonance imaging (MRI) method which enables the measurement of the restricted diffusion of water in tissue in order to produce neural tract images—has revealed structural irregularities in white matter (the part of the brain which ferries electrical signals from one region to another).[49]

The mirror neuron research continues to arouse great interest (see chapter 8). Mirror neurons fire when an individual performs an action but also when that individual watches someone else perform that same action. Neuroscientists believe this "mirroring" is the neural mechanism by which the actions, intentions, and emotions of other people can be automatically understood. Individuals with autism cannot rely on this system to read the minds of other people. Symptoms of autism include varying levels of difficulty with social interaction, including verbal and non-verbal communication, imitation, and empathy. These findings bolster the growing body of evidence that points to a breakdown of the mirror neuron system as the mechanism behind these symptoms.

However, Dr. Geoff Byrd, of the Department of Psychology at University College London, pointed out that studies of mirror system function in ASD had yielded inconsistent findings.[50]

## Language Impairments

The debate will continue as to whether language impairments are specific to autism. This was discussed in detail in earlier chapters. It seems certain that the quest will go on for a psycholinguistic marker. At the moment, none exists. Some autistic children individuals never speak. The sudden, and unexplained, loss of speech in early childhood does appear to be specific to autism, but few studies to date have attempted to analyze the nature of the language used by these children before it disappears. Some of the most detailed research in this area has been conducted by Mercedes Belinchón in Madrid.[51]

One remarkable recent incident gave hope to many parents and professionals, alike. An autistic man in St. Louis, Missouri, spoke his first-ever words at the age of 50. Those words—for the record—were "I don't want that. Get away."

Rebecca Landa in Baltimore believes that there is probably a specific deficit affecting language processing. "But we know, from Helen Tager-Flusberg's work, that not all people with autism have a linguistic impairment. Is making inferences linguistic or is it cognitive?"[52]

## Early Diagnosis

As described in chapter 7, researchers around the world are reducing the proposed earliest age of diagnosing autism, sometimes to close to 1 year of age. Multiple signs indicating early developmental disruptions, according to one team, include abnormalities in initiating communication with others; compromised ability to initiate and respond to opportunities to share experiences with others; irregularities when playing with toys; and a significantly reduced variety of sounds, words, and gestures used to communicate.

It must be emphasized that there are still currently no standardized, published criteria for diagnosing children with autism at or around 1 year of age. Rebecca Landa's goal is to develop these criteria based on this and other autism studies currently under way at the Kennedy Krieger Institute in Baltimore.

## The Savant Syndrome

Thanks to the work of a number of professionals—notably Dr. Darold Treffert in Fond du Lac, Wisconsin—our understanding of the nature of the special skills exhibited by autistic savants (skills already observed by Leo Kanner in his 1943 paper) has increased considerably. Treffert told me he believed the central nervous system was damaged for a variety of reasons and there was left-hemisphere damage with right-brain compensation. "This oversimplifies, but there can be no doubt that there is some degree of specialization in certain functions. There is also a corresponding damage to the higher-level cognitive and semantic memory circuits and their replacement by lower-level circuits. That is not my idea. But I believe there is damage by the same forces to the left hemisphere and higher-level memory circuits and compensation by the lower-level procedural memory."[53]

A surprising study by Pat Howlin in 2009 indicated that the proportion of savants in autism could be as high as 30%—much higher than the figure of 10% normally accepted. Howlin told me she could not really explain the results of her study, especially as it was a systematic and fairly large sample and she was using a more restricted definition of savant skills.[54] She added: "The practical aspects of getting people to use these skills are the challenge. We should put the emphasis on the things they can do, rather than those they can't."[55]

Treffert told me that what Howlin had done in her study was to use some IQ verbal and performance test scales to assess "cognitive" savant syndrome, as opposed to simple observation by parents or others. "While more systematic, I think that would cast a much larger net than just personal observation. For me, savant syndrome is a special skill (art, music, maths, spatial skills) *coupled with* massive memory. I don't classify memory alone in most cases (except Kim Peek perhaps) as a savant skill by itself. Including memory as a special skill alone would also cast a larger net."[56]

Treffert said that, in order to determine the true prevalence of savant skills, there was a need to establish some standard criteria and then test

281

a sufficiently large sample using those criteria. "Pat Howlin did just that, in essence, but I would take issue with the criteria she used, particularly using IQ sub-tests only in some cases. I am not saying that is necessarily wrong, but it may account in part for the difference between 10 and 30%. The time is coming when some scales will be developed to define savant skills both qualitatively and quantitatively. Savant skills are on a spectrum and it would be nice to have less subjective criteria for that spectrum."[57]

Professor Allen Snyder in Sydney, Australia, believes that we all have savant skills and these can be "induced." Treffert is not entirely convinced: "He is talking about the fact that we come to rely on higher-level circuitry in our developments, whereas he identifies autism itself as having privileged access to lower-level circuitry. His idea is not so much inducing savant skills but permitting them to surface. He believes rTMS [repetitive transcranial magnetic simulation] is inhibiting a part of the brain to allow something else to emerge. The idea that you can allow dormant skills to come to the surface is reinforced by the savant. Where Allen and I part a little is that he believes this is a matter of circuitry which is suppressed in most of us. I see it as a compensatory reliance on the left hemisphere of the brain."[58]

Some studies have lent support to Treffert's hypothesis of a compensatory use of different brain circuits in savants. But a very recent functional magnetic resonance imaging study by Richard Cowan and Chris Frith in London indicated that two autistic calendrical savants used the same regions of the brain as a normal adult male when carrying out date calculations.[59]

In another very recent study, a Dutch team postulated that a mutation which gave rise to the development of the positive aspects of the savant syndrome (for instance, an impressive memory capacity), would "virtually always have a deleterious effect on the development of other phenotypic traits (for example, resulting in autism and/or impaired motor coordination)," and that this explained why the savant syndrome had not spread in the general population.[60]

# Recovery and Regression

Meanwhile, the puzzling phenomena of "recovery" from autism and regression seem likely to continue to be the targets of considerable attention from researchers in the years and decades to come.

Ed Ornitz, a pioneer in the field from the 1960s, combines the two phenomena in what he sees as the three main subtypes of autism: "one group with apparently normal development until as late as 30 months and then there is a tremendous regression; a second group that looks very different right from birth; and then there's a third group who between 2 and 3½ have all the symptoms of autism and, when I saw them again as a follow-up at 7 or 8, they no longer met the criteria, and yet I was sure I had not made a mistake in my original diagnosis. It's rare—but it happens," Ornitz told me.[61]

Dr. Rebecca Landa, at the Kennedy Krieger Institute in Baltimore, and Dr. Cathy Lord at the University of Michigan at Ann Arbor also told me that they had seen cases of apparent recovery from autism. But the general feeling among professionals is that complete recovery is unlikely and traits remain, even if distinct improvement occurs.

One of the best-known cases of a man with autism who claims to have recovered completely from an early diagnosis of severe autism is Raun Kaufman, director of the Son-Rise Program in Massachusetts, which itself insists that it has managed to achieve recovery in some of its children.

"I tend to shy away from the word 'cure.' It is a very political term and we are not offering a magic pill," Kaufman told me. "I did have a very interesting interaction once with Eric Schopler. We were both speaking at a conference in Stockholm and we had talked privately beforehand. He was a very intelligent guy, but he didn't seem to be that open to what I was saying—not in a mean way, but he had his own point of view. He said he thought we were advocating false hope. People often say that I must have some remnants of autism or that there must have been a misdiagnosis in the first place. I have a pretty strong reaction to this. I was actually getting worse, not better, when my parents intervened. I was certainly autistic. But I have watched other children recover or do very well. Are we going to assume it was a misdiagnosis in each of these cases? Are we prepared to accept that some people can recover from cancer, but not autism? We write these children off ahead of time."[62]

Kaufman added: "I certainly do not promise parents that their child can recover. Some can. I do feel autism is reversible—because it happened to me. But we need to embrace autism more, embrace the kids the way they are, and help them to be as successful as they can."[63]

Michael Rutter, giving the keynote speech to the Autism-Europe congress in Oslo in 2007, pointed out that it was remarkable how little research had been conducted into the phenomenon of regression. This is, indeed, an area where we have made relatively little advance in understanding—either of the mechanism involved or of its significance for autism.

Some professionals continue to believe that it is very rare. Lorna Wing told me: "In most cases, you find evidence of oddity beforehand. It's just that the autistic-type behavior becomes more obvious later."[64] However, the majority of people working in the field are convinced by studies such as those of Geraldine Dawson, then at the University of Washington in Seattle, of home videos of first- and second-birthday parties that appear to show a clear loss of skills.[65]

Even so, Dawson—who is now Autism Speaks' chief scientific officer—told me: "Our new estimates are actually that true autistic regression—meaning normal development followed by rapid loss of skills in several domains—occurs in only about 10% of children with autism. I do not believe there are any good data indicating an increase in the prevalence of autistic regression *per se*."[66]

Sally Ozonoff, a leading authority on autistic regression, told me: "I do home videos of regression in the infant siblings study. I have a theory that, depending on how you define the word 'regression'—and no one has yet agreed on a definition—it is either very rare or it's almost ubiquitous and almost all children have it. In our infant siblings study, where we track the children from birth, virtually all the children were indistinguishable at 6 months. They look exactly like typical babies: they smile at you. There is eye contact, they engage with you with big facial expressions. They are with you in the relationship. Over time, they lose all that—and we have actual data to show this. What they lose is interest in other people: smiling, eye contact, the baby versions of social interaction. I have great videos showing absolutely clear regression. But other children at 2 months never look at people."[67]

Ozonoff feels there is a continuum in the middle that shows small decreases in eye contact "and then flattens off and never gains other skills. I do feel the super-classic regression where children lose lots of skills is rarer than we think."[68] Ozonoff and Rebecca Landa have tentatively called a group of children "delays-plus-regression."

Landa told me she thought of autism as a progressive disorder: "They start off reasonably OK and then skills decrease in frequency and diversity. Some people would call that a regression. Then you find the emergence of unwanted behaviors like repetitive, stereotyped behaviors. We don't yet know the meaning of regression from a neurobiological perspective. We know something is going terribly wrong some time between six and 36 months."[69]

Is regression specific to autism? "It's extremely rare outside autism," said Ozonoff's MIND Institute colleague, Sally Rogers, "but I don't think it's one of the typical characteristics of autism, either. The majority of children with autism do not show regression."[70]

# Education

Understanding of the educational needs of autistic children has improved immensely—most importantly, through the acceptance that every autistic child is unique and has his or her own specific needs which must be carefully accessed on an individual basis. The idea of one-approach-fits-all has been largely abandoned in the more enlightened parts of the world.

Yet, there are still problems that will need addressing. Autism-specific teacher-training continues to be a rare creature, even in those countries where understanding as a whole is advanced. Ruth Sullivan, director of the remarkable Autism Services Center which celebrated its 30th anniversary in Huntington, West Virginia, on March 27, 2009, told me that, as of 2007, there was still no degree in autism anywhere in the United States.[71]

Throughout the world, services for adults remain poor. This could be, in part, due to an extended influence of the misguided old idea that autism was confined to childhood. In 2002, Ruth Sullivan started an organization for adults with autism. "I could see that very few people were running autism-specific schemes for adults with autism. They're not as cute when they're 22 and weigh 300 pounds. We know how hard it is to keep the staff and train them in how to work with adults with autism. Even parents who have plenty of money have trouble finding placements."[72]

An issue which will continue to rage far and wide is the question of inclusion. Is the best place for autistic children in a mainstream environment? By and large, governments believe that it is, but the reasons may be mixed: a lack of awareness of the sensory and other difficulties faced by pupils with autism in normal classes and very possibly an attempt to save money on the expense of special schools.

Professor Rita Jordan at the University of Birmingham, in the UK, said: "There is always a tension between providing the best environment for the child with autism in terms of reducing stress and increasing relevant attention (which usually means a specialist environment or at least staff who know about autism) and providing the rich social and communication models we know all children (including those with autistic spectrum disorders) need. Research shows that children with autism do benefit most from being with typical peers, but only if that interaction is managed by someone who understands and can organize effective forms of interaction (they do not learn by merely being placed with typical children)."[73]

The ideal, Jordan said, would be to teach some basic skills in an adapted environment and then have some "reverse integration" into that environment by introducing typical children. "Then the child with the ASD knows how to operate in that environment and can concentrate on operating with these new people (one at a time)."[74]

From a practical view, there have been helpful advances. The Picture Exchange Communication System (PECS)—designed by Lori Frost and Andrew Bondy—allows non-verbal autistic children like my son, Johnny, to communicate their needs and, in so doing, to reduce their levels of frustration. While some children with autism may not have a social drive, they do feel the urge to make their requirements known.

## Prevalence

**Figure 80** Peter Tanguay

The veteran autism pioneer, Peter Tanguay, who has been working in the field since the 1960s, told me: "It is very difficult to predict the future in autism, because we are unaware of what new technologies may be developed which could dramatically change our understanding of the nature and treatment of autism. Autism has been shown to have increased 100-fold since the early epidemiological studies of Victor Lotter and his colleague in 1966. Some of this increase must be due to our broader definition of autism, but I can't believe that this would account for a 10-fold increase in prevalence."[75]

Tanguay added that there was no evidence that any of the environmental factors examined so far could account for the increase. "But what if we did find environmental factors that were causing fetal brain malformations which resulted in social communication failures? Now *that* would be a major advance."[76]

The general consensus among professionals is that the rise in diagnoses of autism does not represent an epidemic but is largely due to improved diagnostic instruments, the broadening of the spectrum, and increase awareness and understanding of the disorder. But most concede that an environmental trigger cannot be ruled out.

The prevalence rates do not appear to vary to any great extent geographically. A study by Christopher Gillberg on the Faroe Islands—considered to be a genetic "isolate"—screened all schools for autistic spectrum disorders in an effort to identify a representative cohort for future genetic studies. Of the children aged between 8 and 17 years, just over 0.5% had childhood autism, Asperger's syndrome, or "atypical autism"—a prevalence rate very similar to, or a little lower than, that reported from many Western countries.[77] Gillberg told me that one of the islands had just one child living on it—and he was autistic.

Some bizarre anomalies have emerged in recent years. In 2007, Portuguese researchers reported a prevalence of ASD of 9.2 per 10,000 in mainland Portugal and a much higher prevalence, 15.6 per 10,000, on the Portuguese-owned Azores islands in the Atlantic.[78] Even more puzzlingly, Eric Fombonne claimed that very preliminary results of his study had indicated the absence of a single case of autism among the Inuit of Northern Quebec.[79] In both cases, I have contacted the study authors and they have not been able to explain the findings.

## Legislation

In many parts of the world, governments have introduced legislation to enshrine protection of individuals with autism under the law.

On May 9, 1996, the Charter of Rights of Persons with Autism was adopted as a Written Declaration by the European Parliament. It declares that people with autism "should share the same rights and privileges enjoyed by all of the European population where such are appropriate and in the best interests of the person with autism. These rights should be enhanced, protected and enforced by appropriate legislation in each state." The rights include:

- the right to live independent and full lives to the limit of their potential;
- the right to an accessible, unbiased, and accurate clinical diagnosis and assessment;
- the right to accessible and appropriate education;
- the right to an income or wage sufficient to provide adequate food, clothing, accommodation, and the other necessities of life;
- the right to meaningful employment and vocational training without discrimination or stereotype;
- the right to freedom from fear or threat of unwarranted incarceration in psychiatric hospitals or any other restrictive institution; and
- the right to freedom from pharmaceutical abuse or misuse.

On December 19, 2006, President George W. Bush signed the Combating Autism Act into law. It authorized nearly one billion dollars in expenditures, over five years beginning in 2007, to combat Asperger's syndrome, Rett's syndrome, childhood disintegrative disorder, and PDD-NOS through screening, education, early intervention, prompt referrals for treatment, and services. The new US legislation was welcomed by many around the world, but some activists in the autism rights movement condemned it—for the same reason that they have denounced organizations such as Cure Autism Now and Defeat Autism Now—because they consider it aims to eliminate autism, rather than accommodate it. In the United Kingdom, the 2009 Autism Act received Royal Assent on November 12 of that year. The Act lays down provisions for meeting the needs of adults with autism in England.

On a global level, the United Nations Convention on the Rights of Persons with Disabilities—including autism—was adopted in New York in August 2006. Another encouraging initiative was the United Nations' decision to name April 2 each year in perpetuity as World Autism Awareness Day, starting in 2008. The move—an initiative spearheaded by Qatar—was unanimously approved by the UN General Assembly on December 18, 2007.

## Autism from Within

Some of the most revealing insights about the autistic condition come from the writings of individuals with the disorder. Space does not permit a detailed analysis of any of these writings of articulate high-functioning individuals like Temple Grandin, Donna Williams, and Wendy Lawson. The overlaps between them are striking—as are the differences. All three women describe their confrontation with serious sensory difficulties. But while Grandin is very much a visual thinker, Williams is certainly not. Yet Grandin told me her first job had involved using words not images: she was a reporter for a livestock magazine.

Interestingly, the French psychoanalysts consider these autobiographical writings to be of particular interest—a little ironic, since Temple Grandin often describes the psychoanalytical approach to autism as nonsense and Donna Williams told me she found Bruno Bettelheim's Freudian interpretations "hilarious"[80]). Jean-Claude Maleval, for instance, who is based at the University of Rennes in Brittany, told me: "High-functioning autism seems to me to be the best way in to the logic of autism: it illuminates the deficits as an after-thought."[81]

Donna Williams told me she was "feral" until the age of around 9 to 11. "I'm now someone who can speak fluently. But there's much of me that finds this a foreign system and it's often tiring. I'm far more about being and doing. This is perhaps because I came to understand language quite late . . . or it could be the other way around, that I was late to develop functional speech because the semantic-pragmatic system was not my natural neurological strength. Just because I can learn to do handstands doesn't mean I was designed to walk on my hands. Neurologically, I'm rustier than earlier developers, my batteries go flat more quickly, my natural instincts work in other ways, my soul is geared for a more animalistic style of processing and responding and it takes more effort to dominate that in order to survive in the non-autistic world."[82]

Williams says she sees autism not as one condition but rather as "an

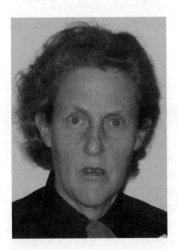

umbrella term for an ongoing collection of autistic responses which can be: compulsive or involuntary, self-stimulatory, self-protective and distancing, distress reactions, the result of addiction to one's own chemical highs, or attempts to connect and make sense of one's experiences when usual channels are emotionally, physically, or otherwise developmentally blocked. There is no one type of autism, because autism is like a fruit salad. . . . For each person diagnosed with autism, the pieces in that fruit salad can be many or few, big or small, exotic or common."[83]

Temple Grandin credited her mother, the actress Eustacia Cutler, for instinctively

**Figure 81** Temple Grandin

forcing her to interact as a severely autistic young girl—and for reject-
ing advice to send her to an institution. "The best thing she did was
send me to my aunt's ranch," Grandin told me."[84] She now designs the
majority of cattle ranches in the United States.

Ros Blackburn, a British woman with autism on whom Sigourney
Weaver's role in the 2006 film *Snow cake* is largely based, told me her
parents forced her to fit in after she was diagnosed as severely autistic
at the age of 1. She certainly seems to fit the theory of mind picture:
"I have been made aware that other people have feelings. But I can't
imagine what other people are thinking or feeling until I'm told. . . . I
don't know from looking at people whether they're happy or sad, interested or bored."[85]

She said that, when she saw wartime footage of a row of houses
being knocked down, she felt more "sympathy" for these houses than
she would if she saw a child falling over in the street. "I'm obsessed
with gables—I'm obsessed with roofs and the angles of roofs in the
skyline. They are my passion. If something is dear to you, you do not
want to see it hurt."[86]

When I asked Blackburn how "disabled" she felt by her autism, she
replied: "I might as well be paralysed from the neck down, and have
no one to push the wheelchair, because of my autism. I do not have
the social ammunition, the flexible thinking, to be able to go out and
handle things."[87]

She certainly regards herself as having autism, rather than
Asperger's syndrome: "I don't want friends. . . . People with Asperger's
syndrome *do* like and wish for the social contact. I know a lot of people
with Asperger's and they all want to be my friends. I *need* people.
It's a totally different thing. They talk about autistic people as being
'trapped' in their own world. I'm not trapped at all—I choose to be in
there."[88]

Dr. Ian Hacking, the Canadian philosopher of science, is critical
of the marketing of books which offer a view from "inside the autistic
mind," as if there were only one kind of such mind.[89] Hacking has
developed a concept called *looping,* by which he means that the label
a child receives may change that child, who may in turn alter the
label. Dr. Douwe Draaisma, of the University of Groningen, in the
Netherlands, agrees: he has warned of the intricate interaction between
the scientific view of autism, the way it is prolifically portrayed in literature and film, and the reality of life for, and with, an individual with
autism.[90]

# DSM-V

The American Psychiatric Association is scheduled to publish DSM-V in 2013. A number of professionals working on the document tell me that sensory issues may well play an important part in its new definition of autism. Temple Grandin, for one, approves: "There are hundreds of papers out there on theory of mind, and it's a fascinating area. But sensory issues are much more debilitating for people with autism," Grandin told me. "Autism is not the only disorder with these issues, of course. They also apply in dyslexia and attention-deficit hyperactivity disorder. I want much more money put into this area. Why do Irlen lenses work on some people and not others?[91] And then we have to figure out therapies. How do we treat sound sensitivity?"[92]

Sally Ozonoff and her MIND colleague, Sally Rogers, have conducted studies on sensory problems in autism, specifically comparing them with children with Fragile X, who also have these difficulties. "Sensory reactivity is different from repetitive behavior," Rogers told me. "We have to get the terminology right. There are a variety of symptoms which fall into that diagnostic category. Children with Fragile X have high levels of repetitive behavior and stronger sensory reactivity than children with autism. It's not an issue restricted to autism. But maybe the internal experience is different—we don't know enough about that area yet."[93]

Interestingly, unlike Francesca Happé—who is a key member of DSM-V's committee working on the new definition of autism and who has suggested that it might be time to move away from a single explanation of autism[94]—Simon Baron-Cohen feels there could be an underlying common factor to autistic talent in the molecular neurobiology of sensory hypersensitivity. In 2008, he and his colleagues published new evidence of superior acuity amongst people with autism across auditory, tactile, olfactory, and visual senses: in the latter, to near the level of birds of prey.[95]

One of the most significant elements of the DSM-V draft revisions released on February 10, 2010, was the proposal to eliminate the diagnosis of Asperger's syndrome as a separate disorder from autism. A new autism spectrum category recognizes that "the symptoms of these disorders represent a continuum from mild to severe, rather than being distinct disorders," said Dr. Edwin Cook, a University of Illinois at Chicago autism researcher and member of the APA working groups proposing the changes.[96]

291

The psychiatrist who coined the term *Asperger's syndrome*, Lorna Wing, told me she would be happy for it to be removed as a separate category. However, she insisted: "The autism spectrum should list the diagnostic subgroups—including Asperger's syndrome—currently in use, but without defining them, because people who have been given these names need to know that they are on the spectrum, and this will also allow them to receive the appropriate services."[97]

## Continuing Confusions and Ignorance

The world's understanding of autism has advanced immensely since the 1940s. Yet as this book has shown, there are startling examples of misconceptions, and the disorder continues to be misunderstood in even the most advanced of nations, as we enter the second decade of the twenty-first century. In the United States, an autistic boy died while undergoing an "exorcism" and a prominent radio talk-show host, Michael Savage, declared:

> Now, the illness *du jour* is autism. You know what autism is? I'll tell you what autism is. In 99% of the cases, it's a brat who hasn't been told to cut the act out. That's what autism is. . . . They don't have a father around to tell them: "Don't act like a moron. You'll get nowhere in life. . . . Don't sit there crying and screaming, idiot."[98]

Even as intelligent a man as the Chilean film director, Alejandro Jodorowsky (who made the extraordinary *El topo*) could be heard telling one Spanish TV interviewer, Fernando Sánchez Dragó, that many autistic children remained non-verbal because they were "hiding a guilty secret" in the family's past, such as incest.[99]

Stigma remains similarly global. At an exhilarating meeting in London organized by the charity Poet in the City in 2008, one of the speakers, the English poet, Selima Hill, suddenly announced to a stunned audience that, for the first time, she was revealing in public that she had been diagnosed with Asperger's syndrome. She had not even told her own children because she was ashamed, she said.[100]

Israel Kolvin's 1971 paper laid down a clear differentiation between autism and schizophrenia. But more than three decades later, individuals with Asperger's syndrome are locked up in mental hospitals in many parts of the world, with a misdiagnosis of schizophrenia. Moreover, the issue has been clouded by several recent studies which have pointed to a possible shared genetic etiology in autism and schizophrenia. Peter Burbach in the Netherlands, for instance, noted that the CNTNAP2 gene had been directly implicated in the two disorders. The research in this and similar cases relates to causes and not manifestations. But as Burbach pointed out in his paper, the fact that the two conditions could arise from similar pathogenic mechanisms raised the question as to what extent the two disorders shared phenotypic aspects.[101]

In contrast, two other researchers—Bernard Crespi and Christopher Badcock—have proposed that autism and schizophrenia exhibit diametrically opposed patterns for traits related to social brain development, including aspects of gaze, agency, social cognition, local versus global processing, language, and behavior. Social cognition, Crespi and Badcock maintain, is underdeveloped in autistic spectrum conditions and hyperdeveloped on the psychotic spectrum. They suggest that the development of these diametrically opposed phenotypes is mediated, in part, by alterations of genomic "imprinting": autistic spectrum conditions, according to Crespi and Badcock, appear to involve increased relative bias towards effects of paternally expressed genes, whereas the etiologies of psychotic conditions involve biases towards increased relative effects from imprinted genes with maternal expression.[102]

Autism remains such a complex and bewildering disorder that agreeing on a definition is virtually impossible, and may even prove meaningless. When I asked the two pioneers in the neurology of autism, Margaret Bauman and Thomas Kemper, whether autism could be described as "brain damage," they could not agree and—even though they have been working together for a quarter of a century—they broke off our interview for a few moments to debate the issue with one another.[103]

\* \* \*

Living with a child with autism remains immensely challenging. The despair of mothers—and it is usually mothers—who take their autistic child's life, and sometimes their own has illustrated the continuing lack of services throughout the world. Yet the allure of *working* with autistic children remains extraordinarily potent for researchers and clinicians. Howard Buten, a French autism clinician who remarkably doubles up as a clown, has observed that, in the 20 years he has been working in the field, he has never met an autistic children he didn't like "nor have I ever been bored by one."[104]

The media have been equally enthralled. The 1988 film, *Rain man*, as we have seen, brought autism to a vast audience, even though the film was originally going to deal with mental retardation, not autism (and an early version of the script seen by one adviser on the film, Peter Tanguay, even featured Raymond Babbitt fleeing white supremacists on a motorcycle![105]) Many other movies have since attempted to portray autism, with distinctly varying success. As Stuart Murray has pointed out, the "autism movie" has virtually become a genre in itself and, in so doing, the complexities of the disorder may have been drowned in stereotypes.[106] In stark contrast, Mark Haddon's 2004 novel, *The curious incident of the dog in the night-time*,[107] featuring a narrator with Asperger's syndrome, was a wonderfully perceptive depiction of a condition thought by many—but by no means all—to be a high-functioning form of autism.

Donna Williams, for one, does not feel we have progressed too far since 1943: "At present, we are merely the fools of tomorrow," she told me, "no more enlightened than those who diagnosed 2-year-olds as psychotic, brain-damaged or emotionally disturbed in the 1940s through to the 1970s."[108]

The remarkable Tian Huiping (Hope) in Beijing shares Williams's skepticism. "The more I know about autism, the fewer expectations I have. I think our greater comprehension of autism should help the whole world understand people with all kinds of disabilities. The best future would be one in which people with autism are respected, accepted and become a real part of our life."[109]

**Figure 82** Robert Hendren

Dr. Robert Hendren, executive director of the MIND Institute, does feel that our understanding has grown. "But in many ways, it is more diverging," he told me. "It used to be seen as a relatively simple disorder to figure out. We now realize how complicated it is. But we have some good theories about mechanisms for what is going on in terms of gene–environment interaction or brain inflammation. What is important is finding treatment targets."[110]

Hendren said that the more sophisticated brain-imaging techniques would help to predict clusters and to make early preventive intervention realistic "within three to five years, possibly. We missed them before because we would do a treatment and put the whole heterogeneous group of autism in it. We are getting better at using biomarkers."[111]

For her part, Lorna Wing emphasized that what mattered most was "that you present findings in a way that is helpful to the individual. The diagnostic labels don't mean a damn thing—just use them to get the person the services they need. What makes me mad is that some people get so wound up about a specific diagnostic label."[112]

The labels can be misleading, and many authorities are misled. Many local authorities in the United Kingdom, for example, are still reluctant to provide services for individuals with Asperger's syndrome because they have an IQ higher than the authorities' "cut-off point" of 70. In this sense, it is a "hidden" disability. But many people with Asperger's do have learning difficulties in the sense that their social and sensory problems represent serious obstacles to normal learning processes.

For Theo Peeters in Antwerp—one of the most compassionate professionals working anywhere in the field of autism today—the "autism" label continues to create misapprehensions about the core problems involved in the condition in many countries: "Autism spectrum disorders are simply too broad a concept—especially at the high end, where people who do indeed have some different personality traits may be labeled as autistic. A society that has such a rigid concept of 'normality' and has so many difficulties with diversity needs 'therapy,'" Peeters told me.[113]

For Peeters, autism is such a complex condition that "exceptional people need exceptional professionals" who have both an in-depth knowledge of the disorder and an ability to be flexible. "When you listen to people with very high-functioning autism, like Jim Sinclair or Claire Sainsbury, they very often use the analogy of a different culture. Sometimes, I say that what we need is not more psychologists but more anthropologists who have learned to look at other cultures without prejudices. We need each other. People with autism need us, because they have to learn about our culture or behavior. But if we want to understand autism better, we need much closer collaboration with people who understand autism from within. So I really feel we are entering a new era in which at least some people with autism will be our collaborators."[114]

Gary Mesibov, until 2010 director of Division TEACCH, sees the future of autism as similar to what has been happening with other developmental disabilities. "Thirty-five years ago, when I started in this field, everyone was very excited about identifying new genetic syndromes and creating medications and other biological approaches to improve outcomes. I think that genetic, brain, and pharmacological research will continue to be helpful for autism spectrum disorders, but I am afraid most of these will not translate into the kind of immediate treatment gains or 'cures' which many consumers are hoping for and many scientists are suggesting. As a result, I am afraid that the hope and promise of scientific biological interventions will continue to proliferate and dominate a lot of the time and energy of many in the field that should be devoted to more promising and empirically validated approaches."[115]

Mesibov lamented the fact that many of the educational interventions and the work with older schoolchildren, adolescents, and adults which had brought about the most important advances in our field would continue to be of lower priority. "Because these techniques are perceived as too slow in producing desired outcomes and do not offer the same promise of achieving the hoped-for cures, they will continue to be second-class citizens in our field. I hope that I am wrong, because I think that if we put more funding and faith into the treatments that have produced the best outcomes in the past decade, then the field would move ahead much more rapidly."[116]

**Figure 83**  Dame Stephanie Shirley

Dame Stephanie Shirley, one of Britain's leading entrepreneurs and autism supporters and the generous sponsor of this book, agrees that serious challenges remain to be tackled. Since her own autistic son, Giles, died at the age of 35, Dame Stephanie has channelled tens of millions of pounds of her own money into autism research and education, launched a school near London, Prior's Court, and founded the British arm of Autism Speaks, dedicated to working with the research community in areas such as autism genetics, autism brain studies and neuro-imaging.

She believes that it is "the gradual and most importantly accelerating accretion of knowledge across many streams of research—genetic, neurological, psychological, biological—and insights that one lends to the other, that will solve the puzzle of autism."[117] She added: "From year to year, it can seem as though some areas of research are not advancing as fast as we'd like. But in reality, it reflects the fact that, as preliminary findings are built on, probed and exploited, we can grow in confidence about their interpretation."[118]

Dame Stephanie, who likes to quote James Joyce's remark that "Mistakes are the portal of discovery," urges researchers not to duplicate research which has already been shown to be solid but to publish all results, including negative ones. She says that her personal mission is that "the causes of the various autisms should be understood by 2012 and the global costs of autism spectrum disorders halved by 2020."[119]

It would be wonderful to be able to share Simon Baron-Cohen's optimism. He told *The Times*:

> It has never been a better time to have autism. Why? Because there is a remarkably good fit between the autistic mind and the digital age. For this new generation of children with autism, I anticipate that many of them will find ways to blossom, using their skills with digital technology to find employment, to find friends and in some cases to innovate.[120]

On the other hand, in 1999, Michael Rutter wrote that we knew a great deal about autism but relatively little about how the various genetic, neuropathological, cognitive, and affective aspects relate to one another.[121] A decade later, I asked Rutter whether he stood by those comments: "We have progressed. There is good cognitive research taking place and we have good imaging studies. We have certainly gained much more information which has brought substantial understanding. But if you asked: can all that be put together into one cohesive unifying view? I would have to say: 'No.' That has to be our goal."[122]

# Notes

## Introduction

1 See Ros Blackburn's interview with the author, *Looking Up*, 2(1) (2000), 19.

2 More detailed accounts of probable pre-Kanner cases can be found elsewhere, for example in Uta Frith's (2003). *Autism: Explaining the enigma* (second ed.). Oxford, England: Wiley-Blackwell.

3 Natalia Challis & Horace W. Dewey (1974). The blessed fools of old Russia. *Jahrbücher für Geschichte Osteuropas*, *20*, 1–11.

4 Uta Frith & Rab Houston (2000). *Autism in history: The case of Hugh Blair of Borgue*, Oxford, England: Wiley-Blackwell.

5 See Ole Sylvester Jørgensen (2002). *Asperger: Syndrom zwischen Autismus und Normalität: Diagnostik und Heilungschancen.* Weinheim, Germany: Beltz Verlag, 78–81.

6 Mitzi Waltz & Paul Shattock (2004). Autistic disorder in nineteenth-century London: Three case reports. *Autism*, 8(1), 7–20.

7 See Darold Treffert (2006). *Extraordinary people: Understanding savant syndrome.* New York, NY: Backinprint.com.

8 Mark Twain writing in the San Francisco newspaper, *Alta California*, August 1, 1869.

9 See Majia Holmer Nadesan (2005). *Constructing autism: Unravelling the "truth" and understanding the social.* London, England: Routledge.

10 Uta Frith (Ed.) (1991). *Autism and Asperger syndrome.* Cambridge, England: Cambridge University Press, 38.

11 Lorna Wing in conversation with the author in Hartfield, UK, August 15, 2007.

12 Lightner Witmer (1919–22). Orthogenic cases, XIV-Don: A curable case of arrested development to a fear psychosis the result of shock in a three-year-old infant. *The Psychological Clinic*, *13*, 97–111.

13 I have decided to use this transliteration of the Russian name on the advice of Olga Bogdashina, to whom many thanks. It appears inaccurately in the German translation and in Sula Wolff's version as Ssucharewa.

14 G. E. Sukhareva (1926). Die schizoiden Psychoathien in Kindesalter [Schizoid psychopathies in childhood]. *Monatschrift für Psychiatrie und Neurologie*, *60*, 235–261.

15 See Sula Wolff (1996). The first account of the syndrome Asperger described? *European Child and Adolescent Psychiatry*, *5*, 119–132.

16 E. Sterba (1936). An abnormal child. *Psychoanalytic Quarterly*, *5*, 375–414, 560–600. My thanks to Anthony Gordon for drawing my attention to this paper.

17 Howard W. Potter (1933). Schizophrenia in children. *American Journal of Psychiatry*, *89*, 1253–1270.

18 C. J. Earl (1934). The primitive catatonic psychosis of idiocy. *British Journal of Medical Psychology*, *14*, 230.

19 Lorna Wing & Amitta Shah (2000). Catatonia in autism. *British Journal of Psychiatry*, *176*, 157–162, and (2006). Psychological approaches to chronic catatonia-like deterioration in autism spectrum disorders, *International Review of Neurobiology*, *72*, 245–264.

20 I am indebted to Dr. Ina van Berckelaer-Onnes, at the University of Leiden for pointing out this pioneering use of the term "autistic" to me. See *Looking Up*, *2*(1), 2000, 14.

21 Maria Asperger Felder in conversation with the author in Zurich, December 5, 2008.

22 Michael Rutter in conversation with the author, Institute of Psychiatry, London, January 27, 2009.

23 Lorna Wing in conversation with the author.

24 Simon Baron-Cohen in conversation with the author at the Autism Research Centre, Cambridge, UK, January 29, 2009. See chapter 8, pp. 211–212 for a discussion of theory of mind.

25 It is anticipated that many of the interviews incorporated in this book will be available on an accompanying website, http://thehistoryofautism.org where contributions and comments from readers are also welcome.

# 1 The Two Great Pioneers

1 Dr. Fred Stone in conversation with the author at his home in Glasgow, July 18, 2007.

2 Ibid.

3 Albert Kanner in conversation with the author in Madison, Wisconsin, October 1, 2007.

4 *Baltimore Sun*, July 13, 1969.

5   Lorna Wing in conversation with the author, in Hartfield, UK, August 15, 2007.

6   Leo Kanner (1943). Autistic disturbances of affective contact. *Nervous Child*, 2, 217–250.

7   Hans Asperger (1944). Die "autistischen Psychopathen" im Kindesalter. *Archiv für Psychiatrie und Nervenkrankheiten*, *117*, 76–136. [Autistic psychopathy in childhood. Trans. Uta Frith. In U. Frith (Ed.) (1991), *Autism amd Asperger syndrome* (pp. 37–92). Cambridge, England: Cambridge University Press].

8   Hans Asperger (1938). Das psychisch abnorme Kind, *Wiener Klinischen Wochenzeitschrift*, *51*, 1314–1317.

9   Maria Asperger Felder in conversation with the author.

10  Maria Asperger Felder (2008). Hans Asperger, 1906–1980: Leben und Werk. In Rolf Castell (Ed.), *Hundert Jahre Kinder- und Jugendpsychiatrie* (pp. 99–117). Göttingen, Germany: V., & R. Unipress.

11  Ibid.

12  Michael Fitzgerald in conversation with the author.

13  Christopher Gillberg in conversation with the author in London, September 4, 2007.

14  Ibid.

15  Leon Eisenberg in conversation with the author at Harvard University Medical School, Cambridge, MA, June 7, 2007.

16  Lorna Wing in conversation with the author.

17  Isabelle Rapin in conversation with the author at the Albert Einstein College of Medicine in New York, June 5, 2007.

18  Gerhard Bosch in telephone conversation with the author from Frankfurt, March 13, 2009.

19  Maria Asperger Felder in conversation with the author.

20  Ibid.

21  Elizabeth Wurst in conversation with the author in Vienna, July 15, 2008.

22  Ibid.

23  Maria Theresia Schubert in conversation with the author in Vienna, July 15, 2008.

24  Ibid.

25  Elizabeth Wurst in conversation with the author.

26  Maria Theresia Schubert in conversation with the author.

27  Hans Asperger interviewed on Austrian radio, 'Geschichte und Geschichten' (History and Histories), December 24, 1974.

28  Franz Hamburger quoted in the *Journal of the American Medical Association*, 1939.

29  Lorna Wing in conversation with the author.

30  Marc Bush in conversation with the author in London. My thanks to Bush, who is currently completing his PhD at the University of

Surrey, for many enjoyable and stimulating discussions on Asperger's writings.

31 Elizabeth Wurst in conversation with the author.
32 Asperger, Das psychisch abnorme Kind.
33 Ibid.
34 Ibid.
35 Elizabeth Wurst in conversation with the author.
36 Maria Asperger Felder in conversation with the author.
37 Asperger, radio interview, December 24, 1974.
38 Maria Asperger Felder in conversation with the author.
39 My thanks to one of Japan's leading child psychiatrists and autism authorities, Dr. Tokio Uchiyama, for pointing out this and many other aspects of the history of autism in that country.
40 Maria Asperger Felder in conversation with the author.
41 Ibid.
42 Gilbert Lelord in conversation with the author, Tours, France, May 9, 2008.
43 Maria Theresia Schubert, in conversation with the author.
44 Albert Kanner in conversation with the author.
45 Leon Eisenberg in conversation with the author.
46 See: Joseph S. Bierman & William H. McClain (n.d.). *An introduction to Leo Kanner the poet.* Archives of Johns Hopkins University, Baltimore, MD.
47 Ibid.
48 *Baltimore Sun,* February 16, 1978.
49 Leo Kanner (n.d.). *Freedom from within* [unpublished autobiography]. American Psychiatric Association library, Arlington, Virginia, USA, p. 347.
50 See: K.-J. Neumärker (2003). Leo Kanner: His years in Berlin, 1906–24. The roots of autistic disorder, *History of Psychiatry, 14*(2), 205–218.
51 Leo Kanner interviewed by Dr. Stafford Ackerly and Dr. Gary May, Louisville, Kentucky, May 15, 1972. Johns Hopkins University archives.
52 Ibid.
53 See Leon Eisenberg (1981). In memoriam Leo Kanner MD 1894–1981. *American Journal of Psychiatry, 138*(8), 1122–1125.
54 See, in particular, a letter from Leo Kanner to Adolf Meyer, October 25, 1942. Johns Hopkins University archives.
55 Leo Kanner (1935). *Child psychiatry.* Springfield, IL: C. C. Thomas Publishing.
56 Leo Kanner *In defense of mothers.* Springfield, IL: C. C. Thomas Publishing.
57 Kanner interviewed by Dr. Stafford Ackerly and Dr. Gary May, Louisville.
58 Leo Kanner interviewed by Tom Sayvetz and Robert Bradsber, September 1976. Johns Hopkins University archives.

59 A year earlier, on September 4, 1937, Kanner nearly died when he fell off a railway bridge into the harbor during a visit to Halifax, in Nova Scotia, Canada. He could not swim but was rescued by the crew of a passing train.

60 Leon Eisenberg in conversation with the author.

61 Ibid.

62 Ibid.

63 Michael Rutter in conversation with the author.

64 Lorna Wing in conversation with the author.

65 Leon Eisenberg in conversation with the author.

66 Michael Rutter in conversation with the author.

67 Ami Klin, speaking to the author during a conference in Baltimore, October 5, 2007; M. Scheerer, E. Rothman, & K. Goldstein (1945). A case of "idiot savant": An experimental study of personality organization. *Psychological Monographs*, *58*(4), 1–63; L. Wing & J. Gould (1979). Severe impairments of social interaction and associated abnormalities in children: Epidemiology and classification. *Journal of Autism and Developmental Disorders*, *9*, 11–29.

68 Albert Kanner in conversation with the author.

69 Christopher Gillberg in conversation with the author.

70 Lauretta Bender (1959). Autism in children with mental deficiency. *American Journal of Mental Deficiency*, *64*(1), 81–86.

71 Bernard Rimland (1964). *Infantile autism*. Englewood Cliffs, NJ: Prentice Hall, 27.

72 Christopher Gillberg in conversation with the author.

73 Ibid.

74 L. Kanner (1949). Problems of nosology and psychodynamics in early childhood autism. *American Journal of Orthopsychiatry*, *19*(3), 416–426.

75 Asperger, Das psychisch abnorme Kind.

76 Asperger, Die "autistischen Psychopathen" im Kindesalter.

77 From Kanner's lecture, *Infantile autism and the schizophrenias* given to an American Psychiatric Association meeting, New York, May 4, 1965, published in *Behavioral Science*, *10*(4) (1965), 412–420.

78 Ibid.

79 Ibid.

80 Arn van Krevelen (1971): Early infantile autism and autistic psychopathy. *Journal of Autism and Childhood Schizophrenia*, *1*(1), 82–86.

81 Cited by Denys Ribas (2006). *Autism: Debates and testimonies*. London, England: Free Association Books, 9.

82 Kathrin Hippler in conversation with the author in Vienna, July 17, 2008

83 Elizabeth Wurst in conversation with the author.

84 Cited by Ribas, *Autism*, 8.

85 Maria Asperger Felder in conversation with the author.

86   Elizabeth Wurst in conversation with the author.

87   Ibid.

88   Marlies Janz (1995). *Elfriede Jelinek*. Stuttgart, Germany: J. B. Metzler; quoted in Leland de la Durantaye (2005, December). *Harvard University Review*, *29*. http://findarticles.com/p/articles/mi_m0RWZ/is_29/ai_n15963997/ (accessed 17 February, 2010).

89   Sula Wolff in conversation with the author in Edinburgh, July 20, 2007.

90   Simon Baron-Cohen in conversation with the author. Indeed, Professor Jeremy Turk, a psychiatrist who examined McKinnon, declared that suicide was "an almost certain inevitability" if he were sent for trial in the US. On January 17, 2010, a High Court judge ruled that the Britain's Home Secretary, Alan Johnson, may have acted unlawfully by failing to halt the extradition to the US and ordered a full judicial review of the case.

91   Simon Baron-Cohen in conversation with the author.

92   Sula Wolff in conversation with the author.

93   Ibid.

94   Lorna Wing (1981). Asperger's syndrome: A clinical account. *Psychological Medicine*, *11*(1), 115–130.

95   Ibid.

96   Elizabeth Wurst in conversation with the author.

97   Maria Theresia Schubert in conversation with the author.

98   Kathrin Hippler in conversation with the author.

99   Ibid.

100  Elizabeth Wurst in conversation with the author.

101  Ibid.

102  *Time* magazine, July 25, 1960.

103  Michael Rutter in conversation with the author.

104  S. Folstein & M. Rutter (1977). Infantile autism: A genetic study of 21 twin pairs. *Journal of Child Psychology and Psychiatry*, *18*, 297–321.

105  Foster Kennedy (1942). The problem of social control of the congenital defective: education, sterilization, euthanasia, *American Journal of Psychiatry*, *99*, 13–16.

106  Leo Kanner in his keynote address to the first annual meeting of the National Society for Autistic Children, Washington, DC, July 1969.

107  Leon Eisenberg in conversation with the author.

108  See Paul E. Stepansky (Ed.) (1988). *The Memoirs of Margaret S. Mahler*. New York: The Free Press, 112–113.

109  Kanner: *Child psychiatry*.

110  Leo Kanner (1973). *Childhood psychosis: Initial studies and new insights*. Washington, DC: Winston, 97–98.

111  Ibid.

112  Leo Kanner (1972). How far can autistic children go in matters of social adaptation? *Journal of Autism and Childhood Schizophrenia*, *2*(1), 9–33.

113 Kanner interviewed by Dr. Stafford Ackerly and Dr. Gary May, Louisville.
114 Ibid.

## 2 The 1950s: The Seeds of Understanding

1 D. A. van Krevelen (1952). Een geval van "early infantile autism." *Nederlands Tijdschrift voor Geneeskunde, 96,* 202–205.
2 Gerhard Bosch in telephone conversation with the author.
3 Peter Tanguay in conversation with the author in Louisville, Kentucky, September 30, 2007.
4 See Kanner, Autistic disturbances of affective contact.
5 Kanner, Problems of nosology and psychodynamics in early childhood autism.
6 J. L. Daniels, U. Forssen, C. M. Hultman, S. Cnattingius, D. A. Savitz, M. Feychting, & P. Sparen (2008). Parental psychiatric disorders associated with autism spectrum disorders in the offspring. *Pediatrics, 121*(5), 1357–1362.
7 Leo Kanner & Leon Eisenberg (1956). Early infantile autism, 1943–55. *American Journal of Orthopsychiatry, 26*(3), 556–566.
8 Ibid.
9 Leon Eisenberg (1956). The autistic child in adolescence. *American Journal of Psychiatry, 112*(8), 607–12.
10 Leon Eisenberg in conversation with the author in Boston, June 5, 2007. This suggestion of a 5-year-old cut-off for prognosis has remained controversial ever since Eisenberg made it in 1956.
11 Leon Eisenberg (1957). The fathers of autistic children. *American Journal of Orthopsychiatry, 27,* 715–724.
12 Rimland, *Infantile autism,* 44.
13 Ibid., 45.
14 Michael Rutter in conversation with the author.
15 Kanner, Problems of nosology and psychodynamics in early childhood autism.
16 Louise J. Despert (1947). Psychotherapy in child schizophrenia. *American Journal of Psychiatry, 104,* 36–43.
17 Peter Tanguay in conversation with the author; I. Kolvin (1971). Studies in the childhood psychoses: Diagnostic criteris and classification. *British Journal of Psychiatry, 118,* 381–384.
18 Ed Ornitz in conversation with the author, UCLA, Los Angeles, June 24, 2008.
19 R. Nesnidalova & V. K. Fiala (1961). On the question of Kanner's early infantile autism. *Ceskoslovenska Psychiatrie, 57,* 76–84.

20  Rimland, *Infantile autism*, 68.
21  Kanner, *Infantile autism and the schizophrenias.*
22  Ibid.
23  Ibid.
24  Ibid.
25  Ibid.
26  Rimland, *Infantile autism*, 68.
27  Cris Bolduc in email communication with the author, February 17, 2010.
28  Christopher Gillberg in conversation with the author. See chapter 8, pp. 211–212 for a discussion of theory of mind.
29  Sula Wolff in conversation with the author.
30  Leon Eisenberg in conversation with the author.
31  Ibid.
32  Fred Stone in conversation with the author.
33  Ibid.
34  Ibid.
35  Bender, Autism in children with mental deficiency, 81.
36  Ibid., 84.
37  Ibid., 85.
38  Ibid.
39  Ibid.; S. Chess (1971). Autism in children with congenital rubella. *Journal of Autism and Childhood Schizophrenia*, *1*(1), 33–47.
40  Bender, Autism in children with mental deficiency, 85.
41  Ibid.
42  Quoted in Barbara Seaman: *Lovely me: The life of Jacqueline Susann*, New York, NY: Seven Stories Press (2003).
43  Ibid.
44  Temple Grandin in conversation with the author, May 23, 2008.
45  Ibid.
46  Ibid.
47  Rimland, *Infantile autism*, 18.
48  Leon Eisenberg in conversation with the author.
49  Helen Tager-Flusberg in conversation with the author at Boston University School of Medicine, October 3, 2007.
50  Michael Rutter in conversation with the author.
51  Leon Eisenberg in conversation with the author.
52  Gerhard Bosch in telephone conversation with the author.
53  James Watson, speaking on DNA and the brain, April 4, 2006; Authors@Google series http://video.google.com/videoplay?docid= -8220394453782681101#. Watson later told the British daily, *The Guardian*, that Rosalind Franklin, believed by many to have played a key role in the discovery of DNA, "was partially autistic." He added: "I'd never

really thought of scientists as autistic until this whole business of high-intelligence autism came up. There is probably no other explanation for Rosalind's behaviour" (*The Guardian*, October 16, 2007).

54 Rimland, *Infantile autism*, 57.

55 Nolan Lewis (1954). In discussion, *Proceedings of the Association for Research into Nervous and Mental Diseases*, *33*, 364.

56 R. J. Schain & H. Yannet (1960). Infantile autism: An analysis of 50 cases and a consideration of certain neurophysiologic concepts. *Journal of Pediatrics*, *57*, 560–567.

57 P. Bergman & Sibylle K. Escalona (1949). Unusual sensitivities in very young children. *Psychoanalytic Study of the Child*, *3–4*, 333–352.

58 H. H. Eveloff (1960). The autistic child. *American Medical Association Archive of General Psychiatry*, *3*, 66–81; W. Goldfarb (1956). Receptor preferences in schizophrenic children. *American Medical Association Archives of Neurology and Psychiatry*, *76*, 643–652.

59 M. S. Mahler (1952). On child psychosis and schizophrenia: Autistic and symbiotic infantile psychoses. *Psychoanalytic Study of the Child*, *7*, 286–305.

60 Ed Ornitz in conversation with the author.

61 Leo Kanner (1954). General concept of schizophrenia at different ages. *Proceedings of the Association for Research into Nervous and Mental Diseases*, *33*, 451–453.

62 J. Simons & S. Oishi (1987). *The hidden child: The Linwood Method for reaching the autistic child*. Bethesda, MD: Woodbine House.

63 As quoted by *The Washington Post* in its obituary of Jeanne Simons on March 12, 2005.

64 Ibid.

65 Ibid.

66 Ibid.

67 See Leo Kanner (1973). Linwood Children's Center: Evaluations and follow-up of 34 psychotic children. In L. Kanner, *Childhood psychosis: Initial studies and new insights* (pp. 223–283). Washington, DC: V. H. Winston & Sons.

68 Ibid.

69 From the transcript of the round-table discussions at the First Leo Kanner Colloquium on Child Development, Deviations and Treatment, held at Chapel Hill, North Carolina in 1973. My thanks to Dr. Brenda Denzler at Division TEACCH for sending me this transcript.

70 Ibid.

71 Ibid.

72 Demetrious Haracapos in conversation with the author, March 5, 2009.

73 Ibid.

## 3  Blaming the Parents

1  Sally Ozonoff in conversation with the author at the MIND Institute in Sacramento, California, June 23, 2008.
2  According to Bent Vandborg Sørensen in conversation with the author in Dortmund, Germany, October 14, 2008.
3  Bruno Bettelheim (1967). *The empty fortress: Infantile autism and the birth of self.* New York, NY: The Free Press, 57.
4  Ibid.
5  See Richard Pollak (1997). *The creation of Dr. B: A biography of Bruno Bettelheim.* New York, NY: Simon & Schuster. 21.
6  As noted by Pollak in ibid., 15.
7  Ibid., 78.
8  Bruno Bettelheim (1943). Individual and mass behavior in extreme situations. *Journal of Abnormal and Social Psychology, 38,* 417–452.
9  Pollak, *The Creation of Dr. B.,* 10.
10  Ibid.
11  *The New York Review of Books,* November 20, 2003.
12  Chloe Silverman (2005). *From disorders of affect to mindblindness: Framing the history of autism spectrum disorders.* Paper presented at the conference Autism and Representation: Writing, Cognition, Disability October 28–30, 2005, Cleveland, Ohio. www.cwru.edu/affil/sce/Texts_2005/Autism%20and%20Representation%20Silverman.htm.
13  Pollak, *The creation of Dr. B.,* 138.
14  Eric Schopler interviwed by his TEACCH colleague, Dr. Brenda Denzler, December 17, 2001.
15  Ibid.
16  Jacquelyn Seevak Sanders in conversation with the author, June 10, 2007.
17  Ibid.
18  Erik Erikson (1950). *Childhood and Society,* New York, NY: W. W. Norton, 181, cited by Bettelheim's former colleague, Karen Zelan (1993). Bruno Bettelheim (1903–1990). *Prospects, 23*(1/2), 85–100.
19  Zelan, *Bruno Bettelheim.*
20  Ibid.
21  Leon Eisenberg in conversation with the author.
22  Pollak, *The creation of Dr. B.,* 147.
23  Jacquelyn Sanders in conversation with the author.
24  Ibid.
25  *New York Review of Books,* November 20, 2003.
26  Jacquelyn Sanders in conversation with the author.
27  Ibid.
28  Quoted in Pollak, *The creation of Dr. B.,* 270.

29  Mary Coleman in conversation with the author in New York, October 2, 2007.
30  Silverman, *From disorders of affect to mindblindness.*
31  Jacquelyn Sanders in conversation with the author.
32  Gilbert Lelord in conversation with the author.
33  Ibid.
34  Ibid.
35  Lee Marcus in conversation with the author, in Chapel Hill, North Carolina, September 28, 2007.
36  Ibid.
37  *Refrigerator mothers*, directed by David E. Simpson, produced by J. J. Hanley. Kartemquin Films, distributed by Fanlight Productions, Boston, MA, 2002.
38  Donata Vivanti in conversation with the author in Oslo, Norway, August 31, 2007.
39  Jacquelyn Sanders in conversation with the author.
40  Ibid.
41  Bruno Bettelheim & Daniel Karlin (1975). *Un autre regard sur la folie.* Paris: Editions Stock.
42  Ibid., 127–128.
43  Clara Claiborne Park (1967). *The siege.* New York, NY: Harcourt, Brace and World, Inc.
44  David Park in e-mail communication with the author, December 12, 2008.
45  Virginia Mae Axline (1971). *Dibs: In search of self: Personality development in play therapy.* London, England: Penguin Books; James T. Fisher, *No search no subject? Autism and the American conversion narrative.* Paper presented at the conference Autism and Representation: Writing, Cognition, Disability October 28–30, 2005, Cleveland, Ohio. http://cwru.edu/affil/sce/Texts_2005/Autism and Representation fisher.htm.
46  James T. Fisher, No search no subject? Autism and the American conversion narrative. In M. Osteen (Ed.), *Autism and Representation* (pp. 51–64). London, England: Routledge, at p. 60.
47  Fisher, *No search no subject?* http://cwru.edu/affil/sce/Texts_2005/Autism and Representation fisher.htm.
48  Ibid.
49  Jacquelyn Sanders in conversation with the author.
50  Bettelheim & Karlin, *Un autre regard sur la folie*, 116–117.
51  Bettelheim, *The empty fortress*, 406.
52  Leon Eisenberg in conversation with the author.
53  Kenneth B. Kidd (2005). Bruno Bettelheim and the psychoanalytic feral tale. *American Imago*, 62(1), 75–99.
54  M. K. DeMyer, W. Pontius, J. A. Norton, S. Barton, J. Allen, & R. Steele (1972). Parental practices and innate activity in normal, autistic and brain-damaged infants, *Journal of Autism and Childhood Schizophrenia*, 2, 49–66.

55 Michael Rutter in conversation with the author.
56 Jacquelyn Sanders in conversation with the author.
57 Bettelheim, Kanner, Rimland, and others. In *The empty fortress*, 425–433.
58 Ibid.
59 Jacquelyn Sanders in conversation with the author.
60 Letter from Bruno Bettelheim to Bernard Rimland, April 9, 1966. Bettelheim Papers, University of Chicago Manuscripts and Archives Collection. See Silverman, *From disorders of affect to mindblindness*.
61 Ibid.
62 Letter from Bruno Bettelheim to Bernard Rimland, April 29, 1966. Bettelheim Papers, University of Chicago Manuscripts and Archives Collection.
63 A. M. Donnellan (ed.) (1985). *Classic readings in autism*. New York, NY. Teachers College Press.
64 Bruno Bettelheim (1959). Joey: A mechanical boy. *Scientific American, 200*, 117–126.
65 Anne Donnellan, in e-mail communication with the author, April 7, 2008.
66 Francesca Happé in conversation with the author at the Institute of Psychiatry, London, November 26, 2008.
67 Quoted in *New York Times*, November 4, 1990.
68 Ibid.
69 See obituary, Bruno Bettelheim dies at 86; Psychoanalyst of vast impact. *New York Times*, March 14, 1990.
70 See Friends pondering Bettelheim death. *New York Times*, March 15, 1990.
71 Jacquelyn Sanders in conversation with the author.
72 Laura Schreibman in conversation with the author in London, May 16, 2008.
73 Donald Meltzer (1975). *Explorations in autism: A psychoanalytic study*. Strathtay, Scotland: Clunie Press.
74 Frances Tustin (1972). *Autism and childhood psychosis*. London, England: Hogarth Press.
75 See Frances Tustin (1991). Revised understandings of psychogenic autism. *International Journal of Psycho-Analysis, 72*(4), 585–591.
76 Dame Stephanie Shirley in conversation with the author, March 6, 2009.
77 IACAPAP Declaration, Venice, 1998.
78 E-mail correspondence.
79 Roger Misès in conversation with the author at his home in Paris, May 13, 2008.
80 David Amaral in conversation with the author at the MIND Institute in Sacramento, California.
81 See Introduction.
82 Simon Baron-Cohen in conversation with the author.
83 Michael Rutter in conversation with the author.

## 4 The 1960s: The Parents Fight Back

1 Lorna Wing. *Forty years on: Memories of an NAS founder member*. Memoir in the archives of the National Autistic Society, unpaginated.
2 Ibid.
3 Ibid.
4 See Michael Rutter (1965). The influence of organic and emotional factors on the origins, nature and outcome of childhood psychosis. *Developmental Medicine and Child Neurology*, 7, 518–528; and (1966). Behavioural and cognitive characteristics of a series of psychotic children, in J. K. Wing (Ed.), *Childhood Autism: Clinical, Educational and Social Aspects*. London: Pergamon Press.
5 Gerhard Bosch (1962). *Der frühkindliche Autismus* (Monographien aus dem Gesamtdebiete der Neurologie und Psychiatrie, Heft 96). Berlin: Springer-Verlag; published in English as *Infantile autism: A clinical and phenomenological-anthropological investigation taking language as the guide*. Springer-Verlag, New York (1970).
6 Bosch: *Infantile autism*, 119.
7 Ibid., 129.
8 Ibid., 130.
9 Gerhard Bosch in telephone conversation with the author.
10 Bosch, *Infantile autism*, 137, 139.
11 Gerhard Bosch in telephone conversation with the author.
12 Sven Bölte & Gerhard Bosch (2004). Bosch's cases: a 40-year follow-up of patients with infantile autism and Asperger syndrome. *German Journal of Psychiatry*, 7, 10–13.
13 Victor Lotter (1967). Epidemiology of autistic conditions in young children: Some characteristics of the parents and children. *Social Psychiatry*, 1, 163–173.
14 Lorna Wing in conversation with the author.
15 Michael Rutter in conversation with the author.
16 J. K. Wing (Ed.) (1966). *Childhood autism: Clinical, educational and social aspects*. London, England: Pergamon Press.
17 L. Wing (1971). *Autistic children: A guide for parents*. London, England: Constable.
18 E. M. Ornitz, C. W. Atwell, A. R. Kaplan, & J. Westlake (1985). Brainstem dysfunction in autism. Results of vestibular stimulation, *Archives of General Psychiatry*, 42(10), 1018–1025.
19 Ed Ornitz in conversation with the author.
20 Philip K. Dick (1964). *Martian time-slip*. New York, NY: Ballantine Books.
21 James Copeland (1973). *For the love of Ann: The true story of an autistic child*. London, England: Arrow Books.

22   Karin Stensland Junker (1961). *De ensamma*. Stockholm, Sweden: Natur och Kultur.

23   Karin Stensland Junker (1964). *The child in the glass ball: A courageous mother's story of hope for retarded children*. Nashville, TN: Abingdon Press.

24   Margaret Golding (2006, October). *The hitch hiker's guide to autism: An educator's unique account of the history of autism and the development of a relevant and empowering curriculum 1959–2005*. Address to the Second World Autism Congress, Cape Town, South Africa.

25   Ibid.

26   Ibid.

27   Lorna Wing in e-mail correspondence with the author, April 26, 2009.

28   Lorna Wing in conversation with the author.

29   Ibid.

30   1999 interview with Peggie Everard. Archives of the National Autistic Society, London.

31   Michael Baron in conversation with the author, London, UK, November 29, 2008.

32   Ibid.

33   Ibid.

34   Golding, *The hitch hiker's guide to autism*.

35   Ibid.

36   Ibid.

37   Lorna Wing in conversation with the author.

38   Helen Allison interviewed by Cindy Andrews, November 14, 1998. Archives of the National Autistic Society, London.

39   Lorna Wing in conversation with the author.

40   Helen Allison interviewed by Cindy Andrews.

41   Ibid.

42   Michael Baron in conversation with the author.

43   Gerald de Groot in conversation with the author in London, December 10, 2008.

44   Richard Mills in e-mail communication with the author, May 7, 2009.

45   Hugh Morgan in conversation with the author in London, December 8, 2008.

46   Ibid.

47   Wendy Brown in e-mail communication with the author.

48   Gerald de Groot in conversation with the author.

49   Ibid.

50   Ibid.

51   David Tomlinson (1990). *Luckier than most: An autobiography*. London: Hodder and Stoughton, 168.

52   Gerald de Groot in conversation with the author.

53   Lorna Wing in conversation with the author.

54  Michael Rutter in conversation with the author.

55  Ibid.

56  Ibid.

57  Phil Christie in conversation with the author, February 16, 2009.

58  Ibid.

59  Paul Tréhin, a leading French autism activist and father of the autistic savant artist, Gilles Tréhin, hypothesizes that many prehistoric artists may well have been autistic because of their focus on detail and their ability to recall precise aspects of an animal long after seeing it, in the same way that the British autistic savant artist, Stephen Wiltshire, is able to reproduce precisely from memory the drawing of a building weeks, even months after seeing it.

60  Phil Christie in conversation with the author.

61  Lorna Wing in conversation with the author.

62  Bent Vandborg Sørensen in conversation with the author, Dortmund, Germany, October 14, 2008.

63  Ibid.

64  Demetrious Haracapos in conversation with the author.

65  Bent Vandborg Sørensen in conversation with the author.

66  Ibid.

67  Ibid.

68  Ibid.

69  Ibid.

70  Ibid.

71  Fred Stone in conversation with the author.

72  See Mark Frankland (1995). *Freddie the weaver: The boy who fought to join the world*. London, England: Sinclair-Stevenson, 113.

73  Marian Critchley in conversation with the author in Edinburgh, July 20, 2007.

74  Ibid.

75  Bob and Yvonne Phillips in conversation with the author at New Struan School, Alloa, Scotland.

76  Marian Critchley in conversation with the author.

77  Chris and Jane Butler-Cole in conversation with the author in Edinburgh, July 20, 2007.

78  Ibid.

79  Ruth Hampton in conversation with the author in Edinburgh, July 20, 2007.

80  Ibid.

81  Jim Taylor in conversation with the author at New Struan, Alloa, Scotland, July 19, 2007.

82  Ibid.

83  Ibid.

84 Ibid. The Curriculum for Excellence, introduced in 2004, is the Scottish Government's major programme of reform for the education sector. It starts in nurseries and continues through schools, colleges, and beyond.

85 Andrew Lester in conversation with the author in Edinburgh, July 20, 2007.

86 Ruth Sullivan in conversation with the author in Huntington, West Virginia, June 8, 2007.

87 Ibid.

88 Ibid.

89 David Park, in e-mail communication with the author, December 18, 2008.

90 Ed Ritvo in conversation with the author, Los Angeles, June 24, 2008.

91 Ibid.

92 Ruth Sullivan in conversation with the author.

93 Ibid.

94 Gilbert Lelord in conversation with the author.

95 Ibid.

96 See Brigitte Chamak (2003). L'autisme: Vers une nécessaire revolution culturelle. *Médecine/Sciences*, *19*, 1152–1159; and (2008). Autism and social movements: French parents' associations and international autistic individuals' organizations. *Sociology of Health and Illness*, *30*, 76–96.

97 Pierre Delion (2003). *Le packing avec les enfants autistes et psychotiques*. Paris: Erès.

98 Theo Peeters in conversation with the author in Antwerp, Belgium, June 3, 2008.

99 Gilbert Lelord in conversation with the author.

100 Isabel Bayonas in conversation with the author, Madrid, Spain, April 11, 2008.

101 Ibid.

102 Ibid.

103 Ibid.

104 Mercedes Belinchón in conversation with the author in Madrid, Spain, April 11, 2008.

105 Ibid. See chapter 8, pp. 211–212 for a discussion of theory of mind.

106 Ibid.

107 Carmen Nieto in conversation with the author in Madrid, Spain, April 11, 2008.

108 Angel Díez-Cuervo in conversation with the author in Madrid, Spain, April 10, 2008.

109 Ibid.

110 Ibid.

111 Ibid.

112 Joaquín Fuentes quoted in the online edition of the Spanish daily, *EcoDiario*, on November 13, 2008. http://ecodiario.eleconomista.es/salud/noticias/860664/11/08/AETAPI-apuesta-por-el-desafio-de-eliminar-las-barreras-a-las-que-se-enfrentan-los-adultos-que-padecen-autismo.html.

113 Isabel Bayonas in conversation with the author.
114 Mercedes Berlinchón in conversation with the author.
115 Donata Vivanti in conversation with the author, Oslo, Norway, August 31, 2007.
116 Ibid.
117 Ibid.
118 Donata Vivanti in conversation with the author.
119 Ibid.
120 Ibid.
121 Marie-Jeanne Accietto quoted in the online edition of the Swiss daily, *Le Courrier*, July 22, 2006. http://lecourrier.ch/modules.php?op= modload&name=NewsPaper&file=article&sid=41857.
122 Theo Peeters in conversation with the author.
123 Ibid.
124 Hilde De Clercq in conversation with the author in Antwerp, Belgium, June 3, 2008.
125 Irène Knodt-Lenfant (2004). *Claudin, classé X chez les dinormos*. Brue Auriac, France: Envol Publications.
126 Irène Knodt-Lenfant in conversation with the author in Brussels, Belgium, June 4, 2008.
127 Ibid.
128 Ibid.
129 Ami Klin in conversation with the author.

## 5  The Two Teaching Pioneers

1 Eric Schopler interviewed by Brenda Denzler in December 2001. TEACCH archives, Chapel Hill, North Carolina.
2 Betsy Schopler in conversation with the author at the TEACCH headquarters in Chapel Hill, North Carolina, September 28, 2007.
3 Susie Schopler in conversation with the author at the TEACCH headquarters in Chapel Hill, North Carolina, September 28, 2007.
4 Eric Schopler interviewed by Gary Mesibov, June 18, 1998. TEACCH archives, Chapel Hill, North Carolina.
5 Robert Reichler in conversation with the author at his home by Lake Washington in Seattle, USA, June 21, 2008.
6 M. Pitfield & A. N. Oppenheim (1964). Child rearing attitudes of mothers of psychotic children. *Journal of Child Psychology and Psychiatry*, 5(1), 51–57.
7 E. Schopler & J. Loftin (1969). Thought disorders in parents of psychotic children: A function of test anxiety. *Archives of General Psychiatry*, 20, 174–181.

8   This was revealed by *Vanity Fair* magazine in its issue of September 2007.
9   Ibid.
10  For example, A. Cox, M. Rutter, S. Newman, & L. Bartak (1975). A comparative study of infantile autism and specific developmental receptive language disorder. II. Parental characteristics. *British Journal of Psychiatry*, *126*, 146–159; and D. P. Cantwell, L. Baker, & M. Rutter (1979). Families of autistic and dysphasic children. I. Family life and interaction patterns, *Archives of General Psychiatry*, *36*(6), 682–687.
11  Ibid.
12  Lee Marcus in conversation with the author.
13  Ibid.
14  Robert Reichler in conversation with the author.
15  Ibid.
16  Mary Lou Warren in conversation with the author in Chapel Hill, North Carolina, September 28, 2007.
17  Ibid.
18  Ibid.
19  Ibid.
20  Betty Camp in conversation with the author in Chapel Hill, North Carolina, September 28, 2007.
21  Robert Reichler in conversation with the author.
22  Ibid.
23  Gary Mesibov in conversation with the author at the TEACCH headquarters in Chapel Hill, North Carolina, September 28, 2007.
24  Ibid.
25  http://www.unc.edu/~annawh/6/history.html.
26  http://ericschopler.blogspot.com/
27  Brenda Denzler in conversation with the author at the TEACCH headquarters in Chapel Hill, North Carolina, September 28, 2007.
28  http://ericschopler.blogspot.com/
29  Ruth Sullivan in conversation with the author.
30  Michael Rutter in conversation with the author.
31  Ribas, *Autism*, 4.
32  Gilbert Lelord in conversation with the author.
33  *Life* magazine (1965, May 7). Screams, slaps, and love: A surprising, shocking treatment helps far-gone mental cripples.
34  Charles B. Ferster & Marian K. DeMyer (1961). The development of performances in autistic children in an automatically controlled environment. *Journal of Chronic Diseases*, *13*, 312–314.
35  Ibid.
36  *Life*, May 7, 1965.
37  Quoted in *Los Angeles* Magazine, April 1, 2004.
38  Ruth Sullivan in conversation with the author.

39  Ibid.

40  Ibid.

41  Laura Schreibman in conversation with the author in London, May 15, 2008.

42  Ibid.

43  Cathy Lord in conversation with the author in Oslo, Norway, August 31, 2007. ABA, or applied behavioral analysis, which derives from Lovaas's original work at UCLA in the 1960s, is a program which involves the teaching of linguistic, cognitive, social, and self-help skills across all settings and breaking down these skills into small tasks which are taught in a highly structured and hierarchical manner. There is a focus on rewarding, or reinforcing, desired behaviors and ignoring, redirecting, or otherwise discouraging inappropriate behaviors. In discrete trial training (DTT)— which is often used as part of a more broadly-based ABA approach— a series of distinct repeated lessons or trials are taught one-to-one. Each trial consists of a "directive" or request for the individual to perform an action; a behavior, or response, from the person; and a consequence, a reaction, from the therapist based upon the response of the person. Positive reinforcers are selected by evaluating the individual's preferences.

44  Paul Chance (1974, January). A conversation with Ivar Lovaas about self-mutilating children and how their parents make it worse. *Psychology Today*, 76. http://www.neurodiversity.com/library_chance_1974.html.

45  Suzie, Bobby, and Tom Schopler in conversation with the author at the TEACCH headquarters in Chapel Hill, North Carolina, September 28, 2007.

46  O. Ivar Lovaas (1981). *Teaching developmentally disabled children: The ME book*. Nerang, Australia: Pro-Ed Books.

47  Quoted in *Los Angeles* Magazine, April 1, 2004.

48  Gary Mesibov in conversation with the author.

49  Michael Rutter in conversation with the author.

50  Cathy Lord in conversation with the author.

51  Ed Ritvo in conversation with the author in Los Angeles, June 24, 2008.

52  Peter Tanguay in conversation with the author.

53  Laura Schreibman in conversation with the author.

54  Catherine Maurice (1993). *Let me hear your voice: A family's triumph over autism*. New York, NY: Fawcett Columbia.

55  Gary Mesibov in conversation with the author.

56  Gary Mesibov, interviewed by the author, *Looking Up*, 2(10) (2001), 20.

57  Ibid.

58  Lorna Wing in conversation with the author.

59  Ibid.

60  Ibid.

61   Peter Tanguay in conversation with the author.
62   Helen Tager-Flusberg in conversation with the author.
63   See Rita Jordan's interview with the author, *Looking Up*, 4(1) (2006), 22.

## 6   The 1970s: Major Steps Forward

1    H. Clancy, A. Dugdale, & J. Rendle-Short (1969). The diagnosis of infantile autism. *Developmental Medicine and Child Neurology*, 11(4), 432–442.
2    Sally Ozonoff in conversation with the author at the MIND Institute in Sacramento, California, June 23, 2008.
3    *British Medical Journal*, 1 (1970), 627.
4    B. Hermelin & N. O'Connor (1970). *Psychological experiments with autistic children*. Oxford, England: Pergamon.
5    Michael Rutter in conversation with the author.
6.   Michael Rutter & Lawrence Bartak (1971). Causes of infantile autism: Some considerations from recent research. *Journal of Autism and Childhood Schizophrenia*, 1(1), 20–32 at p. 22.
7    Ibid., 23.
8    Ibid., 24.
9    Ibid., 25.
10   M. Rutter (1972). *Maternal deprivation reassessed*. London: Penguin.
11   M. Rutter, D. Greenfeld, & L. Lockyer (1967). A five to fifteen year follow-up study of infantile psychosis. II. Social and behavioral outcome. *British Journal of Psychiatry*, 113, 1183–1199.
12   M. Rutter (1968). Concepts of autism: A review of research. *Journal of Child Psychology and Psychiatry*, 9(1), 1–25.
13   Rutter & Bartak, Causes of infantile autism, 27.
14   Ibid.
15   Ibid., 29.
16   Stella Chess (1971). Autism in children with congenital rubella. *Journal of Autism and Childhood Schizophrenia*, 1(1), 33–47.
17   Leon Eisenberg in conversation with the author.
18   Christopher Gillberg in conversation with the author.
19   Kolvin, studies in the childhood psychoses.
20   Kanner, *Childhood psychosis: Initial studies and new insights*.
21   Edward Ornitz & Edward Ritvo (1968). Perceptual inconstancy in early infantile autism. *Archives of General Psychiatry*, 18, 76–98.
22   Ed Ornitz in e-mail communication with the author, February 12, 2009.
23   Not all professionals were convinced by Kolvin's argument that autism and schizophrenia were distinct entities. The Swedish psychiatrist, Dr. Lena Nylander, who has done a great deal of research in this area, told me during the Meeting of Minds autism conference in Herning, Denmark, in

February 2009 that an additional catalyst for the division of the two conditions was the fact that, while there was general recognition in the 1980s that autism was not caused by poor parenting, schizophrenia continued to be widely blamed on the parents. See also chapter 7.

24   I. Kolvin, R. F. Garside, A. R. Nicol, A. Macmillan, F. Woltsenholme, & I. M. Leitch (1981). *Help starts here: The maladjusted child in the ordinary school.* London: Tavistock.

25   Ann Le Couteur in conversation with the author, February 17, 2009.

26   Leo Kanner (1971). Follow-up study of eleven autistic children originally reported in 1943. *Journal of Autism and Childhood Schizophrenia, 1*(2), 119–145 at p. 122.

27   Ibid., 125.

28   Ibid., 129.

29   Ibid., 141.

30   Ibid.

31   Richard Perry in conversation with the author in New York, September 27, 2007.

32   Ibid.

33   Marian DeMyer (1974). In *Psychopathology and child development: Research and treatment (Proceedings of the First International Kanner Colloquium on Child Development, Deviations and Treatment, Chapel Hill, October 30–November 2, 1973)* (pp. 93–94). New York, NY: Plenum Press.

34   Ibid.

35   Ibid., 98.

36   See Mary Coleman (Ed.) (1976). *The autistic syndromes.* Amsterdam: North-Holland Publishing.

37   Mary Coleman in conversation with the author in New York, October 2, 2007.

38   Folstein & Rutter, Infantile autism: A genetic study of 21 twin pairs.

39   Michael Rutter in conversation with the author.

40   Susan Folstein in conversation with the author in Baltimore, October 5, 2007.

41   Ibid.

42   Ibid.

43   Michael Rutter in e-mail communication with the author, February 26, 2009.

44   Susan Folstein in conversation with the author

45   Ibid.

46   Ibid.

47   Ibid.

48   Ibid.

49   See Michael Rutter (1983). Issues and prospects and developmental neuropsychiatry. In M. Rutter (Ed.), *Developmental Neuropsychiatry.* London: Guilford Publications, 589.

50 Susan Folstein in e-mail communication with the author, October 27, 2008.
51 Wing & Gould, Severe impairments of social interaction and associated abnormalities in children.
52 Lorna Wing in conversation with the author, August 15, 2007.
53 Ibid.
54 Ibid.
55 Lorna Wing in conversation with the author.
56 Judith Gould in conversation with the author at Elliot House, the National Autistic Society's diagnostic center in Bromley, Kent, October 12, 2007.
57 Lorna Wing in conversation with the author.
58 Ibid.
59 Judith Gould in conversation with the author.
60 Lorna Wing in e-mail communication with the author, April 26, 2009.
61 Ibid.
62 Theodore Shapiro in conversation with the author at Cornell University, Ithaca, NY, September 27, 2007.
63 Kanner, Infantile autism and schizophrenia.
64 Fred Volkmar in conversation with the author at the Yale Child Study Center, New Haven, CT, September 27, 2007.
65 Ed Ornitz in e-mail communication with the author, May 15, 2009.
66 Ibid.
67 E. M. Ornitz, D. Guthrie, & A. J. Farley (1978). The early symptoms of autism. In G. Serban (Ed.), *Cognitive defects in the development of mental illness* (pp. 24–42). New York, NY: Bruner/Mazel.
68 E. M. Ornitz (1988). Autism: A disorder of directed attention. *Brain Dysfunction*, *1*, 309–322.
69 Ed Ornitz in e-mail communication with the author, May 15, 2009.
70 M. K. DeMyer, S. Barton, G. D. Alpern, C. Kimberlin, J. Allen, E. Yang, R. Steele (1974). The measured intelligence of autistic children. *Journal of Autism and Childhood Schizophrenia*, *4*, 42–60.
71 Lawrence Bartak, Michael Rutter & Anthony Cox (1975). A comparative study of infantile autism and specific developmental receptive language disorder. *British Journal of Psychiatry*, *126*, 127–145.
72 See Lawrence Bartak's interview with the author in Melbourne, Australia, *Looking Up*, *3*(6) (2003), 34.
73 Uta Frith in conversation with the author at the Institute of Cognitive Neuroscience, London, August 12, 2008.
74 Ibid.
75 Francesca Happé in conversation with the author.
76 Ibid.
77 Ibid.

78  Dorothy Bishop (2008). Forty years on: Uta Frith's contribution to research on autism and dyslexia, 1966–2006. *Quarterly Journal of Experimental Psychology, 61*(1), 16–26.

79  Online interview with Simon Mitton at http://www.in-cites.com/scientists/UtaFrith.html.

80  Uta Frith in conversation with the author.

81  Online interview with Simon Mitton.

82  Uta Frith in conversation with the author

83  Ibid.

84  Ibid.

85  Nikolaas Tinbergen (1973, December 12). *Ethology and stress diseases.* Nobel Prize lecture. http://nobelprize.org/nobel_prizes/medicine/laureates/1973/tinbergen-lecture.pdf.

86  Ibid.

87  Ibid.

88  N. Tinbergen & E. A. Tinbergen (1983). *"Autistic" children: new hope for cure.* London, England: Allen & Unwin. Reviewed by Uta Frith (1984). *Psychological Medicine, 14,* 461–463.

89  Michele Zappella in conversation with the author in Oslo, Norway, August 31, 2007.

90  Ibid.

91  Claire Sainsbury, *Holding therapy: An autistic perspective.* http://www.nas.org.uk/nas/jsp/polopoly.jsp?a=2179&d=364; T. Jolliffe, R. Lansdowne, & C. Robinson (1992). Autism: a personal account. *Communication, 26*(3).

92  C. H. Delacato (1974). *The ultimate stranger: The autistic child.* New York, NY: Doubleday.

93  Gerald de Groot in conversation with the author.

94  Ibid.

95  Ibid.

96  Tomlinson, *Luckier than most,* 197.

97  Hugh Morgan in conversation with the author in London, December 8, 2008.

98  Golding, *The hitch hiker's guide to autism.*

99  Ibid.

100  *The Advocate, 7*(5) (1975), 1.

101  Ibid., 2.

# 7  Definition, Diagnosis and Assessment: The History of the Tool

1  L. Wing (1997). The history of ideas on autism: Legends, myths and reality. *Autism, 1*(1), 13–23.

2   American Psychiatric Association (1952). *Diagnostic and Statistical Manual of Mental Disorders.* Washington, DC: American Psychiatric Association.

3   L. Petty, E. Ornitz, J. Michelman & E. Zimmerman (1984). Autistic children who become schizophrenic, *Archives of General Psychiatry, 41,* 129–135.

4   J. Rumsey, J. Rapoport & N. Andreasen (1986). Thought, language, communication and affective flattening in autistic adults. *Archives of General Psychiatry, 43,* 771–777.

5   Fred R. Volkmar (1987). Annotation: Diagnostic issues in the pervasive developmental disorders. *Journal of Child Psychology and Psychiatry, 28*(3), 365–369.

6   Quoted in Kanner, *Infantile autism.*

7   Quoted in Kanner & Eisenberg, Early infantile autism 1943–1955.

8   Fred Stone in conversation with the author.

9   C. G. Polan & B. L. Spencer (1959) A checklist of symptoms of autism of early life. *West Virginia Medical Journal, 55,* 198–204.

10   M. Rutter & L. Lockyer (1965). A five to fifteen year follow-up of infantile psychosis: I. Description of sample. *British Journal of Psychiatry British Journal of Psychiatry, 113,* 1169–1182.

11   Lotter, Epidemiology of autistic conditions in young children.

12   Birte Hoeg Brask (1972). A prevalence investigation of childhood psychoses. *Barne-Psykiatrisk Forening,* 145–153.

13   Darold Treffert (1970). Epidemiology of infantile autism. *Archives of General Psychiatry, 22,* 431–438.

14   Darold Treffert in conversation with the author in Milwaukee, June 9, 2007.

15   Ibid.

16   Clancy *et al.*, The diagnosis of infantile autism.

17   M. K. DeMyer, D. W. Churchill, W. Pontius, & K. M. Gilkey (1971). A comparison of five diagnostic systems for childhood schizophrenia and childhood autism. *Journal of Autism and Childhood Schizophrenia, 1,* 175–189.

18   Ibid.

19   M. Rutter (1978). Diagnosis and definition of childhood autism. In M. Rutter & E. Schopler (Eds.), *Autism: A reappraisal of concepts and treatment.* New York: Plenum Publishing.

20   Ibid.

21   Michael Rutter in e-mail communication with the author, February 26, 2009.

22   Rutter, *Autism: A reappraisal of concepts and treatment.*

23   Michael Rutter in e-mail communication with the author.

24   Ibid.

25   Ibid.

26   Wing & Gould, Severe impairments of social interaction and associated abnormalities in children.

27   Lorna Wing (1993). The definition and prevalence of autism: A review. *European Child and Adolescent Psychiatry*, 2(2), 61–74.

28   Ibid.

29   Ibid.

30   World Health Organization (1987). *The ICD-9 classification of mental and behavioural disorders.* Geneva, Switzerland: World Health Organization.

31   B. J. Freeman, P. Schroth, E. Ritvo, D. Guthrie, & L. Wake (1980). The Behavior Observation Scale for autism (BOS): Initial results of factor analyses. *Journal of Autism and Developmental Disorders*, 10(3), 343–346.

32   D. A. Krug, J. Arick, & P. Almond (1980). Behavior checklist for identifying severely handicapped individuals with high levels of autistic behavior. *Journal of Child Psychology and Psychiatry*, 21(3), 221–229.

33   Robert Reichler in conversation with the author.

34   E. Schopler, R. J. Reichler, R. F. Devellis, & K. Daly (1980). Toward objective classification of childhood autism: Childhood Autism Rating Scale (CARS). *Journal of Autism and Developmental Disorders*, 10, 91–103.

35   Gary Mesibov in conversation with the author.

36   Robert Reichler in conversation with the author.

37   Gary Mesibov in conversation with the author.

38   Theodore Schapiro in conversation with the author.

39   P. Cialdella & N. Mamelle (1989). An epidemiological study of infantile autism in a French department (Rhône): A research note. *Journal of Child Psychology and Psychiatry*, 30(1), 165–175.

40   Wing, Asperger's syndrome: A clinical account.

41   Phil Christie (2006, October). *The distinctive clinical and educational needs of children with pathological demand avoidance syndrome: Guidelines for good practice.* Paper presented at the Second World Autism Congress, Cape Town, South Africa.

42   Lorna Wing in e-mail communication with the author, February 19, 2009.

43   T. Ishii & O. Takahashi (1983). The epidemiology of autistic children in Toyota, Japan: Prevalence. *Japanese Journal of Child and Adolescent Psychiatry*, 24, 311–321.

44   B. J. Freeman, E. R. Ritvo, A. Yokota, & A. Ritvo (1986). A scale for rating symptoms of patients with the syndrome of autism in real life settings. *Journal of the American Academy of Child and Adolescent Psychiatry*, 25(1), 130–136.

45   Ed Ritvo in conversation with the author.

46   I. C. Gillberg & C. Gillberg (1989). Asperger syndrome—some epidemiological considerations: A research note. *Journal of Child Psychology and Psychiatry*, 30(4), 631–638; and P. Szatmari, R. Bremner, & J. Nagy (1989). Asperger's syndrome: A review of clinical features. *Canadian Journal of Psychiatry/Revue Canadienne de Psychiatrie*, 34(6), 554–560.

47   Christopher Gillberg in conversation with the author.

48  Asperger, Autistic psychopathy in childhood.

49  Ami Klin, speaking to the author.

50  Quoted in the American Psychological Association's monthly publication, *APA Monitor*, *29*(11) (1998).

51  A. Le Couteur, M. Rutter, C. Lord, P. Rios, S. Robertson, P. Holdgrafer, & J. McLennan (1989). Autism diagnostic interview: A standardized investigator-based instrument. *Journal of Autism and Developmental Disorders*, *19*(3), 363–387; and C. Lord, M. Rutter, S. Goode, J. Heemsbergen, H. Jordan, L. Mawhood, & E. Schopler (1989). Autism diagnostic observation schedule: A standardized observation of communicative and social behavior. *Journal of Autism and Developmental Disorders*, *19*(2), 185–212.

52  Ann Le Couteur in conversation with the author.

53  Ibid.

54  Susan Folstein in conversation with the author.

55  Michael Rutter in conversation with the author.

56  Cathy Lord in conversation with the author.

57  Dorothy Bishop, in e-mail communication with the author, October 16, 2008.

58  Ibid.

59  Ibid.

60  Ibid.

61  Michael Rutter in conversation with the author.

62  Roger Misès in conversation with the author.

63  Denys Ribas in conversation with the author in Paris, May 10, 2008.

64  S. Baron-Cohen (1987). Autism and symbolic play. *British Journal of Developmental Psychology*, *5*(2), 139–148; and (1989). Perceptual role taking and protodeclarative pointing in autism. *British Journal of Developmental Psychology*, *7*(2), 113–127.

65  Simon Baron-Cohen in conversation with the author.

66  S. Baron-Cohen, J. Allen, & C. Gillberg (1992). Can autism be detected at 18 months? The needle, the haystack, and the CHAT. *British Journal of Psychiatry*, *161*, 839–843.

67  S. Baron-Cohen, A. Cox, G. Baird, J. Swettenham, N. Nightingale, K. Morgan, . . . T. Charman (1996). Psychological markers in the detection of autism in infancy in a large population. *British Journal of Psychiatry*, *168*, 158–163.

68  Ibid.

69  Sally Ozonoff in conversation with the author.

70  Judith Gould in conversation with the author.

71  Ibid.

72  H. N. Massie (1978). The early natural history of childhood psychosis. Ten cases studied by analysis of family home movies of the infancies of

the children. *Journal of the American Academy of Child and Adolescent Psychiatry*, *17*(1), 29–45.

73  J. Rosenthal, H. N. Massie, & K. Wulff (1980). A comparison of cognitive development in normal and psychotic children in the first two years of life from home movies. *Journal of Autism and Developmental Disorders*, *10*, 433–443.

74  P. Teitelbaum, O. Teitelbaum, J. Nye, J. Fryman, & R. G. Maurer (1998). Movement analysis in infancy may be useful for early diagnosis of autism. *Proceedings of the National Academy of Sciences*, *95*(23), 13982–13987; A. R. Damasio & R. G. Maurer (1978). A neurological model for childhood autism. *Archives of Neurology*, *35*(12), 777–786.

75  Colwyn Trevarthen, in a paper to the Awares international online autism conference, 2006. www.awares.org/conferences.

76  Ibid.

77  Ibid.

78  Colwyn Trevarthen, in a response to the author, Awares international online conference, October 4, 2006. www.awares.org/conferences.

79  E. Courchesne, R. Carper, & N. Akshoomoff (2003). Evidence of brain overgrowth in the first year of life in autism. *Journal of the American Medical Association*, *290*(3): 337–344.

80  See Eric Courchesne's interview with the author in Melbourne, *Looking Up*, *3*(6) (2003), 36.

81  Preliminary results from a prospective study by the High-Risk Baby Siblings Research Consortium as reported to the International Meeting for Autism Research in London, 2008.

82  Rebecca Landa in conversation with the author in Baltimore, October 5, 2007.

83  S. J. Rogers, G. S. Young, I. Cook, A. Giolzetti, & S. Ozonoff (2008) Deferred and immediate imitation in regressive and early onset autism. *Journal of Child Psychology and Psychiatry*, *49*(4), 449–457.

84  Sally Rogers in conversation with the author.

85  Sally Ozonoff in conversation with the author.

86  Cathy Lord in conversation with the author.

87  J. H. Miles, T. N. Takahashi, S. Bagby, P. K. Sahota, D. F. Vaslow, C. H. Wang, . . . J. E. Farmer (2005) Essential versus complex autism: Definition of fundamental prognostic subtypes. *American Journal of Medical Genetics*, *135*(2), 171–180.

88  Dorothy Bishop, A. J. O. Whitehouse, H. J. Watt, & E. A. Line (2008). Autism and diagnostic substitution: Evidence from a study of adults with a history of developmental language disorder. *Developmental Medicine and Child Neurology*, *50*(5), 341–345.

89  Ibid.

90  Mary Coleman in conversation with the author.

91 Isabelle Rapin in conversation with the author.
92 Ibid.
93 David Amaral in conversation with the author.
94 Judith Gould in conversation with the author.
95 Christopher Gillberg in conversation with the author.
96 Patricia Howlin in conversation with the author at the Institute of Psychiatry in London, December 15, 2008.
97 Fred Volkmar in conversation with the author.
98 Ibid.
99 See Tony Attwood's interview with the author in Melbourne, *Looking Up*, 3(6) (2003), 28.
100 Ibid.
101 Ibid.
102 Sally Rogers in conversation with the author.
103 S. Ozonoff, B. F. Pennington, & S. J. Rogers (1991). Executive function deficits in high-functioning autistic individuals: Relationship to theory of mind. *Journal of Child Psychology and Psychiatry*, 32(7), 1081–1105.
104 Sally Rogers in conversation with the author.
105 Francesca Happé in conversation with the author.
106 Michael Fitzgerald in conversation with the author.
107 Leon Eisenberg in conversation with the author.
108 Helen Tager-Flusberg in conversation with the author.
109 Ibid.
110 Medical Research Council: *Review of autism research: Epidemiology and causes* 2001 [online]. http://www.mrc.ac.uk/pdf-autism-report.pdf
111 Christopher Gllberg in conversation with the author.
112 Francesca Happé & Angelica Ronald (2008). The "fractionable autism triad": A review of evidence from behavioral, genetic, cognitive and neural research. *Neuropsychology Review*, 18(4), 287–304.
113 Francesca Happé in conversation with the author.
114 Happé & Ronald, The "fractionable autism triad."
115 Ibid.
116 Ibid.

## 8   The 1980s and 1990s: Theories and Concepts

1 Maria Asperger Felder in conversation with the author.
2 See Dr. Franz Wurst (1980, December). In memoriam Univ.-Prof Dr. Hans Asperger. *Heilpädagogik*, 5, 130–133.
3 Elizabeth Wurst in conversation with the author.
4 Lorna Wing in conversation with the author.
5 Judith Gould in conversation with the author.

6   Interview with Leo Kanner, June 30, 1969. Johns Hopkins University archives.
7   See Leon Eisenberg (1981). In memoriam Leo Kanner MD 1894–1981. *American Journal of Psychiatry*, *138*(8), 1122–1125, at p. 1122.
8   Kanner, *Freedom from within*.
9   Albert Kanner in conversation with the author.
10  Christopher Gillberg in conversation with the author.
11  M. Bauman & T. L. Kemper (1985). Histoanatomic observations of the brain in early infantile autism. *Neurology*, *35*(6), 866–874.
12  Margaret Bauman in conversation with the author at Boston University School of Medicine, October 3, 2007.
13  Thomas Kemper in conversation with the author at Boston University School of Medicine, October 3, 2007.
14  Margaret Bauman in conversation with the author.
15  K. Strömland, V. Nordin, M. Miller, B. Akerström, & C. Gillberg (1994). Autism in thalidomide embryopathy: A population study. *Developmental Medicine and Child Neurology*, *36*(4), 351–356.
16  A. Bailey, P. Luthert, A. Dean, B. Harding, I. Janota, M. Montgomery, . . . P. Lantos (1998). A clinicopathological study of autism. *Brain*, *121*, 889–905.
17  Eric Courchesne *et al.*, Evidence of brain overgrowth in the first year of life in autism.
18  M. F. Casanova, I. A. J. van Kooten, A. E. Switala, H. van Engeland, H. Heinsen, H. W. M. Steinbusch, P. R. Hof, . . . C. Schmitz (2006). Minicolumnar abnormalities in autism. *Acta Neuropathologica*; *112*(3), 287–303.
19  Manuel Casanova in conversation with the author in Louisville, Kentucky, September 29, 2007.
20  See, for example, the studies of Gene Blatt and Jane Yip at Boston University School of Medicine: J. Yip, J. J. Soghomonian, & G. J. Blatt (2008). Increased GAD67 mRNA expression in cerebellar interneurons in autism: Implications for Purkinje cell dysfunction. *Journal of Neuroscience Research*, *86*(3), 525–530; and (2009). Decreased GAD65 mRNA levels in select subpopulations of neurons in the cerebellar dentate nuclei in autism: An *in situ* hybridization study. *Autism Research*, *2*(1), 50–59.
21  Thomas Kemper in conversation with the author.
22  Margaret Bauman in conversation with the author.
23  Ibid.
24  Uta Frith in conversation with the author.
25  Online interview with Simon Mitton at http://www.in-cites.com/scientists/UtaFrith.html.
26  Uta Frith, Alan Leslie & Simon Baron-Cohen (1985). Does the autistic child have a "theory of mind"? *Cognition*, *21*, 37–46.

27  Uta Frith in conversation with the author.

28  D. Premack & G. Woodruff (1978). Does the chimpanzee have a theory of mind? *Behavioral and Brain Sciences*, *4*, 515–526.

29  Simon Baron-Cohen in conversation with the author.

30  A useful introduction to theory of mind can be found in S. Baron-Cohen & P. Bolton (1993). *Autism: The facts*. Oxford, England: Oxford University Press.

31  R. Saxe & N. Kanwisher (2003). People thinking about thinking people: The role of the temporo-parietal junction in "theory of mind." *Neuroimage*, *19*(4), 1835–1842; M. Sommer, K. Döhnel, B. Sodian, J. Meinhardt, C. Thoermer, & G. Hajaka (2007). Neural correlates of true and false belief reasoning. *Neuroimage*, *35*(3), 1378–1384.

32  A. Shah & U. Frith (1993). Why do autistic individuals show superior performance on the block design task? *Journal of Child Psychology and Psychiatry and Allied Disciplines*, *34*(8), 1351–1364.

33  Uta Frith in conversation with the author.

34  Simon Baron-Cohen in conversation with the author.

35  Kanner, Autistic disturbances of affective contact,' *Nervous Child*.

36  Ozonoff *et al.*, Executive function deficits in high-functioning autistic individuals.

37  Rebecca Landa in conversation with the author.

38  Michael Rutter in conversation with the author.

39  Rita Jordan (2006, November). *International conceptualisations, theories and treatments: new and valuable?* Address to the Second World Autism Congress, Cape Town, South Africa.

40  Ibid.

41  Simon Baron-Cohen in conversation with the author.

42  Ibid.

43  So well-known by her initials, in fact, that when I referred to B. J. Freeman by her full name in a conversation with Lorna Wing, Lorna suddenly exclaimed: "What? She's a woman!"

44  Marian Sigman in conversation with the author in Los Angeles, June 24, 2008.

45  Ibid.

46  Ibid.; M. Sigman & J. A. Ungerer (1984). Attachment behaviors in autistic children. *Journal of Autism and Developmental Disorders*, *14*(3), 231–244.

47  Sally Rogers in conversation with the author.

48  Ibid.

49  Sally Ozonoff in conversation with the author.

50  Marian Sigman in conversation with the author.

51  Simon Baron-Cohen in conversation with the author.

52  S. Lutchmaya, S. Baron-Cohen, & P. Raggatt (2002). Foetal testosterone and eye contact in 12-month-old infants. *Infant Behaviour and Development*,

25, 327–335; B. Auyeung, S. Baron-Cohen, E. Chapman, R. Knickmeyer, K. Taylor, & G. Hackett (2009). Foetal testosterone and autistic traits. *British Journal of Psychology, 100,* 1–22.

53 Simon Baron-Cohen in conversation with the author. The testosterone findings have been taken up by Professor John Manning, of the University of Central Lancashire in the UK, who has proposed that the greater the ratio between the length of the ring and index fingers the greater the exposure to testosterone in the womb—and therefore, according to Baron-Cohen's hypothesis, the greater the likelihood of an individual having autistic traits.

54 Carol Gray in conversation with the author in Baltimore, October 5, 2007. A Social Story is a short description of a particular situation, event, or activity which includes specific information about what to expect in that situation and why. It has various functions. It can give an individual with an autistic spectrum disorder some idea of how others might respond in a particular situation, thus providing a framework for appropriate behavior. It can also allow other people to view a situation from the perspective of the individual with autism, offering some understanding of why that person may appear to respond or behave in a particular way.

55 See Simon Baron-Cohen's interview with the author, *Looking Up,* 4(6) (2003), 28.

56 Isabelle Rapin in conversation with the author.

57 Ibid.

58 I. Rapin & D. A. Allen (1983). Developmental language disorders: nosological considerations. In U. Kirk (Ed.), *Neuropsychology of language, reading and spelling* (pp. 174–175). New York: Academic Press.

59 Christiane A. M. Baltaxe (1977). Pragmatic deficits in the language of autistic adolescents. *Journal of Pediatric Psychology,* 2(4), 176–180.

60 M. Kjelgaard & H. Tager-Flusberg (2001). An investigation of language impairment in autism: implications for genetic subgroups. *Language and Cognitive Processes,* 16(2–3), 287–308.

61 Ibid.

62 M. Rutter, L. Andersen-Wood, C. Beckett, D. Bredenkamp, J. Castle, C. Groothues, C., . . . T. G. O'Connor (1999). Quasi-autistic patterns following severe early global privation. *Journal of Child Psychology and Psychiatry,* 40(4), 537–549.

63 M. Rutter, J. Kreppner, T. G. O'Connor, and the English and Romanian Adoptees (ERA) study team (2001). Specificity and heterogeneity in children's responses to profound institutional deprivation, *British Journal of Psychiatry,* 179, 97–103.

64 Michael Rutter in conversation with the author.

65 Ibid.

66 Christopher Gillberg in conversation with the author.

67 Ibid.

68 C. Gillberg & M. Coleman (2000). *The biology of the autistic syndromes.* London, England: Mac Keith Press.

69 Michael Rutter, Anthony Bailey, Patrick Bolton, & Ann Le Couteur (1994). Autism and known medical conditions: myth and substance. *Journal of Child Psychology and Psychiatry, 35*(2), 311–322.

70 Ibid.

71 Sally Rogers in conversation with the author.

72 Dorothy Bishop (1989). Autism, Asperger's syndrome and semantic-pragmatic disorder: Where are the boundaries? *British Journal of Disorders of Communication, 24,* 107–121.

73 Robert DeLong in conversation with the author in Chapel Hill, North Carolina, September 28, 2007.

74 Y. Tanoue, S. Oda, F. Asano, & Kawashima, K. (1988). Epidemiology of infantile autism in the Southern Ibaraki, Japan. *Journal of Autism and Developmental Disorders, 18,* 155–167; M. Bohman, I. Bohman, P. Björck, & E. Sjöholm (1983). Childhood psychosis in a northern Swedish county: Some preliminary findings from an epidemiological survey. In M. Schmidt & H. Remschmidt (Eds.), *Epidemiological Approaches in Child Psychiatry II* (pp.164–173). New York: Thieme-Stratton; C. Gillberg (1984). Infantile autism and other childhood psychoses in a Swedish urban region: Epidemiological aspects. *Journal of Child Psychology and Psychiatry, 25,* 35–43; P. McCarthy, M. Fitzgerald, & M. Smith (1984). Prevalence of childhood autism in Ireland. *Irish Medical Journal, 77,* 129–130; P. Cialdella & N. Mamelle, (1989). An epidemiological study of infantile autism in a French Department (Rhône): A research note. *Journal of Child Psychology aud Psychiatry, 30,* 165–176; E. R. Ritvo, B. J. Freeman, C. Pingree, A. Mason-Brothers, L. Jorde, W. R. Jenson, . . . A. Ritvo (1989). The UCLA-University of Utah epidemiological study of autism: Prevalence. *American Journal of Psychiatry, 146,* 194–245.

75 M. King & P. Bearman (2009). Diagnostic change and the increased prevalence of autism. *International Journal of Epidemiology, 38*(5), 1224–1234.

76 Christopher Gillberg in conversation with the author.

77 E. R. Ritvo, B. J. Freeman, C. Pingree, A. Mason-Brothers, L. Jorde, W. R. Jenson, . . . A. Ritvo (1989). The UCLA–University of Utah epidemiological study of autism: Prevalence. *American Journal of Psychiatry, 146,* 194–245.

78 Ed Ritvo in e-mail communication with the author, March 19, 2009.

79 M. A. Farley, W. M. McMahon, E. Fombonne, W. R. Jenson, J. Miller, M. Gardner, . . . H. Coon (2009). Twenty-year outcome for individuals with autism and average or near-average cognitive abilities. *Autism Research, 2*(2), 109–118.

80 Ed Ritvo in e-mail communication with the author, March 24, 2009.

81 A. J. Wakefield, S. H. Murch, A. Anthony, J. Linnell, D. M. Casson, M. Malik . . . J. E. Walker-Smith, J. E. (1998). Ileal-lymphoid-nodular hyperplasia, non-specific colitis, and pervasive developmental disorder in children. *The Lancet, 351*(9103), 637–641.

82 H. Peltola, A. Patja, P. Leinikki, M. Valle, I. Davidkin, & M. Paunio (1998). No evidence for measles, mumps, and rubella vaccine-associated inflammatory bowel disease or autism in a 14-year prospective study. *The Lancet, 2*(351/9112), 1327–1328.

83 Vijendra K. Singh & Ryan L. Jensen (2002). Elevated levels of measles antibodies in children with autism. *Pediatric Neurology, 28*(4), 292–294.

84 Michael Rutter in conversation with the author.

85 Richard Horton quoted in *The Times*, February 21, 2004. http://www.timesonline.co.uk/tol/life_and_style/health/article1027642.ece.

86 *The Daily Telehgraph*, January 29, 2010. http://www.telegraph.co.uk/health/7095145/GMC-brands-Dr-Andrew-Wakefield-dishonest-irresponsible-and-callous.html.

87 *The Times*, February 14, 2009.

88 Ibid.

89 Ibid.

90 Associated Press, February 13, 2009.

91 R. Crossley & A. McDonald (1982). *Annie's coming out.* London: Penguin.

92 D. Biklen (Ed.) (2005). *Autism and the myth of the person alone.* New York, NY: New York University Press.

93 S. von Tetzchner & H. Martinsen (2000). *Introduction to Augmentative and Alternative Communication.* Oxford, England: Wiley-Blackwell.

94 Stephen von Tetzchner (1997). Historical issues in intervention research: Hidden knowledge and facilitating techniques in Denmark. *European Journal of Disorders of Communication, 32*(1), 1–18.

95 Sellin, B. (1993). *Ich will kein inmich mehr sein: Botschaften aus einem autistischen Kerker.* Cologne, Germany: Verlag Kiepenheuer & Witsch; (1995). *I don't want to be inside me anymore: Messages from an autistic mind.* New York, Basic Books.

96 Klaus Brause in conversation with the author in Dortmund, Germany, October 10, 2008.

97 Darold Treffert in e-mail communication with the author, December 1, 2008.

98 Ibid.

# 9 Autism in the Developing Nations

1 Victor Sanua (1984). Is infantile autism a universal phenomenon? An open question. *International Journal of Social Psychiatry, 30*(3), 163–177.

2   Quoted on the website of the Simons Foundation Autism Research Initiative (http://sfari.org/), September 17, 2008.
3   Quoted by Professor Gilbert Lelord in his brilliant book (1998). *L'exploration de l'autisme: Le médecin, l'enfant et sa maman.* Paris: Grasset.
4   Jia Meixiang in conversation with the author in Beijing, June 30, 2008.
5   Ibid.
6   Guo Yanqing in conversation with the author in Beijing, January 29, 2008.
7   Ibid.
8   Ibid.
9   Ibid.
10  Sun Menglin in conversation with the author in Beijing, January 24, 2008.
11  Ibid.
12  Griffin Wang in conversation with the author in Beijing, January 24, 2008.
13  Guo Yanqing in conversation with the author.
14  Ibid.
15  Tian Huiping in conversation with the author.
16  Guo Yanqing in conversation with the author.
17  Jia Meixiang in conversation with the author.
18  Liu Jing in conversation with the author in Beijing, January 25, 2008.
19  Sun Dunke in conversation with the author in Beijing, January 25, 2008.
20  Ibid.
21  See Dr. Tamara Daley's research on the Ronald paper: T. C. Daley. The first reference to autism in the Indian literature? on the Action for Autismwebsite at http://www.autism-india.org/india_research.html.
22  Merry Barua in conversation with the author in New Delhi, January 18, 2008.
23  Ibid.
24  Ibid.
25  http://ibnlive.in.com/news/at-airports-autism-too-is-a-threat/23197-3.html.
26  Merry Barua in conversation with the author.
27  Ibid.
28  Qazi Fazli Azeem in conversation with the author in New Delhi, January 17, 2008.
29  Ibid.
30  Quoted in the *Chicago Tribune*, February 21, 2001.
31  Anwar Hossain in conversation with the author in New Delhi, January 17, 2008.
32  Ibid.
33  Ibid.
34  Margot Prior article on the Academy of Social Sciences in Australia website (http://www.assa.edu.au/international/Reports/prior.htm).
35  Ibid.
36  *Vietnam News*, January 2, 2007.

37   Ibid.
38   Dr. Tokio Uchiyama in conversation with the author at Elliot House, UK.
39   Roy Grinker (2008). *Unstrange minds: Remapping the world of autism.* New York, NY: Basic Books.
40   Victor Lotter (1978). Childhood autism in Africa. *Journal of Child Psychology and Psychiatry, 193,* 231–244.
41   Zemi Yenus in e-mail communication with the author, September 24, 2009, and http://allafrica.com/stories/200603290229.html.
42   Ibid.
43   Quoted in the US National Society for Autistic Children's newsletter, *The Advocate, 8*(2), (1976).
44   Edna Mishori, in e-mail communication with the author, December 20, 2009.
45   Ibid.
46   Ibid.
47   Ibid.
48   See *Looking Up, 2*(8) (2001), 22.
49   Talat al-Wazna in conversation with the author in London, August 21, 2007.
50   Ibid.
51   Ibid.
52   Ibid.
53   IRIN online news report, June 24, 2004. http://www.irinnews.org/report.aspx?reportid=23757.
54   J. Milicic, Z. Bujas Petkovic, J. Bozikov (2003). Dermatoglyphs of digito-palmar complex in autistic disorder: Family analysis. *Croatian Medical Journal, 44*(4), 469–476.
55   Liuba Iacoblev in e-mail communication with the author, April 11, 2008.
56   Ibid.
57   Sergey Morozov & Svetlana Morozova, interviewed by the author at Dobro's headquarters in Moscow, *Looking Up, 3*(9) (2004), 20.
58   Ibid.
59   Ibid., 21.
60   Ibid., 22.
61   Ibid., 22.
62   Ibid., 23.
63   Ibid.
64   Rozagy in conversation with the author in London, October 6, 2008.
65   Olga Bogdashina quoted on the Ukrainian Autism Society's website (http://freewebs.com/autismukraine) in 1995.
66   Olga Bogdashina in e-mail communication with the author, March 7, 2009.
67   Ami Klin, speaking to the author.
68   As reported by the Autism Support Network. See http://www.autismsupportnetwork.com/news/violated-having-autism-776782.

69   Ibid.
70   Judith Martínez de Vaillard in conversation with the author in Mexico City, June 20, 2008.
71   Edna García de Martínez in communication with the author, September 28, 2008.
72   Ibid.
73   Ibid.
74   Ibid.
75   Ibid.
76   Ibid.
77   Quoted at PaginaDigital website, March 30, 2006: http://www.paginadigital.org/articulos/2006/2006prim/Tecnologia5/autistas-300306.asp.
78   See http://parlamentario.com/noticia-9298.html.
79   Theo Peeters in conversation with the author.
80   Lilia Negrón in e-mail communication with the author, July 25, 2007.
81   Ibid.
82   See *People's Weekly World Newspaper*, July 3, 2004.
83   See *Looking Up*, 4(5) (2006), 21.
84   Hugh Morgan in conversation with the author in London, December 8, 2008.
85   Ibid.
86   The British charity, founded by Dame Stephanie Shirley in 2004 to act as a catalyst in increasing the funds available for biomedical autism research in the UK, changed its name to Autistica in January 2010.
87   Arlene Cassidy in conversation with the author in London, December 8, 2008.
88   Ibid.
89   Ibid.
90   Ibid.

## 10   Where the Future Lies

1   Sally Ozonoff in conversation with the author. The book she was writing (together with Sally Rogers and Robert Hendren) was *Autism spectrum disorders: A research review for practitioners* (American Psychiatric Publishing, 2003).
2   Leon Eisenberg in conversation with the author.
3   Maria Asperger Felder in conversation with the author.
4   Mary Coleman in conversation with the author.
5   Jeremy Turk, Martin Bax, Clare Williams, Pooja Amin, Mats Eriksson, & Christopher Gillberg (2009). Autism spectrum disorder in children with and without epilepsy: Impact on social functioning and communication. *Acta Paediatrica*, 98, 675–681.

333

6 Ed Ritvo in conversation with the author.
7 Peter Hobson speaking at the Open University conference, Autism Research: From Diagnosis to Intervention, Milton Keynes, UK, May 11–12, 2007.
8 Sula Wolff in conversation with the author.
9 Rupert Isaacson (2009). *The horse boy: A father's miraculous journey to heal his son.* London: Viking.
10 See *Looking Up*, *3*(6) (2003), 7.
11 Daniel A. Rossignol, Lanier W. Rossignol, Scott Smith, Cindy Schneider, Sally Logerquist, Anju Usman, Jim Neubrander, ... Elizabeth A. Mumper (2009). Hyperbaric treatment for children with autism: A multicenter, randomised, double-blind, controlled trial,' *BMC Pediatrics*, *9*(21). doi:10.1186/1471–2431–9-21.
12 Eric Hollander in comments to the annual meeting of the American College of Neuropsychopharmacology in December 2006. Hollander published his findings in 2007: E. Hollander, J. Bartz, W. Chaplin, A. Phillips, J. Sumner, L. Soorya, L., ... Wasserman, S. (2007). Oxytocin increases retention of social cognition in autism. *Biological Psychiatry*, *61*(4), 498–503.
13 Sula Wolff in conversation with the author.
14 Manuel Ventura in conversation with the author, at Mas Casadevall, Spain, 2001.
15 David Amaral in conversation with the author.
16 Sally Ozonoff in conversation with the author.
17 See *The Times*, London, June 18, 2006.
18 Ibid.
19 Temple Grandin in conversation with the author.
20 Rita Jordan interviewed by the author, *Looking Up*, *4*(1) (2006), 22.
21 Sally Ozonoff in conversation with the author.
22 Susan Folstein in conversation with the author.
23 Mary Coleman in conversation with the author.
24 Simon Baron-Cohen in conversation with the author.
25 Gilbert Lelord in conversation with the author.
26 Marian Sigman in conversation with the author.
27 Susan Folstein in e-mail communication with the author.
28 M. Daly, L. A. Weiss, S. Yiping, J. M. Korn, D. E. Arking, D. T. Miller, ... B.-L. Wu (2008). Association between microdeletion and micro-duplication at 16p11.2 and autism. *New England Journal of Medicine*, *358*, 667–675.
29 M. Alarcón, B. S. Abrahams, J. L. Stone, J. A. Duvall, J. V. Perederiy, J. M. Bomar, ... D. H. Geschwind (2008). Linkage, association, and gene-expression analyses identify CNTNAP2 as an autism-susceptibility gene. *American Journal of Human Genetics*, *82*(1), 150–159.

30   J. Sebat, B. Lakshmi, D. Malhotra, J. Troge, C. Lese-Martin, T. Walsh, . . . M. Wigler (2007). Strong association of *de novo* copy number mutations with autism. *Science, 316*(5823), 445–449.

31   http://www.seattlepi.com/local/307699_geneautism16.html.

32   A. Bird, J. Guy, J. Gan, J. Selfridge, & S. Cobb (2007). Reversal of neurological defects in a mouse model of Rett syndrome. *Science, 315*(5815), 1143–1147.

33   Christopher Gillberg in conversation with the author.

34   S. Jamain, H. Quach, C. Betancur, M. Råstam, C. Colineaux, I. C. Gillberg . . . Paris Autism Research International (2003). Mutations of the X-linked genes encoding neuroligins NLGN3 and NLGN4 are associated with autism. *Nature Genetics, 34*(1), 27–29.

35   Christopher Gillberg in conversation with the author.

36   Ibid.

37   Susan Folstein in conversation with the author.

38   Wakefield *et al.*, Ileal-lymphoid-nodular hyperplasia, non-specific colitis, and pervasive developmental disorder in children. See chapter 8.

39   D. B. Campbell, T. M. Buie, H. Winter, M. Bauman, J. S. Sutcliffe, J. M. Perrin, & P. Levitt (2009). Distinct genetic risk based on association of MET in families with co-occurring autism and gastrointestinal conditions. *Pediatrics, 123*(3), 1018–1024.

40   A. Reichenberg, R. Gross, M. Weiser, M. Bresnahan, J. Silverman, S/. Harlap, . . . E. Susser (2006). Advancing paternal age and autism. *Archives of General Psychiatry, 63*(9), 1026–1032.

41   Susan Folstein in conversation with the author.

42   W. R. Kates, C. P. Burnette, S. Eliez, L. A. Strunge, D. Kaplan, R. Landa, . . . G. D. Pearlson (2004). Neuroanatomic variation in monozygotic twin pairs discordant for the narrow phenotype for autism. *American Journal of Psychiatry, 161*, 539–546.

43   Susan Folstein in e-mail communication with the author, February 21, 2009.

44   Gilbert Lelord in conversation with the author.

45   Monica Zilbovicius in conversation with the author in Oslo, Norway, August 31, 2007.

46   P. H. Chiu, M. A. Kayali, K. T. Kishida, D. Tomlin, L. G. Klinger, M. R. Klinger, & P. R. Montague (2008). Self responses along cingulate cortex reveal quantitative neural phenotype for high-functioning autism. *Neuron, 57*(3), 463–473.

47   R. K. Kana, T. A. Keller, N. J. Minshew, & M. A. Just (2007). Inhibitory control in high-functioning autism: Decreased activation and underconnectivity in inhibition networks. *Biological Psychiatry, 62*(3), 198–206.

48 T. W. Wilson, D. C. Rojas, M. L. Reite, P. D. Teale, & S. J. Rogers (2007). Children and adolescents with autism exhibit reduced MEG steady-state gamma responses. *Biological Psychiatry*, *62*(3), 192–197.

49 Sundaram, S. K., Kumar, A., Makki, M. I., Behen, M. E., Chugani, H. T., & Chugani, D. C. (2008). Diffusion tensor imaging of frontal lobe in autism spectrum disorder. *Cerebral Cortex*, *18*(11), 2659–2665.

50 Comments at a workshop in London organized by Uta Frith, [April 16, 2007].

51 See, for example, Mercedes Belinchón (2001). Lenguaje y autismo: Hacia una explicación Ontogenética. In J. Martos & A. Rivière (Eds.), *Autismo: Comprensión y explicación actual* (pp. 155–204). Madrid: APNA.

52 Rebecca Landa in conversation with the author.

53 Darold Treffert in e-mail communication with the author, February 16, 2009.

54 P. Howlin, S. Goode, J. Hutton, & M. Rutter (2009). Savant skills in autism: Psychometric approaches and parental reports. *Philosophical Transactions of the Royal Society B: Biological Sciences*, *364*(1522), 1359–1367.

55 Patricia Howlin in conversation with the author.

56 Darold Treffert in e-mail conversation with the author, February 16, 2009.

57 Ibid.

58 Ibid.

59 Richard Cowan & Chris Frith (2009). Do calendrical savants use calculation to answer date questions? A functional magnetic resonance imaging study. *Philosophical Transactions of the Royal Society B: Biological Sciences*. doi:10.1098/rstb.2008.0323 65.

60 Ploeger, A., van der Maas, H. L., Raijmakers, M. E., & Galis, F. (2009). Why did the savant syndrome not spread in the population? A psychiatric example of a developmental constraint, *Psychiatry Research*, *166*(1), 85–90.

61 Ed Ornitz in conversation with the author.

62 Raun Kaufman in conversation with the author in London.

63 Ibid.

64 Lorna Wing in conversation with the author.

65 E. Werner & G. Dawson (2005). Validation of the phenomenon of autistic regression using home videotapes. *Archives of General Psychiatry*, *62*(8), 889–895.

66 See *Looking Up*, *2*(10) (2001), 31.

67 Sally Ozonoff in conversation with the author.

68 Ibid.

69 Rebecca Landa in conversation with the author.

70 Sally Rogers in conversation with the author

71 Ruth Sullivan in conversation with the author.

72 Ibid.

73  Rita Jordan interview, *Looking Up*, 4(1) (2006), 22.
74  Ibid.
75  Peter Tanguay in conversation with the author.
76  Ibid.
77  Ellefsen, A., Kampmann, H., Billstedt, E., Gillberg, C., & Gillberg, C. (2007). Autism in the Faroe Islands: An epidemiological study. *Journal of Autism and Developmental Disorders*, 37(3), 437–444.
78  G. Oliveira, A. Ataíde, C. Marques, T. S. Miguel, A. M. Coutinho, B. L. Mota-Vieira, . . . A. Moura Vicente (2007). Epidemiology of autism spectrum disorder in Portugal: Prevalence, clinical characterisation, and medical conditions. *Developmental Medicine and Child Neurology*, 49(10), 726–733.
79  E. Fombonne, J. Morel, & J. Macarthur (2006, June). *No autism amongst Inuits from northern Quebec?* Paper presented at IMFAR (International Meeting for Autism Research) in Montreal, Canada.
80  Donna Williams in e-mail communication with the author, April 4, 2008.
81  Jean-Claude Maleval in e-mail communication with the author, March 25, 2008.
82  Donna Williams in e-mail communication with the author, April 4, 2008.
83  Donna Williams in e-mail communication with the author, October 7, 2007.
84  Temple Grandin in conversation with the author.
85  Ros Blackburn interviewed by the author, *Looking Up*, 2(1) (2000), 18.
86  Ibid.
87  Ibid., 19.
88  Ibid., 20.
89  Ian Hacking speaking at the Talent and Autism conference at the Royal Society, London, September 29–30, 2008.
90  Douwe Draaisma speaking at the Talent and Autism conference at the Royal Society, London, September 29–30, 2008.
91  Irlen colored lenses are designed to correct sensory perceptual distortions and overload which can affect individuals with autistic spectrum disorders, among others.
92  Temple Grandin in conversation with the author.
93  Sally Ozonoff in conversation with the author.
94  Happé, F., Ronald, A., & Plomin, R. (2006). Time to give up on a single explanation for autism. *Nature Neuroscience*, 9, 1218–1220.
95  E. Ashwin, C. Ashwin, D. Rhydderch, J. Howells, S. Baron-Cohen (2008). Eagle-eyed visual acuity: an experimental investigation of enhanced perception in autism. *Biological Psychiatry*, 65(1), 17–21.
96  Associated Press, February 11, 2010.
97  Lorna Wing in conversation with the author in Manchester, March 16, 2010.
98  Michael Savage speaking on Talk Radio Network's syndicated show, *The savage nation*, on July 16, 2008.

99 Alejandro Jodorowsky interviewed by Fernando Sánchez Dragó on *Diario de la Noche*, Telemadrid, June 2, 2005.
100 *Stigma*, London, April 29, 2008.
101 Peter H. Burbach & Bert van der Zwang (2009). Contact in the genetics of autism and schizophrenia. *Trends in Neuroscience, 32*, 69–72.
102 B. Crespi & C. Badcock (2008). Psychosis and autism as diametrical disorders of the social brain. *Behavioral and Brain Sciences, 31*(3), 241–261.
103 Margaret Bauman in conversation with the author.
104 Howard Buten (2003). *Il y a quelqu'un là-dedans: Des autismes*. Paris: Odile Jacob.
105 My thanks to Peter Tanguay for sharing this information with me.
106 Stuart Murray (2008). *Representing autism: Culture, narrative, fascination*. Liverpool, England: Liverpool University Press.
107 Mark Haddon (2004). *The curious incident of the dog in the night-time*. London, England: Vintage.
108 Donna Williams in e-mail communication with the author, September 15, 2008.
109 Tian Huiping in conversation with the author.
110 Robert Hendren in conversation with the author at the MIND Institute in Sacramento, California, June 23, 2007.
111 Ibid.
112 Lorna Wing in conversation with the author.
113 Theo Peeters in e-mail communication with the author, October 3, 2008.
114 Theo Peeters interviewed by the author in Melbourne, Australia. *Looking Up, 3*(6) (2003), 31.
115 Gary Mesibov in e-mail communication with the author, October 13, 2008.
116 Ibid.
117 Quoted in Autism Speaks Annual Review, 2008. http://www.autistica.org.uk/document_downloads/Reports/Annual%20Review%202008.pdf.
118 Ibid.
119 Ibid.
120 *The Times*, January 1, 2007.
121 Michael Rutter (1999). Autism: Two-way interplay between research and clinical work. *Journal of Child Psychology and Child Psychiatry, 40*, 169–188.
122 Michael Rutter in conversation with the author.

# Bibliography

## Books

Although this is the first book to feature interviews with the pioneers in the field dating back to the original colleagues and relatives of Leo Kanner and Hans Asperger, the literature on autism is enormous. Below is a select list of just some of the books which I have consulted while writing this volume.

Alexander, F. G., & Selesnick, S. T. (1968). *The history of psychiatry*. New York, NY: Mentor.

Alvarez, A. (1992). *Live company: psychoanalytic psychotherapy with autistic, borderline, deprived and abused children* (first ed.). London, England: Routledge.

Alvarez, A., & Reid, S. (1999). *Autism and personality: Findings from the Tavistock Autism Workshop* (first ed.). London, England: Routledge.

Asperger Felder, M. (2008). Hans Asperger, 1906–1980: Leben und Werk. In Rolf Castell (Ed.), *Hundert Jahre Kinder- und Jugendpsychiatrie* (pp. 99–117). Göttingen, Germany: V., & R. Unipress.

Asperger, H. (1968). *Heilpädagogik* (fifth ed.). Vienna, Austria: Springer-Verlag.

Attwood, M. (2004). *Oryx and Crake*. London, England: Virago Press.

Attwood, T. (1998). *Asperger's syndrome: A guide for parents and professionals*. London, England: Jessica Kingsley Publishers.

Axline, V. M. (1971). *Dibs: In search of self: Personality development in play therapy*. London, England: Penguin Books.

Badcock, Christopher (2009). *The imprinted brain: How genes set the balance between autism and psychosis*. London, England: Jessica Kingsley Publishers.

Barack, J. A., Charman, T., Yirmiya, N., & Zelazo, P. R. (Eds.) (2001). *The development of autism: Perspectives from theory and research*. Mahwah, NJ: Lawrence Erlbaum Associates.

Baron-Cohen, S. (2003). *The essential difference: The truth about the male and female brain.* New York, NY: Perseus Books.

Baron-Cohen, S. (2008). *Autism and Asperger syndrome: The facts.* Oxford, England: Oxford University Press.

Baron-Cohen, S., & Bolton, P. (1993). *Autism: The facts.* Oxford, England: Oxford University Press.

Baron-Cohen, S., Cosmides, L., & Tooby, J. (1997). *Mindblindness: An essay on autism and the theory of mind.* Boston, MA: MIT Press.

Barron, J., & Barron, S. (2002). *There's a boy in here: Emerging from the bonds of autism.* Arlington, TX: Future Horizons.

Bauman, M. L., & Kemper, T. L. (Eds.) (1997). *The neurobiology of autism.* Baltimore, MD: Johns Hopkins University Press.

Berger, D. S. (2002). *Music therapy, sensory integration and the autistic child.* London, England: Jessica Kingsley Publishers.

Berquez, G. (1983). *L'autisme infantile: Introduction à une clinique relationelle selon Kanner.* Paris: Presses Universitaires de France.

Bettelheim, B. (1967). *The empty fortress.* New York, NY: The Free Press.

Bettelheim, B., & Karlin, K. (1975). *Un autre regard sur la folie.* Paris: Editions Stock.

Biklen, D. (Ed.) (2005). *Autism and the myth of the person alone.* New York, NY: New York University Press.

Blackman, L. (1999). *Lucy's story: Autism and other adventures.* Brisbane, Australia: Book in Hand.

Blastland, M. (2006). *The only boy in the world: A father explores the mysteries of autism.* New York, NY: Marlowe & Company.

Bogdashina, O. (2003). *Communication issues in autism and Asperger syndrome.* London, England: Jessica Kingsley Publishers.

Bogdashina, O. (2003). *Sensory perceptual issues in autism and Asperger syndrome: Different sensory experiences – different perceptual worlds.* London, England: Jessica Kingsley Publishers.

Bogdashina, O. (2005). *Theory of mind and the triad of perspectives on autism and Asperger syndrome: A view from the bridge.* London, England: Jessica Kingsley Publishers.

Bosch, G. (1962). *Der frühkindliche Autismus* (Monographien aus dem Gesamtdebiete der Neurologie und Psychiatrie, Heft 96). Berlin: Springer-Verlag.

Bosch, G. (1970). *Infantile autism: A clinical and phenomenological-anthropological investigation taking language as the guide.* New York, NY: Springer-Verlag.

Boucher, J., & Bowler, D. (2008). *Memory in autism: Theory and evidence.* Cambridge, England: Cambridge University Press.

Brauner, A., & Brauner, F. (1993). *L'enfant déréel.* Paris: Privat.

Buten, H. (2003). *Il y a quelqu'un là-dedans: Des autismes.* Paris: Odile Jacob.

Buten, H. (2005). *Through the glass wall: A therapist's lifelong journey to reach the children of autism.* London, England: Bantam.

340

Cantor, S. (1988). *Childhood schizophrenia*. New York, NY: Guilford Press.

Carruthers, P., & Smith, P. K. (1996). *Theories of theories of mind*. Cambridge, England: Cambridge University Press.

Charman, T., & Clare, P. (2004). *Mapping autism research: Identifying UK priorities for the future*. London, England: National Autistic Society.

Cheng, E. (2007). *Autism and self improvement: My journey to accept planet earth*. Singapore: Eric Chen Yixiong.

Chess, S. (1969). *An introduction to child psychiatry*. New York, NY: Grune & Stratton.

Chilvers, R. (2007). *The hidden world of autism: Writing and art by children with high-functioning autism*. London, England: Jessica Kingsley Publishers.

Claiborne Park, C. (1967). *The siege*. New York, NY: Harcourt, Brace and World, Inc.

Cohen, D. J. (2006). *Life is with others: Selected writings on child psychiatry*. New Haven, CT: Yale University Press.

Cohen, D. J., & Volkmar, F. R. (Eds.) (1997). *Handbook of autism and pervasive developmental disorders* (second ed.). New York, NY: John Wiley & Sons.

Cohen, S. (1998). *Targeting autism*. Berkeley: University of California Press.

Coleman, M. (Ed.) (1976). *The autistic syndromes*. Amsterdam: North-Holland Publishing.

Coleman, M. (Ed.) (2005). *The neurology of autism*. New York, NY: Oxford University Press.

Collins, P. (2004). *Not even wrong: Adventures in autism*. London, England: Bloomsbury.

Copeland, J. (1973). *For the love of Ann: The true story of an autistic child*. London, England: Arrow Books.

Crossley, R., & McDonald, A. (1982). *Annie's coming out*. London, England: Penguin.

Cruthers, B. (1912/2007). *Psychology and psychiatry in pediatrics*. Whitefish, MT: Kessinger Publishing.

Cutler, E. (2005). *A thorn in my pocket: Temple Grandin's mother tells the family story*. Arlington, TX: Future Horizons.

Dawson, J. (2004). *Wild boy*. London, England: Sceptre.

De Clercq, H. (2003). *Mum, is that a human being or an animal?* London, England: Paul Chapman Educational Publishing.

De Clercq, H. (2006). *Autism from within: A unique handbook*. Kungsängen, Sweden: Intermedia Books.

Debray-Ritzen, P. (1998). *La psychanalyse, cette imposture*. Paris: Livre de Poche.

Delacato, C. H. (1974). *The ultimate stranger: The autistic child*. New York, NY: Doubleday.

Delion, P. (2003). *Le packing avec les enfants autistes et psychotiques*. Paris: Erès.

Despert, J. L. (1965). *The emotionally disturbed child: Then and now*. New York, NY: Robert Brunner.

# Bibliography

Dick, P. K. (1964). *Martian time-slip*. New York, NY: Ballantine Books.

Dietz, C. (2007). *The early screening of autistic spectrum disorders*. Enschede, The Netherlands: Gildeprint.

Donnellan, A. M. (Ed.) (1985). *Classic readings in autism*. New York, NY. Teachers College Press.

Durig, A. *Autism and the crisis of meaning*. New York, NY: State University of New York Press.

Ferrari, P. (2004). *L'autisme infantile*. Paris: Livre de Poche.

Fitzgerald, M. (2003). *Autism and creativity: Is there a link between autism in men and exceptional ability?* London, England: Routledge.

Fitzgerald, M. (2005). *Genesis of artistic creativity: Asperger's syndrome and the arts*. London, England: Jessica Kingsley Publishers.

Fitzpatrick, M. (2004). *MMR and autism: What parents need to know*. London, England: Routledge.

Fitzpatrick, M. (2008). *Defeating autism: A damaging delusion*. London, England: Routledge.

Frankland, M. (1995). *Freddie the weaver: The boy who fought to join the world*. London, England: Sinclair-Stevenson.

Frith, U. (Ed.) (1991). *Autism and Asperger syndrome*. Cambridge, England: Cambridge University Press.

Frith, U. (2003). *Autism: Explaining the enigma* (second ed.). Oxford, England: Wiley-Blackwell.

Frith, U. (2008). *Autism: A very short introduction*. Oxford, England: Oxford University Press.

Frith. U., & Hill, E. (Eds.) (2004). *Autism: Mind and brain*. Oxford, England: Oxford University Press.

Frith, U., & Houston, R. (2000). *Autism in history: The case of Hugh Blair of Borgue*, Oxford, England: Wiley-Blackwell.

Gardner, N. (2008). *A friend like Henry*. London, England: Hodder & Stoughton.

Gazzaniga, M. S. (Ed.) (2002). *Cognitive neuroscience: The biology of the mind* (second revised ed.). New York, NY: W. W. Norton & Co Ltd.

Gerlach, E. K. (2004). *Just this side of normal: Glimpses into life with autism*. Arlington, TX: Future Horizons.

Gerland, G. (1997). *A real person*. London, England: Souvenir Press.

Ghaziuddin, M. (2005). *Mental health aspects of autism and Asperger syndrome*. London, England: Jessica Kingsley Publishers.

Gillberg, C., & Coleman, M. (2000). *The biology of the autistic syndromes*. London, England: Mac Keith Press.

Gillberg, C., & Coleman, M. (2002). *The biology of autistic syndromes* (second ed.). Cambridge, England: Cambridge University Press.

Grandin, T. (1996). *Thinking in pictures and other reports from my life with autism*. New York, NY: Vintage Books.

# Bibliography

Grandin, T. (2006). *Animals in translation*. London, England: Bloomsbury Publishing.

Grandin, T. (2008). *The way I see it: A personal look at autism and Asperger's*. Arlington, TX: Future Horizons.

Gray, C. (2001). *My Social Stories book*. London, England: Jessica Kingsley Publishers.

Greenspan, S. I., & Wieder, S. (2008). *Engaging autism: Using the Floortime approach to help children relate, communicate and think*. New York, NY: Perseus Books.

Grinker, R. (2008). *Unstrange minds: Remapping the world of autism*. New York, NY: Basic Books.

Gutstein, S. E. (2000). *Autism: Aspergers: Solving the relationship puzzle: A new developmental program that opens the door to lifelong social and emotional growth*. Arlington, TX: Future Horizons.

Haddon, M. (2004). *The curious incident of the dog in the night-time*. London, England: Vintage.

Hanau, C., & Mariani Cerati, D. (2003). *Il nostro autismo quotidano: Storie di genitori e figli*, Gardolo, Italy: Edizioni Erickson.

Happé, F. (1994). *Autism: An introduction to psychological theory*. London, England: UCL Press.

Hermelin, B. (2001). *Bright splinters of the mind: A personal story of research with autistic savants*. London, England: Jessica Kingsley Publishers.

Hermelin, B., & O'Connor, N. (1970). *Psychological experiments with autistic children*. Oxford, England: Pergamon.

Hesmondhalgh, M. (2006). *Autism, access and inclusion on the front line: Confessions of an autism anorak*. London, England: Jessica Kingsley Publishers.

Hinshelwood, R. D. (2006). *Introducing Melanie Klein*. London, England: Icon Books.

Hobson, P. (2002). *The cradle of thought: Challenging the origins of thinking*. London, England: Macmillan.

Hochmann, J. (1997). *Pour soigner l'enfant autiste*. Paris: Odile Jacob.

Hochmann, J. (2004). *Histoire de la psychiatrie*. Paris: Presses Universitaires de France.

Hochmann, J. (2009). *Histoire de l'autisme: De l'enfant sauvage aux troubles envahissants du développement*. Paris: Odile Jacob.

Howlin, P. (1997). *Autism: Preparing for adulthood*. Hove, England: Routledge.

Howlin, P. (1998). *Children with autism and Asperger syndrome*. Oxford, England: Wiley-Blackwell.

Howlin, P., & Rutter, M. (1987). *Treatment of autistic children*. Chichester, England: John Wiley & Sons.

Isaacson, R. (2009). *The horse boy: A father's miraculous journey to heal his son*. London, England: Viking.

# Bibliography

Iversen, P. (2006). *Strange sons: Two mothers, two sons and the quest to unlock the hidden world of autism.* New York, NY: Riverhead Books.

Jackson, L. J. (2002). *Freaks, geeks and Asperger syndrome: A user guide to adolescence.* London, England: Jessica Kingsley Publishing.

Janz, M. (1995). *Elfriede Jelinek.* Stuttgart, Germany: J. B. Metzler

Jones, G. (2002). *Educational provision for children with autism and Asperger syndrome.* London, England: David Fulton.

Jordan, R. (2001). *Autism with severe learning difficulty.* London, Souvenir Press.

Jordan, R., & Powell, S. (1995). *Understanding and teaching children with autism.* Chichester, England: John Wiley & Sons Ltd.

Jørgensen, O. S. (2002). *Asperger: Syndrom zwischen Autismus und Normalität: Diagnostik und Heilungschancen.* Weinheim, Germany: Beltz Verlag.

Junker, K. S. (1961). *De ensamma.* Stockholm, Sweden: Natur och Kultur.

Junker, K. S. (1964). *The child in the glass ball: A courageous mother's story of hope for retarded children.* Nashville, TN: Abingdon Press.

Kanner, L. (1935). *Child psychiatry.* Springfield, IL: C. C. Thomas Publishing.

Kanner, L. (1941). *In defense of mothers.* Springfield, IL: C. C. Thomas Publishing.

Kanner, L. (1973). *Childhood psychosis: Initial studies and new insights.* Washington, DC: Winston.

Kaufman, B. N. (1994). *Son-rise; The miracle continues.* Tiburon, CA: H. J. Kramer.

Kennedy, A. (2008). *Not stupid: The story of one mother's fight to rescue the lives of her children from autism.* London, England: John Blake Publishing Ltd.

Kessick, R. (2009). *Autism and diet: What you need to know.* London, England: Jessica Kingsley Publishers.

Knodt-Lenfant, I. (2004). *Claudin, classé X chez les dinormos.* Brue Auriac, France: Envol Publications.

Koegel, R. L., & Koegel, L. K. (1996). *Teaching children with autism: Strategies for initiating positive interactions and improving learning opportunities.* Baltimore, MD: Brookes Publishing.

Kolvin, I., Garside, R. F., Nicol, A. R., Macmillan, A., Woltsenholme, F., & Leitch, I. M. (1981). *Help starts here: The maladjusted child in the ordinary school.* London, England: Tavistock.

Lawson, W. (1998). *Life behind glass: A personal account of autism spectrum disorder.* Lismore, Australia: Southern Cross University Press.

Lawson, W. (2001). *Understanding and working with the spectrum of autism.* London, England: Jessica Kingsley Publishers.

Lawson, W. (2008). *Concepts of normality: The autistic and typical spectrum.* London, England: Jessica Kingsley Publishers.

Lefort, R., & Lefort, R. (2003). *La distinction de l'autisme.* Paris: Editions du Seuil.

Leimbach, M. (2006). *Daniel isn't talking.* London, England: Fourth Estate.

Lelord, G. (1998). *L'exploration de l'autisme: Le médecin, l'enfant et sa maman.* Paris: Grasset.

# Bibliography

Lovaas, O. I. (1977). *The autistic child: Language development through behaviur modification.* New York, NY: Irvington Publishers.

Lovaas, O. I. (1981). *Teaching developmentally disabled children: The ME book.* Nerang, Australia: Pro-Ed Books.

Lutz, J. (1961). *Kinder Pyschiatrie* (second ed.). Zurich, Switzerland: Rotapfel Verlag.

Lyons, V., & Fitzgerald, M. (2005). *Asperger syndrome: A gift or a curse?* New York, NY: Nova Science Publishers.

Maleval, J.-C. (2009). *L'autiste et sa voix.* Paris: Seuil.

Maleval, J.-C. (2009). *L'autiste, son double et ses objets.* Rennes: Presses Universitaires de Rennes.

Martos, J. and Rivière, A. (2001). *Autismo: Comprensión y explicación actual.* Madrid, Spain: Ministerio de Trabajo y Asuntos Sociales and APNA.

Maurice, C. (1993). *Let me hear your voice: A family's triumph over autism.* New York, NY: Fawcett Columbia.

May, J. (1958). *A physician looks at psychiatry.* New York, NY: The John Day Company.

McCarthy, J. (2008). *Mother warriors: A nation of parents healing autism against all odds.* New York, NY: Dutton Books.

McGovern, C. (2006). *Eye contact.* London, England: Viking.

McGregor, E., Núñez, M., Cebula, K., & Gómez, J. C. (2008). *Autism: An integrated view from neurocognitive, clinical and intervention research.* Oxford, England: Blackwell Publishing.

Meltzer, D. (1975). *Explorations in autism: A psychoanalytic study.* Strathtay, Scotland: Clunie Press.

Mesibov, G. B., Shea, V., & Schopler, E. (2004). *The TEACCH approach to autism spectrum disorders.* New York, NY: Plenum Publishing.

Mistura, S. (2006). *Autismo: L'Umanità nascosta.* Turin, Italy: Einaudi.

Mitchell, P. (2000). *Introduction to theory of mind: Children, autism and apes.* London, England: Hodder Arnold.

Moon, E. (2002). *Speed of dark.* London, England: Orbit.

Moore, C. (2005). *George and Sam.* London, England: Penguin Books.

Mor, C. (2007). *A blessing and a curse: Autism and me.* London, England: Jessica Kingsley Publishers.

Morgan, H. (1996). *Adults with autism: A guide to theory and practice.* Cambridge, England: Cambridge University Press.

Mukhopadhyay, T. R. (2000). *Beyond the silence: My life, the world and autism.* London, England: National Autistic Society.

Murray, D. (Ed.) (2005). *Coming out Asperger: Diagnosis, disclosure and self-confidence.* London, England: Jessica Kingsley Publishers.

Murray, S. (2008). *Representing autism: Culture, narrative, fascination.* Liverpool, England: Liverpool University Press.

Nadesan, M. H. (2005). *Constructing autism: Unravelling the "truth" and understanding the social.* London, England: Routledge.

Napear, P. (1974). *Brain child: A mother's child.* New York, NY: Harper & Row.

Nazeer, K. (2006). *Send in the idiots.* London, England: Bloomsbury.

Osteen, M. (2007). *Autism and representation.* London, England: Routledge.

Ozonoff, S., Rogers, S., & Hendren, R. (2003). *Autism spectrum disorders: A research review for practitioners.* Arlington, TX: American Psychiatric Publishing.

Park, C. C. (1967). *The siege.* New York, NY: Harcourt, Brace and World, Inc.

Park, C. C. (2001). *Exiting Nirvana: A daughter's life with autism.* London, England: Aurum Press Ltd.

Peeters, T. (1997). *Autism: From theoretical understanding to educational intervention.* London, England: Whurr Publishers.

Peeters, T., & Gillberg, C. (1999). *Autism: Medical and educational aspects.* Oxford, England: Wiley-Blackwell.

Perron, R., & Ribas, D. (1997). *Autismes de l'enfance.* Paris: Presses Universitaires de France.

Piaget, J. (1962). *Dreams, play and imitation in childhood.* London, England: Routledge and Kegan Paul.

Pollak, R. (1997). *The creation of Dr. B: A biography of Bruno Bettelheim.* New York, NY: Simon & Schuster.

Rey-Flaud, H. (2008). *L'enfant qui s'est arrêté au seuil du langage: Comprendre l'autisme.* Paris: Editions Flammarion.

Ribas, D. (2004). *Controverses sur l'autisme et témoignages.* Paris: Presses Universitaires de France.

Ribas, D. (2006). *Autism: Debates and testimonies.* London, England: Free Association Books.

Rimland, B. (1964). *Infantile autism.* Englewood Cliffs, NJ: Prentice Hall.

Ritvo, E. R. (2006). *Understanding the nature of autism and Asperger's disorder: Forty years of clinical practice and pioneering research.* London, England: Jessica Kingsley Publishers.

Rivière, A. (2001). *Autismo: Orientaciones para la intervención educativa.* Madrid, Spain: Editorial Trotta.

Roth, I. (Ed.) (2007). *Imaginative minds: Concepts, controversies and themes.* Oxford and London, England: Oxford University Press and the British Academy.

Rutter, M. (1972). *Maternal deprivation reassessed.* London, England: Penguin.

Rutter, M. (Ed.) (1983). *Developmental neuropsychiatry.* London, England: Guilford Publications.

Rutter, M., & Schopler, E. (Eds.) (1978). *Autism: A reappraisal of concepts and treatment.* New York, NY: Plenum Publishing.

Sacks, O. (1995). *An anthropologist on Mars,* London, England: Picador.

Sainsbury, C. (2000). *Martian in the playground: Understanding the schoolchild with Asperger's syndrome.* Bristol, England: Lucky Duck Publishing.

# Bibliography

Sanders, J. S. (1989). *A greenhouse for the mind.* Chicago, IL: University of Chicago Press.

Schopler, E., & Mesibov, G. B. (Eds.) (1987). *Neurobiological issues in autism.* New York, NY: Springer Publishing.

Schopler, E., & Mesibov, G. B. (Eds.) (1988). *Diagnosis and assessment in autism.* New York, NY: Springer Publishing.

Schopler, E., Yirmiya, N., Shulman, C., & Marcus, L. M. (2001). *The research basis for autism intervention.* New York, NY: Springer Publishing.

Schreibman, L. (1988). *Autism.* Newbury Park, CA: Sage Publications.

Schreibman, L. (2007). *The science and fiction of autism.* Cambridge, MA: Harvard University Press.

Sellin, B. (1993). *Ich will kein inmich mehr sein: Botschaften aus einem autistischen Kerker.* Cologne, Germany: Verlag Kiepenheuer & Witsch.

Sellin, B. (1995). *I don't want to be inside me anymore: Messages from an autistic mind.* New York, Basic Books.

Serruys, M. (2005). *Aan de rand in het midden.* Antwerp, Belgium: Fontys.

Shattock, P., & Savery, D. (1997). *Autism as a metabolic disorder.* Sunderland, England: Sunderland University, Autism Research Unit.

Shore, S. M. (2003). *Beyond the wall: Personal experiences with autism and Asperger syndrome.* Shawnee Mission, KS: Autism Asperger Publishing Co.

Sicile-Kira, C. (2003). *Autism spectrum disorders: The complete guide.* London, England: Vermilion.

Siegel, B. (1996). *The world of the autistic child: Understanding and treating autism spectrum disorders.* New York, NY: Oxford University Press.

Sigman, M. (1997). *Children with autism: A developmental perspective.* Cambridge, MA: Harvard University Press.

Simmons, K. L. (2008). *Official autism 101 manual: Everything you need to know about autism from experts who know and care.* Autism Today. http://www.autism101manual.com/

Simons, J., & Oishi, S. (1987). *The hidden child: The Linwood Method for reaching the autistic child.* Bethesda, MD: Woodbine House.

Stehli, A. (1991). *The sound of a miracle: A child's triumph over autism.* New York, NY: Doubleday.

Stevens, C., & Stevens, N. (2008). *A real boy: How autism shattered our lives: and made a family from the pieces.* London, England: Michael OMara Books.

Szatmari, P. (2004). *A mind apart: Understanding children with autism and Asperger syndrome.* London, England: Guilford Press.

Tammet, D. (2006). *Born on a blue day: A memoir of Asperger's and an extraordinary mind.* London, England: Hodder and Stoughton.

Tammet, D. (2009). *Embracing the wide sky: The enormous potential of your mind.* London, England: Hodder and Stoughton.

Tantam, D. (2009). *Can the world afford autistic spectrum disorder? Nonverbal communication, Asperger syndrome and the interbrain.* London, England: Jessica Kingsley Publishers.

Tardif, C., & Gepner, B. (2007). *L'autisme.* Paris: Armand Colin.

Tetzchner, S. von & Martinsen, H. (2000). *Introduction to Augmentative and Alternative Communication.* Oxford, England: Wiley-Blackwell.

Tomlinson, D. (1990). *Luckier than most: An autobiography.* London, England: Hodder and Stoughton.

Treffert, D. (2006). *Extraordinary people: Understanding savant syndrome.* New York, NY: Backinprint.com.

Tréhin, G. (2006). *Urville.* London, England: Jessica Kingsley Publishers.

Trevarthen, C., Aitken, K., Papoudi, D., & Roberts, J. (1996). *Children with autism: Diagnosis and interventions to meet their needs.* London, England: Jessica Kingsley Publishers.

Tuchman, R., & Rapin, I. (Eds.) (2006). *Autism: A neurological disorder of early brain development international review of child neurology.* London, England: MacKeith Press.

Tustin, F. (1972). *Autism and childhood psychosis.* London, England: Hogarth.

Tustin, F. (1981). *Autistic states in children.* London, England: Routledge.

Tustin, F. (1986). *Autistic barriers in neurotic patients.* London, England: Karnac Books.

Waterhouse, S. (1999). *A positive approach to autism.* London, England: Jessica Kingsley Publishers.

Whitman, T. L. (2004). *The development of autism: A self-regulatory perspective.* London, England: Jessica Kingsley Publishers.

Williams, D. (1996). *Autism: An inside-out approach: An innovative look at the mechanics of autism and its developmental cousins.* London, England: Jessica Kingsley Publishers.

Williams, D. (1998). *Autism and sensing: The unlost instinct.* London, England: Jessica Kingsley Publishers.

Williams, D. (1998). *Like colour to the blind: Soul searching and soul finding.* London, England: Jessica Kingsley Publishers.

Williams, D. (1998). *Nobody nowhere: The remarkable autobiography of an autistic girl.* London, England: Jessica Kingsley Publishers.

Williams, D. (1998). *Somebody somewhere: Breaking free from the world of autism.* London, England: Jessica Kingsley Publishers.

Williams, D. (2002). *Exposure anxiety: The invisible cage: An exploration of self-protection responses in the autism spectrum and beyond.* London, England: Jessica Kingsley Publishers.

Williams, D. (2004). *Everyday heaven: Journeys beyond the stereotypes of autism.* London, England: Jessica Kingsley Publishers.

Williams, D. (2005). *The jumbled jigsaw: An insider's approach to the treatment of autistic spectrum fruit salads.* London, England: Jessica Kingsley Publishers.

# Bibliography

Wiltshire, S. (1987). *Drawings*. Tokyo, Japan: Suemori Books.

Wiltshire, S. (1989). *Cities*. Tokyo, Japan: Suemori Books.

Wiltshire, S. (1991). *Floating cities*. London, England: Michael Joseph.

Wing, J. K. (Ed.) (1966). *Childhood autism: Clinical, educational and social aspects*. London, England: Pergamon Press.

Wing, L. (1971). *Autistic children: A guide for parents*. London, England: Constable.

Wing, L. (1996). *The autistic spectrum: A guide for parents and professionals*. London, England: Constable.

Wolff, S. (1995). *Loners: The life path of unusual children*. London, England: Routledge.

Zappella, M. (2006). *Autismo infantile* (second ed.). Rome, Italy: Carocci.

Zelan, K. (2003). *Between their world and ours: Breakthroughs with autistic children*. New York, NY: St. Martin's Press.

Zunshine, L. (2006). *Why we read fiction: Theory of mind and the novel* (Theory and interpretation of narrative). Columbus: Ohio State University Press.

## DVDs

(The dates refer to when the DVD was released)

*A is for autism* (2004), director Tim Webb, BFI Video.

*After Thomas* (2007), director Simon Shore, 2 Entertain Video.

*The autism puzzle* (2003), director Saskia Baron, BBC Television.

*Ben X* (2008), director Nic Balthazar, Momentum Pictures.

*Black balloon* (2009), director Elissa Down, Icon Home Entertainment.

*Cube* (2000), director Vincenzo Natali, First Independent Video.

*Elle s'appelle Sabine* (2008), director Sandrine Bonnaire, Ica Films.

*Mercury rising* (2008), director Harold Becker, Uca.

*Mozart and the whale* (2006), director Petter Naess, Bridge Entertainment.

*Rain man* (1989), director Barry Levinson, MGM.

*Refrigerator mothers* (2002), director David. E. Simpson, Kartemquin Films.

*Silent fall* (2000), director Bruce Beresford, Warner Home Video.

*Snow cake* (2007), director Marc Evans, Cinema Club.

## Websites

*Looking Up*, the monthly international autism newsletter, www.lookingupautism.org

AutismConnect, www.autismconnect.org.uk

Awares, www.awares.org

# Other works cited in the text

Adrien, J. L., Ornitz, E., Barthélémy, C., Sauvage, D., & Lelord, G. (1987). The presence or absence of certain behaviors associated with infantile autism in severely retarded autistic and non-autistic retarded children and very young normal children. *Journal of Autism and Developmental Disorders*, *17*(3), 407–416.

Alarcón, M., Abrahams, B. S., Stone, J. L., Duvall, J. A., Perederiy, J. V., Bomar, J. M. . . . Geschwind, D. H. (2008). Linkage, association, and gene-expression analyses identify CNTNAP2 as an autism-susceptibility gene. *American Journal of Human Genetics*, *82*(1), 150–159.

Anthony, J. (1958). An experimental approach to the psychopathology of childhood: Autism. *British Journal of Medical Psychology*, *31*, 211–225.

Asarnow, R. F., Tanguay, P. E., Bott, L., & Freeman, B. J. (1987). Patterns of intellectual functioning in non-retarded autistic and schizophrenic children. *Journal of Child Psychology and Psychiatry*, *28*(2), 273–280.

Ashwin, E., Ashwin, C., Rhydderch, D., Howells, J., & Baron-Cohen, S. (2008). Eagle-eyed visual acuity: an experimental investigation of enhanced perception in autism. *Biological Psychiatry*, *65*(1), 17–21.

Asperger, H. (1938). Das psychisch abnorme Kind, *Wiener Klinischen Wochenzeitschrift*, *51*, 1314–1317.

Asperger, H. (1944). Die "autistischen Psychopathen" im Kindesalter. *Archiv für Psychiatrie und Nervenkrankheiten*, *117*, 76–136. [Autistic psychopathy in childhood. Trans. Uta Frith. In U. Frith (Ed.) (1991), *Autism amd Asperger syndrome* (pp. 37–92). Cambridge, England: Cambridge University Press].

Auyeung, B., Baron-Cohen, S., Chapman, E., Knickmeyer, R., Taylor, K., & Hackett, G. (2009). Foetal testosterone and autistic traits. *British Journal of Psychology*, *100*, 1–22.

Bailey, A., Luthert, P., Dean, A., Harding, B., Janota, I., Montgomery, M., . . . Lantos, P. (1998). A clinicopathological study of autism. *Brain*, *121*, 889–905.

Baltaxe, C. A. M. (1977). Pragmatic deficits in the language of autistic adolescents. *Journal of Pediatric Psychology*, *2*(4), 176–180.

Baron-Cohen, S. (1987). Autism and symbolic play. *British Journal of Developmental Psychology*, *5*(2), 139–148.

Baron-Cohen, S. (1989). Perceptual role taking and protodeclarative pointing in autism. *British Journal of Developmental Psychology*, *7*(2), 113–127.

Baron-Cohen, S. (2002). The extreme male brain theory of autism. *Trends in Cognitive Sciences*, *6*, 248–254.

Baron-Cohen, S., Allen, J., & Gillberg, C. (1992). Can autism be detected at 18 months? The needle, the haystack, and the CHAT. *British Journal of Psychiatry*, *161*, 839–843.

Baron-Cohen, S., Cox, A., Baird, G., Swettenham, J., Nightingale, N., Morgan, K., . . . Charman, T. (1996). Psychological markers in the detection of autism in infancy in a large population. *British Journal of Psychiatry*, *168*, 158–163.

Baron-Cohen, S., Wheelwright, S., Cox, A., Baird, G., Charman, T., Swettenham, J., . . . Doehring, P. (2000). The early identification of autism: The Checklist for Autism in Toddlers (CHAT). *Journal of the Royal Society of Medicine*, *93*, 521–525.

Baron-Cohen, S., Wheelwright, S., Skinner, R., Martin, J., & Clubley, E. (2001). The Autism-Spectrum Quotient: Evidence from Asperger syndrome/high-functioning autism, males and females, scientists, and mathematicians. *Journal of Autism and Developmental Disorders*, *31*, 5–17.

Bartak, L., Rutter, M., & Cox, A. (1975). A comparative study of infantile autism and specific developmental receptive language disorder. *British Journal of Psychiatry*, *126*, 127–145.

Barthélémy, C., & Lelord, G. (1987). Autism and psychoses in children. Treatment and practical measures. *Soins Psychiatriques*, *82–83*, 18–19.

Bates, G. (2010). Autism in fiction and autobiography. *Advances in Psychiatric Treatment*, *16*, 47–52.

Bauman, M., & Kemper, T. L. (1985). Histoanatomic observations of the brain in early infantile autism. *Neurology*, *35*, 866–874.

Belinchón, M. (2001). Lenguaje y autismo: Hacia una explicación ontogenética. In J. Martos & A. Rivière (Eds.), *Autismo: Comprensión y explicación actual* (pp. 155–204). Madrid: APNA.

Bender, L. (1959). Autism in children with mental deficiency. *American Journal of Mental Deficiency*, *64*(1), 81–86.

Bergman, P., & Escalona, Sibylle K. (1949). Unusual sensitivities in very young children. *Psychoanalytic Study of the Child*, *3–4*, 333–352.

Berney, T. P. (2000). Autism—an evolving concept. *British Journal of Psychiatry*, *176*(1), 20–25.

Bettelheim, B. (1943). Individual and mass behavior in extreme situations. *Journal of Abnormal and Social Psychology*, *38*, 417–452.

Bettelheim, B. (1959). Joey: A mechanical boy. *Scientific American*, *200*, 117–126.

Bierman, J. S., & McClain, W. H. (n.d.). *An introduction to Leo Kanner the poet*. Archives of Johns Hopkins University, Baltimore, MD.

Bird, A., Guy, J., Gan, J., Selfridge, J., & Cobb, S. (2007). Reversal of neurological defects in a mouse model of Rett syndrome. *Science*, *315*(5815), 1143–1147.

Bishop, D. (1989). Autism, Asperger's syndrome and semantic-pragmatic disorder: Where are the boundaries? *British Journal of Disorders of Communication*, *24*, 107–121.

Bishop, D. (2008). Forty years on: Uta Frith's contribution to research on autism and dyslexia, 1966–2006. *Quarterly Journal of Experimental Psychology*, *61*(1), 16–26.

Bishop, D., Whitehouse, A. J. O., Watt, H. J., & Line, E. A. (2008). Autism and diagnostic substitution: Evidence from a study of adults with a history of developmental language disorder. *Developmental Medicine and Child Neurology*, *50*(5), 341–345.

Bohman, M., Bohman, I., Björck, P., & Sjöholm, E. (1983). Childhood psychosis in a northern Swedish county: Some preliminary findings from an epidemiological survey. In M. Schmidt and H. Remschmidt (Eds.), *Epidemiological Approaches in Child Psychiatry II* (pp. 164–173). New York: Thieme-Stratton.

Bölte, S., & Bosch, G. (2004). Bosch's cases: a 40-year follow-up of patients with infantile autism and Asperger syndrome. *German Journal of Psychiatry*, *7*, 10–13.

Boucher, J. (1976). Is autism primarily a language disorder? *International Journal of Language and Communication Disorders*, *11*(2), 135–143.

Brask, B. H. (1972). A prevalence investigation of childhood psychoses. *Barne-Psykiatrisk Forening*, 145–153.

Brock, J., Brown, C. C., Boucher, J., & Rippon, G. (2002). The temporal binding deficit hypothesis of autism. *Development and Psychopathology*, *14*(2), 209–224.

Brownlow, C. (2010). Presenting the self: Negotiating a label of autism. *Journal of Intellectual and Developmental Disability*, *35*(1), 14–21.

Burbach, P. H., & van der Zwang, B. (2009). Contact in the genetics of autism and schizophrenia. *Trends in Neuroscience*, *32*, 69–72.

Campbell, D. B., Buie, T. M., Winter, H., Bauman, M., Sutcliffe, J. S., Perrin, J. M., & Levitt, P. (2009). Distinct genetic risk based on association of MET in families with co-occurring autism and gastrointestinal conditions. *Pediatrics*, *123*(3), 1018–1024.

Cantwell, D. P., Baker, L., & Rutter, M. (1979). Families of autistic and dysphasic children. I. Family life and interaction patterns, *Archives of General Psychiatry*, *36*(6), 682–687.

Casanova, M. F., Kooten, I. A. J. van, Switala, A. E., Engeland, H. van, Heinsen, H., Steinbusch, H. W. M., Hof, P. R., . . . Schmitz, C. (2006). Minicolumnar abnormalities in autism. *Acta Neuropathologica*; *112*(3), 287–303.

Castelli, F., Frith, C., Happé, F., & Frith, U. (2002). Autism, Asperger syndrome and brain mechanisms for the attribution of mental states to animated shapes. *Brain*, *125*(8), 1839–1849.

Challis, N., & Dewey, Horace W. (1974). The blessed fools of old Russia. *Jahrbücher für Geschichte Osteuropas*, *20*, 1–11.

Chamak, B. (2003). L'autisme: Vers une nécessaire revolution culturelle. *Médecine/Sciences*, *19*, 1152–1159.

Chamak, B. (2008). Autism and social movements: French parents' associations and international autistic individuals' organizations. *Sociology of Health and Illness, 30,* 76–96.

Chance, P. (1974, January). A conversation with Ivar Lovaas about self-mutilating children and how their parents make it worse. *Psychology Today.* http://www.neurodiversity.com/library_chance_1974.html.

Chess, S. (1971). Autism in children with congenital rubella. *Journal of Autism and Childhood Schizophrenia, 1*(1), 33–47.

Chiu, P. H., Kayali, M. A., Kishida, K. T., Tomlin, D., Klinger, L. G., Klinger, M. R., & Montague, P. R. (2008). Self responses along cingulate cortex reveal quantitative neural phenotype for high-functioning autism. *Neuron, 57*(3), 463–473.

Christie, P. (2006, October). *The distinctive clinical and educational needs of children with pathological demand avoidance syndrome: Guidelines for good practice.* Paper presented at the Second World Autism Congress, Cape Town, South Africa.

Cialdella, P., & Mamelle, N. (1989). An epidemiological study of infantile autism in a French Department (Rhône): A research note. *Journal of Child Psychology aud Psychiatry, 30,* 165–176.

Clancy, H., Dugdale, A., and Rendle-Short, J. (1969). The diagnosis of infantile autism. *Developmental Medicine and Child Neurology, 11*(4), 432–442.

Courchesne, E., Carper, R., & Akshoomoff, N. (2003). Evidence of brain overgrowth in the first year of life in autism. *Journal of the American Medical Association, 290*(3): 337–344.

Cowan, R., & Frith, C. (2009). Do calendrical savants use calculation to answer date questions? A functional magnetic resonance imaging study. *Philosophical Transactions of the Royal Society B: Biological Sciences.* doi:10.1098/rstb.2008.0323 65.

Cox, A., Rutter, M., Newman, S., & Bartak, L. (1975). A comparative study of infantile autism and specific developmental receptive language disorder. II. Parental characteristics. *British Journal of Psychiatry, 126,* 146–159.

Creak, M. (1963). Childhood psychosis: A review of 100 cases. *British Journal of Psychiatry, 109,* 84–89.

Crespi, B., & Badcock, C. (2008). Psychosis and autism as diametrical disorders of the social brain. *Behavioral and Brain Sciences, 31*(3), 241–61.

Daly, M., Weiss, L. A., Yiping, S., Korn, J. M., Arking, D. E., Miller, D. T., . . . Wu, B.-L. (2008). Association between microdeletion and microduplication at 16p11.2 and autism. *New England Journal of Medicine, 358,* 667–675.

Damasio, A. R., & Maurer, R. G. (1978). A neurological model for childhood autism. *Archives of Neurology, 35*(12), 777–786.

Daniels, J. L., Forssen, U., Hultman, C. M., Cnattingius, S., Savitz, D. A., Feychting, M., & Sparen, P. (2008). Parental psychiatric disorders associated with autism spectrum disorders in the offspring. *Pediatrics*, *121*(5), 1357–1362.

Dawson, G., Estes, A., Munson, J., Schellenberg, G., Bernier, R., & Abbott, R. (2007). Quantitative assessment of autism symptom-related traits in probands and parents: broader phenotype autism symptom scale. *Journal of Autism and Developmental Disorders*, *37*, 523–536.

DeMyer, M. (1974). In *Psychopathology and child development: Research and treatment (Proceedings of the First International Kanner Colloquium on Child Development, Deviations and Treatment, Chapel Hill, October 30–November 2, 1973)* (pp. 93–94). New York, NY: Plenum Press.

DeMyer, M. K., Barton, S., Alpern, G. D., Kimberlin, C., Allen, J., Yang, E., & Steele, R. (1974). The measured intelligence of autistic children. *Journal of Autism and Childhood Schizophrenia*, *4*, 42–60.

DeMyer, M. K., Churchill, D. W., Pontius, W., & Gilkey, K. M. (1971). A comparison of five diagnostic systems for childhood schizophrenia and childhood autism. *Journal of Autism and Childhood Schizophrenia*, *1*, 175–189.

DeMyer, M. K., Pontius, W., Norton, J. A., Barton, S., Allen, J., & Steele, R. (1972). Parental practices and innate activity in normal, autistic and brain-damaged infants, *Journal of Autism and Childhood Schizophrenia*, *2*, 49–66.

Despert, L. J. (1947). Psychotherapy in child schizophrenia. *American Journal of Psychiatry*, *104*, 36–43.

Earl, C. J. (1934). The primitive catatonic psychosis of idiocy. *British Journal of Medical Psychology*, *14*, 230.

Eisenberg, L. (1956). The autistic child in adolescence. *American Journal of Psychiatry*, *112*(8), 607–12.

Eisenberg, L. (1957). The fathers of autistic children. *American Journal of Orthopsychiatry*, *27*, 715–724.

Eisenberg, L. (1981). In memoriam Leo Kanner MD 1894–1981. *American Journal of Psychiatry*, *138*(8), 1122–1125.

El-Fishawy, P., & State, M. W. (2010). The genetics of autism: Key issues, recent findings, and clinical implications. *Psychiatric Clinics of North America*, *33*(1), 83–105.

Ellefsen, A., Kampmann, H., Billstedt, E., Gillberg, C., & Gillberg, C. (2007). Autism in the Faroe Islands: An epidemiological study. *Journal of Autism and Developmental Disorders*, *37*(3), 437–444.

Eveloff, H. H. (1960). The autistic child. *American Medical Association Archive of General Psychiatry*, *3*, 66–81.

Farley, M. A., McMahon, W. M., Fombonne, E., Jenson, W. R., Miller, J., Gardner, M., . . . Coon, H. (2009). Twenty-year outcome for individuals with autism and average or near-average cognitive abilities. *Autism Research*, *2*(2), 109–118.

Ferster, C. B. (1961). Positive reinforcement and behavioural deficits of autistic children. *Child Development*, *32*, 437–456.

# Bibliography

Ferster, C. B., & DeMyer, M. K. (1961). The development of performances in autistic children in an automatically controlled environment. *Journal of Chronic Diseases, 13,* 312–314.

Fisher, J. T. (2005). *No search no subject? Autism and the American conversion narrative.* Paper presented at the conference Autism and Representation: Writing, Cognition, Disability October 28–30, 2005, Cleveland, Ohio. www.cwru.edu/affil/sce/Texts_2005/Autism and Representation fisher.htm.

Fisher, J. T. (2008). No search no subject? Autism and the American conversion narrative. In M. Osteen (Ed.), *Autism and Representation* (pp. 51–64). London, England: Routledge.

Folstein, S., & Rutter, M. (1977). Infantile autism: A genetic study of 21 twin pairs. *Journal of Child Psychology and Psychiatry, 18,* 297–321.

Fombonne, E. (2005). The changing epidemiology of autism. *Journal of Applied Research in Intellectual Disabilities, 18*(4), 281–304.

Fombonne, E., du Mazaubrun, C., Cans, C., & Grandjean, H. (1997). Autism and associated medical disorders in a French epidemiological survey. *Journal of the American Academy of Child and Adolescent Psychiatry, 36*(11), 1561–1569.

Fombonne, E., Morel, J., & Macarthur, J. (2006, June). *No autism amongst Inuits from northern Quebec?* Paper presented at IMFAR (International Meeting for Autism Research) in Montreal, Canada.

Freeman, B. J., Ritvo, E. R., Yokota, A., & Ritvo, A. (1986). A scale for rating symptoms of patients with the syndrome of autism in real life settings. *Journal of the American Academy of Child and Adolescent Psychiatry, 25*(1), 130–136.

Freeman, B. J., Schroth, P., Ritvo, E., Guthrie, D., & Wake, L. (1980). The Behavior Observation Scale for autism (BOS): Initial results of factor analyses. *Journal of Autism and Developmental Disorders, 10*(3), 343–346.

Frith, U., Leslie, A., & Baron-Cohen, S. (1985). Does the autistic child have a "theory of mind"? *Cognition, 21,* 37–46.

Garreau, B., Barthélémy, C., Sauvage, D., Leddet, I., & Lelord, G. (1984). A comparison of autistic syndromes with and without associated neurological problems. *Journal of Autism and Developmental Disorders, 14*(1), 105–111.

Garreau, B., Tanguay, P., Roux, S., & Lelord, G. (1984). Brain stem auditory evoked potentials in the normal and autistic child. *Revue d'électroencéphalographie et de neurophysiologie clinique, 14*(1), 25–31.

Ghaziuddin, M. (2002). Asperger syndrome: Associated psychiatric and medical conditions. *Focus on Autism and Other Developmental Disabilities, 17*(3), 138–144.

Ghaziuddin, M., & Mountain-Kimchi, K. (2004). Defining the intellectual profile of Asperger syndrome: Comparison with high-functioning autism. *Journal of Autism and Developmental Disorders, 34*(3), 279–84.

355

Gillberg, C. (1984). Infantile autism and other childhood psychoses in a Swedish urban region: Epidemiological aspects. *Journal of Child Psychology and Psychiatry, 25,* 35–43.

Gillberg, I. C., & Gillberg, C. (1989). Asperger syndrome—some epidemiological considerations: A research note. *Journal of Child Psychology and Psychiatry, 30*(4), 631–638.

Glessner, J. T., Wang, K., Cai, G., Korvatska, O., Kim, C. E., Wood, S., . . . Hakonarson, H. (2009). Autism genome-wide copy number variation reveals ubiquitin and neuronal genes. *Nature, 459*(7246), 569–573.

Goldfarb, W. (1956). Receptor preferences in schizophrenic children. *American Medical Association Archives of Neurology and Psychiatry, 76,* 643–652.

Golding, M. (2006, October). *The hitch hiker's guide to autism: An educator's unique account of the history of autism and the development of a relevant and empowering curriculum 1959–2005.* Address to the Second World Autism Congress, Cape Town, South Africa.

Gray, C. (2004). Social Stories 10.0: The new defining criteria. *Jenison Autism Journal, 15,* 1–21.

Hacking, I. (2009). Humans, aliens and autism. *Daedalus, 138*(3), 44–59.

Happé, F. and Ronald, A. (2008). The "fractionable autism triad": A review of evidence from behavioral, genetic, cognitive and neural research. *Neuropsychology Review, 18*(4), 287–304.

Happé, F., Ronald, A., & Plomin, R. (2006). Time to give up on a single explanation for autism. *Nature Neuroscience, 9,* 1218–1220.

Hippler, K., & Klicpera, C. (2004). A retrospective analysis of the clinical case records of "autistic psychopaths" diagnosed by Hans Asperger and his teaching at the University Children's Hospital, Vienna. In U. Frith and E. Hill (Eds.), *Autism: Mind and Brain* (pp. 21–42). Oxford, England: Oxford University Press.

Hollander, E., Bartz, J., Chaplin, W., Phillips, A., Sumner, J., Soorya, L., . . . Wasserman, S. (2007). Oxytocin increases retention of social cognition in autism. *Biological Psychiatry, 61*(4), 498–503.

Howlin, P. (2000). Outcome in adult life for more able individuals with autism or Asperger syndrome. *Autism, 4*(1), 63–83.

Howlin, P., Goode, S., Hutton, J., & Rutter, M. (2009). Savant skills in autism: Psychometric approaches and parental reports. *Philosophical Transactions of the Royal Society B: Biological Sciences, 364*(1522), 1359–1367.

Ishii, T., & Takahashi, O. (1983). The epidemiology of autistic children in Toyota, Japan: Prevalence. *Japanese Journal of Child and Adolescent Psychiatry, 24,* 311–321.

Jamain, S., Quach, H., Betancur, C., Råstam, M., Colineaux, C., Gillberg, I. C., . . . Paris Autism Research International (2003). Mutations of the X-linked genes encoding neuroligins NLGN3 and NLGN4 are associated with autism. *Nature Genetics, 34*(1), 27–29.

# Bibliography

Jarrold, C., & Boucher, J. (1997). Language profiles in children with autism: theoretical and methodological implications. *Autism*, *1*(1), 57–76.

Jolliffe, T., Lansdowne, R., & Robinson, C. (1992). Autism: a personal account. *Communication*, *26*(3).

Jordan, R. (2006, November). *International conceptualisations, theories and treatments: new and valuable?* Address to the Second World Autism Congress, Cape Town, South Africa.

Kana, R. K., Keller, T. A., Cherkassky, V. L., Minshew, N. J., Just, M. A. (2009). Atypical frontal-posterior synchronization of theory of mind regions in autism during mental state attribution. *Society for Neuroscience*, *4*(2), 135–152.

Kana, R. K., Keller, T. A., Minshew, N. J., & Just, M. A. (2007). Inhibitory control in high-functioning autism: Decreased activation and underconnectivity in inhibition networks. *Biological Psychiatry*, *62*(3), 198–206.

Kanner, L. (n.d.). *Freedom from within* [unpublished autobiography]. American Psychiatric Association library, Arlington, Virginia, USA.

Kanner, L. (1942). Exoneration of the feeble-minded. *American Journal of Psychiatry*, *99*, 17–22.

Kanner, L. (1943). Autistic disturbances of affective contact. *Nervous Child, 2*, 217–250.

Kanner, L. (1949). Problems of nosology and psychodynamics in early childhood autism. *American Journal of Orthopsychiatry*, *19*(3), 416–426.

Kanner, L. (1954). General concept of schizophrenia at different ages. *Proceedings of the Association for Research into Nervous and Mental Diseases, 33*, 451–453.

Kanner, L. (1965). *Infantile autism and the schizophrenias.* [Lecture given to an American Psychiatric Association meeting, New York, May 4, 1965, published in *Behavioral Science*, *10*(4) (1965), 412–420.]

Kanner, L. (1971). Follow-up study of eleven autistic children originally reported in 1943. *Journal of Autism and Childhood Schizophrenia*, *1*(2), 119–145.

Kanner, L. (1972). How far can autistic children go in matters of social adaptation? *Journal of Autism and Childhood Schizophrenia*, *2*(1), 9–33.

Kanner, L. (1973). Linwood Children's Center: Evaluations and follow-up of 34 psychotic children. In L. Kanner, *Childhood psychosis: Initial studies and new insights* (pp. 223–283). Washington, DC: V. H. Winston & Sons.

Kanner, L., & Eisenberg, L. (1956). Early infantile autism, 1943–55. *American Journal of Orthopsychiatry*, *26*(3), 556–566.

Kates, W. R., Burnette, C. P., Eliez, S., Strunge, L. A., Kaplan, D., Landa, R., . . . Pearlson, G. D. (2004). Neuroanatomic variation in monozygotic twin pairs discordant for the narrow phenotype for autism. *American Journal of Psychiatry*, *161*, 539–546.

# Bibliography

Kennedy, F. (1942). The problem of social control of the congenital defective: education, sterilization, euthanasia, *American Journal of Psychiatry*, 99, 13–16.

Kidd, K. B. (2005). Bruno Bettelheim and the psychoanalytic feral tale. *American Imago*, 62(1), 75–99.

King, M., & Bearman, P. (2009). Diagnostic change and the increased prevalence of autism. *International Journal of Epidemiology*, 38(5), 1224–1234.

Kjelgaard, M., & Tager-Flusberg, H. (2001). An investigation of language impairment in autism: implications for genetic subgroups. *Language and Cognitive Processes*, 16(2–3), 287–308.

Kolvin, I., Ounsted, C., Humphrey, M., & McNay, A. (1971). Studies in the childhood psychoses. *British Journal of Psychiatry*, 118, 381–419.

Krug, D. A., Arick, J., & Almond, P. (1980). Behavior checklist for identifying severely handicapped individuals with high levels of autistic behavior. *Journal of Child Psychology and Psychiatry*, 21(3), 221–229.

Laffont, F., Jusseaume, P., Bruneau, N., Dubost, P., & Lelord, G. (1975). Conditioning of evoked potentials in normal, mentally retarded and autistic children. *Revue d'électroencéphalographie et de neurophysiologie clinique*, 5(4), 369–74.

Le Couteur, A., Rutter, M., Lord, C., Rios, P., Robertson, S., Holdgrafer, P., & McLennan, J. (1989). Autism diagnostic interview: A standardized investigator-based instrument. *Journal of Autism and Developmental Disorders*, 19(3), 363–387.

Leboyer, M., Osherson. D. N., Nosten, M., & Roubertoux, P. (1988). Is autism associated with anomalous dominance? *Journal of Autism and Developmental Disorders*, 18(4), 539–551.

Lelord, G., Barthélemy, C., Sauvage, D., & Ragazzoni, A. (1978). Autism, inhibition, electrophysiology and biochemistry. *Encéphale*, 4(5) [Suppl.], 489–501.

Lelord, G., Garreau, B., Barthélemy, C., Bruneau, N., & Sauvage, D. (1986). Neurological aspects of infantile autism. *Encéphale*, 12(2), 71–76.

Lelord, G., Muh, J.-P., Sauvage, D., & Hérault, J. (1996). Neurobiologie des syndromes autistiques de l'enfant. *Médecine/Sciences*, 12, 715–722.

Lewis, N. (1954). In discussion, *Proceedings of the Association for Research into Nervous and Mental Diseases*, 33, 364.

*Life* magazine (1965, May 7). Screams, slaps, and love: A surprising, shocking treatment helps far-gone mental cripples.

Lind, S. E., & Bowler, D. M. (2009). Language and theory of mind in autism spectrum disorder: The relationship between complement syntax and false belief task performance. *Journal of Autism and Developmental Disorders*, 39(6), 929–37.

Lord, C., Rutter, M., Goode, S., Heemsbergen, J., Jordan, H., Mawhood, L., & Schopler, E. (1989). Autism diagnostic observation schedule: A standardized observation of communicative and social behavior. *Journal of Autism and Developmental Disorders*, *19*(2), 185–212.

Lotter, V. (1967). Epidemiology of autistic conditions in young children: Some characteristics of the parents and children. *Social Psychiatry 1*, 163–173.

Lotter, V. (1978). Childhood autism in Africa. *Journal of Child Psychology and Psychiatry*, *193*, 231–244.

Loucas, T., Charman, T., Pickles, A., Simonoff, E., Chandler, S., Meldrum, D., & Baird, G. J. (2008). Autistic symptomatology and language ability in autism spectrum disorder and specific language impairment. *Child Psychology and Psychiatry*, *49*(11), 1184–1192.

Lutchmaya, S., Baron-Cohen, S., & Raggatt, P. (2002). Foetal testosterone and eye contact in 12-month-old infants. *Infant Behaviour and Development*, *25*, 327–335.

Mahler, M. S. (1952). On child psychosis and schizophrenia: Autistic and symbiotic infantile psychoses. *Psychoanalytic Study of the Child*, *7*, 286–305.

Martineau, J., Garreau. B., Barthélemy, C., Callaway, E., & Lelord, G. (1981). Effects of vitamin B6 on averaged evoked potentials in infantile autism. *Biological Psychiatry*, *16*(7), 627–641.

Massie, H. N. (1978). The early natural history of childhood psychosis. Ten cases studied by analysis of family home movies of the infancies of the children. *Journal of the American Academy of Child and Adolescent Psychiatry*, *17*(1), 29–45.

Matson, J. L., Wilkins, J., & Fodstad, J. C. (2010). Children with autism spectrum disorders: A comparison of those who regress versus those who do not. *Developmental Neurorehabilitation*, *13*(1), 37–45.

McCarthy, P., Fitzgerald, M., & Smith, M. (1984). Prevalence of childhood autism in Ireland. *Irish Medical Journal*, *77*, 129–130.

Medical Research Council (2001). *Review of autism research: Epidemiology and causes*. http://www.mrc.ac.uk/Utilities/Documentrecord/index.htm?d=MRC002394.

Miles, J. H., Takahashi, T. N., Bagby, S., Sahota, P. K., Vaslow, D. F., Wang, C. H., . . . Farmer, J. E. (2005). Essential versus complex autism: Definition of fundamental prognostic subtypes. *American Journal of Medical Genetics*, *135*(2), 171–180.

Milicic, J., Bujas Petkovic, Z., & Bozikov, J. (2003). Dermatoglyphs of digito-palmar complex in autistic disorder: Family analysis. *Croatian Medical Journal*, *44*(4), 469–476.

Mnukhin, S. S., Isaev, D. N., & O'Tuama, L. (1975). On the organic nature of some forms of schizoid or autistic psychopathy. *Journal of Autism and Developmental Disorders*, *5*(2), 99–108.

Nesnidalova, R., & Fiala, V. K. (1961). On the question of Kanner's early infantile autism. *Ceskoslovenska Psychiatrie*, *57*, 76–84.

Neumärker, K.-J. (2003). Leo Kanner: His years in Berlin, 1906–24. The roots of autistic disorder, *History of Psychiatry*, *14*(2), 205–218.

Oliveira, G., Ataíde, A., Marques, C., Miguel, T. S., Margarida Coutinho, A., Mota-Vieira, L., . . . Moura Vicente, A. (2007). Epidemiology of autism spectrum disorder in Portugal: Prevalence, clinical characterisation, and medical conditions. *Developmental Medicine and Child Neurology*, *49*(10), 726–733.

Ornitz, E. M. (1969). Disorders of perception common to early infantile autism and schizophrenia. *Comprehensive Psychiatry*, *10*(4), 259–274.

Ornitz, E. M. (1988). Autism: A disorder of directed attention. *Brain Dysfunction*, *1*, 309–322.

Ornitz, E. M., Atwell, C. W., Kaplan, A. R., & Westlake, J. (1985). Brain-stem dysfunction in autism. Results of vestibular stimulation, *Archives of General Psychiatry*, *42*(10), 1018–1025.

Ornitz, E. M., Guthrie, D., & Farley, A. J. (1978). The early symptoms of autism. In G. Serban (Ed.), *Cognitive defects in the development of mental illness* (pp. 24–42). New York, NY: Bruner/Mazel.

Ornitz, E. M., & Ritvo, E. R. (1968). Perceptual inconstancy in early infantile autism. *Archives of General Psychiatry*, *18*, 76–98.

Ornitz, E. M., & Ritvo, E. R. (1976). The syndrome of autism: a critical review, *American Journal of Psychiatry*, *133*(6), 609–621.

Ornitz, E. M., Ritvo, E. R., & Walter, R. D. (1965). Dreaming sleep in autistic and schizophrenic children. *American Journal of Psychiatry*, *122*(4), 419–424.

Ozonoff, S., Pennington, B. F., & Rogers, S. J. (1991). Executive function deficits in high-functioning autistic individuals: Relationship to theory of mind. *Journal of Child Psychology and Psychiatry*, *32*(7), 1081–1105.

Peltola, H., Patja, A., Leinikki, P., Valle, M., Davidkin, I., & Paunio, M. (1998). No evidence for measles, mumps, and rubella vaccine-associated inflammatory bowel disease or autism in a 14-year prospective study. *The Lancet*, *2*(351/9112), 1327–1328.

Pennington, B. F., & Ozonoff, S. (1996). Executive functions and developmental psychopathology. *Journal of Child Psychology and Psychiatry*, *37*, 51–87.

Petty, L., Ornitz, E., Michelman, J., & Zimmerman, E. (1984). Autistic children who become schizophrenic, *Archives of General Psychiatry*, *41*, 129–135.

Pitfield, M., & Oppenheim, A. N. (1964). Child rearing attitudes of mothers of psychotic children. *Journal of Child Psychology and Psychiatry*, *5*(1), 51–57.

Ploeger, A., van der Maas, H. L., Raijmakers, M. E., & Galis, F. (2009). Why did the savant syndrome not spread in the population? A psychiatric example of a developmental constraint, *Psychiatry Research*, *166*(1), 85–90.

Polan, C. G., & Spencer, B. L. (1959). A checklist of symptoms of autism of early life. *West Virginia Medical Journal, 55,* 198–204.

Potter, H. W. (1933). Schizophrenia in children. *American Journal of Psychiatry, 89,* 1253–1270.

Premack, D., & Woodruff, G. (1978). Does the chimpanzee have a theory of mind? *Behavioral and Brain Sciences, 4,* 515–526.

Rapin, I., & Allen, D. A. (1983). Developmental language disorders: nosological considerations. In U. Kirk (Ed.), *Neuropsychology of language, reading and spelling* (pp. 174–175). New York: Academic Press.

Reichelt, K. L., & Knivsberg, A. M. (2003). Can the pathophysiology of autism be explained by the nature of the discovered urine peptides? *Nutritional Neuroscience, 6*(1), 19–28.

Reichenberg, A., Gross, R., Weiser, M., Bresnahan, M., Silverman, J., Harlap, S., . . . Susser, E. (2006). Advancing paternal age and autism. *Archives of General Psychiatry, 63*(9), 1026–1032.

Ritvo, E. R., Freeman, B. J., Pingree, C., Mason-Brothers, A., Jorde, L., Jenson, W. R., . . . Ritvo, A. (1989). The UCLA–University of Utah epidemiological study of autism: Prevalence. *American Journal of Psychiatry, 146,* 194–245.

Ritvo, E. R., Yuwiler, A., Geller, E., Ornitz, E. M., Saeger, K., & Plotkin, S. (1970). Increased blood serotonin and platelets in early infantile autism. *Archives of General Psychiatry, 23*(6), 566–572.

Rogers, S. J. (2004). Developmental regression in autism spectrum disorders. *Mental Retardation and Developmental Disabilities Research Reviews, 10*(2), 39–143.

Rogers, S. J., Young, G. S., Cook, I., Giolzetti, A., & Ozonoff, S. (2008). Deferred and immediate imitation in regressive and early onset autism. *Journal of Child Psychology and Psychiatry, 49*(4), 449–457.

Rosenthal, J., Massie, H. N., & Wulff, K. (1980). A comparison of cognitive development in normal and psychotic children in the first two years of life from home movies. *Journal of Autism and Developmental Disorders, 10,* 433–443.

Rossignol, D. A., Rossignol, L. W., Scott Smith, C. S., Logerquist, S., Usman, A., Neubrander, J., . . . Elizabeth A Mumper (2009). Hyperbaric treatment for children with autism: A multicenter, randomised, double-blind, controlled trial,' *BMC Pediatrics, 9*(21). doi:10.1186/1471-2431-9-21.

Rumsey, J., Rapoport, J., & Andreasen, N. (1986). Thought, language, communication and affective flattening in autistic adults. *Archives of General Psychiatry, 43,* 771–777.

Rutter, M. (1965). The influence of organic and emotional factors on the origins, nature and outcome of childhood psychosis. *Developmental Medicine and Child Neurology, 7,* 518–528.

Rutter, M. (1966). Behavioural and cognitive characteristics of a series of psychotic children, in J. K. Wing (Ed.), *Childhood Autism: Clinical, Educational and Social Aspects.* London, England: Pergamon Press.

Rutter, M. (1968). Concepts of autism: A review of research. *Journal of Child Psychology and Psychiatry, 9*(1), 1–25.

Rutter, M. (1972). Childhood schizophrenia reconsidered. *Journal of Autism and Childhood Schizophrenia, 2*(4), 315–337.

Rutter, M. (1978). Diagnosis and definition of childhood autism. In M. Rutter & E. Schopler (Eds.), *Autism: A reappraisal of concepts and treatment.* New York: Plenum Publishing.

Rutter, M. (1999). Autism: Two-way interplay between research and clinical work. *Journal of Child Psychology and Child Psychiatry, 40,* 169–188.

Rutter, M. (forthcoming). A selected scientific history of autism. In E. Hollander, A. Kolevzon, & J. Coyle (Eds.), *Textbook of autism spectrum disorders.* Arlington, VA: American Psychiatric Association.

Rutter, M., Andersen-Wood, L., Beckett, C., Bredenkamp, D., Castle, J., Groothues, C., . . . O'Connor, T. G. (1999). Quasi-autistic patterns following severe early global privation. *Journal of Child Psychology and Psychiatry, 40*(4), 537–549.

Rutter, M., Bailey, A., Bolton, P., & Le Couteur, A. (1994). Autism and known medical conditions: myth and substance. *Journal of Child Psychology and Psychiatry, 35*(2), 311–322.

Rutter, M. & Bartak, L. (1971). Causes of infantile autism: Some considerations from recent research. *Journal of Autism and Childhood Schizophrenia, 1*(1), 20–32.

Rutter, M., Greenfeld, D., & Lockyer, L. (1967). A five to fifteen year follow-up study of infantile psychosis. II. Social and behavioral outcome. *British Journal of Psychiatry, 113,* 1183–1199.

Rutter, M., Kreppner, J., O'Connor, T. G. and the English and Romanian Adoptees (ERA) study team (2001). Specificity and heterogeneity in children's responses to profound institutional deprivation, *British Journal of Psychiatry, 179,* 97–103.

Rutter, M., & Lockyer, L. (1965). A five to fifteen year follow-up of infantile psychosis: I. Description of sample. *British Journal of Psychiatry British Journal of Psychiatry, 113,* 1169–1182.

Sainsbury, C. *Holding therapy: An autistic perspective.* http://www.nas.org.uk/nas/jsp/polopoly.jsp?a=2179&d=364.

Sanua, V. (1984). Is infantile autism a universal phenomenon? An open question. *International Journal of Social Psychiatry, 30*(3), 163–177.

Saxe, R., & Kanwisher, N. (2003). People thinking about thinking people: The role of the temporo-parietal junction in theory of mind. *Neuroimage, 19*(4), 1835–1842.

# Bibliography

Schain, R. J., & Yannet, H. (1960). Infantile autism: An analysis of 50 cases and a consideration of certain neurophysiologic concepts. *Journal of Pediatrics*, *57*, 560–567.

Scheerer, M., Rothman, E., & Goldstein, K. (1945). A case of "idiot savant": An experimental study of personality organization. *Psychological Monographs*, *58*(4), 1–63.

Schopler, E., Chess, S., & Eisenberg (1981). Our memorial to Leo Kanner. *Journal of Autism and Developmental Disorders*, *11*(3), 257–269.

Schopler, E., & Loftin, J. (1969). Thought disorders in parents of psychotic children: A function of test anxiety. *Archives of General Psychiatry*, *20*, 174–181.

Schopler, E., Reichler, R. J., Devellis, R. F., & Daly, K. (1980). Toward objective classification of childhood autism: Childhood Autism Rating Scale (CARS). *Journal of Autism and Developmental Disorders*, *10*, 91–103.

Sebat, J., Lakshmi, B., Malhotra, D., Troge, J., Lese-Martin, C., Walsh. T., . . . Wigler, M. (2007). Strong association of de novo copy number mutations with autism. *Science*, *316*(5823), 445–449.

Shah, A., & Frith, U. (1993). Why do autistic individuals show superior performance on the block design task? *Journal of Child Psychology and Psychiatry and Allied Disciplines*, *34*(8): 1351–1364.

Sigman, M., & Ungerer, J. A. (1984). Attachment behaviors in autistic children. *Journal of Autism and Developmental Disorders*, *14*(3), 231–244.

Silani, G., Bird, G., Brindley, R., Singer, T., Frith, C., & Frith, U. (2008). Levels of emotional awareness and autism: an fMRI study. *Society for Neuroscience*, *3*(2): 97–112.

Silverman, C. (2005). *From disorders of affect to mindblindness: Framing the history of autism spectrum disorders.* Paper presented at the conference Autism and Representation: Writing, Cognition, Disability October 28–30, 2005, Cleveland, Ohio. www.cwru.edu/affil/sce/Texts_2005/Autism%20and%20Representation%20Silverman.htm.

Singh, V. K., & Jensen, R. L. (2002). Elevated levels of measles antibodies in children with autism. *Pediatric Neurology*, *28*(4), 292–294.

Smalley, S., Smith, M., & Tanguay, P. (1991). Autism and psychiatric disorders in tuberous sclerosis, *Annals of the New York Academy of Sciences*, *615*, 382–383.

Sommer, M., Döhnel, K., Sodian, B., Meinhardt, J., Thoermer, C., & Hajaka, G. (2007). Neural correlates of true and false belief reasoning. *Neuroimage*, *35*(3), 1378–1384.

Sterba, E. (1936). An abnormal child. *Psychoanalytic Quarterly*, *5*, 375–414, 560–600.

Strömland, K., Nordin, V., Miller, M., Akerström, B., & Gillberg, C. (1994). Autism in thalidomide embryopathy: A population study. *Developmental Medicine and Child Neurology*, *36*(4), 351–356.

# Bibliography

Sukhareva, G. E. (1926). Die schizoiden Psychoathien in Kindesalter [Schizoid psychopathies in childhood]. *Monatschrift für Psychiatrie und Neurologie, 60,* 235–261.

Sundaram, S. K., Kumar, A., Makki, M. I., Behen, M. E., Chugani, H. T., & Chugani, D. C. (2008). Diffusion tensor imaging of frontal lobe in autism spectrum disorder. *Cerebral Cortex, 18*(11), 2659–2665.

Szatmari, P., Bremner, R., & Nagy, J. (1989). Asperger's syndrome: A review of clinical features. *Canadian Journal of Psychiatry/Revue Canadienne de Psychiatrie, 34*(6), 554–560.

Szurek, S. A. (1956). Childhood schizophrenia; symposium, 1955. IV. Psychotic episodes and psychotic maldevelopment. *American Journal of Orthopsychiatry, 26*(3), 519–543.

Tager-Flusberg, H. (2000). Understanding the language and communicative impairments in autism. In L. M. Glidden (Ed.), *Autism* (pp. 185–205). San Diego, CA: Academic Press.

Tanguay, P. E., Edwards, R. M., Buchwald, J., Schwafel. J., & Allen, V. (1982). Auditory brainstem-evoked responses in autistic children. *Archives of General Psychiatry, 39*(2), 174–180.

Tanoue, Y., Oda, S., Asano, F., & Kawashima, K. (1988). Epidemiology of infantile autism in the Southern Ibaraki, Japan. *Journal of Autism and Developmental Disorders, 18,* 155–167.

Teitelbaum, P., Teitelbaum, O., Nye. J., Fryman, J., & Maurer, R .G. (1998). Movement analysis in infancy may be useful for early diagnosis of autism. *Proceedings of the National Academy of Sciences, 95*(23), 13982–13987.

Tinbergen, N. (1973, December 12). *Ethology and stress diseases.* Nobel Prize lecture. http://nobelprize.org/nobel_prizes/medicine/laureates/1973/tinbergen-lecture.pdf.

Treffert, D. (1970). Epidemiology of infantile autism. *Archives of General Psychiatry, 22,* 431–438.

Turk, J., Bax, M., Williams, C., Amin, P., Eriksson, M., & Gillberg, C. (2009). Autism spectrum disorder in children with and without epilepsy: Impact on social functioning and communication. *Acta Paediatrica, 98,* 675–681.

Tustin, F. (1991). Revised understandings of psychogenic autism. *International Journal of Psycho-Analysis, 72*(4), 585–591.

van Krevelen, D. A. (1952). Een geval van early infantile autism. *Nederlands Tijdschrift voor Geneeskunde, 96,* 202–205.

van Krevelen, D. A. (1952). Early infantile autism. *Zeitung für Kinderpsychiatrie, 19,* 91–97.

van Krevelen, D. A. (1971). Early infantile autism and autistic psychopathy. *Journal of Autism and Childhood Schizophrenia, 1*(1), 82–86.

Volkmar, F. R. (1987). Annotation: Diagnostic issues in the pervasive developmental disorders. *Journal of Child Psychology and Psychiatry, 28*(3), 365–369.

# Bibliography

von Tetzchner, S. (1997). Historical issues in intervention research: Hidden knowledge and facilitating techniques in Denmark. *European Journal of Disorders of Communication, 32*(1), 1–18.

Wakefield, A. J., Murch, S. H., Anthony, A., Linnell, J., Casson, D. M., Malik, M., . . . Walker-Smith, J. E. (1998). Ileal-lymphoid-nodular hyperplasia, non-specific colitis, and pervasive developmental disorder in children. *The Lancet, 351*(9103), 637–641. [*The Lancet* retracted this article in February 2010; *The Lancet 375*(9713), 445.]

Waltz, M., & Shattock, P. (2004). Autistic disorder in nineteenth-century London: Three case reports. *Autism, 8*(1), 7–20.

Wang, K., Zhang, H., Ma, D., Bucan, M., Glessner, J. T., Abrahams, B. S., . . . Hakonarson, H. D. (2009). Common genetic variants on 5p14.1 associate with autism spectrum disorders. *Nature, 459*(7246): 528–533. (2009). Autism genome-wide copy number variation reveals ubiquitin and neuronal genes. *Nature, 459*(7246): 569–573.

Werner, E., & Dawson, G. (2005). Validation of the phenomenon of autistic regression using home videotapes. *Archives of General Psychiatry, 62*(8), 889–895.

Wilson, T. W., Rojas, D. C., Reite, M. L., Teale, P. D., & Rogers, S. J. (2007). Children and adolescents with autism exhibit reduced MEG steady-state gamma responses. *Biological Psychiatry, 62*(3), 192–197.

Wing, L., & Shah, A. (2000). Catatonia in autism. *British Journal of Psychiatry, 176*, 157–162.

Wing, L., & Shah, A. (2006). Psychological approaches to chronic catatonia-like deterioration in autism spectrum disorders, *International Review of Neurobiology, 72*, 245–264.

Wing, L. (1981). Asperger's syndrome: A clinical account. *Psychological Medicine, 11*(1), 115–130.

Wing, L. (1993). The definition and prevalence of autism: A review. *European Child and Adolescent Psychiatry, 2*(2), 61–74.

Wing, L. (1997). The history of ideas on autism: legends, myths and reality. *Autism, 1*(1), 13–23.

Wing, L., & Gould, J. (1979). Severe impairments of social interaction and associated abnormalities in children: Epidemiology and classification. *Journal of Autism and Developmental Disorders, 9*, 11–29.

Witmer, L. (1919–22). Orthogenic cases, XIV-Don: A curable case of arrested development to a fear psychosis the result of shock in a three-year-old infant. *The Psychological Clinic, 13*, 97–111.

Wolff, S. (1996). The first account of the syndrome Asperger described? *European Child and Adolescent Psychiatry, 5*, 119–132.

World Health Organization (1987). *The ICD-9 classification of mental and behavioural disorders*. Geneva, Switzerland: World Health Organization.

Wurst, F. (1980). In memoriam Univ.-Prof Dr Hans Asperger. *Heilpädagogik, 5*, 130–133.

Yip, J., Soghomonian, J. J., & Blatt, G. J. (2008). Increased GAD67 mRNA expression in cerebellar interneurons in autism: Implications for Purkinje cell dysfunction. *Journal of Neuroscience Research*, *86*(3), 525–530.

Yip, J., Soghomonian, J. J., & Blatt, G. J. (2009). Decreased GAD65 mRNA levels in select subpopulations of neurons in the cerebellar dentate nuclei in autism: An *in situ* hybridization study. *Autism Research*, *2*(1), 50–59.

Zelan, K. (1993). Bruno Bettelheim (1903–1990). *Prospects*, *23*(1/2), 85–100.

Zilbovicius, M., Garreau, B., Tzourio, N., Mazoyer, B., Bruck, B., Martinot, J. L., . . . Lelord, G. (1992). Regional cerebral blood flow in childhood autism: a SPECT study. *American Journal of Psychiatry*, *149*(7), 924–930.

Zwaigenbaum, L. (2010). Unique developmental differences associated with ASD. *Autism*, *14*(1), 5–7.

# Index

Page numbers in *italic* indicate photographs

367

*Index*